# IN THE COMPANY OF FRIENDS

*Exploring Faith and Understanding*

*with Buddhists and Christians*

JOHN ROSS CARTER

SUNY PRESS

Published by
STATE UNIVERSITY OF NEW YORK PRESS, ALBANY



For information, contact State University of New York Press,
Albany, NY
www.sunypress.edu

Production, Laurie Searl
Marketing, Kate McDonnell

Library of Congress Cataloging-in-Publication Data
Carter, John Ross.
In the company of friends : exploring faith and understanding with Buddhists and Christians / John Ross Carter.
p. cm. Includes bibliographical references (p. ) and index.
ISBN 978-1-4384-4279-2 (hardcover : alk. paper)
1. Christianity and other religions—Buddhism. 2. Buddhism—Relations—Christianity. I. Title.
BR128.B8C37 2012
261.2'43—dc23 2011033669

10 9 8 7 6 5 4 3 2 1

To Sandra

*With Whom I Have Walked Along The Way In The Company Of Friends*

# Contents

# Foreword

## *That Other Practice that Guides Our Understanding*

Matthew's biography of Jesus in the New Testament recounts an exchange between Jesus and his disciples: "Now when Jesus came into the district of Caesarea Philippi, he asked his disciples, 'Who do people say that the Son of Man is?' And they said, 'Some say John the Baptist, but others Elijah, and still others Jeremiah or one of the prophets.' He said to them, 'But who do you say that I am?'" (Matthew 16:13–16). This familiar incident has been emblematic in Christian piety and theology across the centuries, a paradigm for many that truth—or better, Truth—is best understood as a quality of personal living, something that is best understood when spoken in the first person. By extension, this evocative incident can also be made paradigmatic for some of the basic challenges that inevitably engage every student of humanity's many and diverse religious traditions, and especially about what might be entailed when one gives answers to questions about other persons with respect to who they are and what they say. Another obvious challenge evoked by extension from the incident is about whether our answers to questions about other persons with respect to who they are and how they see the world are best given somehow in the first person, but if this is so, how can this be done in the public discourse expected in scholarship? Another challenge evoked by extension from the incident is the need for a student of particular religious traditions and communities to cultivate scholarly skills of imagination and empathy that can aid him or her in taking the measure—from the inside, as it were—of the qualities of personal living found in different religious communities. And yet another challenge evoked by extension from the incident is the need for students of religion themselves to learn a lesson from one aspect of this account, but an aspect that is actually a common theme in many religious traditions: that what are the most important things for a person to know are also very easy to get wrong. Being mindful of the ease with which important things are misperceived and thus misunderstood is, of course, a primary scholarly virtue, and not only for those engaged in the study of human religiousness. It is also a virtue too that remains effective and generative best when exercised in disciplined self-consciousness among others.

That it is easy to get important things wrong—whether by overlooking them, misperceiving them, or misunderstanding them—may be a sad feature of human life, but it is still a commonplace that is worth pausing over and reconsidering again and again and especially by students of religion. That it is easy to get important things wrong is not only true for what is preserved in the heritages of religious communities. It is also easy to get important things wrong about religious persons themselves in how we see them and in what we say about them.

We should also remember, by a second-order extension, that it is just as easy to get important things wrong when we read works of scholarly interpretation about religious traditions and religious persons. In contributing a foreword to this second collection of John Ross Carter's essays, I would like to mark a small amount of my respect for and gratitude to my teacher by taking up just one of the issues that I find especially instructive in his work for all students of human religiousness, but it is an issue in our activities of understanding that I think is all too easy to overlook, misperceive, or misunderstand: Why it is that scholarship about humans is properly pursued *in the company of friends,* as the title of this collection has it?[2]

That many commonly refer to academic fields and specializations as "disciplines" is a still-useful reminder that our desire to interpret and to understand humans properly leads us to engage in certain practices of knowing that are self-consciously learned and equally self-consciously employed. Just as commonly, in discussions about "hermeneutics" and "methodology," in which we reflect on these practices of ours, we bring them to our collective consciousness in order to refine them and to get better at employing them, but, as is also well known now, such discussions, as valuable and necessary as they may be, can become ends in their own right and distract our attention from other important concerns about the formation of a scholar and the place of a scholar in his or her larger moral and political context.[3] In other words, our concern to employ publicly techniques of interpretation in our practices of knowing is necessary to the activity of understanding, but learning these techniques or methods is not sufficient to account for the formation of a competent scholar, and much less is their employment sufficient to account for the activity of understanding itself. In this collection of essays, John Ross Carter makes a case by example that a capacity for friendship is also necessary to the formation of a competent scholar and that engaging *in the company of friends* in practices of interpretation and knowing is also key to the activity of understanding. In making his case, Carter also gives us insight into friendship as an aspect of the activity of understanding itself, an aspect that we have not given in our scholarly lives—unfortunately, for each and all of us—the collective self-reflection and self-conscious personal cultivation that it deserves. *In the Company of Friends* is thus hardly a sentimental but otherwise vacuous title for essays that appeared originally in scattered publications but which are now brought together mainly for ease of others' access. Rather, the title should be taken as an aphorism that participates itself in a deeply challenging vision of the activity of understanding in which we engage as students of the human in general and students of religion in particular. What I want to emphasize here might best be conveyed with a paraphrase of what Paul Ricoeur said about the aphorism that guides his *The Symbolism of Evil*—"the symbol gives rise to thought": the notion of *In the Company of Friends,* which enchants me, says two things: friendship gives; but what it gives is occasion for thought, something to think about.[4]

## THE ACTIVITY OF UNDERSTANDING ON THE MODEL OF FRIENDSHIP

We can begin to consider friendship as something to think about in the life of a student of human religiousness, as a conative practice that is constitutive of the activity of understanding itself, by taking up what might appear to be an aside in one of the essays included in this collection. It comes late in the book, in chapter 17, "Buddhists and Baptists: In Conversation into our Common Future,"[5] the chapter being an essay that was originally published in Sri Lanka in a festschrift for the great Sinhala scholar of Theravāda Buddhism, O. H. de A. Wijesekera. Because the essay was originally presented as a memorial oration in honor of Professor Wijesekera and subsequently published separately in Sri Lanka, we might be disposed, as readers, to be momentarily touched by the warmth of the personal memories that Carter includes in his essay, since the inclusion of personal memories is a feature of the peculiar academic genre of a memorial oration to honor a scholar, but to leave the passage aside then. While it would be completely understandable were we to do so, if we did, I think we would miss something quite important. To try to attend to what Carter is saying to us in this "aside" is in the vein with which I began this foreword: what is important is all too easy to get wrong. I want to suggest that this "aside" be read paradigmatically, and that we take Carter's memories of studying with Wijesekera as a frame within which all of the essays collected here should be read and understood. In that respect, this passage is an instance of what Thomas Aquinas called *manuductio,* an example that can *take us by the hand and lead*, in a manner analogous to the way that a friend takes us by the hand and leads in the activity of knowing. It should be no surprise, then, that Carter's memories of studying with Wijesekera are, in the end, about friendship.

Indeed, Carter gives to us quite something important-that-is-easy-to-get-wrong even when he prepares us for this passage with what might be taken as a few atmospheric details about the occasions when he met Professor Wijesekera as a student at Wijesekera's home "on High Level Road just south of the Nugegoda intersection and north of the Gangodawila junction."[6] As Carter says earlier in this chapter, "this paper arises from *particularity*"[7] and there is something important for us to take into account here about the activity of scholarly understanding and its embeddedness in particularity:

> I warmly recall the hours spent with Professor Wijesekera in his home on High Level Road, working through portions of the Pali *Aṭṭhakathā* of the *Sutta-nipāta.* A Buddhist and a Baptist were working together in an old Indian language, studying ancient words of wisdom, ever new and refreshing. A teacher was also being *patient* with an appreciative student. When I entered the house, he would always receive me warmly. Almost on every occasion during those afternoon sessions he would be in his sarong, cigar sometimes lit, sometimes not, ever enjoyed. Partially reclining in his chair, a leg comfortably raised and resting on a leg-brace swung from beneath his chair's right arm, we wandered through text and translation, grammar and syntax, concepts and customs, cheerful tales and laughter. It was during that time that I first learned the widespread Sri Lankan custom of reading aloud letters received to enable one's attendant friend to become a party to the correspondence and the communication—a wonderful custom greatly appreciated, one that we might have put aside in the United States to our loss.[8]

The very casualness of this account belies the significance of what we are offered here. It would take some sustained effort to see all of the lessons that are offered here in this anecdote, but I think we will be well rewarded by trying to discern them from a variety of perspectives. Following Carter's comment that "this paper arises from *particularity,*" we might begin by simply noticing the insistence on particulars throughout the passage: texts are named, persons are identified, places located, intellectual practices specified even as they are embedded—not coincidentally—in personal habits. We thus see here an account of a kind of apprenticeship in coming to know particular *goods,* an apprenticeship that in some way depends upon friendship in order for those involved to become alert to what goes beyond any particular goods, alert to what might be suggested to be, in Aristotle's account, *the* good: the *Aṭṭhakavagga* of the *Sutta-nipāta,* "old, ancient words" that become "ever new and refreshing" through this apprenticeship.

We might engage this passage again by glimpsing in and through it a vision of a key component to the activity of understanding that every scholarly exploration of human religiousness assumes. Clearly, the activity of understanding depicted here depends upon generosity. As was said above, friendship *gives.* In this passage, it may be Carter who is the one who desires to learn about Buddhists in Sri Lanka, and this desire is what has brought him to Wijesekera's house but it is Wijesekera who makes learning, knowing, and understanding possible by *his* generosity to Carter, by welcoming Carter into his home. It is important for us to remember not only that friendship gives something to think about, but that friends literally give. How do we acknowledge in our self-reflections on the activity of understanding that generosity is constitutive of understanding itself? How might we make generosity more effective in our activity of understanding? Shouldn't we keep such questions in mind in our contemporary reflections on the hermeneutic conundrums of understanding what we have become wont to call "The Other"? Moreover, we will also want to remember that the friendship that grounds our understanding of particular goods—because there is a friend who takes us by the hand and leads us to the good—is a friendship that must be understood as both synchronic and diachronic, involving friends[9] both past and present. It can deepen our appreciation of the lessons about time and friendship in this passage—and in this collection of essays—if we recall here something that Carter wrote in his preface to his earlier collection of essays, *On Understanding Buddhists: Essays on the Theravāda Tradition in Sri Lanka*:

> This is a study about friends of old and of today, a study offered in response to their friendship. It is an attempt to glimpse what they beheld, to come to understand a little, perhaps, of what undergirds their lives.
>
> I speak of friends of old, having in mind those Buddhists who have gone on before us, who speak to us through their recorded words, words shared by them and remembered by countless others through the centuries, words that have come before the eyes of a person living today. And by writing of friends of today I mean the numerous men and women who are Buddhists who have been faithful and caring in enduring friendship.
>
> It takes time for friendship to form and hold.

Yes, it does take time for friendship to form and hold, but where does friendship begin? We can answer that, in part, friendship begins perhaps in spontaneous generosity, such as was first given by Wijesekera to Carter, but is an occasion of spontaneous generosity enough to say friendship is there? When do we feel warranted to say that *friendship* itself *gives*? Perhaps friendship *gives* especially when it is seen in retrospect (as a memorial oration is an occasion for), because it is easy to get friendship wrong when the gifts of a friend are offered to us the first time. And this necessary practice of seeing gifts and generosity in retrospect reminds us that any activity of understanding on one's own part is not possible apart from the unknown activities of understanding done by others before us, "shared by them and remembered by countless others" before oneself.

Alternatively, we might engage Carter's passage about Wijesekera again from yet another vantage point, now considering how Carter's vision here of what is involved in the activity of understanding shows us that it involves profound transformations of persons. To glimpse the course of these transformations, occurring in and through activities that run the gamut between work and pleasure (and is this not naturally so, insofar as the activity of understanding itself is both hard work and deep pleasure?), we should note the sequence of identity terms as they are introduced in the passage, alert to how each subsequent identity implicitly transforms the previous one, even as the former also seems to ground and to sustain the latter: "a Buddhist and a Baptist" without any relationship specified between them, individuals just "working together;" then a relationship appears—a teacher and a student appear[10]—with qualities appropriate to each—a patient teacher and an appreciative student—but there is still a crucial distinction between them in which the nominal equivalency between "the Buddhist" and "the Baptist" is now relationally inflected by the lack of moral equivalence between teacher and student; and then yet another relationship is named—friendship—that changes how both individuals—one still Buddhist, the other still Baptist, one still teacher, the other still student—relate to "a letter" that has been received by one and is being read to the other. Running through the anecdote is a movement, a transformation, that assumes the possibility of both change and continuity in persons: Wijesekera begins as a Buddhist and ends as a Buddhist, Carter begins as a Baptist and ends as a Baptist, but should we not discern that Wijesekera is transformed as a Buddhist when he becomes a teacher and friend to the student and friend Carter, who is equally transformed as the Baptist he continues to be? Carter ends this chapter with a reaffirmation of the particular:

> We begin afresh where we human beings have always begun—with the *particulars,* in the details, in the bedrock of our individual experiences and personal realizations. Truth also lies in the particular—as it did in a study and a living room in a home on High level Road just south of the Nugegoda intersection and north of the Gangodawila junction in Sri Lanka, as it does afresh today.[11]

This repeated evocation of Wijesekera's home is a reminder that any truth that emerges in the activity of understanding always lies in particular relationships, in the relations between particular teachers and students and in the particular relations between friends. Because of these particular relationships of mutuality, the "bedrock of our individual experiences" is, and can only be, something that is shared with particular others. So much so, that one thing that we come to know in friendship, that good friends (or in Pali, *kalyāṇamitta*) teach us afresh again and again, is that the bedrock of our individual experiences and personal realizations lies not only within us, but also beyond us. It is for this reason that, as students concerned with understanding religious persons, we will want to allow our practices of friendship to guide us, to take us by the hand and lead us in our studies, as well as in any attempts on our part to understand the fragile and dependent nature of our own activities of understanding.

Let's engage Carter's passage once again by asking another question, one that yields yet another vantage point on its significance, something else that we can learn from it. What is the "letter" that the Buddhist Wijesekera reads to the Baptist Carter? I am sure, of course, that sometimes there really was a letter from a friend read by Wijesekera to Carter—that particular custom, perhaps the particular good of laughter shared when the letter was read, was necessary to learn well *the* general good displayed here, but which is "perhaps lost" among some of us—but in the structure of this passage and in the light of what Carter wrote in his preface to *On Understanding Buddhists,* it is equally clear that the "letter" that Wijesekera is reading to Carter is the *Sutta-nipāta* and that by reading it to the Baptist Carter, the Buddhist Wijesekera makes the Baptist Carter, his student and friend, *party* to it. In suggesting that the *Sutta-nipāta* is like a letter received by Wijesekera, we can see that Carter is following his own teacher, Wilfred Cantwell Smith, in construing texts such as the *Sutta-Nipāta,* as scriptures, a class of texts that, according to Smith, are best interpreted relationally; in Smith's conceptualization of scriptures, particular texts only *become* scriptures to someone, in a manner analogous to how a person only becomes a *friend* to someone or a house only becomes a *home* to someone.[12] Carter is a master in the use of relational categories such as scripture, friend, home, and by adding the implications that the particular Sri Lankan custom of reading letters received to friends and thereby making the friends *party* to the letter, Carter is able to make a case for construing the "subject-position" of a student of religion relationally, that is, in a manner that is quite different from the epoché described by phenomenologists, or the emic perspective described by anthropologists, or maintaining the primacy of insider's point of view or letting members of particular religious communities speak for themselves as is commonly advocated in the academic study of religion. All of these conventional construals of the proper subject-position of the student assume the value of some sort of temporary erasure of the ordinary personhood of the student for the sake of understanding another, but in considering the subject-position of the student on the model of friendship no such erasure is desirable, much less is it necessary. And isn't it the case that we can only become *party* to the letters of friends because of some constitutive quality of friendship itself, that quality that Aristotle marked when he said that the friend is "another self," a challenging locution that demands both identity and difference between friends at the same time? And isn't it the case that, through friendship, through our openness to having a friend, we gain another self within ourselves? Or, as Carter says, "because one has learned, while *seeking* to understand, one has grown, one has become other than what one was, yet not in every way different."[13]

Let me suggest, then, that we, as readers, should try to read the chapters on Buddhist ideas that Carter includes in this collection as accounts of the contents of letters to which Carter is party because of the generosity of friends, and that in some way he is, in turn, trying to make us party to their letters. And to return to the notion that truth is best understood as a quality of personal living, something that is best understood when spoken in the first person, let me suggest, then, that we, as readers, try to hear the implicit "my friends say," everywhere present in the chapters on Buddhist ideas that follow, and understand that Carter is striving in these chapters for a kind of speech that is implicitly, but self-consciously always in the first person, voicing a conational recognition of truth as a quality of personal living, both with respect to Carter himself and to the friends whose ideas he is relating to us. Similarly, the chapters on Christian ideas and Christians included here we should read as "letters" that we are overhearing Carter reading to Buddhist friends, to give them an opportunity to become party to what he has happily received as a Christian. These chapters about Christian ideas are not irrelevant to a student of Buddhist communities by any means, either. Indeed, Carter is quite creative in recognizing that those of us who are primarily students of Buddhism can learn something important about Buddhists, "glimpse what they [have] beheld [and now behold], to come to understand a little, perhaps, of what undergirds their lives,"[14] if we can catch a bit of how Buddhists listen to a Christian friend speak about Christianity; what we learn will be quite different from and more important than a Buddhist "theology of other religions." By taking up the individual chapters in this book as "letters," we too, as readers, have a chance to become party to them, but to relate to them in this way is something that will be quite demanding of us. The account of listening to letters read in Wijesekera's home can help us, take us by the hand and lead us, even if it also can make it seem that this will be easy. It is not. Important things are easy to get wrong. I have worried over this one passage—perhaps excessively—in an attempt to show how it can be used paradigmatically and productively as a "how to" manual on how to read Carter's essays collected here. But if important things are easy to get wrong, it is also equally true that it is hard to get them right, especially in the sense of doing justice to them, and I am aware that I have only begun to discern a few of the important epistemological and moral lessons that Carter's paradigm teaches us about the activity of understanding. I am sure that readers will be able to see more than I have in the company of their own friends.

## TRADITIONS, COMMUNITIES, FRIENDSHIPS

In *In the Company of Friends,* Carter not only teaches us a rich way of coming to some self-understanding of what we do, and what we should expect of ourselves, in our activity of understanding human religiousness, by asking us to look at our activity on the model of friendship. He also gives us a rich way of reimagining what is now conventionally dubbed "interreligious dialogue," again on the model of friendship. He does this explicitly, for example, in the chapters grouped together in Part IV of this book, "Building from our Past into Our Common Future," but it is again in a short narrative included in chapter 13, "From Controversy to Understanding: More than a Century of Progress," that Carter offers a paradigmatic incident that can guide those who come to formal as well as informal encounters between members of different religious communities:

> On August 13, 1967, a Catholic priest received a message from the Venerable Walagedera Somaloka Tissa Nayaka Thera, a patient at the Ayurvedic Hospital in Colombo. The Catholic priest went straightway to the hospital. After a pleasant conversation, when the Catholic priest stood to leave, the venerable Thera said to his friend: "Now bless me according to your faith, and I will bless you according to mine." This they did.[15]

Carter offers a rich reflection on this incident right after citing it, a reflection that is explicitly about friendship as a context for the activity of understanding. And in a comment that reminds us, as our paraphrase of Ricoeur above put it, "friendship gives, it gives an occasion for thought," Carter describes friendship as "a context that generates the activity of granting the benefit of the doubt that, on the one hand, holds in check a rapid drive to analysis and assertion of claims and, on the other hand, leads to further reflection and inquiry."[16] Moreover, we see in the anecdote that there is a need at the heart of this exchange: in a hospital, there is a sick friend who asks. I think there is something richly suggestive in this particular detail for us to ponder when we take up the anecdote as a paradigm for interreligious encounter. What is the need that one can address in another in interreligious encounter?

Carter's explanation of friendship as a context of understanding is worth quoting as a way of giving it emphasis. What he says is both familiar as well as surprising. It is familiar in the way that it speaks of friendship that seems to recall Aristotle, that the friend is another self. It is surprising because Carter does not claim, as many often do, that friendship with members of another religious community gives one a privileged insight into what members of a community see and experience; that friendship is proof of a deeper "participant observation." Instead, again to refer to our paraphrase of Ricoeur, Carter makes it clear that "friendship gives something to think about":

> In the blossoming of friendship with persons of other religious communities a complex, occasionally inchoate, incipiently inarticulate orientation evolves. Another person has now become a meaningful part of one's life; what happens to him or her in life matters, really matters, to one. One's friends, if clarity and honesty of relationship are considered important, contribute to one's orientation in the religiously plural setting and that which obstructs this clarity, inhibits this depth, tends to impede, is, in some instances, disruptive of relationship, divisive of community and destructive of integrity. The meaning of one's life in the context of a particular religious tradition becomes deepened, more subtle, by the catalytic sincerity of friendship with persons of other religious traditions. Defensive structures tend to become dismantled, barriers of closed systems, disassembled; plate glass windows through which one can look

> out to others but which nevertheless separate persons are removed in the context of friendship.[17]

Carter is wondering here over something that is of great significance for our religiously plural contemporary world. As David Burrell has said in his own reflections on *Friendship and Ways to Truth*,[18]

> If truth is to be had, it will only be had in a tradition, within a community, in the company of friends. For each of these terms implies the other: tradition without a sustaining and connecting community is nothing but past history; and we are formed into communities by the cross-hatching of friendships, and especially of friends bound together by their shared faith in a communal goal.

Then what are we to expect of situations such as what Carter describes as happened in the Ayurvedic Hospital in Colombo in August 1967. "Friends were there," as Carter says, but shouldn't we expect that the cross-hatching of friendships such as this, between members of different religious communities, will generate future communities of vitality, respect and caring of faith, the contours of which remain quite inchoate and indescribable to us? When Carter suggests that interreligious colloquia should be pursued on the model of friendship he is making the case that some sort of transcendence will occur between friends that will allow us to be "formed into new communities by the cross-hatching of friendships."

Perhaps it is at this point that we can see clearly why friendship is illuminating for understanding our activity of understanding, even as it is also, as Carter reminds us again and again throughout these essays, a constitutive practice in the activity of understanding. Friendship is about self-transcendence. It is in our very human ability to have friends and be a friend, to find another self in another person, that most of us experience for the first time, the pleasures, the goods, and the good of self-transcendence.

And self-transcendence is at the very heart of the activity of understanding. Wilfred Cantwell Smith has argued that

> [h]umane learning is not a methodological system for gratifying desires, however worthy. It is an exploration of what man as such is; what he has been, what he may be. Or shall we not, rather, say: of what we men have been, may be, and we women; and thereby what we men and women truly, ultimately, are. The individual who enters upon it is therefore exposing his actual self to his potential self; is participating in that process of self-transcendence in which being human in part consists.[19]

What John Ross Carter gives us in this collection, *In the Company of Friends,* is the opportunity to reflect on humane learning, on the activity of understanding, using the model of friendship to invite us to participate *afresh* in a process of self-transcendence that is simultaneously ordinary and extraordinary. He invites us to consider that in the blossoming of friendship, in that inchoate orientation in which we are fully human, it is there that we can best see ourselves as we are when we are engaged in the activity of understanding. What John Carter gives us in this collection is the always needed reminder: friendship gives.

CHARLES HALLISEY

Cambridge, Massachusetts

# Acknowledgments

This book, like most things in our lives, could not have appeared without the contributions of others. Over the years, and in previously published volumes, I have indicated many persons who have worked with me in our joint efforts to understand the subject of humankind's religiousness and of our own religious orientations. Among them, persons who have led me into the study of religious texts have my gratitude because, by doing so, I have been enabled to learn from others, particularly those who speak to us in different languages from the past, and consequently I have had the opportunity of hearing their voices as they have called me out of a tendency to be preoccupied by current assumptions of what it is to be genuinely human. At the same time, this grounding in the cumulative process of religious traditions has helped me to discern, however falteringly, the assumptions of religious men and women living around the globe today.

I am grateful for persons who have taught me, in Texas, Kentucky, and Massachusetts, in England, Sri Lanka, and also in Japan, who have enabled me, at least to some degree, to understand some of our languages. Languages enable us to speak among ourselves; English, of course, becoming more and more dominant today. But it is the language of another person that is closest to his or her heart and it is through that language that one draws nearer to the fundamental basis of, foundation for self-disclosure in, another's thought. When that is done, even approximated—even attempted as a person with my limited abilities might—one is called out from oneself and enters into an inter-penetrative intellectual process giving rise to an appropriation of concepts once thought peculiarly foreign, now found to be primarily human. For these language teachers, their knowledge and patience, I remain grateful.

One of the pressing concerns for Buddhist men and women in the twenty-first century is to gain a more comprehensive and self-conscious understanding of their religious affirmations and the quality of personal faith both within the Buddhist tradition at-large and in the religious history of humankind generally, including, of course, our global religious context today. This study explores dimensions of faith and understanding comparatively within the Buddhist tradition and also within the Christian.

After graduating from a Southern Baptist university, in Texas, and seminary, in Kentucky, with primary focus on Western history and Christian studies—prior to the rise of fundamentalist paternalism that now dominates the seminary and, to some degree, continues to threaten the open inquiry of the university—I began my study of what were then called "non-Christian religions" at King's College and the School of Oriental and African Studies, of the University of London, concentrating on the Buddhist tradition with a thesis on the Bodhisattva doctrine in early Indian Mahāyāna and subsequently launched a sustained study of the Theravāda during my doctoral work at Harvard. As is so often the case, one's friendship with and respect for another colleague can be of lasting influence. I found this so with the late Minor Lee Rogers, formerly of Washington and Lee University, author, with Ann T. Rogers, of *Rennyo: The Second Founder of Shin Buddhism—with a translation of his letters* ("Nanzan Studies in Asian Religions," Berkeley: Asian Humanities Press, 1991). Recognizing in Minor Rogers an impressive commitment to the subject and an involvement with the issues of religious living as Jōdo Shinshū or Shin Buddhists have demonstrated in the past *and* today, I became interested, too, in pursuing studies in the Jōdo Shinshū tradition and among Shin Buddhists. Two decades ago I began working with Dennis Hirota, a scholar and translator of the first order, who with patience led me into the magnificent heritage and vision of Jōdo Shinshū. Too numerous are the significant works by Dennis Hirota on which I have relied in my studies for me to note here. My indebtedness to his guidance will become clear as we turn our attention to Jōdo Shinshū. One is deeply moved by one's good fortune to have been able to work alongside men of such stature and insight.

I have learned enormously from Buddhist men and women, particularly in Sri Lanka and in Japan. Their faithfulness to their religious heritage, to the subject, and to me, has been uninterrupted over the years providing both a compass for living life well and a map demonstrating how it can be done.[1] I express here my admiration for numerous dear colleagues at the universities of Colombo, Kelaniya, Jayawardhenepure (Vidyodaya), and Peradeniya, in Sri Lanka, particularly W. S. Karunatillake and the late G. D. Wijayawardhana, and for those at the universities of Otani, Ryukoku, and Kyoto Women's University, in Kyoto, Japan, particularly Minoru Tada, Meiji Yamada, Hisao Inagaki, Michio Tokunaga, Nobuo Nomura, with N. Kashiwahara, and the late Bando Shojun.

I have had the deep satisfaction of working closely with Professor Mahinda Palihawadana over many years, both in Sri Lanka and in the United States. We have been mutually supportive as our families have moved through vicissitudes of life, have entered lively discussions on grammatical forms, on occasion have tried our hands at debate with each other, but consistently, coherently, we have fashioned an understanding of our joint work, our continuing study of ourselves in the dimensions of our lives that we take most seriously. For Mahinda Paliha-wadana's enduring friendship and collaboration with me over the years, I here express my deep gratitude.

My indebtedness to Wilfred Cantwell Smith, my advisor during my years at Harvard, will become abundantly clear throughout this work. The personal and existential perspective I have maintained through the years and here, in this study, was launched in response to Smith's wide-ranging and insightful work. One is fortunate, indeed, to have been introduced to a procedure of humane scholarship in learning of humankind's religiousness.

Jean Getchonis, Clara B. Lantz, and Naveed Ghannad, one of my students at Colgate, have patiently and meticulously reviewed my typed manuscript and made numerous helpful suggestions contributing to stylistic consistency. Clara Lantz carefully reviewed the notes to assure uniformity. Nancy Ellegate, of the State University of New York Press, consistently demonstrated patience and support throughout this publication process. Laurie D. Searl provided editorial assistance in the production of the final text. I am pleased to extend my thanks to them. What errors might remain are, of course, mine.

And my sense of gratitude is also extended to the students with whom I have worked for very nearly four decades, and who have demonstrated for me, ever refreshingly, that becoming personally engaged in an academic subject, especially when that subject rigorously investigates and seriously considers the great human issues, tends to give rise to sustained reflection on that subject and faithfulness among fellow inquirers. Some of these students have gone on to hold professorships in religious studies and have become colleagues from whom I continue to learn. One student has moved along a path similar to mine and has traveled farther, showing me new vistas along the way. Charles Hallisey's graduate students are aware of his extraordinary talent in offering constructive suggestions about their written work. He has done this for me with this book by seeing the point of what I am attempting to communicate and by setting this before the reader in his "Foreword," for which I am grateful.

JOHN ROSS CARTER

Hamilton, New York

# Introductory Note

This volume offers neither a survey of the Buddhist tradition nor a synopsis of Christian systematic theology. It is a collection of a series of reflections that attempts to explore two fundamental dimensions of human religiousness: faith and the activity of understanding. We begin with theoretical issues involved in one's quest for religious understanding by considering briefly the way interreligious understanding could be restricted by maintaining primary loyalty or commitment to one's discipline, especially, in our case, with a sociological approach to the study of what is considered "Religion" (our section I). Becoming engaged in a process leading to understanding religious men and women is, of course, set in history, and we will consider ramifications of one's view of history as an arena for discerning truth. In raising these two areas for consideration, the suggestion is advanced that interreligious understanding itself is a religious quest.

Of course, this would require some careful study of faith, not in isolation but in the context of an ever-expanding community of friends (our section II). At this point we go into some depth considering what others have said about human realizations clustering around that to which English readers refer as "faith," we broaden our inquiry to consider fundamental affirmations about the foundations of religious awareness (our section III).

At this point we move to a more specifically focused review of developments in the island nation of Sri Lanka and the ongoing reciprocal influence of Buddhists and Christians, and other religious persons, in building from our common past into our common future (our section IV). The study ends not with a conclusion, but in raising a question that might be, in the final answer, the ultimate question for men and women living today (our section V).

This study arose from reflections presented to Buddhist hearers and readers well versed in the subjects being considered, primarily drawn from their own religious tradition with observations shared from within a Christian perspective. I hope that what follows will contribute to further constructive considerations among Buddhists and Christians, and others among us too, as we become more self-conscious of the religiously plural world in which we are living and as we continue to lay the foundations for greater mutual self-understanding as we move into our future.

The focus on the Buddhist tradition which we will develop in these pages is on two of its major strands: the Theravāda, primarily present in Sri Lanka and Southeast Asia, and the Jōdo Shinshū, or "Pure Land School," considered within the Mahāyāna movement and representing the largest form of Buddhist piety in Japan.[1] Studies that develop this particular binocular focus are rare. Although an enormous amount of superb scholarship has been produced treating the Buddhist tradition in isolated segments, either geographically or in historical periods, or general surveys, perhaps in future scholars will broaden the scope of their inquiries to include *also* points of view from multiple dimensions of contemporary Buddhist piety in the context of intellectually rigorous global religious colloquia.

We here are not aligning parallel lists of doctrines, running the risk of pulling them out of the dynamic and developing context in which they were formulated and in light of which they have been maintained. And our study is neither static nor defensive speculative inquiry that limits itself to disciplinary assumptions with a sense of objectivity thereby achieved. We seek to understand religious life in a pluralistic context with comparative reflections. We know that the entire matter is ever in process: cumulative, sparkling with the unexpected, regularly instructive; both in the ongoing development of scholarship and in our own personal development. And this process, we have come to learn, is hardly chaotic but suggests purposeful movement. A sense of "*path awareness*," for ourselves, as we carry forward our thoughts into the unfolding years, and for those men and women we study and seek to understand, provides a rewarding orientation in which to launch our study.

Religious persons around the globe have testified that the religious life is a process involving both decision and transition or transformation. They have frequently found the image of a path, or of a way of proceeding, to be helpful in communicating a sense of direction, or orientation, following upon decision, and transition in process suggested by movement along such path or in following such a way. The notion of *a way* of living or *a path* to follow with its concomitant sense of stepping onto and moving forward in the way or path appears throughout Buddhist and Christian literature. We provide a discussion of the most important dimension of the notion of "path"as *magga/mārga* in a sense not very familiar to English readers but long known to Theravāda Buddhists, as the arising of salvific efficacy, as a moment of dawning liberating awareness. This might strike one as *a novel way of speaking* of a path, as something that arises, but the point is that such a path constitutes *a new orientation of life,* a new, assured, tried and true way of living because something profoundly new is seen providing direction supportively.

And as soon as one meets the Sanskrit word *mārga,* "path or way," one thinks of the great Hindu testimony of salvific accessibility that lies at the heart of reality, that there are *ways* of living authentically, religiously, frequently referred to as the "three paths" or "three ways" (*trimārga*). A person, in the process of determining which way is more conducive in leading onward, which one enables a person to become more completely attuned to the salvific reality undergirding all that can be known, discerns how he or she can become more fully integrated, "yoked" (*yoga*), with himself or herself and that reality, whether by the quality of action (*karmayoga*) or through loving devotion (*bhaktiyoga*) or in liberating insight (*jñānayoga*). The *Bhagavadgītā,* that magnificent scripture that today is hardly limited to the Hindu tradition, provides a lasting testimony to the importance of these ways in the context of liberation. We become aware of an important affirmation of Hindu men and women that there are *more than one way* by means of which one might become enabled to find salvific liberation.

When considering that great portion of human history, and human lives and traditions and records—and one can go on and on, significantly so—of what one might call "East Asia," having moved beyond the self-centered nomenclature of "the Far East," we see the enormously consequential notion of *Dao/Tao,* "way or path," and how human life has been largely what it has been in that part of our world because that notion was present, with which men and women could become engaged. It has loomed large in Chinese religiousness, in the Tradition of the Way (*tao-chiao,* what some have called "Taoism," more recently written as "Daoism"), and in the Classical Tradition (*ju-chiao*, what some have called "Confucianism") and has played an important role in the religious orientations of men and women in Japan whose religious engagement was given a name by the Chinese, Shintō (*shen-tao*, pronounced in Japanese [*kun* reading] as *kami[-no-] michi*, "the way of the *kami*").

Other than the Theravāda Buddhist tradition, our considerations of the Buddhist case will deal with the Pure Land Buddhist tradition (*Jōdo Shinshū*) in Japan. In that remarkable heritage, there is a well-known image of "the White Way/Path" (*byaku-dō*), in the parable of "the two rivers," which portrays the condition of men and women, confronted with fearful disorientation and threatening perplexities of life, having the opportunity of walking a narrow and difficult path between storm-tossed water on one side and raging fire on the other, being enabled, once stepping forth, to hear the encouraging words of Śākyamuni speaking from the hither side and of Amida Buddha beckoning from the other. Difficult the way might well be, as historians of religion and other scholars frequently note about difficult soteriological crossings depicted in the religious imagination, but one notes that in this crossing, as metaphorically depicted by Pure Land Buddhists, a starting point is in the realization that one is hardly left to one's wits alone.

Turning to the three major streams of the Western religious heritage stemming from the eastern Mediterranean region and becoming ever more self-consciously global, we find, first, with the Hebrew Bible/Old Testament, a term for "way" or "path" (*derekh,* as at Gen. 18:19, for example, and *ōrakh*, as at Ps. 25:4 and 27:11, for example),[2] as one would fully anticipate, given the context. As the tradition continued, a profound sense of movement, expressed in a notion of going accordingly, living aright, fully, was given focus in the notion of religious law (*halakhah,* derived from *halakh*) which continued to be developed through the centuries to make clearer and continually more relevant the understanding of God's teaching, Torah (תּוֹרָה).

The early followers of Christ were referred to as "men and women being of the Way" (*tēs hodou ontas, andras te kai gunaikas* / τῆς ὁδοῦ ὄντας, ἄνδρας τε χαὶ γυναῖκας, Acts 9:2)[3] by Paul, when he was known as Saul, before the arising of the salvific insight of the risen Christ, and again by Paul, this time on trial, who refers to himself as worshiping according to "the Way" (*kata tēn hodon* / κατὰ τὴν ὁδόν), which he acknowledges some call a "sect" (*airesin* / αἵρεσιν, Acts 24:14; see also an outsider's designation, to which Paul is apparently referring, "sect of the Nazarenes," *tōn Nazōraiōn aireseōs* / τῶν Ναζωραίων αἱρέσεως, Acts 24:5). A complaint by one Demetrius about the economic pressure brought on his livelihood as a silversmith and that of other artisans in Ephesus and elsewhere engaged in providing customary ritual objects, because of Paul's restlessness about such things, gave rise to "considerable disturbance concerning the Way" (*taraxos ouk oligos peri tēs hodou* / τάραχος οὐκ ὀλίγος περὶ τῆς ὁδοῦ, Acts 19:23).

And, of course, there is that weighty response by Jesus at John 14:6 to the sincere question raised by a perplexed Thomas, to which we will return in a note to chapter 17, "Buddhists and Baptists: In Conversation into Our Common Future." Jesus utters one of his significant "I am [myself, indeed (*egō eimi* / ἐγώ εἰμι)]" statements making it clear that dynamic engagement with God as *Father* is open as the way for those who truly understand the unique life and ministry of Christ. This, of course, was of profound significance for those who held dear John's Gospel as they were becoming more self-conscious of the Way and of their supportive religious community in distinction from the Jewish community and the larger sociocultural world at the time.

Those of us who are Muslims have celebrated the "straight path"(*as-sirāt al-mustaqīm*) as providing the means whereby one can enhance one's life through submission (*islām*) to God's guidance on this given straight path. This Way of God, Muslims aver, encapsulates all that is in the heavens and on the earth, and tends toward God.[4] The grand concept of religious law is also held warmly and centrally in the Islamic heritage. This practice is a way of recognizing divine involvement in one's routine living making it, thereby, hardly routine but remarkably refreshing. "Law" tends to weigh heavily in the thinking of contemporary North Americans, carrying connotations running from proscriptions and prohibitions to obligations and duties. For Muslims, and Jews, religious law is a gift. This sense of religious law demonstrates that it is also refreshingly life-sustaining, a sense captured by Muslims in the Arabic word *sharī'a* in its fundamental sense of "the road to the watering place."[5]

Pilgrims walking in different directions, in different centuries, with different messages, seeking different ends, have, in their simultaneous personal inward movement, graced both our planet and our humanity. Persons have been on the move both literally and metaphorically. It is in this metaphorical sense that I introduce the theme of "Way" in this volume. Part of what is involved in the study of the religious lives of men and women is to be conscious of the point on which one, the student, stands as one launches this study—an ever-cumulative dynamic process conducted among friends. When an academic, who aspires to be Christian, spends more than forty years studying the religious traditions of humankind with some focus given to the Buddhist and Christian traditions, the engagement of mind and of intellect yields in that person a consciousness of himself as being a student of other persons while simultaneously grounding him in the patent historical fact that he, insofar as he is human and seeks, however faultily, to live religiously, is studying persons who in their humanity and aspirations are not unlike himself. In the course of forty years, in the United Kingdom, in the United States, in India, Sri Lanka, and in Japan, I have been in motion: spatial, intellectual, and personal—inseparably so.

An astute observer, keen listener, humane companion will naturally learn from others with whom he or she has studied as in the company of friends. One realizes what others have helped to make available for one's benefit, and gathers it in the process, little by little through the years and around the world. Most of the chapters that follow were not originally offered as major breakthroughs in Buddhist scholarship or as standard, official, or orthodox formulations of Christian doctrinal positions for Buddhist-Christian colloquia. They were written initially mostly in response to invitations extended by Buddhists and represent an engagement with issues that matter; and for some, matter cosmically. Most were presented as papers or lectures or talks in the presence of Buddhists from whom I have gleaned much about a religious tradition and also about how to attempt to live life well. It would be inappropriate for me to claim that I have, solitarily, ploughed new soil in developing this volume, uniformly exposing new levels in Buddhist Studies. It would be arrogant to suggest that I, myself, have harvested that for which Buddhists, religious persons, are aspiring. On the contrary, gradually, over the years, important dimensions in learning how to live life well have been exposed, considered, offered by Buddhists, and I have been sufficiently fortunate to come along and glean what was already there. It is in this sense, and with a sense of gratitude to others, that I have collected articles previously deliberately placed separately for publication and now present them with appropriate revisions as a body of work providing interpretations of Buddhist life and practice and reflections arising from a Christian's engagement with those interpretations. Among the different paths, ways of life, modes of living made manifest by religious men and women, it has been my good fortune to have caught a glimpse primarily of two: the Buddhist and the Christian.

And so we begin our inquiry, aware of who we are, with an engaged and disciplined intellectual commitment utilizing as many relevant factors arising from the complex cluster of lived experiences as we are capable. We place this inquiry into religious understanding as itself a religious activity, a religious quest among friends, with the recognition that these paths or ways, these modes providing fundamental orientation in life, are part of *our* ways, paths discovered and continued from century to century in *our one* global religious history.

Recognizing and subsequently affirming what constitutes a path that provides both support and orientation in life is not automatic, of course. Nor is it merely an unengaging speculative activity. It seems to require, on the part of those persons discerning the creative edge in finding meaning in life by following those paths, a deeply profound affirmation of commitment, of trust in and simultaneously responsibility to the process of discoveries it opens before one. In English, we often speak of this profound affirmation as "faith," a quality at the foundations of the religious life. Reflecting on the evidence arising from colloquia with Theravāda and Jōdo Shinshū Buddhists we uncover subtle issues perhaps broadening, surely refining, our articulation of this quality of faith while, at the same time, recognizing that all of us involved have a sense of what we are considering. Although we are aware that these paths are not necessarily multidirectional, we are also not in position boldly to argue that there will indeed be ultimate convergence. At the same time, we know what it is to walk along a path, both literally and in the metaphorical sense we have noted, and we know the persons that we are, in the particularity of our given life contexts, while recognizing that we are not unfamiliar with an orientational and directional process involving both decision and transition or transformation.

In this inclusive awareness of familiarity with what is going on, both in our studies and in our religious lives, we also become aware that, from our differing perspectives, we have made, both personally and communally now and through the centuries, affirmations about faith that suggest a tendency toward convergence. This awareness occurs in colloquia, where we speak with each other about ourselves. In this intellectual and necessarily honest procedure, we come to realize that we "have been in this together"—and this for quite some time, through millennia. We thereby come to endorse through these colloquia that whatever the future might be that arises from these colloquia, it will be *our* future. But the future remains open to us, to do as we think best, best for ourselves of course, and, inseparably, what is best for others too. This will depend to a great extent on what we take ourselves to be, religious men and women, genuinely human, ever seeking to understand, as an expression of faith, ourselves, our neighbor, our friend, the world in which we find ourselves—persons and things—and in the process creatively responding to the challenges of the future and thereby, in the face of these challenges, disclosing a future that is friendly for all of us.

# Abbreviations

| | |
|---|---|
| C: | Chinese |
| Grk: | Greek |
| *HOS*: | Harvard Oriental Series |
| J: | Japanese |
| P: | Pali |
| *PTS*: | The Pali Text Society |
| *RTS*: | Ryukoku Translation Series |
| *RSV*: | Revised Standard Version of the Bible |
| S: | Sinhala |
| *SBTS*: | Shin Buddhism Translation Series |
| Skt: | Sanskrit |
| *SSZ*: | Shinshū Shōgyō Zensho |

# I

# The Quest for Religious Understanding with Theravāda, Jōdo Shinshū Buddhists, and Christians

# 1

# On Understanding Religious Men and Women

*We are entering an exciting period in the history of our global religious self-consciousness. It is no longer a period in which persons study others and offer their findings to audiences back home, to a few hundred participants in one's academic discipline. It is a time that enables one to live alongside friends, to learn about them and with them, their vision for and struggles with life, and to learn from them about how to live life well. The inquiry invites us to look and listen, and not to frame a picture.*

## WHAT IS BEING ATTEMPTED

When I first shared the words that follow in this chapter, some years ago, I began by saying, "I am honored to be here to speak to you today," indicating both the context—a speaker addressing an audience—and an attitude on the part of the speaker, now the writer. The invitation to speak at Otani University, Kyoto, Japan, took the form, "Speak to us about what you are doing."[1]

What am I doing? It seems to me that this is one of the great questions. When asked, "Who are you?" most of us begin to define ourselves by our names and occupations, our jobs, mode of employment. When asked "What are you?" our tendency has been, in the last half-century or so, to turn the search for an answer over to our university colleagues in the natural sciences or social sciences. We sometimes seek, surprisingly, an empirical or, disappointingly, an impersonal reply to this question: I am made of water, bone, flesh, and so forth, or I am a species or a social animal, a Caucasian male or female, an Afro-American, Asian American, a minority, and so forth.

Nevertheless, in the development of the Western religious heritage, one question has loomed large: "What am I?"—providing a personal orientation to the issue raised more indirectly by our questions, "Who are you?" and "What are you?" "What am I?" is the kind of question that gives one pause to begin the search for fundamental criteria, foundational orientations, in light of which one shapes one's identity. "What am I?" is one of those great questions, and the Western heritage has had a great deal to say in response to it.

Among the answers that have been given to the question, "What am I?" one finds, "I am a Jew," or "I am a Muslim," or "I am a sinner saved by the grace of God," or "I am a child of God." Another response, representing also a major strand in the Western heritage, is, "I am a rational being." Perhaps we have weathered the faddish reply of saying, in response to this question, only "I am an individual." It appears that we in the West are moving into (back to?) a more engaging formulation of "I am a person" in response to the question, "What am I?" We are learning (again?) that one moves from being an individual into becoming a person as one moves from isolation into meaningful relationships.

The assignment put to me, to talk about what I am doing, gave me pause, made me ask, "What *am* I doing?" That, I suggest, is a question that will repay reflection. As is the case with most engaging questions, there can be levels in one's reply. One can reply to the question by noting a particular concurrent action, for example, that one is speaking at a Japanese university to a group of scholars who are Buddhists. But this is hardly the full extent to which one could reply to the question "What am I doing?" Sensing the levels in the responses one might make to this question could well indicate, for example, the development of a child through adolescence into the maturity of adulthood as those responses move from being simple, to becoming complex, more subtle, perhaps to move again to a profound simplicity.

There also might be a dimension in responses to this question that could indicate the sensitivity one might have in attempting to live one's life religiously. There is a story passed around among persons who have chosen to aspire to live life Buddhistically through the Zen medium. You readily recall how a child will play outside, or in his or her room, for hours, playing intently, moving buses, houses, even continents, it seems, with total concentration and creative interest. Mother or father will call to the child: "What are you doing?" The child answers without a moment's delay, "Nothing." This little example suggests a way of living that is consonant with the Buddha's intention: to be engaged with the moment, creatively so, as the moment unfolds, ever with it, right there, and yet, as it were, doing nothing. I have shared this example in a sermon offered in the First Baptist Church of Hamilton, New York,[2] indicating what it might be like to live as a child of God; just there, right there, ever creatively so, responding freely, lovingly—doing nothing.

There are dimensions suggested when emphases and intonation are given to the question when spoken—

> ***What*** are you doing?
> What ***are*** you doing?
> What are ***you*** doing?
> What are you ***doing***?

Not only might this question be asked of the men and women of Otani University, but also of all of us on this globe: What are we doing? But the question has been put to me—and I am grateful for the pause that it has given me and the opportunity to attempt to formulate an initial response.

*What am I doing*? I am attempting to understand the religious life of men and women, what they hold most dear, what they cherish, choose to live life by because they have found thereby that life has meaning, choose to remember and pass on to their children—and why they have done all of this. More customarily formulated in academic circles, I am attempting to understand *homo religiosus,* religious persons. As a person who is inadequate *in being Christian* but who, nevertheless, aspires to continue living with an awareness of this inadequacy, and as a person who is *a Christian,*[3] I have been introduced to a religious dimension in human life that is old, as old as *homo sapiens,* discerning persons, and continually new in its formulations and manifestations, in ancient civilizations, in the great continuing traditions, and in the nonliterate or extracivilizational societies, in the past and today, around the globe.

I seek to understand not only things, but persons; not solely the operations or patterns or constellations of objects or events, but also what those operations or patterns have meant to persons, or wherein no meaning was found in or through them by persons; most fundamentally, I seek to understand what it means to be genuinely human, authentically a person. The historical record leaves no doubt that wise people have lived, thought, and died, have indicated, too, that being born into our species does not, of itself, provide an answer to what human life is, that being born a human being is a biological process, of itself insufficient to provide an answer to what it is to become genuinely human.

## THE LIMITATION OF ANY ONE METHOD: THE SOCIOLOGICAL

As is the case when generalizations are made about any group of persons, one can misrepresent the important insights of a few in speaking broadly of the many. The sociological approach to the study of religion, germinating within and expanding beyond a particular scholarly discipline within what is called the social sciences, has been handled deftly, although to limited results, by a few leading sociologists of religion, and some cultural anthropologists, too. But the particular method has been so prevalently applied uncritically by so many writers that lesser lights in the discipline have apparently failed constantly and consistently to evaluate the method itself, tending to accept it as an objectively verified and scientifically established method of procedure rather than as a matter of consensus.

Some social scientists—I, rather, prefer to call them social theorists—have attempted explanations for the process of acquiring meaning in life, for discerning how we ought to live to become genuinely human. We human beings, we are told, have little instinctual equipment to prepare us for living in the uncertain complexities of life. We search for meaning, for a normative pattern of understanding that will enable us to make sense of the unfolding of our fears, anxieties, and uncertainties. Society, we are told, over the years fashions these normative patterns and introduces us to them as we grow older. Through education, a society leads its members, and, it would follow, therefore, we ourselves are led, to embrace the models for interpreting meaning which a society, in its wisdom, has fashioned for us, models that tend also to perpetuate a society's particular understanding of itself. This is a neat explanation, and one that has been around for about a century or so with recurring modifications and reformulations, but one that, upon analysis, has strands going back to ancient times.

It is easier to say that something called "society" does this than to say that persons do, much easier to move from the complex, variegated, multifaceted reality of persons to a theoretical level and to talk about a formal reified grouping of persons, whether in village or massive civilization, that operates on an abstract level as something called "society," as something perpetuating its norms. It is difficult for me to say that the wise persons who have gone before us in history were, in effect, not very smart, that they took to be the basis of reality, the source of meaning, what in reality was only their inheritance from society, merely the normative patterns society had projected in order to perpetuate itself.

But a social theorist would have little difficulty with my restlessness. I would be told that it is part of the operation of society, in this process of establishing and perpetuating meaning, that it projects this meaning onto what is now called another order of reality in a very subtle way so that it is then, subsequently, discerned as actually being other than, apart from, the ordinary realm of human experience. I would be told that when this projected meaning is reappropriated by a person it is discerned as possessing a distinct quality, as being other, as striking a person from "the other side," as it were, but now endowed with new force and significance.

Yet I am still restless with this. Wise persons have indicated to me, through their writings, and also by what has been written about them, that they are more reflective than they have been judged by some to be, more analytical, more subtle, more self-conscious, even more humane. They have not indicated that they have committed their lives to what society has structured for them, have not oriented their future to a projection of normative meaning put out there somehow by something called society. They do not seem to have been hit, as it were, by a projection from something called the social reality which somehow "came to them" from another, fanciful, order of existence.

At least two inferences can be drawn from a consideration of this general sociological approach to the study of something called "religion." Some social theorists, who have adopted this approach, have studied some of the variegated forms of religious systems in different contexts and various periods around the globe, and have drawn from their comparative studies a theoretical explanation for differences while maintaining that we humans are similar in our conceptual processes and group dynamics. Their work has shed some light on interpreting the *differences between societies* and the religious systems within those societies. The second inference is more problematic. It suggests, from this mode of analysis frequently uncritically applied, resulting in a theory becoming the norm, that it is, in fact, "the social scientist" who really knows; the religious person really does not, does not know the real, only thinks he or she knows the real, which, for our social theorists, is merely a discernment of a social projection appropriated and perceived as having unusual significance.

My point is this: this particular approach to the study of something called "religion" can be instructive when investigating differences among religious systems in different societies, but it also frequently, if not regularly, involves another discernment of difference, one that leaves me restless. That difference seems to be *the difference between the social theorist and religious persons*. There is great irony in this: the social theorist knows the basis for all of this; the religious person only thinks he or she knows.

Religious traditions have been shaped mightily by the societies of which they have been a part, certainly, and they have contributed weightily to the formation of the cultures that have supported the civilizations in which societies have participated, assuredly. There is a dynamic process involved in this, a dialectic of a religious tradition and the history of societies, of course. One would be obstinate not to see this. Yet, one would be obdurate were one to maintain that the position represented by this particular sociological approach is comprehensive of truth, that this interpretation of religious phenomena is all that is real, even that this approach is the only one that a social scientist or social theorist can endorse as a social scientist or theorist. One wonders whether a person might too readily submit the human mind to a discipline, willing to allow his or her study to be defined not by *what* is being studied, that is, the subject, but by *how* the study is to be conducted, the method. Not infrequently does one meet this, as in the case of a social scientist saying that he or she cannot speak about a subject insofar as that subject might extend beyond his or her particular method of approach. One wonders what happened to the intellectual, what happened to the unlimited scope of inquiry launched by the human mind into a subject. It seems to me that this particular sociological approach to the study of religious persons is culturally specific, is Western, is recent, and, in a comparative context today, is certainly limited, tends to be a whit arrogant, and hence, obviously, is, in itself, inadequate.

I recall the teaching of the Buddha, recorded in the Pali texts, which urges us never to fall into the trap of saying "this alone is true, all else is false." One wonders whether a person who has seen the point of the creative edge of this advice could maintain an interpretation of religious life that sees it *only* as one dimension of a society's self-preservation, as really only being based on the only basis of reality available to the inquiring mind, namely, something called society, all else being conjecture at best, open to question, certainly ontologically unreal, probably, or epistemologically false, possibly. There might be an attempt to say that such a remark as this one by the Buddha is merely a social projection put into the words of a socially sanctioned holy figure. But in attempting to do this, one fails to see the cutting edge of the remark: not to become stuck in any way, or with any method or approach, by saying "This alone is true, all else is false."

Or let me put it another way. It would seem unlikely that a student of the religious heritage that has come to be called Jōdo Shinshū would have achieved understanding of Shinran were that person to argue that Shinran represents someone so overwhelmed by a sense of personal inadequacy and so at a loss at how to save himself (of course this statement *already* represents a fundamental misunderstanding of Shinran) that he had no recourse but to accept what society had already projected as "other-power." The same would hold were such student to say that Shinran was a religious genius but one who broke the established order of meaning by reinterpreting previous projections made by something called "society" in such a way that a person ridden with guilt as he was could still find salvation.

## LIVING AND LEARNING IN THE COMPANY OF FRIENDS

Nearly a half-century ago, after completing undergraduate studies in history, philosophy, and religion at Baylor University, a Southern Baptist university, and general postgraduate Christian theological studies in The Southern Baptist Theological Seminary, I began a concentrated study of the Buddhist tradition at the University of London. It was primarily library work, with some amount of sympathy and historical sensitivity. Four decades ago, while working in a doctoral program at Harvard University, I arrived in Sri Lanka, that ancient country and idyllic setting where Dharma has been long remembered by persons because they have been long nurtured by Dharma as the Buddha rediscovered it and shared it by speaking it and by living it. I then began to rely on friends in Sri Lanka who helped me, who worked with me, who taught me, who gave of their time, energy, and care. I lived with dear Buddhist friends, and continue so to do today, who, in their friendship and caring, introduced me, however falteringly on my part, to that quality of life to which they, too, aspired, and led me to discern their faith—not Buddhism, mind you; faith is much more fundamental than a reified concept called "Buddhism." I began to learn of the faith of Buddhist men and women, the way they placed their hearts and minds on Dharma, Dharma that enabled Gautama to become enlightened when he realized it, Dharma which supports these friends, our Sri Lankan Buddhist brothers and sisters, as they move through the experiences of human life.

I was writing a PhD thesis at the time entitled "Dhamma: Western Academic and Sinhalese Buddhist Interpretations—A Study of a Religious Concept."[4] I lived in Sri Lanka for three years during that time and have since returned frequently, even on three occasions bringing groups of Colgate undergraduate students to learn there with me. I continue to learn about Dharma, how lives have been changed by coming in touch with it, how hopes have been buttressed by hearing it, how wrongs have been righted by responding to it, how life is lived with dignity, grace, and beauty by being supported by it. I have learned that the heritage of Sinhala Buddhists, which they have come more recently to call the Theravāda, and some Buddhists today continue mistakenly to call "Hīnayāna" (although in the early formative stage of the Mahāyāna the use of the term *hīnayāna* I consider a *creative* mistake), is rooted in a calm certainty that growth in one's life can be ever new and consistently, constructively, creative in the context of uncertainties, in the face of doubt and the unknown, precisely because Dharma abides and it supports the one living it—*dhāretī ti dhammo*, freely, but adequately, translated, "It is called 'Dhamma' because 'it holds, supports,'" the old texts tell us, and, I will add, empirical evidence makes manifest.

These persons in Sri Lanka have taken refuge in the Buddha, what he represents as a glorious exemplar for our lives, with the hope that they, too, might realize Dharma that served as the foundation for that quality of his life. They have taken refuge in Dharma, in the Salvific Truth that abides, is there/here, realizing that it is entirely capable of supporting the heart and mind that is placed on it, that we can take it up and hold in mind and in heart, that we can give expression to it readily in living freely, abundantly, come what may, and that it leads on, without fail, to the occasion when reality is known and truth realized, and completed is what was to have been completed, and done is what was to have been done (P: *katam karanīyam*). We let our words stop there because *no* projections of any kind are adequate, neither those of society nor mine. We move into silence, comfortably, without fear and trembling, because Dharma abides.

These people of Sri Lanka also take refuge in the Saṅgha, by no means the local order of monks—fellows known in most cases since their childhood days. The robes are honored, of course, not because the monastic institution "denies this world," as some might put it, but because the robes symbolically represent a mode of life other than this life that we are living, a mode of life that puts this life into a broader context than the ordinary limits set on it, a mode of life that enables us to see *this* life precisely as it is—*ordinary*. The monastic institution constantly reminds us that this life is not the only life for living, is not all that there is to living, either. Refuge is taken in the Saṅgha, not in the monks but in those who have gone far in the soteriological process, those countless worthies of the past who also have demonstrated qualities of life that are worthy of emulation, who have shown us the way of Dharma-living, who have set the examples for Dharma-realization.[5]

Now, it has been my pleasant opportunity to have studied in Japan.[6] I am not here attempting to understand the historical institution that has come to be called Jōdo Shinshū. I can do that, perhaps, with more reading and language study in libraries in the United States. I am seeking to understand *why I have been at home here* among Jōdo Shinshū Buddhist men and women.

I am not planning to understand fully *shinjin* (true, honest, sincere heart/mind) or *shinjitsu shingyō* (true and real pure heart/mind) or the number of related concepts or expressions. I have learned enough during this period of study in Japan to say that I am at ease with the thought of going to my grave without ever fully achieving an understanding of *shinjin.* I will keep working on these notions, realizing that this particular struggle is both immensely rewarding and, to use Christian theological terms in response to what I have learned from friends here, this struggle is divine. I am forming tentative conclusions about *shinjin,* one of which I will briefly mention here while holding a more thorough inquiry for our chapter 5.

I am only just beginning to grapple with this issue. It appears that *shinjin* is not best translated into English as "faith." Christian theological categories do not seem to have a word to match *shinjin.* From a Christian theological perspective, if one were to seek for a dimension in the religious experience of Jōdo Shinshū men and women that represents a quality in the religious orientation of persons to life, about which one could speak in a general context utilizing the English term *faith,* one might turn to what I might tentatively translate as "refuge," to *kimyō* (taking refuge) or *kie* (to turn around, to turn toward), with their implications of responding to a summons to return home, to turn around (with something of the sense of the New Testament Greek verb *metanoeō* [μετανοέω] and noun *metanoia* [μετάνοια]) and to return to the source in which to place one's commitment of one's life. But one moves carefully in this consideration, being fully aware that a notion of self-power, ego-agency (*jiriki*), might be lurking in the subliminal psychic operation involved in this refuge seeking, this turning and responding.

I am not suggesting that there is something like a movement from *kimyō* to *shinjin,* as one might mistakenly indicate by drawing a line on a chart, from "A to B," as it were. I sense that *shinjin* is present in *kimyō,* but also that there might be a slight difference. It appears that in *kimyō* one is self-consciously aware that one is doing the action, that one is doing, *while receiving, kimyō,* that one is returning home in response to Amida's gentle but authoritative summons. In *kimyō* one is aware that one is giving expression to *kimyō,* has responded, is responding, but in *shinjin* one is not aware that one has or possesses *shinjin. Shinjin,* rather, permeates one's heart and mind and *possesses* one.

There might be something more basic, more fundamental, involved in all of this that might be suggestive of what Christians tend to mean when they speak of faith. Perhaps what I mean by faith is much more readily at hand than the subtleties found in the dialectic structure of "deep" *shinjin* (*jinshinjin*). There appears to be a moment in one's religious life when one really *hears* (*mon*: *ki*[*ku*])—not just "listens to" (*chō*)—really hears the *sūtra*s, really hears a sermon, really hears the well-spoken and timely word. There is a moment in a person's life when one tends to lean in the direction of making a response, leans to respond, as it were, moves with an inclination into responding, and makes a response.

At this moment, in this movement of really hearing and in responding, perhaps initially responding only in deeply authentic receiving, perhaps, also initially, with commitment, is the dimension of human religious experience that represents the dawn of faith, as it appears that Christians have been enabled to discern it. In a sense, then, in the act of really *hearing, kimyō* is taking place. An engaged consideration of whether or not *shinjin* has arisen is rather a question *of* faith, arising *from* faith, a question *for* faith; it does not entail whether or not we have faith, it is not a question about faith. Faith is already present. And so it is with *kimyō*. Let me turn the point succinctly: *shinjin* is important for us not because we have *shinjin,* it seems, but because we have faith.

## LOOKING FORWARD INTO OUR COMMON FUTURE

Of more than passing note, however, is recognizing that a man from Texas, more recently of New York, a Southern Baptist having served on the diaconate of an American Baptist church, an ordained minister of the Gospel of Jesus Christ, a student of the Theravāda Buddhist tradition who has also turned his attention also to Jōdo Shinshū, is speaking about attempts to understand the religious life of men and women before a group of Buddhist scholars at a well-known Japanese Buddhist university. Could this have happened before the latter half of the twentieth century? I do not think so.

Although you have heard frequent references to history and to the past, mention of tradition and heritage, I do not want to leave you with the thought that I am looking backward, looking into the past. I see my task as looking forward, toward the future. I fear that too many of our Buddhist young men and women are being trained to become scholars of the past with little concern, based on disciplined scholarly interest, for the present or the future. In the Buddhist case, it is important to study the past, of course; I would be the last to deny this. However, I think it is inadequate to have experts on the early formation of the monastic discipline (*vinaya*) who do not have also a scholarly grasp on the function of that discipline in the lives of Buddhists today, or to have Japanese Buddhist experts on something called early folk religion in India who do not have also a disciplined intellectual interest in the intricacies of Japanese religious life. And the examples could continue. It is very important to have an understanding of the history of the Buddhist tradition, even of the early period of the tradition in India, indeed, of its movement through Central Asia, China, Korea, and Japan, certainly. But there are Buddhists living *today* in South and Southeast Asia who share with Japanese Buddhists the quest for enlightenment. What do Buddhists in contemporary Japan know of them?

Similarly, if I were asked how doctoral students in the area of the comparative study of religion should select a subject for study, I would suggest that they choose the most engaging dimension of a religious heritage that is currently unfolding and is still developing in a major cultural complex and civilization today. That would assure that these doctoral students will look to the past, of course, but also to the future where they would also stand alongside intelligent, insightful, reflective friends, participating in the religious tradition being studied, who would instruct them when they are on the right track, take issue with them when they go astray, point the doctoral students both in the direction of their inquiry and in the direction of life as it is to be lived religiously.

I am looking to the future, to greater understanding of us as persons aspiring to live religiously. I think there is purpose in what I am doing.

We mentioned a little story about a mother or father calling out to a child intent at play, "What are you doing?" and the child's quick and spontaneous reply, "Nothing." Will I find myself sometime in the future replying to the question, "What am I doing?" or "What are you doing?" by saying "Nothing"? I do not know. Perhaps you will allow me to wait to respond to that question, to hold it for the future when that question will be asked with finality and perhaps I might be summoned. Perhaps at that time I might know completely what I am doing. Perhaps then I might reply.

# 2

# Truth and History in Interreligious Understanding

## *A Preliminary Inquiry*

*The record of scholarship in religious studies in the past century, the impressive amassing of reliable information, is remarkable. It has enabled us to move beyond anecdotal reports about exotic others to the attainment of knowledge. But knowledge, in the enterprise of becoming authentically human, is not enough. We are no longer to ask what persons believe, but what they have come to understand and why that understanding matters.*

Any particular day is a day humankind has never before witnessed. A conference of engaged persons, Buddhists and Christians, representing primarily two universities, Chikushi Jogakuen of Dazaifu, Japan, and Loyola Marymount University of Los Angeles, in September 2001, was an event that had never occurred before in the history of humankind. This much we know. The newness of every situation in which we enter colloquia, and the consequential novelty in innovative thinking required of us, should not be put aside lightly. Innovative thinking is monumentally important. Obviously, on the basis of the fact of the gathering at Loyola Marymount we are aware that the Christian and Buddhist traditions are in process.

Much of what I have to say in this context and for this chapter is derived from the thinking of two Protestant Christians. The prospects of drawing upon the work of Protestants is particularly delightful for me in the presence of Roman Catholics, as at Loyola Marymount of Los Angeles, who, I am sure, will make it clear to me wherein my Protestant assumptions could be limiting, or wherein they fail to incorporate other promising avenues of inquiry into truth and history in interreligious understanding. The two Protestant thinkers are H. Richard Niebuhr (1894–1962), who was Sterling Professor of Theology and Christian

Ethics at Yale University Divinity School, and Wilfred Cantwell Smith (1916–2000), who was Professor of the Comparative History of Religion and Chair of the Committee on the Study of Religion at Harvard University.

H. Richard Niebuhr presents three fundamental convictions underlying his splendid study of revelation in his book, *The Meaning of Revelation*. The first is "the conviction that self-defense is the most prevalent source of error in all thinking and perhaps especially in theology and ethics." The second is the awareness that "the great source of evil in life is the absolutizing of the relative, which in Christianity takes the form of substituting religion, revelation, church or Christian morality for God." And the third "is that Christianity is 'permanent revolution' or *metanoia* which does not come to an end in this world, this life, or this time."[1] This brilliant Christian theologian, while writing primarily for the Christian community a little more than a half-century ago, addresses our setting today with remarkable relevance: we are to strip ourselves of defensiveness, open ourselves before God, and recognize the ongoing "metanoic" process of repentance into the divine newness of life, which Niebuhr calls "permanent revolution."

Buddhists have no difficulty applying these recommendations in our context, surely, for the testimony of Buddhists throughout the centuries reminds one not to set about to defend one's ideas, not to become disoriented about what is absolute, and also, especially with Jōdo Shinshū Buddhists, persons of the Pure Land heritage, the dialectic with regard to *shinjin* is not unlike a continuing "metanoic" process. The Buddhist tradition, too, is in process, as is all life. Niebuhr's observations certainly set a creative orientation for our considerations. But is one left only to one's wits alone if one refrains from a defensiveness, from a tendency to absolutize, and from a static view of one's tradition? Not at all, upon becoming aware of our religious communities in which we participate and of our ever more extending and inclusive community of religious intellectuals around the globe.

Wilfred Smith has suggested another threefold orientation, which complements nicely the observations by Niebuhr. Smith recommends, first, that we seek to maintain a loyalty to our own religious heritage, and to the faith that we have been enabled to discern and to embrace through that heritage; and, second, that we enter into interreligious understanding without negating either the religious traditions or the faith of other persons; and, third, that we not disregard the facts involved in the process of understanding.[2] Elsewhere, and in a different context, Smith introduces three modes for interpreting key issues in interreligious understanding: historical, theological, and personalist.[3] And, further, we want to be aware of the context in which we do our thinking, both personally and, now, here, spatiotemporally—the intellectual heritage of the academic tradition puts a check on antirationalism, or whimsical, arbitrary pronouncements.

Buddhists and Christians were at the Loyola Marymount conference largely because of loyalty to received religious heritages and as an expression of the faith we were therein enabled to discern. This loyalty can be a foundation for openness to others, to our disciplined self-consciousness, which simultaneously contributes to a lack of defensiveness and to an ability not to absolutize what is relative. In this process of understanding others we come to understand ourselves more comprehensively, which is an activity entirely consonant with continuing renewal and reformation. Required of us throughout this process is the activity of the inquiring mind, rigorous in uncovering facts, self-aware of its activity in the particularity of time and place, of context and culture. In our work as intellectuals becoming ever more aware of our global religious history, in our inquiry as Christians and Buddhists into our religious traditions and religious faith, we recognize, indeed celebrate, an irrefutable foundation for meaning in life: each other—the persons we are, as *loci* of truth, of faith, of meaning in history.

## RESPONSIBILITY FOR WHAT WE KNOW OF OUR HISTORY

Our first move is to recognize how novel our situation is. If it were not for the creative life-experiences of the Loyola Marymount conference organizers, the particular persons would not have been gathered there. The situation was new! Monumentally so! Smith speaks to persons in the current situation as indicating

> the unimaginably promising venture of becoming authentically aware of each other, and thereby of themselves, and of their several participation in the whole . . . and aware of their own and other's participation in the process of unending transition. . . . For the first time there is for all of us an increasingly common consciousness of the world around us, given by science, and of the total process of our human history, including religious history, and of the fact that this is currently entering a strikingly new phase in all its parts.[4]

If we are not among the first group, we are certainly *Nisei,* as it were, a second generation, in this ever-new phase of mutual and corporate awareness. We are, indeed, becoming ever more self-conscious of each other and of our global religious history.

We, of the twenty-first century, know well the thought of the thirteenth-century theologian Thomas Aquinas (1225–1274). We know, also, a good deal about his contemporaries, among whom were Madhva (1238–1317), a theologian who formulated the *dvaita* interpretation of Vedānta with special reference to Krishna in India; Jalāl ad-Dīn Rūmī (1207–1273), a theologian and mystic of Konya in eastern Anatolia, a lover of God; our great Japanese religious geniuses, Shinran (1173–1262), Dōgen (1200–1253), and Nichiren (1222–1282)—to name a few. Not only have we learned a great deal more within the Christian heritage since the thirteenth century, we have come to know much more about the thirteenth century in our global religious history, more than was available to Thomas. Ignatius of Loyola (1491–1556), illustrious initiator of the Jesuits and the first general of this impressive religious order, canonized in 1622, and important for Loyola Marymount University, had his contemporaries also: Martin Luther (1483–1546), a German Protestant reformer; John Calvin (1509–1564), a French Protestant reformer who flourished in Geneva; Vallabha (1479–1531), a Telugu theologian who flourished in Vrindaban, India, stressing theistic pure nonduality in Krishna; Caitanya (1486–1533), an outstanding theologian of the Vaiṣṇava movement in eastern India who was devoted in love to Krishna, and after whose death was viewed as embodying Krishna and also Rādhā. We know far more about these contemporaries of Ignatius of Loyola, their lives, their views, their contributions in our global religious history, than he did.[5] These facts are significant for our consideration without even having to mention the Buddha, K'ung Tzu, Lao Tzu, or Śaṅkara, or Rāmānuja, or the *Dhammapada,* the *Upaniṣads,* the *Bhagavadgītā,* the *Lotus Sutra,* or the central *sūtras* for Jōdo Shinshū. And, of course, a parallel observation can be made regarding Shinran, who lived and made his enormous contribution to our religious life without the slightest idea of the role of grace in later Christian theology or *prasāda* (Sanskrit), and *aruḷ* (Tamil) in the richly devotional heritage of Śaivasiddhānta, particularly in South India.

However, we, living and working and thinking today, are responsible for our knowledge of our religious history. What do we make of this enhanced knowledge and broadened awareness? How will we respond with responsibility to God, to our religious heritage, to each other in the midst of this new knowledge which yields among us, as Smith has put it, a corporate self-consciousness? There is need for a firm recognition of the significance of history, but by this I do not mean another reified "great something."[6] When pressed, it seems the significance of history comes down to two important foundations: causality and personhood. By causality I mean the historical causal sequence in space and time of events, whether these events be geological, biological, even species evolution, or social. The *significance* of history, rather, is to be found in the lives of persons; their thoughts, their actions, aspirations, accomplishments, failures, contributions, their human lives lived out in both space and time. If our history is *ONE,* it is the *OUR* in this phrase that makes it so. It is the recognition that we human beings have been involved in living and in dying in space and time. One could surely say that dropping the atomic bombs on Hiroshima and Nagasaki were enormously significant events in history. They were, and continue to be significant events. In the final analysis this significance rests on the fact that some of us did the dropping, and others of us experienced the death and destruction, and still others of us are doing the remembering. That grounding in personhood is the final foundation for historical significance.[7]

Our Hindu testimony suggests this. If *saṃsāra* has any meaning it is to be found not in some purposeful mass movement of human events—as perhaps Hegel and Marx might have thought[8]—as though *saṃsāra,* misunderstood if a reified concept, had some kind of inherent worth. Meaning is to be found in the soteriological arena of the human heart. There is where Śiva dances. It is because

Śiva continues to dance in the human heart that Śiva dances at Chidambaram in South India. A kind of complementariness, rather than contradiction, is offered to us by those of us who are Hindus: deity gives to us *darśan,* we receive *darśan* in the context of our living. In this way, God appears and in that appearing offers a way of knowing that is soteriologically efficacious. Whereas Christians, in what appears to be an ever-narrowing focus on Jesus the Christ, have stressed primarily, and on occasion solely, the appearance of God in Christ in the reality of what is the past, in the reality of history, Hindus suggest to the Christians among us that the discernment of the Christ of faith in the Jesus of history is a matter of the human heart in response to God's initiative quite analogous with the discernment of the beholding of God, and being so beheld by God, in the act of *darśan.*

Theological implications for Christians are swirling in these considerations of history. They urge nothing more than that we apply the comprehensive and integrative symbol of the Holy Trinity more broadly; that Christians are monotheists after all and that God has become revealed to Christians as Father, as Son, and as Holy Spirit. The narrow focus on the Son tends to give undue emphasis on what some have called "real history," to the sequence of events of a particular time, without recognizing simultaneously that the universe revolves around God who, through the Holy Spirit, continues instant by instant to be involved with human beings. History, too, is in process.

I do not want to say God is in process, as some process theologians might. But God, as demonstrated by the life of Jesus the Christ, has not left humankind without witness to the abiding presence of transcendence in the ongoing process of human events. H. Richard Niebuhr has referred to God, in the final analysis, as "the nameless ultimate Transcendent and Circumambient."[9] Christian theologians have tended to stress the transcendent dimension which has broken into history sometime in the past. Our Hindu colleagues and, too, those of us who are Jōdo Shinshū Buddhists, would heartily concur that the salvific efficacy compassionately at the center of reality is also Circumambient. The locus of significance in history, it seems to me, is also, if not primarily, in persons.

## REVELATION IN HISTORY

This developing historical self-consciousness gives rise to questions of religious truth with new and vibrant relevance in a religiously plural setting. The point of view tends to shift from argumentative confrontation highlighting contradictions to engaged participation seeking to discern one's place in a cumulative and global process. A central question we might ask in this context is, What happens to revelation? Is this an entirely relativistic matter? A critical historical theology seeks to respond to this question. Niebuhr writes,

> A critical historical theology cannot, to be sure, prescribe what form religious life must take in all places and all times beyond the limits of its

> own historical system. But it can seek within the history of which it is a part for an intelligible pattern; it can undertake to analyze the reason which is in that history and to assist those who participate in this historical life to disregard in their thinking and practice all that is secondary and not in conformity with the central ideas and patterns of the historical movement. Such theology can attempt to state the grammar, not of a universal religious language, but of a particular language, in order that those who use it may be kept in true communication with each other and with the realities to which the language refers.[10]

And, he continues,

> Such a theology of revelation is objectively relativistic, proceeding with confidence in the independent reality of what is seen, though recognizing that its assertions about the reality are meaningful only to those who look upon it from the same standpoint.[11]

Understanding aright the relation of history to revelation we would recognize that the history of events as observed impartially by an observer does not constitute revelation. The history that is associated with revelation is history that is seen from within revelation, from within *our* revelation and *our* history for those of us who are Christians. And the case is similar for those of us who are in the lineage that has enabled us to become known as Jōdo Shinshū Buddhists.[12]

Wilfred Smith brings the issue clearly into focus and in doing so elaborates Niebuhr's metaphor of revelation as the grammar of communal religious language, noting how this language is most forceful in the present tense. Smith writes,

> The good news is not that God did something centuries ago in Palestine, however big that bang; but that He can and may do something, and something salvific, however small our capacity, for you and me today. *The locus of revelation is always the present, and always the person* [emphasis added]. The channel of revelation in the Christian case, Christ, is a figure in history. But history, I have insisted, moves forward, and is the process by which He comes to us; is not something to be studied backwards, as the process by which we try to recapture Him.[13]

Often, among Christians in particular who tend to stress an objective historicity of the revelation of God in Christ, great weight is placed on what is called scripture, a body of authoritative writings, from which some draw what is taken as irrefutable and irrepressible evidence to this historicity of God's revelation in Christ. Scripture, in this case, becomes in itself and of itself a basis for religious truth, a kind of theologically revelatory given providing a canon for conceptualizations and for the religious life. Setting scripture as the definitive mode for interpreting Christian life and thought not only runs the risk of absolutizing the relative, as Niebuhr warned, but also of misunderstanding scripture as well as misapprehending transcendence itself. Smith has proposed that we consider scripture to be at its most fundamental an *engagement*. In bringing to a close his book, *What Is Scripture?,* Smith offers "the further refinement, to do justice to what we have observed throughout: that it [scripture] is best characterized as, rather, trilateral: referring to a relation—an *engagement*—among humans, the transcendent, and a text."[14] The point is that when this trilateral interrelation is fragmented, becomes disintegrated, there is no longer scripture through which and in response to which persons are introduced to transcendence and by means of which persons enter into community. One is left with a text or texts. This disintegration could well happen, in the Christian case, conceivably in the Buddhist case, too, in this century. And if it should, Christians and Jōdo Shinshū Buddhists would no longer have scripture.

Things change in a cumulative tradition, obviously, and to a significant degree this is due to the faith, or lack of it, of men and women, century by century, year by year, month by month, even day by day. The revelation of which we speak, the matter of scripture to which we refer, both fall within history, a process of time and events. Neither revelation nor scripture would have occurred, surely, also, neither would they have continued, had it not been for the faith of persons. In the final analysis, Smith quite rightly affirms, the locus of faith is persons.[15]

## "FOR GOD INDEED FOR TRUTH"

These comments about history, in which revelation occurs and faith becomes manifest, set the backdrop for our brief considerations about truth in interreligious understanding. We have, to our good fortune, weathered the period of roughly seventy-five years when Western academic scholarship first began earnestly grappling with the ever-increasing data collected in the previous half-century about the great religious traditions of the world. Frequently one hears "conflicting truth claims," or "the issue of truth claims," no doubt arising from an assumption that the most important matter in understanding religious living is what persons believe and, as the data suggests, beliefs vary, even conflict. And, it is further assumed, if there are conflicting truth claims, all assertions cannot be right. And the issues are joined!

I find considerable delight in the motto of my university, which was created some decades after the university was founded as The Hamilton Literary and Theological Institution (in 1819) to serve, initially, as a Baptist seminary—*deo ac veritati*—"For God indeed for Truth." The insight of the motto makers of over a century ago is instructive for our inquiry today. As deeply meaningful as the notion of God is for us, so also should be the notion of Truth. One does not so much go around asserting before all comers this or that about God as one would want to be enabled to say, more humbly, that one is spoken for by God, held by

God, claimed by God. So, it is also with Truth. Admirable is the person who is, as it were, claimed by Truth, taken by Truth, maintained by Truth. The dynamic involved in one's relationship with God, daily, conceivably hourly, along one's way while recognizing in that relationship the dimension wherein transcendence begins is parallel to one's dynamic involvement with Truth, knowing wherein one has been true and is true and in that awareness also discerning wherein transcendence begins. A joy in one's faith is in realizing, however incompletely or inadequately, wherein there is convergence in this discernment and awareness of God and of Truth. True faith becomes true not by laying it alongside belief systems, doctrines, and dogmas and arguing over conflicting claims, but in coming to understand wherein there is this convergence of truth within the person of faith, of being true to God, to Truth, to one's neighbor and to a stranger—and one could continue"Religious truth," Smith writes,

> is utterly crucial; is the paramount and inescapable issue, before which all other religious matters, however mighty, must bow. It is final. The great question, however, is where does it lie—and the immediate question, does it lie in the religions. I am suggesting that it does not (that it lies elsewhere; namely, in persons).[16]

In our study of humankind's religiousness, we, as intellectuals—especially those of us in the academic setting—would want to try earnestly, with utmost rigor, to get the facts straight: the historical events, the doctrines, the beliefs and teachings, the texts, the liturgies and rituals, the art, architecture, poetry, and music. We do this because these matters are before us as a result of something more fundamental: the faith of persons in their response to transcendence through history and of their being true to the Truth to which their cumulative and continuing religious insight points.[17] But we do well not to stop there. We do not achieve understanding without taking the further step, moving into the unobservables to infer the humility before God and the honesty before Truth converging in the hearts of men and women. This dimension of our seeking to understand can become the most delightful, informative, enhancing, realization in our inquiry into interreligious understanding. It might arise for us when no longer reified systems are being compared, when no longer conceptually isolated traditions are being set down beside each other, when no longer faces remain primarily turned inward to one's own religious community with the overtone of communal loyalty, but, rather, when our faces become aligned with others of us—Buddhists and Christians—toward a center of value in the presence of transcendence.

It is fundamentally, and cosmically, the *person* for whom God has initiated revelation as God the Father, the Son, the Holy Spirit, gratefully received by some of us, and also, fundamentally and cosmically, it is the person for whom Truth/Reality has initiated revelation of Amida the Buddha, giver of his mind as *shinjin,* by means of which persons can grasp with understanding the abiding truth that compassion undergirds the structure of reality.[18] God is in this. Truth is in this. Persons have seen this, and have affirmed this in their lives in our common history.

Smith writes, "If God is not the truth, what is God, and what is truth? But these are rhetorical questions; God *is* truth, and one must take this intimate fact very, very seriously. Wherever truth is found, there is God. And wherever truth is stated, there God is speaking."[19] And let me note an old and greatly cherished Latin refrain sung through the centuries,

> *ubi caritas et amore, deus ibi est*
>
> "Where there is charity and love, God is there."

Sincere persons today are speaking truly, attempting, in colloquia, to be true to each other and to their heritages as they seek for Truth and in the process they are giving expression of their religious faith in seeking to understand each other in their religious lives and the mutual affirmation of the salvific core at the heart of the universe.

# 3

# Interreligious Understanding as a Religious Quest

*Among the many profound concepts involved in interreligious understanding are truth, which is of such quality that one can discern it, find it alluring, and know that it finally exceeds one's grasp both cognitively and personally, qualitatively, and also history, which also exceeds one's grasp, the ever-changing arena and events of human activity. Our quest for truth is ancient but the setting in which we are now working is new, enhanced by our knowledge of our one global religious heritage. Our task is not to know all the answers but to be responsible for what we know.*

"I understand" are welcomed words whenever one hears them from another. The phrase does not necessarily indicate an agreement between or among persons. When spoken in good faith the phrase suggests an ability on the part of the speaker to find coherence in information provided that relates to one's life experience and to discern continuity in ideas that introduce one to new interpretations of human events. "I understand" is among the first and most fundamental statements of our being discerning beings, human, *homo sapiens.* With the sincere repetition of the phrase when new information is assimilated, new dimensions of inquiry are launched and, through the years of one's life, one learns more and the horizons of one's intelligible life-context are ever expanded. Interreligious understanding establishes rapport among persons of faith leading to an appreciation of each other. This understanding requires both intellectual honesty and moral sincerity. When these associated qualities combine in a person of faith seeking to understand religious men and women, a religious activity is underway.

We continue our preliminary inquiry, launched in our preceding chapters, to consider the process of interreligious understanding as a religious activity. The scope of the inquiry is enormous; one would anticipate a thorough and an inclusive investigation to involve contributions by psychologists and philosophers, historians and theologians, major authorities working in several more recent intellectual pursuits, even neurology. What I am proposing, however, in this brief chapter is that we pause to consider preliminarily what might be occurring when we speak of ourselves as reaching an understanding; an understanding of a proposition, a mathematical formula, a musical score, an instruction given to us, or a carpenter's skill, and, more particularly, of another person, especially another person in that person's religious life, especially, in this case, in the religious life of Theravāda Buddhists and Christians. Let it be known at the outset, that this preliminary inquiry will remain incomplete, will hardly offer a definition of "to understand," surely will remain inconclusive. Its objective will have been achieved if serious consideration is given to the human process of understanding as a distinctively and authentically human activity, as a religious activity, not solely as a cognitive enterprise posing an epistemological issue, as David Hume (1711–1776) and subsequent generations of competent thinkers have considered it to be in the canon of the received tradition in the Western philosophical heritage.[1] This kind of understanding is central in understanding a religious tradition other than one's own, and in achieving this understanding one becomes religiously self-conscious not unlike the dawning of self-consciousness in the developmental process and growth of the human personality.

Consider this. A student ponders over and memorizes a mathematical formula but cannot see the principle involved, fails to align the sequence of steps leading to the integration of the formula, and cannot discern the comprehensive structure of the formula or the foundation provided, consequently, by the formula for the next, more advanced, sequencing of mathematical principles. Now, consider a student who, with insight, sees the point of it all and realizes a delightful sense of contentment. Or, try as one might, a *raga* remains opaque—a disconnected cluster of ad hoc sounds incapable of being discerned as providing musical structure, cadence, and counterpoint in temporal sequence. Yet one marvels at a *sitar* or *vina* player who soars, as it were, with impressive freedom of improvisation entirely taken up in a delicate sense of joy, apparently unimpeded by scale or rhythmic beat. What makes the difference between an arithmetician and a mathematician, between a musician and an accomplished performing artist? In both cases, while the former can reproduce what others have discerned, even created, the latter understands, sees through to the point of, mathematical order and musical genius. The former would be one who is capable of knowing something presented and learned. The latter would be one who understands, who has been enabled to give expression to a foundational structure of truth that, as it were, stands under him or her. The parallel would suggest that in the study of Buddhist religiousness, the former would represent one who has knowledge about the Theravāda Buddhist tradition. The latter would be one who understands Theravāda Buddhists.

We can recall the observation, now widespread and perhaps trite, that there is a response referred to as an *ah-ha* moment, an instant, perhaps, when something becomes clear, when the point is seen, when comprehension arises and one learns, knows, indeed, understands for oneself what is presented or has arisen. It is in this very familiar and broad dimension of human experience, not entirely dissociated from a religious realization, that I would like to place this brief inquiry on the search for understanding—of the world, of oneself, of others, including others of differing religious traditions, and, ultimately, of responses to transcendence.

The Theravāda Buddhist tradition has been studied by outsiders for well over a century, and a great deal has been learned: languages, literary heritages, customs, practices, institutions, and much more. Philologists have made their important contributions, as have historians, linguists, anthropologists, historians of religion, sociologists, theologians, political scientists, and one could continue. Their work has been enormously significant in adding to our knowledge. But wherein does this work cohere? What is the foundation for the appearance in space and time of the items or topics of these studies? The subjects being studied by means of these disciplines are rooted in the persons being studied, whether of the eleventh century or today, and the search for understanding must, to be comprehensive, involve an understanding of persons, which understanding, insofar as it is realized by a person who is engaged in the study, is not unlike a religious activity.

Within religious studies, whether in the frame of reference known as history of religion or that of Christian theology, intellectual progress seems to have stalled: our academic disciplines have tended to offer us important but disparate details and theological approaches have been diverted to internal concerns and debates. It is not possible to tell the meaning of that which is being studied or to present something in understandable terms without involving how the meaning is grounded in persons and how what is made understandable has become understood by persons. It is in the dimension of inquiry in which persons are engaged in understanding persons in their religious life that the process of understanding becomes a religious act.

Aristotle nudged this notion by showing us how the process of reflection is participatory in the inherent intelligibility of the cosmos. The person engaged in that activity of coming to understand, which, of course, would require sincerity in the enterprise and commitment to the process, would be a participant in a religious activity. So also is the case of Christians seeking to understand Theravāda Buddhists, with the obvious implication that such is also involved when Buddhists seek to understand Christians, which could be extended to all attempts, honestly, seriously, and rigorously, in interreligious colloquia leading to understanding. Although this brief inquiry is written somewhat broadly without tradition-specific analyses, the general context from which the concern of the chapter arises is primarily Buddhist-Christian colloquia, more specifically Theravāda Buddhist and Christian academic.

## MOVING BEYOND CATEGORIES TO UNDERSTAND PERSONS

When we consider what might be involved in the human activity of understanding persons participating in religious traditions, important issues arise. We have found that this activity is sufficiently comprehensive that some of us in the academic arena have instituted distinct disciplines as separate modes of knowing whereby we can handle, it is assumed, facets of our more comprehensive subject, namely, the authentic human being, *homo religiosus,* humankind in its religiousness. But one wonders whether modes of understanding, disciplines yielding "ways of knowing," will ever satisfy an intellectual's search for understanding, a search ever more inclusive, comprehensive, integrative, converging. And when we turn our attention to an attempt to understand others in the most value-centered core of their lives, the dimension that gives meaning to life and that beyond life, understanding is, I am becoming more and more persuaded, a religious activity. For example, for a Christian or a secular Western scholar to understand *dāna,* "giving," or the heart of Buddhist meditation, or the meaning of *Dhamma* (P:, in Skt: *Dharma*) requires the acquisition of knowledge, rigorously so. Understanding demands more than this, requiring a discernment of the cohesive supportiveness that these concepts, practices, notions, and religious symbols provide for other human beings, and in so gaining this one's own humanness will have been thereby enhanced. This is a suggestion that will hardly be readily endorsed today by students of humankind's religiousness. But the suggestion should be taken seriously and in time, I would argue were length of no concern, will become more central as a subject for further investigation in considerations of our one global human religious history: past, present, and future.

There are studies, for example, dealing with the task of understanding *Religion,* as the task and subject have been worded. Initially the approach to understanding *Religion* was one of "origin and development," with the customary cultural assumptions of the nineteenth century out in front of the investigator, as it were. Then, and more recently, studies have attempted to define *religion,* occasionally have offered lengthy and cumbersome definitions or characteristics of the concept *religion,* and then have continued with the word and presupposed notion itself. We have learned a great deal from such studies by patient and committed scholars. But we have tended, now, to move beyond this approach.[2]

More recently, one notes attempts at understanding the *Study of Religion.* Here, the task has been to demarcate an area of intellectual inquiry called the "Study of Religion," proposing acceptable hermeneutical approaches—even a "hermeneutic of suspicion"—particular definitional categories, technical terms of and for analysis—myth, pilgrimage, ritual, purity, sacred space, and the like—composing an accepted vocabulary and a disciplinary canon of received scholarly texts almost all of which have been written by Western investigators (often drawn from several separate disciplines, leading to a kind of premature celebration of an unintegrated interdisciplinary scholarship in this study). Important as this has been, and one applauds the commitment of scholars working in this manner, an intellectual seeking to understand tends to press this procedure asking whether it takes one far enough, or, rather, whether, in reality, it only parries one's inquiry into the primary source for understanding, from human beings to constructed systems, from the *subject* of the inquiry to the *way* legitimate inquiries are to be conducted. It is one thing to understand a particular discipline with its demarcated nomenclature, with analyses appropriate to religious studies or sociology or anthropology or political science, and quite another—and much more—to understand another human being.

Along with the scholarly involvement in studying *Religion* (a human activity) and, more recently, the study of a "field [*NB*] of study," namely, the *Study of Religion* (also a human activity) has come a consideration of how to interpret religiously the presence of *Religions*. Some scholars, particularly engaged Christian theologians, currently speak of interpretive positions as "exclusivism," "inclusivism," and "pluralism." One readily discerns a pattern of designation whereby positions are given their labels from a preferred, distinctive, and distinguishing point of view, much like the categorization of the so-called "worlds": "first world," "third world," and "second world." "First worlders," of course, coined the phrasing so to speak of others. And, today, although we have more or less lost the "second world," persons continue to speak of "the third world," and persons have adopted this label to refer to themselves, alas, as persons "living in the third world." Our world is and has been one throughout human history, for better or worse, in sickness and in health, too.

"Exclusivism," in Christian interpretations of the presence of other religious men and women, has been around for quite some time. "Radical discontinuity" was a phrase often heard about a half-century or more ago, and also "Christian absolutism." Often, scriptural bases for this position were found in those biblical passages reflecting a growing particularity of "peoplehood" and the covenantal acts of God recorded in the Old Testament together with the early Christian community's attempt to discern self-definition, adjusting to a new self-consciousness as a confessional community with *membership* formed by adult affirmations and acceptance vis-à-vis a fluid but relatively cohesive Jewish community, under Roman political hegemony, within Hellenistic culture, as reflected in the New Testament. Surely, an exclusivistic syllogism in this case would be consistent with the heritage stemming from those times.[3]

"Inclusivism" has been taken to refer to an interpretation of other religious traditions that incorporates their presence within the doctrinal frame of reference of the interpreter's religious worldview, quite apart, on occasion, from whether or not persons participating in the other religious traditions endorse such interpretations or find them relevant to their own self-understanding. In short, this position is said to represent those attempts that *include* within one's own doctrinal scheme the doctrinal schemes and practices of persons of other religious traditions. And, indeed, biblical passages are found to provide a basis for this interpretation, too, particularly those that reflect the early Christian community's sense of giving expression to God's redemptive act of reconciling the world in Christ.

"Pluralism," apparently the home position for the label makers in these recent categorizations, admirably recognizes the reality of faith on earth, its variety of manifestations, and the unquestionable facticity of the historical record—that we men and women have expressed our religiousness variously through the centuries and magnificently so in numerous ways in great traditions. Pluralism, therefore, recognizes both a validity in the faith of religious men and women around the globe and also the abiding presence of transcendence in light of which, in an engagement with which, persons have discovered, or have been enabled to find, the ability to live life authentically as human beings, to live life religiously. This position, taking full notice of a global religious history unknown to the biblical writers, has been called, consequently, "liberal," no doubt because of attempts to construct a Christian theology appropriate for the fact of human faith as it can be discerned or inferred around the world in different religious traditions throughout our human history.

One, in the search for understanding religiousness, seeks to understand also the persons who are "exclusivistic," "inclusivistic," and "pluralistic," otherwise the search is incomplete, certainly biased. And one recognizes quickly that in this attempt these categories, although providing topics of conversation, even, perhaps, for broad and imprecise analyses, are not particularly helpful. To understand an "exclusivist," for example, one would want to consider, as thoroughly as one's wits allow, the vibrant relevance of that person's relationship with God, the particularity of the revelatory moment, the singularity of the Christ-event, the reliability through history of the testimony of the Church regarding thought and practice in integrating one's human life in a changing world, whether in the fourteenth century in southern France or eighteenth-century London, or twenty-first-century North America.

Regarding the "inclusivist," there might well be significant movements yet to be launched in one's utilization of received doctrinal formulations in an attempt to understand others participating in the religious traditions of the world. Whether a Hindu might see himself or herself within categories developed through Christian reflections over the centuries in Europe, say, is an important matter. But one wonders whether inclusivist moves and methods have been written off too quickly as being inappropriate, with a sense that somehow conversation cannot take place between persons participating in different religious traditions, that somehow systems must be constructed in isolation, in books, for the intellectual enterprise to be legitimate, expressed on panels at conferences, without recognizing what has always been the case—that persons of different religious traditions can talk among themselves and seek understanding. For example, an inclusivist in considering, say, the case of Islam, might speak of the activity of the Holy Spirit and of General Revelation through history and around the world. Such inclusivist would be advised not to give up too quickly in probing what he or she means by these terms and, for that matter, a Muslim would do well not to react too quickly to that Christian's attempt to give expression to these notions in a multifaceted religious context. In responding constructively to those notions a Muslim might assist a Christian inclusivist to discern new depth of meaning in those cherished ideas.

A pluralist recognizes the fact of the variety of religious expressions, the differing forms of religious institutions, the numerous religious traditions, faith among men and women, and seeks to interpret this reality in an innovative mode, trusting both the value of the religious life clearly manifested around the globe and the abiding quality of transcendence, an engagement with which gives rise to that religious life.

But the categories tend to become blurred. One can be a pluralist in this sense while being an exclusivist in recognizing the uniqueness of the Christ-event in one's life and in human history, while being an inclusivist in discerning in that event a manifestation of the integrative, reconciling reality of transcendence to which persons refer as "God." When we seek to understand another, our categories of "exclusivist," "inclusivist," and "pluralist" do not take us far enough. We should understand what is being stated by these terms, but be aware that the scope of inquiry is not adequately framed by them.

## ON BECOMING FULLY HUMAN IN THE ACTIVITY OF UNDERSTANDING

The search for understanding has long been a part of our human record, and we note its distinguished presence in the Western intellectual heritage, indicating an inquisitiveness to grasp why things happen, how things occur, a puzzlement encountered in our attempts to come to grips with our surroundings, including others and ourselves, too. We have sought to understand how things—bricks, microbes, quarks, *stūpas* (Skt:, P: *thūpa*), *pirit* (S:, P: *paritta*), and symbols—have come to be (compare the insightful Buddhist phrase, *yathābhūtam*, "as it has come to be," which term communicates a fundamental affirmation about human understanding, that one becomes free of ego-ensnaring projected volitional impositions when one recognizes the causal sequentiality that has given rise to the thing before one's senses or idea in one's thinking). For Aristotle, who has cast a long shadow through Western intellectual history, including, of course, its religious history, understanding is an authentically human activity. In a splendid book, *Aristotle: The Desire to Understand*, Jonathan Lear provides an insightful observation:

> We want to know *why* the heavens move that way, *why* the phenomena are as they are. We are after more than knowledge, we are after understanding. Aristotle was, I believe, aware of this. Although "to know" is an adequate translation of the Greek *"eidenai,"* Aristotle used this term

> generically to cover various species of knowing. One of the species is *"epistasthai"* (literally, to be in a state of having *epistēmē*) which has often been translated as "to know" or "to have scientific knowledge," but which ought to be translated as "to understand."[4]

Systematic inquiry, inquisitiveness and continuing explorations into everything around one are natural activities in being human that involve *epistēmē,* which, Lear stresses, *"is by its nature reflective: one cannot understand the world unless one understands the place of understanding within it."*[5] In this process of understanding one's understanding, one also understands the desire to understand, leading to the understanding of "first principles," which reflective process of understanding is participating in Mind (*nous/νοῦς*), and, for Aristotle, this activity is participating in the divine. Lear puts it succinctly:

> [W]hen man acquires this understanding, he is not acquiring understanding of a distinct object which, as it turns out, is divine [as one might consider God as a first principle]: the understanding is itself divine. Thus in the acquisition of this understanding—in philosophical activity—man partially transcends his own nature.[6]

I would add to Lear's observation "in philosophical activity," the point that such philosophical activity is also, at the same time, religious activity. I would also want to indicate that the point at issue is not that "man partially transcends his own nature," as Lear puts it, but that in this way men and women achieve their true nature, what they can become—authentically, genuinely human.

"Aristotle believed," Lear makes clear, "that to understand ourselves we must understand the world" and continues, "his insistence that understanding and self-understanding are each dependent on the other is . . . a truth whose depth we have only begun to appreciate."[7] And Lear provides a summation:

> Such investigation and understanding, the complete satisfaction of the desire to understand, ultimately constitute the highest form of self-understanding. That is, once we have penetrated deeply into the world's intelligible structure, we come to understand God—or, equivalently, God's understanding. But divine understanding simply *is* the intelligible ground of the world. And so we discover that what we have been thinking (in our investigation of the world) simply *is* Mind. At this point, our thinking is imitating and re-enacting God's thinking. It is in this re-enactment that man comes to understand the world and to understand God, but he also comes to understand himself.[8]

Lear's interpretation of Aristotle demonstrates his apprehension of the integrated reality of an intelligible world—of one's capacity to discern intelligibility, of one's fulfilling oneself as a human being in the activity of understanding—which activity participates in a divine order that depends upon the activity of that which Aristotle perceived to be God. Aristotle's worldview is hardly the one shared today. However, it is remarkably instructive to learn that he found the activity of understanding to be uniquely human, that one becomes fully human, rises to what is best in being human, in the activity of understanding the world (bones, bushes, birds, and neighbors), which process involves self-understanding and is nothing other than participating in the divine. Understanding, for Aristotle, is hardly limited to control of information, handling data, or systems analysis. Insofar as understanding involves participating in the divine intelligibility of the world in which one finds oneself, engaging in an activity that is both distinctly human and at the same time enables one to become genuinely human, fully human, the best that it is humanly possible to become, *that activity is religious,* enabling one, as it does, to live with meaning in life, to relate with things and with persons in an orderly and responsible manner, a way that is both moral and consistent with the order of the universe.

Twenty-four centuries after Aristotle lived and thought and died, H. Richard Niebuhr observed about the reflective method, which we have seen was stressed in Lear's interpretation of *epistēmē,* that it

> is not solipsistic. We can carry on our effort to understand ourselves only in the company of other selves whom we are trying to understand and who are trying to understand themselves and us. The reflective method is always interpersonal, dependent on communication, seeking verification, correction, guidance from the reflections of others as these are mediated through statements about faith and definitions of the idea of faith. We do not even seem to know ourselves as selves in isolation but only in interpersonal society, in which we communicate with each other about common objects, whether these be the objects of perception or of reflection.[9]

One of H. Richard Niebuhr's major contributions to our thinking is his thematic stress and structural clarification of the social context of human valuations and the degree to which faith, as trust and responsibility among persons, lies at the heart of human attempts to understand. Although Niebuhr is fully conversant with Aristotle's thinking, and although he acknowledges that his ethical position, presented succinctly in one of his chapters, "The Center of Value," is more indebted to G. H. Mead than to Aristotle,[10] had Lear's interpretation been available for Niebuhr one might well conjecture he would have found himself standing to a considerable degree in agreement with Aristotle, man of the *polis.* Niebuhr instructs us, in a chapter, entitled "The Reconstruction of Faith,"

> Without acknowledgment in trust of other persons who have bound themselves to us in loyalty and without a covenanting binding of

> ourselves to them as well as to causes that unite us, we do not exist as selves; we cannot think, we cannot communicate with objects or with one another. Without interpersonal relationship in faith, in the great triadic interaction of self, companions and cause, we might perceive the data offered to our senses but it is questionable whether we would possess concepts.[11]

But, as Niebuhr stresses, "Our human dilemma is this: we live as selves by faith but our faith is perverted and we with it."[12] "This is our anxiety," he writes, "a result not of our finiteness but of our dependence on an infinite and on finites which have the freedom to deceive us. There is no escape from this dilemma."[13] Niebuhr, the faithful Christian theologian, points out that there is a promise of healing of what he calls this "diseased faith," namely, "the New Covenant."[14]

The interpersonal basis of understanding runs throughout Niebuhr's writings, highlighting a triadic sense: of person and person(s) and object, which object, ultimately, for Niebuhr, is "the nameless, ultimate Transcendent and Circumambient."[15] This triadic structure of faith is entirely relevant and operable in seeking understanding of humankind's religiousness: oneself, the other religious person(s), and the ultimate Transcendent and Circumambient. It is largely due to one's having discerned wherein one is dependent on, is responsible to, other human beings while ascertaining a ground upon which those human relations can be discerned as fitting, as being supported by a moral order, and to one's becoming engaged with a transcendent reference made available to human apperception and memory, that one can begin to have a glimpse of the profound significance of Dhamma in the lives of Buddhist men and women. Although Niebuhr would have moved to this notion of "the nameless, ultimate Transcendent and Circumambient" through an apprehension of a personal deity, which, in the grammar of his religious language he would refer to as God, Theravāda Buddhists would find his phrase helpful in pointing to Dhamma in the highest sense of Salvific Truth, that truth which is transcendent and also circumambient, that surrounds us and is not apart from us.

## BECOMING GENUINELY HUMAN IS A RELIGIOUS QUEST

The search for understanding is familiar to us all, and Aristotle, surely, endorsed its centrality in a quest to become fully human. In considering issues of religious pluralism, efforts to seek understanding of others, giving rise to a concomitant process of self-understanding, provide a category of religious thought more promising for further inquiry than we, perhaps, might have previously thought. Understanding requires knowledge, of course, but knowledge alone does not necessarily include understanding. Understanding, rather, is a supplement of knowledge, and by adding to it understanding completes it. Wilfred Smith puts it this way:

> In the study of human affairs, "to know and to understand" must be the twin objectives of intellectual inquiry. It is easy for a person to be ignorant of the data of human history, in general or for a particular sub-process; it requires much effort to come to know, even in small part. Yet to know but not to understand (to know what human beings have done or do, but not to understand them or it) is in its turn all too possible. It is, also, manifestly inadequate intellectually. This is conspicuously so in the history of religion, where knowledge without understanding has been common, and continues into our day. The category of understanding could, I suggest, become of potentially much greater significance than that of believing. It could prove more helpful, more illuminating, even decisive.[16]

Of course, what Aristotle meant by Mind (*nous*) or by God is not the same as what a Christian theologian might mean by God, nor would it be what a Theravāda Buddhist might mean by God. The movement in understanding that is involved, the activity of seeing the point, is not that of incorporating into one's own worldview a notion taken from another worldview and inserted into a paradigmatic complex circumscribed, defined, by a pattern of meanings with which one is already familiar, but to understand *as others have understood*.[17] We turn again to an insightful observation by Smith.

> By "understanding" here I intend his [a Theravāda Buddhist's] apprehending not what the term "God" means in his own worldview, where it refers to something that perhaps does not exist or is unworthy, but rather what it has meant to those who have used it to denote and to connote a great range of their life in the world, and the universally human reaching beyond the world: their perception both of empiricals and of ultimates.[18]

This orientation toward understanding of the world, of persons and the centers of value in terms of which they, themselves, find personal integration, responsible relationships with others, and orientation to the world, can move us beyond the inadequate fixation on belief systems, syllogistic arguments, and theoretical models such as "exclusive," "inclusive," and "pluralistic," with associated cudgel-like categories of "true" and "false" disconcertingly applied to something simultaneously more engaging and more productive of convergence: seeking to become ever more true to the truth one has been enabled to discern, on the one hand, and, on the other, seeking to deepen one's understanding of the apprehensions of transcendence to which others bear witness.

Primary focus need not remain on what *Religion* is or on what has been written and discussed in the *Study of Religion,* or on what all *Religions* might have or not have in common. Utmost importance need no longer to be placed on whether one is an "exclusivist" or an "inclusivist" or a "pluralist" as one attempts to sort out a position among positions within current Christian reflection. One can place aside the patterns of judging reified concepts of "religions" as being true or false—a really surprising practice in light of the overwhelming and variegated movements and dimensions of the ever-changing religious traditions through many cultures over the centuries. How is one to "freeze-frame" the dynamic and cumulative global historical process in order to set up mutually agreed upon syllogistic formulae by means of which to judge this or that religious tradition as true or false? And, further, grappling with the particulars of a religious tradition, the facts of the case, checking them, testing them rigorously as serious inquirers, would not require that one maintain an impersonal distance, a kind of so-called objectivity, a matter-of-fact lack of involvement face to face with profound human concerns. Understanding leads beyond all of this, is required of us and in it we discover, refreshingly, a genuinely human activity. As Smith says, "The requirement that one's own ideas be true is a moral demand; the requirement that others' be understood is a moral demand also."[19] This search for understanding is not restricted to the acquisition of facts and assimilation of information, nor is it mere speculation, an abstract armchair activity. This search for interreligious understanding requires the discipline of an intellectual, the humane sensitivity of a self-conscious human being, and the commitment to truth that provides both motivation and orientation. This search for understanding is at the heart of what it means to be genuinely human, and the quest to become such is a religious quest.

# II

# The Dynamics of Faith and Beyond: Personally and in an Ever-Expanding Community

# 4

# *Saṃvega* and the Incipient Phase of Faith

*The more we learn, the more we become other than what we were before. So it is with the magnificent human quality to which the English word* faith *points, which* faith *represents. We do not expect every religious tradition to say the same thing about this extraordinarily personal and dynamic quality, of course. But as we carefully consider what others of us have to say, we can find our understanding enhanced among friends which would also involve a deepening understanding of ourselves. Theravāda Buddhists have written of this quality of* faith *and aver that it is incipiently present in one's becoming deeply moved.*

One of the most engaging dimensions of human self-understanding that becomes available to the student of humankind's religiousness is a continuing process of watching unfold the depth and the complexities of what is involved in being human religiously, or of becoming fully, authentically human. One comes to understand that being religious involves the totality of the human personality: one's thinking and acting, one's feelings, perceptions, and responses. The grander in historical continuity the religious tradition being studied, the more comprehensive are the analyses of the human person that become apparent. A student of the Theravāda tradition, and of the men and women who have perpetuated this heritage by participating in it, is not without examples depicting acute sensitivity to mental processes from which one can learn more about the variegated components of religious awareness.

There are key terms in the Theravāda Buddhist tradition awaiting patient, thorough, exhaustive treatment, terms a fuller understanding of which enhance our knowledge of this tradition and the religious staying power it has had in human history. We still have not exhausted the need to study further *paññā,* that entirely admirable insight that one might achieve (on the *lokiya,* customary, level) and also that life-altering spontaneous salvific realization that is available (on the *lokuttara,* world-transcending, level), or *saddhā,* a sense of entrusting, of placing one's heart on something, of commitment (both in a *lokiya* and *lokuttara* sense). Nor have we learned all we can about *pasāda,* that remarkably delicate awareness of serenity that arises concomitantly with a sense of being taken up. One key term that awaits our further inquiry is *saṃvega.*

This chapter has a narrow objective of pointing to the significance of the notion of *saṃvega* and indicating how we might begin to discern its place in the dynamics of Theravāda Buddhist religious awareness. There is no attempt to determine historical strata representing stages or development of interpretation of this term, although that would be a splendid objective for a longer and more exhaustive study. The task here is primarily to call attention to a subject that would repay our further reflection.

The etymological derivation of *saṃvega* is conveniently straightforward: from the root *vij,* "to tremble," with the prefix *sam,* suggesting, here, intensity.[1] But its force, on the basis primarily of the Pali canonical texts, is both subtle and comprehensive. The great Pali lexicographers who went before us, and in whose shadows we continue to a considerable degree to do our work, communicate their awareness of the scope of meaning the notion of *saṃvega* apparently carries. One notes at various entries in the *Pali Text Society's Pali-English Dictionary*[2] the following suggestions for English equivalents: of the noun, "agitation, fear, anxiety; thrill, religious emotion"; of the verb, "to be agitated or moved, to be stirred," also appearing as a past participle, with a middle force of "filled with fear or awe, made to tremble," and a passive sense of "felt, realized"; and appearing also in the causative, imperative, and aorist, together with an infinitive, as a gerund with the basic force of "to be agitated or moved, to be stirred"; as a gerundive, that is, "that which should cause awe"; and also as an adjective, "agitating, moving," or "apt to cause emotion." Ven. A. P. Buddhadatta works only with three key interpretations: "emotion" or "religious emotion," "anxiety," and "agitation."[3] Ven. Nyanatiloka incorporates the familiar term of "emotion" but adds the notion of "a sense of urgency."[4] A. K. Coomaraswamy mentions, further, that our basic term, *saṃvega*, "implies a swift recoil from or trembling at something feared."[5] Franklin Edgerton adds, for the noun in Buddhist Hybrid Sanskrit, "perturbation" and for the gerundive, "to be shuddered at."[6] Upon glancing at the meanings offered for what is going on in the *saṃvega* complex or event, let us call it, we recognize that we are on to something weighty, even *tremendous* (from Latin *tremere,* to tremble). It appears that we are dealing with a human feeling of emotion that features the qualities of disturbing, of discomposing, perturbing, causing one to tremble from fear (rather than fatigue), to quake with agitation, to shudder, quiver with a sense of dread. However, this same emotive complex can arise in contexts involving veneration, even reverence. One becomes deeply moved, aroused to act.

Beneath it all there seems to be a kind of perspectival transition occurring at the arising of the *saṃvega* event, a paradigmatic shift that temporarily leaves one suspended at the transitional instant or moment when what strikes one as unusual in an existentially attention-grabbing way is beginning to be discerned as not unusual in a cosmically and soteriologically extended context. Let me try to elaborate.

There is a story about Jīvaka, a physician, who suggests that King Ajātasattu visit the Buddha and thereby find that the matrix for/of his thinking would become serene (*cittaṃ pasīdeyyātim*). Ajātasattu, we are told, approached a group of more than one thousand bhikkhus in the presence of the Buddha. They appeared to him to be absolutely silent, and this stunning stillness led Ajātasattu to be grasped by fear (*bhīto*), characterized by *saṃvega* (*saṃviggo*), having the hair of his body standing erect (*lomahaṭṭhajāto*). If not eerie, the sight was sufficiently unusual, according to the story, to give rise to this emotive disposition on the part of Ajātasattu.[7] We see the same semantic field arising in another story, this one having to do with a *brahmaṇa*, Mahāgovinda by name. It seems that when Brahmā Sanaṃkumāra suddenly appeared before him, Mahāgovinda was "*bhīto saṃviggo loma-haṭṭha-jāto*," grasped by fear, becoming one characterized by *saṃvega*, having the hair of his body standing on end.[8] His reaction was because he saw something he had never seen before (*tam adiṭṭha-pubbaṃ rūpaṃm disvā*). We see a very similar circumstance occurring with a householder named Citta. It seems he asked venerable Mahaka to do some special magical act. So Mahaka, in response, caused a bolt of fire to go through the apertures of a door to ignite grass placed on a cloak without burning the cloak. Citta, upon seeing this, was one characterized by *saṃvega,* having the hair of his body standing on end (*saṃviggo lomahaṭṭhajāto*).[9]

There are other stories involving personalities experiencing the *saṃvega* complex, having their "hair standing on end." One story has to do with bhikkhus who, in colloquial English one might say, were apparently "horsing around" on the ground floor of a terraced dwelling belonging to a woman known as Migāra's mother. It seems that the Buddha wanted Venerable Mahāmoggallāna, again in colloquial English, "to go and shake 'em up" (*gaccha Moggallāna te bhikkhū saṃvejehi*) in order to stop the "horseplay," to get the bhikkhus serious again in their more noble pursuits. So, the story goes, Moggallāna, with only his big toe, shook that terraced house with its quake-proof, deep foundations. Then the bhikkhus, agitated, stricken by what they had seen, said to the Buddha, "How surprising [in the sense of occurring quickly, suddenly, *acchariyam*]! Bhante. How extraordinary [in the sense of abnormal, unanticipated, *abbhutam*]! Bhante."[10] Moggallāna with his big toe causes trepidation by making to shake another impressive structure, this time the Vejayanta Palace. There, referring to Sakka, the lord of gods (*devas*), as a mere spirit (*yakkha*), and noting that he together with a great king, Vessavaṇa, and the *devas* of the Tāvatiṃsā heavens, were indolent and indifferent (*pamatto*) in their behavior, Moggallāna, intent on agitating Sakka by means of his psychic power (*iddhi*), took his big toe and shook the palace. Upon seeing this, they were of one mind; "How surprising! How extraordinary!" Moggallāna was fully aware that Sakka was deeply moved and had his hair standing on end.[11] The commentary on this passage glosses "deeply moved" or "agitated" (*saṃviggaṃ*) with an allied form, which we might translate as "flurried" (*ubbiggaṃ* from *ud+vij),* and indicates that this "having hair standing on end" emotion can arise either from happiness (*somanassa*) or grief (*domanassa*). In this particular case, Sakka's emotive condition causing his hair to stand on end and experiencing the *saṃvega* event arose from happiness or joy. We have seen thus far that the emotional condition or situation indicated by the term *saṃvega* arises in a striking circumstance and, as in the case of Moggallāna, can be a disposition engendered for a purpose, namely, again in colloquial English, "to shake up" in order "to shape up," that is, to encourage, to stimulate, to quicken one in pursuing worthwhile goals.

A person can be characterized as having an intelligent temperament (*buddhicarita*) and also a *saṃvega* disposition, being quickened with regard to matters properly engaging (*saṃvejanīyesu thanesu saṃvego, saṃviggassa . . .* ),[12] which Ven. Ñyāṇamoli translates as "a sense of urgency about things that should inspire a sense of urgency."[13] And we learn of a householder who has attained the state of "fruit of stream attainment" (*sotāpattiphala*) experiencing this *saṃvega* event and subsequently "going forth" into the monastic order, thereafter attaining Arahantship.[14]

When that which was considered to be abnormal now becomes discerned to be normal, one's complete structure of meaning is turned topsy-turvy, put into an inverted state giving rise to a condition of confusion. This is the moment when one brings to bear on the situation all of one's faculties of cognition, with intensity, trying hard to make some sense of the wholly unusual. Mental activity is keenly engaged, the emotions are charged, one is moved into reflection, made to reconsider existentially matters profoundly operating on one's life. This is part of what we have called the *saṃvega* event. We note, also, that in each case presented to us in the stories, the person realizing the *saṃvega* event is neither left alone nor abandoned without recourse to resolution of this moment of transitional dislocation. And this is a key facet in the *saṃvega* event, already adumbrated in our previous cases, namely, the motivational force exerted by being quickened, deeply moved, to launch one's life (*yoniso padahati*)[15] in noble pursuits in a soteriological process. With this in mind, the Buddha sought to stir, as it were, an ascetic who subsequently asked permission to "go forth."[16] And a *deva,* out of compassion, was desirous of quickening a bhikkhu, to lead him from distracting thoughts.[17]

In the case of the Buddha, this *saṃvega* complex can arise in response to one's realizing the plight of humanity, leading, as in the Buddha's case, to a magnificent pronouncement of guidelines for a life sublime. Observing armaments, quarrels, having a sense that people are flapping about like fish in a dried-out pond, and opposing each other gave rise to this *saṃvega* complex in the Buddha. And further, seeing how the world was without substance, fleeting, in enmity, the Buddha, when a Bodhisattva, found the barb in the human heart, which, when extracted, one no longer runs about nor sinks down (despairs? *sīdati*). It is with this awareness that the Buddha offers guidelines for a life sublime.[18]

Affliction and the reality of death can quicken one into disciplining one's life much as a stick might do for a thoroughbred horse. A report heard about the affliction or death of another can lead one to become stirred, agitated, quickened much as the shadow of a stick, a thoroughbred horse. The sight of an afflicted or dead man or woman would be like a stick that pricks the skin, causing one to quiver, as that stick would, a horse. Learning that one's relative is afflicted or dead would be like a stick piercing the flesh of a thoroughbred horse. One's own affliction, distracting pain, emaciating, grievous, like a stick stuck into the flesh of a thoroughbred, would serve to quicken one, a bhikkhu, like a thoroughbred horse.[19] In general, awareness of one's body (*kāyagatā-sati*) can bring with it a lesson providing somber motivation (*saṃvegāya saṃvattati*) leading to wholesome ends in this life.[20] The same pattern is present in another passage but, in this case, with cultivation of the idea of cessation (*Nirodhasaññā . . . bhāvitā bahulīkatā*).[21]

Just as a lion's roar reminds animals within range how contingent their continuity in this life really is and thereby causes the *saṃvega* complex or event to arise, so also the annunciation of Salvific Truth by the Buddha indicating the contingency of one's perceived corporal individuality—the arising of perception, the cessation of this perception, and the process leading to the destruction of this perception—initially gives rise to the *saṃvega* complex.[22] And, ordinary human reflections are put into the minds of *deva*s when they hear this reality check embedded in the teaching of the Buddha. That which is to be inferred from the experience of those in whom the *saṃvega* complex has arisen is, in effect, realizing that we who thought ourselves to be permanent, stable, and lasting, now know ourselves to be impermanent, unstable, and transitory.[23]

The tradition has retained an episode in which *deva*s cause to arise, before the Bodhisattva Siddhattha, appearances of a wasted old man with rotted teeth and grey hair, bent over supporting himself with a stick, an appearance subsequently of a sick man and a dead man. With the *saṃvega* complex arisen in the Bodhisattva's heart, he is said to have returned to his palace.[24] The literary heritage that gave rise to the *Milindapañha* tradition continued to relate the activities of *deva*s with the going forth of the Bodhisattva, noting that a *deva* who made the *saṃvega* complex to arise in the Bodhisattva is to be reckoned as the Bodhisattva's third teacher.[25]

One becomes deeply moved in the *saṃvega* event upon frequently developing meditational cultivation of an idea of a skeleton or of the sign of a bone,[26] or in letting awareness settle down with death as its object of consciousness,[27] or upon one's seeing a single grey hair on one's head,[28] or, among humans and earth-*devas,* upon hearing the announcement of the end of the world as far as the *brahmaloka,*[29] or, among *yakkha*s, when the Buddha caused darkness and a rainstorm to arise.[30] Even passages in a text received from tradition can, if listened to with proper disposition, give rise to both serenity (*pasāda*) and the *saṃvega* complex.[31]

This complex is not to be understood as bad, as somehow abnormal or leading to distortion. This emotional response has a generative effect. One of two supportive factors, recorded as having been proclaimed by the Buddha for the welfare of sentient beings, is "Being deeply moved and the committed application of one so moved with regard to the matters that engender such disposition."[32]

There are particular sites that give rise to the *saṃvega* complex in the mind and heart of a reflective person. One would anticipate a cemetery being such a site, in light of what we have read regarding systematic meditation on the idea of a skeleton or of the sign of a bone. The four sites that the heritage has celebrated for educing this complex are quite opposite to these topics of meditation, suggesting to us the breadth of the notion of *saṃvega* as it applies to the activity of religious awareness. "Ānanda, for a person of good family, of faith, these four places, giving rise to a sense of trembling, are to be visited. What four?" a passage asks, and goes on to mention those places where a person of faith could say, (1) "Here the Tathāgata was born"; (2) "Here the Tathāgata was completely awakened to the incomparable proper enlightenment"; (3) "Here the incomparable wheel of Salvific Truth (*dhammacakka*) was set turning"; (4) "Here the Tathāgata attained the state of Nibbāna without residue."[33] A parallel passage continues to say that persons with serene heart (*pasanna-citta*) who die while on this *caitya* pilgrimage, all, "after the breaking up of their bodies, shall arise, after death, in a happy realm in heaven (*sugatiṃ saggaṃ lokaṃ*)."[34] Do we let an English word such as "awe" move to center stage in a translation process here, perhaps something like "reverence," to provide some representation of the religious awareness of a person of faith visiting these sites?

Buddhaghosa, that learned commentator of the fifth century CE, recorded a summary of sorts indicating one scope of reference for our term *saṃvega*. He wrote,

> How does *one cause the heart (cittaṃ) to be gladdened at a time in which the heart should be gladdened*? When one's heart is discontented because of sluggishness in the commitment to wisdom or failure to achieve the ease of quietude, then one should quicken (*saṃvejeti*) it by review of the eight bases [that give rise to] the *saṃvega* complex. The eight . . . are [1–4] the four, namely, birth, old age, sickness and death, [5] the fifth, misery of *apāya* [hells], [6] the misery of the past, rooted in the whirl [of rebirths], [7] misery in the future rooted in the whirl, and the misery in the present rooted in the search for nutriment. And one brings forth one's serenity by recollecting the qualities of the Buddha, Dhamma and Saṅgha. Thus, [the meaning of] *causes the heart (cittaṃ) to be gladdened at a time in which the heart should be gladdened.*[35]

In the *Dhampiyā-aṭuvā-gäṭapadaya,* a Sinhala text dating from the tenth century CE, a summary statement is provided regarding what constitutes *dhammasaṃvega,* a Pali compound that is difficult succinctly to translate into

English. It could mean something like an existential response to reality, or a soteriologically efficacious emotive response, or being deeply moved in the context of reality. The general notion would be that the processes that are going on in the honest and receptive reflection of a person upon perceiving and becoming engaged with the human predicament are not isolated, erratic impulses of depression and despondency but are sober, grave, deeply moving, humane responses taken within a supportive context, namely, that Salvific Truth abides and appropriating that truth into one's life involves knowledge and understanding of the way things really are. One reads, in effect, that *dhammasaṃvega* is the understanding which arises for an Arahant that the elements constituting individual identity are not to be found in deathless Nirvāṇa (P: Nibbāna), that all contingent processes are replete with defects, that they are imbued with the qualities of wasting away and decline.[36]

Our brief consideration of *saṃvega* has given us a glimpse into the religious dynamic at work in the Theravāda Buddhist tradition, a dynamic that is not entirely foreign to experiential processes other persons participating in other religious traditions have known in their religious lives. When the *saṃvega* complex arises—this sense of fear, awe, reverence, of being stirred, deeply moved, agitated, stunned, surprised, and so forth—one is now at the very beginning of the religious life, it seems. One has already entered into a shift of perspective, adopted an alternative perspective in light of a discerned broader soteriological context. One is shifting lineage, as it were, moving into an engaged perspective of the way things really are and one is responding to that confrontation with reality through an emotional readjustment of perspective, a readjustment of a cognitive evaluation of oneself, one's setting in life, the world, and all that one has previously known.

This *saṃvega* complex or event is a kind of "fear and trembling" that is the end result of human reflection on both the finite and the infinite, a kind of pervasive dread that arises from the recognition of the limitations of human existence and of the extent of human agency. This *saṃvega* complex or event arises within a supportive reality context, namely, Dhamma, Salvific Truth, and hence it concomitantly yields to faith (*saddhā*), and not to despondency or ultimate despair. This new orientation of one's personality complements, by being involved in its incipience, an arising of serenity of heart and mind, a clarity and lucidness communicated in another word from of old, *pasāda*.

# 5

# *Shinjin*

## *More than "Faith"?*

*In the previous chapter we considered saṃvega, a Pali term to which one might not initially turn to consider dimensions of an incipient movement of faith and, hence, not many have considered its relation to the arising of faith. In this chapter, however, something of the opposite seems to have occurred when we find that our attempts to understand a word most prominently given to us by Jōdo Shinshū Buddhists,* shinjin, *might become inadequate by introducing the English word* faith.

We come now to give focal attention to a great human word, a word that points to the heart of what it means to be genuinely human. That word is a Japanese word, *shinjin* (信心). *Shinjin is alluring.* Let me begin to respond to this. *Shinjin* is attractive, or at least some of us find this notion of the goal of human life to be eminently worth pursuing, or at least seriously pondering. I am not sure that I fully understand why. Perhaps it is part of our human "makeup," part of what it means to be human, that men and women are so constituted that when we "hit upon" a notion such as *shinjin* it gives us pause and makes us consider what we have come upon. It is possible that this observation reflects my anthropology, a systematic reflection on the behavior that constitutes human existence. It is also possible that my perception is associated with what it means to be a discerning human being, *homo sapiens*. Assuredly, this observation has direct bearing on my understanding of religious men and women, persons becoming genuinely, authentically human, *homo religiosus*. What is it about us, or within us, that makes us take *shinjin* seriously, that makes us want to understand it, as reasonable men and women, that leads us to pursue it, initially to try to find at least some perspective for it if not to hope for its arising or occurrence ?

Some of us who are Jōdo Shinshū or Shin Buddhists have thought that realizing *shinjin* would be the fulfillment of our lives. One wonders why. For those of us who are Jōdo Shinshū or Shin Buddhists, *shinjin* represents salvation, our final and only hope. Others of us who are students of this tradition, and primarily of men and women who participate in it, seek to understand too. We seek this understanding because through it, if we have the patience and humane sensitivity to discern it, we might come to learn something more about ourselves, about ourselves as men and women, about ourselves as religious persons. Shinran seems never to have told us exactly what *shinjin* is, nor did he give us a path with methodical stages whereby we might follow into *shinjin,* nor did he represent himself as an example of a person who has *shinjin.* Yet, he spoke and wrote from within *shinjin.* How might we begin a consideration of *shinjin*? Of course, we might turn to Shinran, but what do we find—a shaveling simpleton, a person who called himself "short-haired stupid person (*Gutoku*)," and we are immediately knocked off balance because we readily perceive that Shinran became a profoundly insightful man, that he was enabled to unmask our human deceptions and thereby to help us find the source of our healing by letting us see ourselves *exactly as we are* in a context, indeed in a cosmos, that is fundamentally, ineradicably, compassionate.

Shinran was powerful in his meekness, a forceful presence in his radical self-effacement, profoundly simple in his observations about the complexities of the human condition, dynamic in his quiet gentleness. While living in exile he was reaching out to be supportive of others. He was a person exerting great influence without self-assertiveness, a person who communicated to us the bondage that is our experience and who thereby led us to a position to discern wherein our freedom might begin. When we consider a figure such as Shinran, evaluations by customary analysis tend somehow to miss the mark. Yet millions of men and women since the lifetime of this person have found this focal figure worthy of deepest admiration. Would you agree with me that this is fascinating?

Speak about *shinjin,* write about the conditionless, about that which is fundamentally inconceivable—that is impossible, and yet we continue.

I will consider two general points in this chapter: (1) reasons for one's thinking that *shinjin* seems to mean more than the customary English and/or Christian notion of "faith," that it is a manifestation of faith,[1] and (2) wherein a Christian might find a deep commonality of religious experience long understood by Jōdo Shinshū men and women.

## SHINRAN: RELIGIOUS GENIUS—LIVING THROUGH LIFE IN A CONTEXT BROADER THAN LIFE

Some years ago, Kenneth W. Morgan and I were standing in the music room of the beautiful Chapel House located on Colgate's campus. We were looking at a rubbing of Bodhidharma, with bulging eyes and standing on a single floating reed while crossing a river. Morgan said, with a sparkle in his eyes, "You have to be a little mad to be religious." Within a Japanese Buddhist perspective, there is some truth in this, I think, if the point is that one discerns the limits of reason and rationality and at those limits determines whether one meets the source of compassionate understanding, whether at the limits of rationality is irrationality or whether at the limits of rationality one finds that which simultaneously totally negates rationality itself, subsumes it, and transforms it into a mode of human understanding that enables one to become aligned within oneself and also with the cosmos, into an alignment that undergirds human action that is something like consistent spontaneity.

Shinran, it appears, has told us everything that one needs to know. He has not told us everything about *shinjin*; such would not be in keeping either with this notion or with this man.[2] He has not explained *shinjin*. He has merely told us where to begin to look.[3]

One of the first things that we find in attempting a serious textual study of *shinjin* is the way many terms become gradually associated with this one key notion, as we will see in our consideration of a coherent attitudinal field in our chapter 8. There seems to be a funneling effect; many ideas initially form a cluster to become more fully understood as they tend to be interpreted from the perspective of *shinjin,* become merged in, if not collapsed into, the notion of *shinjin.* Once this process of understanding occurs, there is an "out-pouring" process of seeing how the many terms expand with heightened nuances into a broadening spectrum of meaning. All through the texts we see a centripetal movement by Shinran, pulling all of these notions together, giving to his readers some hint of how these notions, perceptions, ideas, tend to converge in *shinjin.* Further, and also all through the texts, we see a centrifugal movement launched by Shinran, letting these notions extend the matrix of *shinjin,* spreading out into a widening spectrum. But it seems that more is going on. There is evidence that Shinran spreads it out before us, so to speak, presenting an elaborate display of initially apparently dissociated ideas. Just at the moment that this is sensed, Shinran makes another move, to hold the idea in focus, as it were, carefully turning it around, letting us see flashing reflections of Amida's light, as we would look at the slowly revolving diamond that is *shinjin.* And all the while, if we were to look for a statement by Shinran telling us that he has *shinjin,* we would look in vain.

We realize that this is the life and work of a person who referred to himself as something like a "simple shaveling." We realize, too, that he was a remarkable religious genius providing us with a paradigm of religious language at work, moving with purpose by refraining from attempts to be explicit about *shinjin,* knowing that refraining from explicitness on this point would yield a more fundamental paradox, allowing us to reconsider the issue again and again at our present level of understanding by means of creative, catalytic contradiction.[4]

In a brief consideration of *shinjin* we must deal with a disappointing requirement of being selective. In meeting this requirement we realize that there is a serious possibility that the whole might be misrepresented, that we run the risk of failing to communicate the interlinkage of subtle notions. Consequently, my decision to select one cluster of terms and not another might result in failing to communicate the core dimension of *shinjin,* might also give rise to a situation in which some are able to see the point of this chapter while others might not. Selectivity on an author's part also requires, to some extent, "filling in" on the part of the reader.

Shinran discovered the integrating singularity of what the texts presented to him as a threefold mind or heart (*shin* 心) seen as one (*isshin* 一心). We read that "sublime mind or heart" (*shishin* 至心), "genuine serenity" (*shingyō* 信楽), and "assurance of birth" (*yokushō* 欲生) are not penetrated by doubt and are the one mind or heart (*shin*) that is the cause for Nirvāṇa.[5] Shinran concludes that it is the one mind which is true and real (*shinjitsu no isshin* 真実一心), which is called "Adamantine True Mind" (*kongō no shinshin* 金剛之眞心), which is itself *shinjin* that is true and real (*shinjitsu no shinjin* 真実之信心).[6]

There are two important dimensions in the notion of "aspiration for birth" or "desire to be born," even "assurance of birth," (*yokushō*) in the Pure Land that might provide a helpful analogy to what I will have to say regarding *shinjin.* It is not difficult to understand how a person might desire to be born in the Pure Land; our human predicament impinges upon us with sufficient dislocation that further elaboration on this point is not necessary. However, in the thought of Shinran, even this aspiration or desire, when it is authentic, genuine, sincere, and true, and, hence, also efficacious, is not a self-creation but is turned over to us by the Buddha Amida. A dynamic arises—our readily understandable human response to the potential for transcending the life-context by seeking to live through life in a broader context, in light of the Pure Land, and yet, try as we might, in the final analysis, it is not our desiring or our aspiring that gives rise to true and real "assurance of birth" *yokushō.*

Keeping this dynamic in mind, we will focus briefly on the "diamond-like" *shin* before turning to consider two other weighty perspectives: *shinjitsu no shinjin* (真実之信心) and *jinshin* (深心).

## Diamond-Like Genuine Serenity: kongō no shingyō (金剛之眞心)

When the diamond-like genuine serenity (*kongō no shingyō*) arises one is no longer in doubt and perplexity because one realizes the true operating and sustaining principle of what we call reality, that to which the word reality (*shinri* 真理) points.[7] When this diamond-like (*kongō no*) quality of mind (*shingyō*)—impregnable from without, invulnerable from assault from within—arises, one is brought to the attainment of enlightenment.[8] This is diamond-like *shinjin* (金剛之眞心). When this arises, one is not getting a glimpse of something, is not seeing "through a glass darkly," not committing oneself to something in the sense of responding within current uncertainty in the hope of a future attainment—there is nothing more to which to commit oneself, if, indeed, according to the thought of Shinran, one can even *do* this. This diamond-like *shinjin* arises at the rebirth of those who are definitely settled to become born in total consummation in the Pure Land at the demise of this body, then fully to realize enlightenment.

A person in whom the diamond-like *shinjin* arises is "the absolute and incomparable practicer."[9] This diamond-like quality of heart or mind is not one's doing; one receives it by means of the power of the Primal Vow (*honganriki* 本願力) of Amida as the Bodhisattva Dharmākara.[10] Further, this diamond-like mind, we are told, is the Bodhi Mind (mind for enlightenment, *bodai-shin* 菩提心) which is "other-power" (*tariki* 他力).[11] A realization of this diamond-like heart or mind, or *shinjin,* which is given to us, which is based on the working of Amida, is not the kind of state that would entail doubt; doubt about the soteriological efficacy of the Vow of Amida, about attainment of consummating birth in the Pure Land, doubt about the textual heritage, about the reality of the source of one's realization of reality, that is, Amida. This heart or mind suggests *certain* insight into the nature of things, as things really, presently—and lastingly—fundamentally are. Involved in this activity is the act of personalizing truth (*shin* 信), when truth permeates the heart or mind (*shin* 心). This heart/mind recognizes that it is the heart/mind of Amida, that this heart/mind cannot become dissociated from the heart/mind of Amida, is assured of fully becoming one with Amida's heart/mind because the person's heart/mind, by being honest and sincere (*shin* 信) *is* true, and naturally is thereby embraced in Truth which is also Reality, never to be dislodged. This sequence of linguistic expressions nudges the edge of discourse about ultimate reality that is formless yet yields itself into discernible form.

## Shinjin (信心) that Is True and Real: shinjitsu no shinjin (真実之信心)

If a single English term is required for the second member of the compound *shinjin*, to wit, *-jin/shin* (心), it can be translated "mind," although I am becoming more at ease with the translation "heart." Still the subtle first member of the compound, *shin* (信), is present. Without attempting to translate *shinjin* let us consider the two adjectives in *shinjitsu* (真実).

What is the force of this *shin* (真) and this *jitsu* (実) in the compound *shinjitsu*? Almost in every case, when these terms are combined, they have been translated by superlative translators as "true and real." This in itself is an extraordinarily weighty pair of adjectives in the English language. On occasion one finds *shinjitsu* translated with the one English term *true.*[12] Often this phrase, *shinjitsu no shinjin,* appears in a semantic cluster involving the activity of "other-power" (*tariki*) or of "benefiting others" or for "other's benefit" (*rita*) in the sense that it is resultant from "other-power." The *shin*-clusters lie behind a significant passage taken from the *Kyōgyōshinshō*:

> Since this *shin* [(心)] the context seems to allow us to take it either as *shingyō* (信楽), "genuine serenity" or as *shishin*: "sublime *shin*" (至心) is the Tathāgata's Great Compassionate *shin* [*daihishin* (大悲心)], it

> necessarily becomes the rightly determinant cause for . . . the Recompensed Land. The Tathāgata, pitying the sea of suffering multitudes, endowed the unhindered, great Pure *shin* [*jōshin* (浄信) "unblemished sincerity"], to the ocean of all beings. This is called the . . . [*shinjitsu no shinjin*] of the Other-Power.[13]

One's *shin* (心) and Amida's *shin* (心) meet when, as a result of Amida's great compassionate *shin,* pure *shin* (*jōshin*) is given to one, causing to arise in one the *shinjin* (信心) that is *shinjitsu no shinjin.* In other words, the mind or heart of a person becomes the mind or heart of Amida when the person's mind or heart is permeated by *shin* (信 salvific authenticity?), and, consequently, also becomes worthy to be called "true and real" (*shinjitsu*). This is a point to remember, because our theoretical problem of whether the notion "faith" is adequate as a translation for *shinjin* is not a problem in the notion of *shinjin,* of course, but primarily with the denotations and connotations of an English word.

But we should not focus too narrowly on this oneness of heart/mind of Amida and the person in whom *shinjin* has arisen. Were we to do so we might lose sight of a dynamic that Shinran realized, and many have since: a dynamic that one senses in genuine encounter of oneself—the stumbling, incorrigible, fragmented person that one is—and the salvific source of reality. *Shinjin* appears to be the actualization within oneself both of that encounter of oneself and that encounter within the salvific source of reality. So also is *shinjitsu no shinjin,* which also has been given to one by Amida.

What is the sense of "true" in the term *shin* (真) of *shinjitsu*? What is the sense of "real" in *jitsu* (実) of *shinjitsu*?[14] "True" is a great English word and, for that matter, it represents a great human concept, without which one wonders whether our human life on this globe could have continued and would have been worth living. But "true," in customary English discourse, has as its contrasting notion, "false." If one were to take *shinjin* to mean "faith," one might say in customary English that one could have "true faith." But without further elaboration, this usage could also give rise to the serious question whether it might be possible for someone to have "false faith." Persons either have faith or they do not, although their faith might be more true, more genuine, more authentic one day and less so on another. It would be presumptuous of me as a person, inadequate for me as a historian of religion, uncharitable of me as a Christian, to say that persons might have "false faith."

Let me suggest what *shinjitsu no shinjin* means. It means "true and real *shinjin,*" but "true and real" in a way that personalizes our customary categories of epistemology and ontology in one's becoming oneself "authentic and actual" or "genuine and non-ephemeral." It could mean, most engagingly, "honest or sincere heart and mind that is rooted in Truth and in Reality." It seems that this kind of *shinjin* is not merely an individual's opinion, not merely a psychological state of mind, neither is it impersonally true or false, existing "out there" as something about which we could argue propositionally or verify through syllogistic inquiry. This *shinjin* suggests that when one's heart is sincerely honest, genuinely so, to the core, from the heart (which also carries with it the realization of one's dishonesty, genuinely so, to the core, from the heart) such heart and mind is also real, authentic.

One ramification of this way of thinking might lead us to see that personal truth, that is, sincerity and honesty, is fundamentally aligned, both epistemologically and ontologically, with truth in the highest sense, even Salvific Truth, and that this truth *is* Reality in the highest sense, else, of course, it would be neither true nor real. In *shinjitsu no shinjin,* one's mind/heart merges with and is permeated by truth-reality, never to be separated by either one's actions or those of any other agent. The person of *shinjitsu no shinjin becomes* true and real; the heart that is honest, sincere, true, is the heart that is real, genuine.[15] This has come about through the power of Amida's Vow, especially the Eighteenth Vow, as an expression of Amida's compassionate light and life. When this occurs, one is lifted up and embraced by Amida, never to be forsaken.

## Deep Heart or Mind: jinshin (深心)

Deep heart or mind, *jinshin* is another interesting dimension in this human realization. Shinran discerned, in a statement by Shan-tao, an insight of significant import: Shan-tao tells us that *jinshin* is *shinjitsu no shinjin.*[16]

> One truly knows[17] oneself to be a foolish being full of blind passions, having scant roots of good and transmigrating in the three worlds unable to emerge from this burning house. At the same time, one truly knows without so much as a single thought of doubt, that Amida's universal Primal Vow decisively enables all to attain birth. . . .[18]

Now, this "truly" knowing (*makotoni shinnu* 信知) is, as we would put it in colloquial American English, really and truly knowing, that is, something is both genuinely, authentically known and at the same time it is actually, factually, empirically the case. This mind or heart, this deep and profoundly insightful mind or heart, knows that one is oneself fundamentally inadequate, bound by disorienting passions, fragmented, awry, that one's life is out of joint (*ki no jinshin* 機の深心) and, *at the same time,* this deep mind or heart knows Salvific Truth (*hō no jinshin* 法の深心), genuinely knows it.

This is the creative catalytic awakening that enables one to know oneself as one truly is without committing suicide, to see the reality of oneself without attempting to destroy it or suppress or repress it. One is enabled to do this because of the certainty of the constructive context in which this awakening occurs, in the embrace of Amida through the efficacy of the Vow. One is enabled to see oneself as simultaneously childish (*bonbu*) and childlike, as foolish and as grasped by Salvific Truth, because one's mind or heart (心) has been permeated by *shin* (信).

In the *jinshin* that is *shinjitsu no shinjin,* this realization is certainly not a theory, nor is it something held to be the case by trusting that it is the real state of affairs. It is not a situation the full disclosure of which will come in the future. It no longer seems to be primarily a matter of entrusting. It is the *realization* of the actual situation, the way things really are. It is both within and simultaneously throughout the sincere heart, which is true and real, that this realization has arisen.

## FAITH AND THE ARISING OF THE DIALECTIC OF *SHINJIN*

We have generally refrained from translating our key notion, *shinjin.* In a symposium held at Harvard Divinity School in the spring of 1984, representatives of the heritage of Shinran were divided in their judgment whether *shinjin* should be translated as "faith." Christian theologians frequently make the point that the word *faith* means many things, and then they often set about to tell us what *faith* really means. However, one moves closer to the thought of Shinran when one refrains from translating *shinjin* into the English word *faith.*

It appears that *shinjin* is a particularly impressive manifestation of faith, shared by men and women in the Jōdo Shinshū heritage, that should be shared in its fullness and in its magnificence as a creative testimony in the religious history of humankind. I think this testimony is best discerned by others, if Japanese Buddhists will allow me this observation, by keeping the term *shinjin* untranslated, by trying to elaborate it, rather, by sharing it, by introducing the term into the English vocabulary, and, perhaps, a decade or so from now, if not today, by participating with those religious persons who have been nurtured in the Christian tradition through the Western heritage, and also through the English medium, in building a deeper, perhaps revitalized notion of the way faith has been and can continue to be made manifest.

But there is another side to this perspective, too, one that is also important. In making translations into English, we are not translating merely for Christians of the West. We are doing our work for English-reading Christians in Japan, for English-reading Jōdo Shinshū or Shin Buddhists in Japan and elsewhere, for English-reading Hindus, Muslims, Theravāda Buddhists, Jews, and others (including Humanists, Western secularists, and atheists, too). Persons in the religious traditions have their notions of faith, and, obviously, have expressed their faith differently. Are we moving to the depth of meaning in the notion of *shinjin* in this pluralistic context when we translate it, now, at this time, in our generation, by "faith"?

There is a rather recent movement called Shinran-kai, which has generated some restlessness among Buddhist colleagues in Kyoto because of possible ramifications of this movement's emphasizing the assured and ready acquisition of *shinjin* or attainment of *shinjin.* Jōdo Shinshū ministers in the United States, and elsewhere, might find some concern among their parishioners who live in areas where the evangelical Christian witness is strong. In these Christian circles, great stress is placed on attaining faith, in some cases "getting faith," right now, or as soon as possible, or recalling when one "got faith." For this reason, too, I would suggest that American Jōdo Shinshū ministers and parishioners not translate *shinjin* by "faith."

In our first chapter, we explored a little the notion of *shinjin,* suggesting along the way that *shinjin* was an expression of faith, that persons have expressed their faith this way. I turned, rather, to the notion of "refuge" *kimyō* (歸命), and followed upon that with a brief consideration of the idea of *hearing*, not merely listening to (*chō* 聽), but *really* hearing (*mon* 聞). I was searching for a dimension in human religious experience that might be prior to *shinjin,* not in a sense that one begins there at that beginning place and methodically moves through stages to *shinjin.* I have not found that idea in Jōdo Shinshū texts. I was looking for an incipient dawning or initial response that would tend to signal to me the presence of what I have been enabled to discern to be a response of faith.

It is possible that in the *chō-mon-kimyō* complex, if Jōdo Shinshū Buddhists will forgive my putting it this way for brevity, one finds an initial dawning of faith. In quoting a line from the *Larger Sūtra,* "will serenely listen to [*chō*] and hear [*mon*] the teaching of the World Honored One," Shinran, writing from within *shinjin,* indicates that we are enabled to listen (*chō*) to the teaching, we are allowed to listen (*yurusarete kiku*), and that when one really hears (*mon*), one hears by sincerely entrusting (*shinjite kiku*).[19] We also read, "Hear [*mon*] is a word indicating *shinjin*."[20] Closely associated with this is the notion of refuge. We read, "*Take refuge* [*kimyō*] translates *namu* (南無). It means to follow the command of the *Tathāgata*."[21] And further, we are told, "*Namu* means 'to take refuge [*kimyō*].' 'To take refuge' is to respond to the command and follow the call of the two honored ones, Śākyamuni and Amida."[22]

One can listen to teachings without seeing the point, without hearing. One can read the words, or listen to them, without hearing a command or gentle summons. One can simply not understand what is going on. More boldly put, one could even say No! And one could continue to say No! But one does not, and history testifies that persons have not. One can say the *nembutsu* without taking refuge, of course—the *nembutsu* could be merely a physiological articulation of sound. One can, of course, simply mimic an action. One could say that it is merely a ritual—but one does not, and history testifies that persons have not. One manifests one's faith by saying YES to *shinjin,* by initially giving oneself to the ongoing salvific dialectic of *shinjin.* When one first hears (*mon*), when one first takes refuge (*kimyō/namu*), one has already said Yes! One would expect Shinran, writing from within *shinjin,* to remind one that in the breakthrough of the salvific realization of *shinjin,* in hearing (*mon*), in truly, sincerely saying the name, *THERE* is the activity of Amida. But one's faith is to be seen in one's responding to the hope for this occurrence, in sincerely affirming this event would be the pilgrim's blessed realization.

I am not saying that there is no faith involved in *shinjin*—quite the contrary; one finds the fullest expression of one's faith in and through *shinjin.* I am suggesting that *shinjin* includes faith and yet *means more than faith,* that it is a manifestation of faith and the consummation of faith in this present life.

One of the fundamental points of the religious life, globally considered, is that, in the final analysis, one does not save oneself. The way of salvation remains, at its irreducible center, *given.* Even in one of the traditions that at first glance would appear most in keeping with "self-effort," namely, the Theravāda Buddhist tradition, there is a basic triple assertion: (1) that the preexistent Dhamma, Salvific Truth, was not and is not of one's making, that the Buddha realized it, the Awakened One awoke to it, and shared it, without alteration; (2) that it is the kind of salvific process that enables one to participate in it through discipline, that it supports one in working through it, that it yields its fruit as the person follows it; (3) and that at the moment of salvific insight (Skt: *prajñā*/P: *paññā*, salvific insight-wisdom = Pali, *magga-dassana*, "path insight" or "vision of the path") there is no self-effort, no striving of the will or of the mind, that the salvific moment of insight arises of itself—such being the natural order of things—and subsequent occurrences lead naturally to full penetration of Salvific Truth. We will return to this soteriological structure in our chapter 11, "The Arising of Salvific Realization as Buddhists and Christians Have Affirmed."

There is no recorded passage where Shinran used the expression "*shinjin* in or of self-power" (*jiriki no shinjin*). There are several occasions on which he spoke of "self-power mind or heart" (*jiriki no shin* °心) and only two where he mentioned "trust in self-power" (*jiriki no shin* °信). This strikingly substantiates our interpretation. It is possible that *shin* (信), when it stands alone, and especially in the self-power complex (*jiriki*), is *not* synonymous with *shinjin.* Hence, one could take the phrase *jiriki no shin* (°心) to mean something like "mind or heart characterized by self-power," and *jiriki no shin* (°信) to mean "self-willed conviction"[23] or "trust in the efficacy of one's own [acts]," being aware that in this latter usage, the trust involved recognizes concomitantly the penultimate utility of one's own acts and the fundamental supportiveness of the Dharma-way. One might still choose to refer to the Theravāda Buddhist case as *jiriki no shinjin,* but one would fail to understand the process or the persons involved were one to say this is "faith in self-power or self-power faith." There is faith, certainly, but not in self-power, not even faith characterized by self-power. There is faith that Dhamma, to use the Pali form, is such that one can commit oneself in living it, and thereby will find it to be supportive.

One might propose that *jiriki no shin* means something like "a mind/heart committed to self-effort," committed to a way of discipline. This quality of being sincere in self-exertion, entrusting to the reliability of the way in supporting one's self-effort, *jiriki no shin,* is *already* an expression of faith, faith that expresses itself in commitment, in discipline, in self-power *only* insofar as Dharma is such that it enables this process of religious living to lead onward to enlightenment.

There is another manifestation of faith, and that would be a sincere mind/heart totally turned over to and turned around by other-power, *tariki no shinjin.* This is the manifestation of faith so prevalent in the aspirations in Jōdo Shinshū. From within the Jōdo Shinshū heritage, this commitment in and through self-exertion has been understood as "self-power within Other Power."[24]

There is a corollary to this interpretation. There is a complete parallelism in the way Shinran was enabled to discover that birth in the Pure Land can be birth, *now,* in this life, and realized in consummation, in enlightenment, in the Pure Land at the falling away of this physical body in death. The direction of the soteriological process is *from* Amida's side, so radically, so compassionately, pervasively so that one no longer "takes refuge" (*kimyō*) at one's own initiative, as formerly was the case in the Buddhist tradition and still is now also for some persons in the Mahāyāna movement and almost all in the Theravāda. Even in the moment of really hearing with depth of insight, there one finds the arising of *shinjin,* which is the activity of Amida. Just as the full soteriological realization has been brought closer to the "now" that one is presently living, from the moment of one's physical death to the moment of the demise of one's self-centeredness, so also the activity of the salvific agency has been discovered *in* the act of one's taking refuge, *in* the act of one's really hearing. And, it appears, in this arising of *shinjin* there is not only the arising of salvific insight in and of reality but also the concomitant arising of compassion in and of truth.

If I were to search through the concepts of the Indian phase of the Buddhist movement for a term that would tend to parallel *shinjin,* I would tend not to find it in "faith" (Skt: *śraddhā,* P: *saddhā*) but in the arising of salvific insight-wisdom (Skt: *prajñā,* P: *paññā*) present in dynamic equipoise within a heart and mind that is serenely lucid (Skt: *prasāda,* P: *pasāda*). Thinking through the vocabulary of our contemporary Theravāda Buddhist colleagues, who have followed and have been supported by a tradition at least 1,500 years, if not roughly 2,500 years, old, I would tend not to find the parallel of *shinjin* in *saddhā* but in *lokuttarapaññā,* in "world-transcending salvific insight-wisdom," which explicitly is not the activity of one's mind and at the same time is the awareness of reality that yields genuine compassion for others as seen in the Buddha, the One of Great Compassion (*mahākaruṇāvant*).

I have not found another term in the writings of Shinran that can be translated readily into "faith." The reason is obvious, one might say; *shinjin* means faith. But still I continue to ponder this. Could it be that Shinran, in writing from the perspective of *shinjin,* was taking something for granted, and so did not stress a point because it did not need stressing ? Shinran was not primarily concerned with the matter of, or question of, faith,[25] but with an awareness that could be realized as authentic, sincere, and true, being given in its realization and consummation by Amida in the degenerate age in which he was living (*mappō*). Wherein might one find this religious sense that I am calling "faith"—a religious sense for which, apparently, there was not a Japanese word used by Shinran? I think one might say that it is present initially in discerning *the alluring quality of shinjin*, at least in our first sensing this quality and responding to it, saying, in effect, "Yes," affirming both our commitment to attaining it and also, inseparably, our openness to receiving it. *Shinjin* is seen but not yet really seen, acknowledged as worthy of aspiration, but not yet received, affirmed as goal but not yet realized.

Two observations are timely before proceeding: (1) to consider Shinran's view of human beings and (2) to comment on how *shinjin* would be understood in this case. First, we acknowledge that when Shinran spoke primarily from his own self-understanding, we see ourselves as being addressed as fundamentally bound by our incorrigible human inadequacy, by the disorienting duplicity of our detrimental, deceitful thoughts, words, and deeds. He spoke at a time when the vitality of Dharma was no longer readily discerned in the hearts of men and women (*mappō*). One wonders to what extent this sense of *mappō* still applies to our world today. We are passion-ridden folks, we come to agree. And yet, Shinran spoke from within *shinjin*. It has been said that Shinran had a pessimistic view of us, but this appraisal of him and of us is incomplete.

There is another dimension in Shinran's view of us that is singularly engaging. He had a very penetrating sense of the way any person of any rank and of any length of training could be open to the salvific activity of Amida at any time and at any place. This is remarkable! It suggests not only the comprehensiveness of Amida's compassion but also of a soteriological sensitivity on the part of men and women that is so keen there is no need for one to lay out stages or methods for pursuing the goal. Of course, in the thought of Shinran, one could not "do the doing" that would be necessary to pursue those stages or methods in the first place. But I am drawing our attention to the other side of the dialectic. "*Just hear,*" we are told, "*just say the name.*" Just as one is, it can happen! That, we can agree, is fairly good news about us and, of course, about Amida's relation to persons.

I venture to say that for Jōdo Shinshū or Shin Buddhists who have lived with, even if not also within, the notion of *shinjin,* it is possible to say that one discovers the trustworthiness of this *shin*-oriented way of life, "this side of *shinjin,*" and that one entrusts oneself (verb, *shinzuru*) to it, and to that which this way of life holds out before one (as a person who knows oneself sufficiently well, and feels deeply that even on this initial level one is not initiating this "true-ing," this act of deep, sincere, honest alignment of mind and heart, *shinzuru*), because the context that enables one to give expression to one's entrusting of oneself has been sensed, although not fully understood, to be supportive—no matter which way it goes, so to speak; no matter how things might turn out. Moreover, one can have a sense of *shinjin* that one's heritage has handed down to one, that the texts have placed before one, that one's mind has dwelled upon, that leads one to keep it in one's heart and mind—a *jiriki* action that is not in discord with *shinjin* farther down the way, so to speak. One can have a glimpse of *shinjin* "this side" of *shinjin* that, farther along, should *shinjin* arise, one could then look back to find that glimpse, then given, now fully attained in a gift that establishes one in certainty of enlightenment.

Now, in making these observations it appears that I might be creating a *gap* of sorts, one between something like a *jiriki-shinzuru,* entrusting in self-power, or a first glimpse of yielding to a full awakening of *shinjin.* At this point a dialectic arises,[26] when one gains a glimpse of what *shinjin* might mean, aspires for it, but realizes the self-oriented calculation (*hakarai*) that lurks in the depth of all one's actions. This creative dialectic would itself undercut any attempt to create "stages along the way." Behind every so-called "stage" would lie one's calculation, whether one can perceive it or not.

Yet, *shinjin is alluring.* Why ? And the dialectic is in full swing.

This dialectic is first discerned as a process, one never ending except, perhaps, upon realizing consummating enlightenment upon birth in the Pure Land. The dialectic seems to express itself initially at the dawning of one's discovery of the alluring quality of *shinjin.* At this dawning, the dialectic takes place between the person—involving heart and mind; this is not merely a cognitive exercise only—and the idea of *shinjin,* the notion of *shinjin.* Deep introspection appears to be a part of this dialectic, an honest self-appraisal, a developing self-consciousness of the pervasiveness of one's shrewd calculations, the inadequacy of all one's designing—even of all one's imagining (*hakarai*). This first phase of the dialectic occurs in the *context of one's existential uncertainty*; there is *anxiety* in this. Precisely on the issue that concerns one most, one's ultimate and only hope, one begins to see that one is absolutely helpless. And yet, one does not put aside the idea of *shinjin,* one hopes for it, knowing that this hope is *one's own* hope and is itself ineffectual. Yet one will not step away from this dialectic, which, when engaged, is a manifestation of one's faith. One wonders whether Amida is already at work in such persons.

There is a second level in this dialectic, not in the sense of a stage, but more in the sense of an unfolding of the former dialectic process. Whereas the former process was a dialectic *between* oneself and the idea of *shinjin,* the unfolding opens *within* oneself, as the dialectic of *bonbu/bodhi* mind, of one both foolish (*bonbu*) *and* possessed of the mind of enlightenment (*bodhi*). Whereas the former process operates in the context of one's existential uncertainty, it becomes transformed into and occurs within the *context of Amida's salvific reality*; it is freed from anxiety.

Faith is present when one first discerns that fundamental meaning in life is found within this dialectic, even in its incipient phase, when one is enabled to respond to the idea of *shinjin,* to find a dialectic with an idea yielding to a notion, to be enabled to respond to what the notion might mean, to be enabled to enter into the fullness of the dialectic into the reality of what one truly is—foolish and of one mind with Amida.

When, then, would *shinjin* arise ? One does not know. Assuredly it has arisen within some—always, it seems, some *others.* And others might have left a testimony that can be read today, that for them the realization of *shinjin* was an "all-of-a-sudden" kind of thing. And so it seems that others have spoken using temporal metaphors to refer to the immediacy of an actualization that one cannot cultivate. But, for oneself, one does not know except *by the absence of anxiety*[27] when the dialectic continues, but totally within Amida's embrace.

One gives expression to one's faith by living within this dialectic, even initially, even haltingly, ever refreshingly so, with a deepening awareness that this dialectic is divine, will yield salvific fruition in certainty of birth and enlightenment some way, somehow along the way, and that when it does so, it will then be seen fully as the natural and consistent action of Amida. Coming to see oneself as inadequate and, at the same time, finding *shinjin* alluring, profoundly realizing the incisive edge of the self-power/other-power dialectic, might already be the action of Amida. If this dialectic has been deeply sensed, through the action of Amida, in the natural course of things, one has hope that *shinjitsu no shinjin* will arise—not beyond the dialectic, but at its most sincere and honest core, in the unfolding of *bonbu/bodhi* mind. It is, after all, pebbles or tile chips that are turned into gold, Jōdo Shinshū Buddhists have averred.

## A CHRISTIAN'S RESPONSE TO *SHINJIN* AS MORE THAN FAITH

What might one who aspires to live Christianly say in response to all of this ? If *shinjin* is not best translated as "faith" and if it remains a fundamental religious insight, and if Christian men and women are also religious, wherein might there be convergence in religious experience on the theme of our subject?

First of all, one can acknowledge that from "the Christian side" it is rather easy to take *shinjin* as the equivalent of *faith* because at first glance the superficial internal structures of the two traditions appear similar: through a response of faith, which ability is given to one, one is born again and is saved to attain heaven at death. One can readily determine the parallel in Jōdo Shinshū. But turning our attention from structures to persons living in the two traditions, to the meaning that they have found in their religious lives, this analogy breaks down.

In the Christian tradition, the *homologous* dialectic is not faith, but the salvific dialectic that arises in one's heart when one expresses one's faith in the act of becoming honest about oneself and sincere in one's aspiration to become Christlike, a dialectic that unfolds, through God's grace, into a deeper dialectic—one free from anxiety—of the knowledge of what one is in oneself and, at the same time, acknowledging the dwelling of Christ in one's heart, a dialectic wherein one yet aspires to become "Christlike" (to become Christian as an adjective), falteringly, while Christ is in one's heart. What *shinjin* means to persons of *shinjin* is homologous to what "Christ in me—this particular 'me'," or "in-Christ-but-not-Christlike" would mean to those persons in whom Christ abides or who live in Christ and know all along the persons they are. And further, the faith of those of us who aspire for the arising of *shinjin* is not foreign to the faith of those of us who aspire to be Christlike.

Wilfred Smith has written a sterling piece entitled "Christian—Noun or Adjective?" to which we have referred.[28] In that work, Smith reminds some of us of the casual way we tend to speak of ourselves as Christians, that is, in the sense of the noun, and how we are given pause, frequently embarrassingly so, at the thought of whether we are Christian, that is, whether we are characterized by the adjective, Christlike. This is a "matter of the closet," so to speak, for the personal privacy of one's life. The same would tend to hold true for those of us who are Jōdo Shinshū Buddhists, for those of us who prefer to call ourselves Shin Buddhists, when we pause for a moment to reflect on whether we are characterized by the true purport of the message of the Pure Land—*shinjin.*

Although I am a Christian, I am not successful, I must say, in being Christlike, alas. This is the dialectic in which I find my faith being given its fullest expression. I am sure that there are those who could or who have lived this Christlike way, always, it seems, *others*—the great children of God of the past and somewhere, surely, today. There is not yet sufficient evidence that I can. Related to this comment that I have just made about "always, it seems, *others,*" a Jōdo Shinshū Buddhist would readily spot the creative dialectic that the "wonderfully marvelous people" (*myōkōnin*), who are immersed in the compassionate mind of Amida, set loose in one's heart and mind today.

The word *Christian* occurs in the Greek New Testament. Outsiders used it to designate a group of people; insiders used it to designate only those who were prepared to live like Christ, even to the extent of giving up one's life by crucifixion as Christ did, and later in martyrdom, in a Christlike way. Perhaps it is possible that *I* can never *be* Christian. Let me put it this way; it is possible that the particular person that I am, this *bonbu,* is so constituted that it is impossible for me ever to *be* in a state that is Christlike. Perhaps the very most that I can aspire to is that I might be present at a moment when an *act*—not me in myself—is done that is Christlike. At such moment, the *I* that I *am* would not be self-consciously present—I am not there at all, nor, I suppose, would *hakarai* be active. The act that is Christlike occurs, and in that act is Christ, is God enacted, and that act is in Christ by the grace of God. And so we say again, *ubi caritas et amore, deus ibi est*—"Where there is charity and love, God is there."

If I were a Roman Catholic Christian I might say that the realization of *shinjin* is homologous to the realization of the Sacred Heart, the very Heart of God in Christ, the realization of it, the actualization in reality of it, not only entrusting to it or hoping for it in the future. As a Protestant Christian, I turn to the life of Christ, the quality of that life, as the unfolding within time and space of the revelation of God that enables me in aspiring to, and in failing to, live like that life, to come to know what God is like. My faith rests in the heart of God's redeeming love as held before me in the event of Jesus Christ. I have been enabled, by God's gift of faith, to place my heart in God through Christ. Somehow, the person that I am trusts that in God's love there is something in me that is salvageable, that if I were left to my wits alone I would be no more than a clanking sound of dull brass, both in quality of tone and in endurance of sound. Yet God accepts this person that I am; God gives to me the ability to receive this acceptance, which acceptance I aspire again to offer to God through Christ. In Christ one finds evidence of one's fundamental inadequacy, of one's failure, and simultaneously, inseparably, one's salvation. And the dialectic has begun, perhaps beginning years ago when one responded to an idea, discerning through the dialectic that the idea becomes a notion, even thereafter becoming aware of a notion yielding, in a sophisticated sort of way, to a religious symbol, but finding, eventually, that the dialectic is, and has been, with and at the heart of reality.

Protestant Christians, in whose fold I am warmed to recognize myself, have held that one is saved by faith through God's grace, and not, of course, through acts of one's own: ecclesiastical disciplines or self-imposed regimens. This faith, of course, is seen to be a gift. But Christians who have written such things, as Martin Luther did, have spoken from within *the gift* of God in Christ. This is *the gift,* the unconditioned gift, the inconceivability of which is brought within our range of understanding by our speaking of it as the love of God for us, for all of us. This gift of Christ is *the gift,* and one's appropriation of its givenness is also a gift of God, *and* a manifestation of one's faith.

If I were a Jōdo Shinshū or Shin Buddhist who set about to communicate with persons in the *nembutsu*-way the religious affirmations shared by Christians, I think I could do worse than to say that Christians, *as a manifestation of their faith,* have affirmed that the cosmic salvific activity that we Buddhists have discerned to be the Universal Primal Vow has become "enfleshed" in Jesus, the Christ. Although when they stand before God in Christ they always measure themselves and find themselves to be wanting, they simultaneously receive the reconciling activity of God in Christ. They, as an expression of their faith, have called "grace" what we tend to refer to as Amida's designing (*hakarai*). They seek the fulfillment of human life in simultaneous self-effacement and in giving praise to God in a way closely akin to the *nembutsu* when it is sincere, honest, true, and real. For them, God in Christ makes life worth living—and death worth dying. For us, Amida's gift of *shinjin* has a similar depth of meaning.

What does *shinjin* mean ? It assuredly means more to a Jōdo Shinshū Buddhist than it does to an outsider. What does *shinjin* mean ? I suggest that it means more than "faith." I suggest that it means for Jōdo Shinshū Buddhists something like what I mean by the salvific activity of God in Christ, by the engagement with the dialectic of being inadequate and accepted, of being a failure in becoming Christlike and yet saved by God through Christ in the indwelling of Christ in one's life. Hence, I think *shinjin* is a manifestation of faith. And the dialectic that is an expression of the faith of Jōdo Shinshū Buddhists is a dialectic known also to Christians who would seek for the continual Gethsemane of the heart: "not my will but thine be done."

But at the depths of the dialectic of *shinjin,* there is a plus factor, touched upon above in the brief comments about *shinjitsu no shinjin.* The point seems to be that when *shinjin* arises, truth/reality is known in truth, the equal of enlightenment. As a Christian, I am not able to see this yet; perhaps I must await death, when perhaps I shall know in truth. Then, in the presence of God—my heritage has spoken of this as heaven—what would be the meaning of faith ? I celebrate the availability of *shinjin* as deepening dialectic and as realization of truth in fullness. I also celebrate the outpouring of compassion (Skt: *karuṇā*) that flows freely through the heart and mind that realizes the salvific insight-wisdom (Skt: *prajñā*) into reality that is made available. The outpouring of compassion I have been enabled to see in God through Christ. The salvific dialectic I find friendly. I will have to wait before I will know in truth—and I suppose in the presence of such weighty and marvelous matters, a decade or so makes little difference.

I am not qualified to write about what it means to be Christlike. There is a superficial level in this observation of course, but there is a profoundly subtle level, too. I think a Jōdo Shinshū or Shin Buddhist would be able to understand, deeply understand, the point of the sentence, and, indeed, celebrate with me this fact, in my awareness of not being so qualified. An ability to celebrate this awareness is a manifestation of our faith, Christian and Buddhist.

# 6

# Celebrating Our Faith

*As we have come to learn more about our faith, as Buddhists and Christians have demonstrated it in responding to despair and aloneness prevalent in its absence, we find that this quality enables us to offset self-centeredness and simultaneously discover equipoise. The assumption working in this company of friends is that truth is liberating and unfolds compassionately, not as the result of our agency. This is a mutual awareness worth celebrating.*

It is difficult to translate this title into Japanese for Jōdo Shinshū or Shin Buddhists. This fact substantiates to a considerable degree the point that I have been making. We need to think more about what we mean when we use the English word *faith.* When I first suggested this title for a lecture that I was asked to give at Ryukoku University in Kyoto, a distinguished Japanese Buddhist professor responded, "Do you mean your Christian faith?" I replied, "No, I mean the faith of all of us who will be in the room." That is what I continue to celebrate.

But first, let us lay the groundwork to see wherein we might share this quality of life.

## WHERE DOES ONE BEGIN IN CELEBRATING OUR FAITH?

There are several ways that Christian thinkers might set about to discuss what has been called Christianity and Buddhism. Their initial assumptions, occasionally not self-consciously acknowledged, are regularly intriguing. Have any of us who are Buddhists attended a conference with Christian thinkers at which a Christian thinker began his or her presentation of a scholarly paper by offering a prayer? Would it seem inappropriate to begin a paper with an authentic prayer of the heart, or would such behavior be considered out of place? There have been conferences at which representatives of the various religious traditions have met for a day or two, or more, to study together, to hear papers presented, and, as a *separate part* of the program, to meet together for devotional activities, usually meditation, prayer, chanting, and song. But why not begin an academic paper with a sincere prayer?

Moreover, Christian thinkers, in considering other religious traditions, have tilted toward, or have stressed, or have given primary emphasis to the Greek heritage of the Western intellectual tradition. However, on some occasions, when these thinkers deal with the strands of our human religious history that have derived from a Semitic background, the tendency has been to dwell more centrally on biblical concepts, on the Semitic heritage that Jews, Christians, and Muslims share. It seems that when discussions are held with Buddhists, and to some extent with Hindus, there is a tendency on the part of Christian thinkers to move into a Greek arena of discourse, to discuss problems of time, say, or the notion of the absolute, or causality, or the question of ontology, of being and becoming, or of substance and substancelessness, of fundamental reality, and so forth. The Greek heritage in the West has often been the strand of our intellectual thought to which we have turned for rational arbitration. We call the mental activity, in this process of rational discourse, "reason." We become engaged with reason with great respect for it, and we participate in this process with genuine and deep commitment. Our academic tradition is largely based upon this commitment to reason and to each other. Whereas the biblical view suggests that men and women are to decide whether to say Yes or No to God's salvific activity, the Greek view suggests that we are to decide whether to say Yes or No to the honest inquiry of reason. The dynamic between these two stances has also led some to promote a mode of philosophical inquiry that seeks to investigate what would constitute that to which we should say Yes or No.

Joachim Jeremias, to whom we will return in our penultimate chapter, has demonstrated that a key theme in the message of Jesus, seen particularly in his prayers, was a creative and vibrant orientation to God as Father.[1] Although the argument advanced by Jeremias, and widely endorsed—that *'abbā* = "Daddy"—is no longer persuasive,[2] the centrality of Jesus' relationship with God as Father, to whom and about whom he spoke as "Father," was at the heart of his own self-understanding and ministry. "Father," as a sincere mature address to God, then, for Christians, is a New Testament concept, and hence a biblical concept. "The Absolute" is not. Ideas such as "ontology," "substance and substancelessness," and so forth, even the idea of "problem," as an intellectual issue to be discussed, decided upon and resolved through reason, are not primary biblical categories. If there is a "problem" in the Bible, either in the Hebrew or Greek portions, or both, it is the problem that some persons neither heed nor respond to the salvific activity of God.

How might one draw upon our Palestinian and Greco-Roman sources in considering a celebration of our faith? We can begin with concepts. Let me note that I am fully aware that part of the value of the concepts that I will mention is that they are also notions, that is, they tend toward vagueness, they extend in nuance and scope of meaning, they are not entirely precise and clear, and that in their usage there is a sense that they cannot be limited through definition. The notion of religious symbol, though helpful when it came along not so very long ago, might lead us to stop with it, to consider symbol as being as far as we can go in our efforts to understand, so to speak. The problem with speaking only, or even primarily, of religious symbols is that such discussion, although occasionally of creative potential in one's reflection about one's own religious tradition, nevertheless tends to misrepresent, or inadequately to understand, the positions of other persons. The Hindu heritage, for example, has been rich and multifaceted, and Hindus have tended to speak of rites and doctrines, persons and events, as manifestations of the divine. Christ, in this sense, would be seen as an *avatāra,* a manifestation of the divine or of the absolute. For many Hindus, this way of viewing Jesus the Christ is both coherent within the general Hindu perspective and impressive in its openness to the activity of the divine among men and women in various ways. For some Christians, however, this interpretation of the Christ-event might fail to represent their apperception of God through Christ. Or, consider the case of one speaking of God, known to us also as Allah, primarily as a religious symbol. Speaking in this way would hardly take the measure of the reverberating vitality in the life of a Muslim who becomes engaged with, who becomes a submitter (*muslim*) to, the will of God in the act of submission (*islām*) to that will. Thinking in terms of religious symbols is helpful only insofar as this way of thinking assists us in moving beyond the older and surprisingly tenacious approach in interreligious understanding, that considers propositional statements or so-called truth-claims to be of paramount importance, in order to understand more adequately the persons for whom that relationship with what some have preferred to call "religious symbols" takes on dramatic, deeply meaningful immediacy.[3]

## BECOMING SALVIFICLY AWARE OF THAT WHICH TRANSCENDS OUR CONCEPTUALITY

For two generations, some Christians have thought that they were forging a new theological expression when they talked about "God above God," overlooking, perhaps, the keen religious sensitivity of the contemplatives in the Christian tradition and the Christian mystics, too; also not acknowledging, perhaps, that reflective persons have rarely said that they knew all that there was to know about God. The notion of "God above God" can be formulated in another way; that God *is* God, which means that God, by definition, transcends my or your idea of God. Some Christian theologians rather recently have emphasized "radical monotheism," where the reality of the oneness of God transcends in value and worth all other things to which we might commit our loyalty. All other things which we value—"gods," with a little "g"—pale into insignificance in the presence of the One God, a radical monotheism. Whereas the "God above God" mode of speaking focused on the transcendence of God, the "radical monotheism" discourse, launched by H. Richard Niebuhr, tended to draw one's attention to one's relationship with God and the ensuing realignment of one's orientation to one's life-context. Both frames of discourse were directed to Christians within the intellectual heritage of the West, and directed to Christians of the twentieth century.

"Father" cuts right through this! "Father" is not talking *about* God, it is not talking about God above God, it is not even talking about radical monotheism. It is not talking *about* anything. "Father" is a term of address, full of the immediacy of relationship, vibrant and personal, alive and engaging. Jesus, of course, was a Jew of his time. And those of us who are Jewish have heard in silence the name of God—not the *term* "God," but the giving of God's own name. I do not think those among us who are Jewish would say that God, in giving us his name, gave us a secondary religious symbol by means of which we might know a superordinate religious symbol. I wonder whether, in an attempt to understand the prayers of Jesus, we have understood *him* when we speak of "Father" as a religious symbol. My concern is that we do not direct our attention solely to the concepts, notions, and symbols, but that we also, and primarily, seek to understand the persons who have held these ideas and symbols in mind and heart, how they have committed their lives *not* to the concepts, notions, and symbols, but through them to that which resolutely supports those minds, hearts, and lives.

Christians have worshiped God through Christ. They have found in the Christ-event—the life, ministry, death, and resurrection of Jesus of Nazareth—the disclosure of the heart of God, the salvific manifestation of God in flesh, "enfleshed." Christians have worshiped God as father, as parent, having come to see this vibrantly dynamic and inescapable relationship with God through the Christ-event. And Christians have lived through life and through human history and have done so not without thinking and reflecting on God.

Christians are monotheists. One might need to mention this from time to time because of the difficulty persons might have in understanding the notion of the Trinity, which took the early Christians some time to formulate—the notion of God as Father, Son, and Holy Spirit, although we do not hear so much about the Holy Spirit these days except, perhaps, in evangelical churches. We will return to the notion of the Trinity later in this study. One wonders why the Holy Spirit was not featured more prominently among Christian theologians or in interreligious discussions. Christians, to repeat, are monotheists. And yet, there have been, for centuries, attempts to hold distinctions in oneness, or unity of inseparable dimensions. Christians are monotheists, to say yet again: only one God is worshiped, and yet library shelves in the West groan under the weight of volumes that provide interpretations of God. It is obvious, too, that Christians worship God who *is God,* not the *concept* "God," not one particular concept of God, or one particular notion or even religious symbol.

Those among us who are Jōdo Shinshū or Shin Buddhists have also affirmed that there is that which transcends conceptuality, namely that to which we refer when we use the Japanese term *hosshin* (Skt: *dharmakāya*). We have found that within this oneness there are integral, inseparable, dimensions, spoken of by representative translators as "dharmakāya-as-suchness (J: *hosshō hosshin*)" and "dharmakāya-as-compassionate-means (J: *hōben hosshin*)."[4] We have found that this fundamental principle of Salvific Truth, *dharmakāya,* enters our awareness as an activity of compassion rooted in and forming an inseparable part of this Salvific Truth, as Amida, who has acted on our behalf and continues ever to act on our behalf. It enters our awareness not as a result of our designing. Christians, too, have found that God—as God—transcends our conceptuality, lies beyond our ability to comprehend, and yet as Salvific Truth enters our awareness through an activity of compassion not fundamentally dissociated from the oneness of God, who has acted on our behalf and continues ever to act on our behalf. It enters our awareness not as a result of our designing.

Moreover, Amida, in the form of the Bodhisattva Dharmākara (J: Hōzō), uttered the Primal Vow, made the Vow, gave the Vow. This Primal Vow is not merely a statement; it is, when understood more fully, an act, an event. It is not an isolated act, but an act that permeates all dimensions of human understanding and yet also transcends those dimensions. It is an act that functions in time but is itself timeless, an act that breaks into the realm of human moral aspirations and human moral failure, spoken of as a moral order (J: *gō,* Skt: *karma*), and transforms that order. As an act within the realm of human perception (*gō*) the act is efficacious (J: *honganriki*) in a remarkably dynamic way; it occurs within karma and works through karma and severs the bonds of karma, but derives from a source not of karma, a source behind and beyond karma. Not only is the Primal Vow efficacious because Dharmākara became the Buddha Amida, and hence the Vow was fulfilled, but also because Amida was Dharmākara, and hence the Vow will be efficacious because it is a pure expression, falling within our awareness, of the fundamental reality of truth which, in the highest sense, is salvific, of truth, which, in the highest sense, is not dissociated from compassion either in the order of things or in the hearts and minds of persons.

Christians have encountered an act also, but similarly, also, much more. Those among us who are Christians have encountered God who acts in human history. Some of us have found the Christ-event to be the act of God in space and time, an act that is in time but also is timeless, an act that permeates all dimensions of human understanding, and yet transcends them. One courageous person in our human history chose a magnificent Greek notion, *logos,* to which we have previously referred, to try to give expression to what he discerned to have been a core principle "enfleshed" in this act and, at the same time, expressed his Semitic roots by saying this *logos* was with God, face to face with God, was and is God, and became "enfleshed" and "pitched a tent" among us. So he wrote in what is known as the prologue to the Gospel according to John. Those among us who are Christians have found that this act is efficacious, that through the Christ-event compassion is disclosed as being at the heart of Salvific Truth, that the heart of

God is one with the way things truly are, that Salvific Truth is available, that it abides, that it is not remote from persons. The Christ-event has been seen to transform not only the relationship between persons and God in a global sense but also the relationship of one's self-understanding of one's self and of one's neighbor.

How does this salvific realization, this transformation, come about? With this question, let me turn to what I consider to be the central point of the matter, what I take to be the core issue in our religious lives. This is a point with which religious persons around the globe have been familiar for a long time, and yet it is an issue that we need to study with each other and to understand more fully about each other.

## SALVIFIC REALIZATION AND THE ARISING OF FAITH

How does this salvific realization, this transformation, come about? It comes about by what is so very easy to say and yet so very difficult to realize; it comes about by means of death to the self. In the Christian heritage the rite of baptism has been institutionalized as a commemorative and exemplary rite leading to membership in a local church, discovered by some to be a sacrament, a channel of divine grace. The imagery of the rite of baptism that has had a major developmental influence within the Christian tradition was expressed by Paul in his letter to the Christians in Rome: "We are buried with Christ through baptism into death," he said, "that like Christ, who was raised from death by the glorious power of the Father, we also might rise to walk in newness of life" (Romans 6:4). When we die to the self, we enter into a new understanding. The self to which we die is the self that was known, the self that looked out from itself and measured all things in light of itself, even measured itself by its own standards. There is involved in this activity not only a shifting away from self-centeredness, but a placing of the previously known self into an entirely new context. The old self is now seen for what it was, and, engagingly, this new perspective has for its foundation that viewpoint that enables one to see what that old self might now aspire to become.

A psychologist unaccustomed to religious discourse might think we have a case of "split personality" on our hands. More reflective persons would tend to find in this religious discourse a way of talking about human self-understanding that has been placed into a broader and deeper context. Unless the context for self-understanding is broad and deep, the person who thinks he or she has a well-integrated identity might, in time, become the person of psychological instability. Consider, in this regard, why a Christian might speak of himself or herself as a child of God. There is personal identity in that way of speaking, of finding self-understanding as *a child,* and also an identity that is placed within the broadest context that the mind of a Christian can reach—a child *of God.* Death to self is not synonymous with death of self, of course. About the former, most accounts left to us from persons who have contributed mightily to our global religious history would concur—we must die to self. About the latter, we have chosen to speak otherwise, to express it differently.

Christians have spoken and written, not only in European languages, a great deal about faith, and a great deal of what has been said about faith is, no doubt, true. Christians have had faith and have had, also, a doctrine of faith. Christians, however, have not placed their hearts on the Christian doctrine of faith, but in God through Christ. And yet, what faith is tends to escape a quick and brief definition. Christians, of course, have learned many things, and they are still learning. One of the most interesting developments that has recently reappeared on the scene in human history is that Christians are learning from men and women who have been nurtured by other religious traditions. What Christians have meant by faith, and this is no little topic in itself, might change, conceivably might develop more fully as a result of conversations with Theravāda and Jōdo Shinshū Buddhists and others on this globe. And yet, we would do well to move carefully in these delicate matters of the heart, to move with the study, skill, and dedication comparable to that of a surgeon who works with the heart's tissues.

A global study of ourselves has indicated that men and women around the world, and for centuries, have communicated a quality of life, have demonstrated a distinctive way of living through life, of transcending the ordinary, have made manifest our humanity as a process of becoming genuinely human that most of us have found alluring, singularly engaging, worthy of emulation. In most cases compassion has been seen as a reliable manifestation of that quality of life. But that quality, that affirmation, that placing of the human heart, that fundamental orientation and continuing willingness to be so oriented, has been expressed differently, has been manifested differently through the media at our human disposal: in art, in music, in architecture, in prose and poetry, in metaphors, allegories, and, yes, in concepts, notions, and symbols; and yet also converging in love and loyalty, in a sense of humor and in faithfulness, in truth speaking and promise keeping, in reverence and responsibility, and, significantly for us today, in deep and lasting friendship.

The study of the great religious traditions in our one human history tends to teach a great deal about us, and, in this process, a student, in studying human beings, comes to understand himself or herself more fully. We cannot be sure that we, through the study of our human religious history, will come to find out what the Absolute in reality actually is—most of the great religious thinkers have tried to make it clear that more would be expected of us than historical study, even discussion at conferences. Nor does it appear that solely by lexical work and textual analysis, doctrinal investigation and comparative categorization, will we find disclosed in the dynamic center of the life-context that to which we can give our hearts, the path that we can follow and be supported as we walk it, the great treasure ocean into which we can plunge.

We study, of course, and study diligently in order to understand, not only to understand doctrinal expressions or other modes of expression, but also and primarily to understand what meaning persons have given to these expressions, or have found in them, or have discovered through them (or have failed to find in them or through them). It is because of this commitment to the understanding of persons, our own understanding of ourselves, that I would suggest we move very slowly, deliberately, subtly, with scholarly acumen and personal caring, as we make comparative analyses and tentative interpretations of our religious affirmations.[5]

Faith is a global fact of our one global human religious history. But can we say more about this, can we share more among ourselves about our faith? How can we set about to do it? I have previously adumbrated several doctrinal points that would indicate a rough doctrinal parallelism between two systems of thought, one Jōdo Shinshū and the other Christian. This is interesting, it seems to me, not because of Jōdo Shinshū or Shin Buddhism as a doctrinal system or because it tells me something about conceptualizations such as Buddhism and Christianity. It tells me something about myself and something about Buddhists. I want to celebrate that recognition. Jōdo Shinshū Buddhists have made a distinctive contribution to our human religious history. They have shared it with all who have been interested—they have been truth-bearers without being missionary.

In our consideration of *shinjin* in chapter 5, we noted that it has been translated by some Buddhists and Christians with the English term *faith.* I take that translation seriously. But other Buddhists have decided not to translate *shinjin* by "faith." We have seen that *shinjin* is both a *manifestation* of faith and *more* than faith. *Shinjin* has points of convergence with what Christians have tended to mean by "faith," yet *shinjin* has very important dimensions formulated within the Buddhist heritage which would run the risk of becoming lost in English were one to translate it by "faith." These dimensions pertain to a distinctive testimony to self-understanding in the soteriological process as Jōdo Shinshū Buddhists have discerned it. Losing the particularity of *shinjin* would make our global understanding of ourselves as religious persons less exhilarating in its variety, less alluring in its richness, less complete in its comprehensiveness. A Christian generally knows whether he or she has faith and is prepared, with appropriate modesty, to talk about it; that it might be more authentically expressed one day, less so on another. It is a different matter with *shinjin* among Jōdo Shinshū Buddhists.

We have seen that in a consideration of *shinjin* one sooner or later has to consider, among several important notions, the important ideas of "self-power" (*jiriki*) and "other-power" (*tariki*). With great existential force, we realize that *jiriki* is the only way open to us in the religious life. When Shinran writes that we must understand *jiriki* well, I think he meant it.[6] Shinran, speaking from within *shinjin,* was advising us that the only way for *shinjin* to arise is for one to understand "self-power" (*jiriki*), that is, to see "self-power" for what it is, precisely the power of the self, and not only "the self" in an abstract way but also this particular self. That is part of his courageous contribution, which has placed him in the first rank of religious geniuses that has augmented marvelously our human history. To see "self-power" as "self-power" means that we have no way to proceed other than through "self-power." That is the only way we can know "self-power," to press it to its fullest, to be enabled to find wherein it is inadequate. Just as we cannot really know "self-power" without "other-power" which contextualizes "self-power," places it into a context that is both broad and deep, so also we cannot really know the limits of "self-power" without trying, without really and earnestly trying to transcend it with our best wits, with our most sincere commitment, with our most sensitively tuned calculations (*hakarai*), knowing all the while that every attempt to transcend "self-power," to bring it to a halt, is "self-power." When *shinjin* arises, one is assured that "other-power" is recognized.

No one would tell another that it is not proper to aspire to be born in the Pure Land, or to want to say the *nembutsu,* or to desire to study the honored texts, or earnestly to seek for the arising of *shinjin.* Why? Because this aspiring, this wanting, this desiring, this earnest seeking is already the activity of the human heart that indicates the presence of what I have been enabled to know of faith. Shinran put it this way, "Thus, we must carefully understand the importance of threefold shinjin and aspire for its realization."[7] But is this aspiring, this earnest seeking, evidence that *shinjin* has arisen? We will be led into the answer to this question by our Jōdo Shinshū friends.

Faith has been described as an activity of commitment, of affirming, of placing one's heart in the source of the salvific reality that abides. It has tended to involve volition, a willingness and ardent desire to submit to, to give one's heart, that is, to give the totality of one's human personality, to God, indeed, to Salvific Truth.[8] Christians have reflected on this matter and have found that this capacity so to live, so to commit one's life, is not of one's own designing (*hakarai*) but is the result of the initiative of God through Christ and the Holy Spirit, in grace: (1) prevenient grace, (2) preparatory grace, (3) grace of conversion, and (4) cooperating grace. The capacity has been given to one, as it were, but one also commits oneself this way—a kind of "self-power" within "other-power," of which Jōdo Shinshū Buddhist are familiar—failing miserably here, gloriously manifesting this faith there, differently as a teenager, ideally, one supposes, more maturely, richly, more pervasively as one grows older. Christians have expressed their faith in God's act through Christ as an event in the past and ever reoccurring afresh, even this morning. It is the salvific act of God in Christ on which and in which persons, by becoming Christians, have placed their hearts and, possibly, by placing their hearts more authentically, more genuinely, more wholeheartedly, have come to know what it might be like to be Christian, Christlike. God, therefore, has given the gift of Christ, the full and unqualified gift, and also gives the capacity to persons to respond to this Christ-event. But persons could choose not to respond to it, and persons have chosen not to respond to it, to be indifferent toward it, even to reject it.

A Christian might find himself or herself able to say that even at an incipient moment in realizing the dawning of the religious life, on this initial level of response, of initial orientation, of affirmation, one can find the presence of faith and the activity of God. And such Christian could very well say the same thing both for his or her Christian experience *and* for the experience of Jōdo Shinshū men and women. Similarly, persons can respond to the notion of *shinjin,* to aspire for its occurrence, to place their hearts on the possibility of its arising in one's lifetime or thereafter. I leave it to Buddhists to elaborate whether one might find on this incipient level of commitment to the arising of *shinjin* the prior activity of Amida, whether in one's initial commitment to the Jōdo Shinshū way, in the original exalted sense of this phrase, one already has manifested one's faith. And I leave it to Buddhists to elaborate whether the experience of Christians has been a response to that which Buddhists have known to be both compassionate reality and real compassion.

We do not save ourselves, religious persons have long affirmed. Christians have found that the indwelling of Christ in the human heart is the indwelling of Salvific Truth within the heart that is in every way human, the heart that is one's heart, this heart that one knows full well in all its frailty, designing, even imagining. Yet, Christ dwells therein, it is affirmed. This is an affirmation of faith, a manifestation of faith, profoundly so.[9]

And in the description of the diamond-like heart (*kongō no shin*), Buddhists affirm the possibility of that indwelling and yet ever indestructible quality of Salvific Truth that dwells within one, yet is not of one's making or doing or designing, even imagining. This awareness of the activity of Salvific Truth within one is a manifestation of faith, profoundly so.

"Faith is the substance of things hoped for, the evidence of things not seen," one of the writers of the New Testament has averred (Hebrews 11:4). For those of us who stand "this side" of *shinjin* this sense of faith might be intelligible. When Christ enters the human heart, Christians have held, and by so holding have been themselves supported through the vicissitudes of life, things become seen anew, including, also, oneself, and one relies upon the compassion of God for salvaging the remainder of one's life for the remainder of the day, next week and into the future, and in the hope of that to which Christians refer when they speak of heaven.[10]

Manifestly, Buddhists and Christians are persons of faith. That we assuredly celebrate.

# 7

# Colloquia in Faith

*In the age of communication satellites, cell phones, nonstop flights around half the world, interreligious marriages that endure, old reified conceptual entities thought of as distinct religions are dissolving. Persons are meeting now, happily, not religions. And persons are becoming more engaged not in arguing or converting as was the practice of self-denying and courageous Christian missionaries of a century ago, but in speaking among ourselves about ourselves, of learning from each other in the company of friends.*

## MOVING BEYOND DIALOGUE

Leading representatives of the major religious traditions have been talking about dialogue for half a century or more. We have come a long way, indeed, from the days of public debates, from a time of studying another religious tradition in order for some to know its strengths, contributing to a sense of respect for it, in order for others to know its weaknesses so that one might present more effectively one's own religious views. We have arrived at the stage of dialogue. But nowadays, people tend to think of dialogue, instead of its basic sense of communication, to be, rather, a discussion between *two* parties, suggesting that those speakers who are participating in the discussions are engaged in their activity primarily insofar as they are seen as representing two positions. And straightway we have "dialogue conferences" in which we invite a few Christians to talk about Christianity and a few Jōdo Shinshū Buddhists to talk about Jōdo Shinshū, or even Buddhism, and before we have had time to read the papers of the conference, or even the newspapers the next day, we are told that dialogue is underway between Christianity and Buddhism, or, in those refined reports or newspaper accounts, between Christianity and Jōdo Shinshū or Shin Buddhism. This is interesting, to say the least.

There is no person alive today who knows all that there is to be known about Christianity; no one alive who knows everything about Jōdo Shinshū.

Have we given thought to the procedure by which a person or a committee goes about selecting or inviting a scholar to represent a position? How do we pick the scholar to "speak on behalf of" Christianity? How do we select and to whom do we turn to "speak on behalf" of Jōdo Shinshū? Usually, and recently, for international conferences two requirements have been proposed: (1) some knowledge of the tradition from which one speaks, and (2) a command of the English language. It appears that, rather recently, a third requirement has been added; (3) some familiarity with the other tradition that is being "represented" in the dialogue.

We have entered the so-called Buddhist-Christian dialogue phase of our global human religious history, with some sense of accomplishment and not a little fanfare. But, alas, it appears that this phase has already passed us by and we are being called upon to enter an even newer phase. This more recent phase is even more demanding of us: we are called upon to enter into a multifaceted colloquium that at one and the same time beckons us to speak about ourselves among persons of other religious traditions and also among ourselves within our own religious heritage.

Let me take Jōdo Shinshū as a case in point. There is some excitement in some circles now about Buddhist-Christian "dialogue," meaning, in this particular case, Shin Buddhist and Christian "dialogue." But one is struck by an apparent absence of Shin Buddhist and Zen Buddhist "dialogue," or—and stand by for this one—Jōdo Shinshū and Nichiren-shū "dialogue." As students might put it, "Why aren't Buddhists getting their act together?" One wonders why.[1] And further, there are conferences already scheduled for a continuation of Jōdo Shinshū Buddhist and Christian "dialogue," conferences that are important and suggestive of ways of developing and deepening our self-understanding in the future. But one wonders why we have not yet seen a conference on Jōdo Shinshū Buddhist and Theravāda Buddhist "dialogue."

I wonder whether those of us who are Jōdo Shinshū Buddhists have had a conference on why we want to have conferences with anyone, especially why we want to have conferences with Christians? And which Christians? Has there been a conference within the past three decades among Japanese Jōdo Shinshū ministers and Japanese Christian ministers—priests, monks, and pastors—*in Japan*? If such a conference has not been held, indeed, if several have not been held, one wonders why. Some time ago I learned of a quiet and steady series of small meetings held annually for several years among Zen Buddhists and Christians in the Tokyo area. One prominent Jōdo Shinshū Buddhist scholar who participated has now left us. (Incidentally, and worthy of note, these persons covered their own expenses, personally, in arranging for and in attending those sessions.) If our goal in "dialogue" is a deeper understanding of the spiritual life of our own Japanese neighbors, one would have thought that such local conferences among Japanese Jōdo Shinshū thinkers and priests and officials and Christian priests, monks, and ministers in Japan would have been held, and frequently held again and again. But have we seen such conferences?

What is going on? And why? Why are we in Japan interested in what a so-called representative from the other side of the globe might say about a religious tradition that has had its formative history in a European context? What do we think we might learn today from such spokesperson that might open new understanding for our own religious lives in this century in Japan: in Kansai or Kanto, even in Kyushu? Where are we headed in our "drive for dialogue" and why? What are we seeking to learn? And why? Is it not the case that our Japanese Christian friends, in sharing the same linguistic and cultural context, are in position to work with us in developing startling and creatively refreshing new interpretations of both our Buddhist and Christian heritage *in Japan*? Is it too far-fetched to think that Japanese Buddhists and Japanese Christians already have at their fingertips, if not at the top of their minds or in the depths of their hearts, the foundations on which the rest of us on this globe might build into more adequate understanding of our religiousness in the future? That is a thought, I suggest, worth considering, certainly worth calling a committee meeting to discuss. There are two deeper issues, two fundamental questions: the first one asks of us rather simply why we are interested in "dialogue," and the second asks us rather straightforwardly why we are still interested in "dialogue" when "dialogue" has already passed us by, when we are actually in a multifaceted and variegated religiously plural world, empirically, inescapably.

The unavoidable religious issue for those of us who are Jōdo Shinshū or Theravāda Buddhists or Christians is as follows: How do we find within our religious heritages a view that accounts for the presence of the other religious traditions and, at the same time, how do we find in this view an interpretation of our own religious lives that is simultaneously faithful to the vision of our own tradition, which includes, of course, not only the development within our traditions—a loyalty to our religious forebears—but also to the development of our own personal religious lives, which also involves a loyalty to our own personal receptivity of Salvific Truth?

Why are Jōdo Shinshū Buddhists interested in "dialogue" with Christians and not *also* with Muslims or Hindus? One might have thought that perhaps there is an apparent similarity with Christians, or at least with some Christian thinkers, that appears to us at first glance to be interesting, or intriguing and, hence, this apparent similarity would provide the motivation for further inquiry, for "dialogue." But why does this strike us as of primary importance? Is it not already the case that there is much more in common that Jōdo Shinshū Buddhists share with Zen Buddhists, or among the various subsects of Jōdo Shinshū Buddhists? When was the last conference involving scholars who have come together to work on central themes in the Jōdo Shinshū Buddhist heritage from the academic institutions associated with Highashi Hongwanji and Nishi Hongwanji?

Why the focus on Christians? And which Christians? How do we determine which theologians to invite?[2] One might establish two criteria: invite those who have already written on the theme of a conference to be held or who have already published on issues in Buddhist-Christian understanding, or invite those who hold positions at the prestigious universities and divinity schools in the United States. These are fine criteria, of course. But one wonders why these criteria have been important. Let me propose another: invite those Christian thinkers who are being *quoted from the pulpits* in the churches across North America, or in the United Kingdom, Germany, or elsewhere in Europe, and in the churches in Asia, too. We would want to have present at such conference one or more of those theologians who are shaping the interpretation of the Christian heritage for Christians in the context of their religious lives in the contemporary world. But who are they?

Suppose, then, that those of us who are Jōdo Shinshū or Shin Buddhists had completed our series of preparatory conferences on why we wish to have conferences with other religious groups, including conferences with other Japanese Buddhist representatives, as well as conferences with our Theravāda Buddhist friends, and suppose we were clear in our thinking on why we sought to hold conferences with others, what kind of conference might be most productive of further inquiry?[3] The point is straightforward. Jōdo Shinshū Buddhists are becoming self-conscious of their minority status. The overwhelming majority of religious persons on this globe have never heard of this heritage, nor of the message that has made lives worth living and death worth dying. We are coming to see that this religious tradition has its own particularity. Christians are beginning to see this, too. But particularity will continue in Buddhist-Christian "dialogue," that is, the particularity of the Buddhist (let me say Jōdo Shinshū Buddhist) experience and the particularity of the largely Protestant Christian witness. But Buddhists and Christians, although nurtured by immensely important strands of our human religious history, have not existed in a vacuum; do not, and will not.[4]

The only comprehensive course open to us is to move into "colloquia," to leave "dialogue" behind. But are we prepared for it? Perhaps we might want to consider the following theoretical setting as an example, if not also a test case. Suppose for the next conference to which Jōdo Shinshū representatives and Christian representatives are invited to engage in Buddhist-Christian "dialogue," we might also invite Theravāda Buddhist, Hindu, Muslim, Jewish, and Shinto scholars. Suppose, after the Jōdo Shinshū Buddhists and Christians have presented their papers and have completed their discussions, we invited the other guests to share their views on the theme that was discussed. I wonder what we might learn upon hearing what they would say? I think we might find our Buddhist-Christian "dialogue" considerations to have been interesting but provincial, as it were, as a consequence of, for example, a Theravāda spokesperson pulling us back to a central concern in Buddhist soteriology, say, or a Hindu sharing a strand of convergence, as, for example, with Rāmānuja and dimensions of *viśiṣṭādvaita* thought, far more similar, provocatively so, than we might have anticipated even among Christian "counterparts," or a Muslim pressing us on the matter of personal accountability, or a Jew carefully laying bare our massive assumptions in, perhaps, overlooking the supportiveness of particularity, or a participant in Shinto quietly asking why we put such emphasis on founders, patriarchs, texts, and doctrines and not on family and the life context of community in which one finds oneself.

Anything less than colloquia will be inadequate.

## WHAT WOULD WE CONSIDER IN COLLOQUIA?

What might be themes that we might address? For quite some time we have considered doctrines, and doctrines are important, of course. But the importance of doctrines is to be found in the way persons have responded to those doctrines, have responded through them, have changed them, altered them, revised them, even how persons have forgotten them. For quite some time we have considered texts. But the important thing about texts is found in the way persons have responded to them (either as oral expressions or written documents), have responded through them, remembered them, cherished them, how persons have been introduced to transcendence and have found community through them and in this multifaceted process to discover scripture, as Wilfred Smith has shown in our global context. Also instructive would be a study of how scripture becomes a text when persons have failed to find them of profound significance for the living of their lives or to have forgotten them.[5]

A remarkable conference was held about thirty-five years ago at Washington and Lee University in Lexington, Virginia. The theme of the gathering was "Christian Faith in a Religiously Plural World." The conference organizers arranged the conference in an ingenious and provocative way. A Muslim, a Hindu, a Theravāda Buddhist, and a Jew responded to a major presentation by a Christian theologian, and Christian theologians, Protestant and Catholic, responded to a major presentation by a Christian historian of religion. Also forming a part of this conference were smaller study sessions treating one or more issues from the different perspectives of the major religious traditions. A comparable setting for our days, for example, would be for a Jōdo Shinshū thinker to offer an interpretation from within the Jōdo Shinshū heritage that would account for the presence of the great religious traditions of humankind, and to be *assisted* in this effort by Christians, Hindus, other Buddhists, Muslims, and others. How do those of us who are Jōdo Shinshū or Theravāda Buddhists account for the unquestionable fact that the majority of us are not Buddhists and will probably live our days without ever hearing of Jōdo Shinshū or Theravāda, much less becoming Buddhists?

Can there be the arising of *shinjin* without *nembutsu*? Can there be an arising of *magga* at the moment when the self is crucified with Christ?

Wherein do we find the core of our religious heritage, the deep religious current that has been passed down from life to life in our tradition, the depths of our own religious sensitivity and commitment, and how might we seek to study it in the presence of and with the cooperation of persons living in other religious traditions? Colloquia would be the context that enables us, all of us, to talk about ourselves in our religious life more fully and to understand ourselves more adequately. Colloquia would also represent the only future that we have in a world that might or might not have a future. The inescapable fact of our global religious pluralism makes it clear that colloquia is our only proper, comprehensive, response. The alternative, "dialogue," seems at worst piecemeal; at best it seems preparatory.

What might be a theme for such colloquia in our near future? I think one such theme that would be worthy of our best work and diligent preparation would be for us to work together to understand more fully "Faith in a Religiously Plural World." Is it the case that, in the final analysis, the only adjective that can stand before the word "faith" is "human," as in "human faith"? We might not have seen it, preferring, rather, to speak of Buddhist faith or Christian faith or Muslim faith and the like. But this is something for us to study *together,* to come to know more thoroughly.

Another possible theme that would repay our careful thinking might be "The Religious Community as Social Institution," a theme that would enable all of us to consider the forms in which our religious heritages have become socially institutionalized through history: the fluidity and variety of this in the Hindu experience, the monastic complex in Theravāda, the sense of community in Islam, the elaborate structure of the Church in the Roman Catholic tradition, the autonomy of the local church in many Protestant strands, the blood-lineage system in Jōdo Shinshū, the pattern of temple membership without vitality in temple community that we often find in Japan, the sense of "peoplehood" and the role of the synagogue among those of us who are Jewish, and on and on we might go.

Another possible topic might be "Religious Themes in the Art of Healing" where we might work together to understand more fully the working of the human mind and the process of dying (in the very act of living) and the way religious themes from our religious traditions have contributed to the healing process in clinical psychology and also to the more comprehensive healing process of persons who are dying.

Perhaps another theme might be "Truth As Personal," in which we consider that zone of human experience, and dimension of our religious and intellectual heritages, that has to do with fundamental reality, hitherto more frequently discussed in the context of "myth and history," but now, more engagingly formulated as "Truth As Personal." This would suggest an inquiry into the interrelationship of religious insight in the complex of spatial and temporal coordinates, of the interrelationship of history and of truth in the complex of religious insight and actual reality.[6]

Still another theme might be "On Being Genuinely Human," a theme that would lead us to consider thoroughly our self-understanding in light of our religious insights. This theme would provide a context that might enable us to see how others of us have understood human life at its most mundane, ordinary level, and at its noblest, most authentic, genuine. This would also enable us to understand the working of our religious insights precisely at the center of our own human self-understanding.

And there are other possible themes, of course. These five suggestions should be enough to point the direction one hopes to continue to move in the future.

## "WHAT OF FAITH IN A RELIGIOUSLY PLURAL WORLD?"

"Faith in a Religiously Plural World" was the first of the five possible themes that were mentioned, and the one that has caught my attention most. I do not fully understand "faith." It does not follow that this means "faith" cannot be understood, although some Protestant theologians might take issue with me on this point. Nor does it follow that should one come to understand faith one would no longer have faith. Such might be the case, but we—all of us—would have to discuss it more fully.

If faith is fundamental to the religious life, and if we wish to understand this quality of religious living, then we need others to help us: Muslims to share their insights into the distinctively human act of submission (*islām*); Jōdo Shinshū Buddhists to inform us about why *shinjin* is important, its importance being discerned as an affirmation of faith; Hindus, to instruct us in the act of self-effacement through devotional love (*bhakti*); Jews *and* Muslims, to teach us how a life is lived freely with a sense of blessing in response to God's continuing teaching; Theravāda Buddhists, to bear witness to the supportive dimensions of the Dhamma-way.

I am coming to share more fully the position developed first by Wilfred Smith, that the more thoroughly one studies the religious traditions of humankind, the more one comes to find a quality of person that is found within them, nurtured by them, discovered anew by each person participating in those religious traditions. This quality of person in living life seems to be something like what one means by faith. Contributing to this quality of life, and yet at the same time arising from it, have been manifestations of faith—doctrines, rites, institutions, practices, and so forth—the so-called externals, or perhaps more accurately phrased, the manifestations arising from a prior and more foundational orientation of persons. Precisely how we are to set about to define this quality of life that cannot exactly be seen, that cannot be measured, but only inferred to be within the hearts of persons, is not an easy task. We need to study it more thoroughly. We need to hear from more of us about it. Although we cannot actually see this quality of life in the hearts of persons, we can infer its presence because we have within our own religious sensitivity, and within our own acknowledgment of the modes of response given by the human heart in the presence of transcendence, the means by which our inferences on this particular matter can be coherent. This way of understanding us as religious men and women enables us to see the variety in which we have given expression to our faith and at the same time enables us to touch the foundations on which we can begin to discern in that quality of life, that faith, the commonality of our religious lives.

That we might find convergence in some of our doctrinal formulations would seem to be only of secondary importance with regard to the validity or accuracy of our perceptions of the so-called objective world. However, this discovery of convergence would be of primary importance in its indication of the distinctively human quality of life that has supported the continuity of the doctrinal formulations and, at the same time, has found those doctrinal formulations expressive of one's understanding of oneself and of one's life. Were we to extract faith from this study and focus solely on doctrines, we would cut away the foundation for those doctrines, and also the ground of both our sense of our common humanity and of our sense of what it is to be genuinely human.

We have known for some time that religious traditions change in the historical process, because of the socioeconomic setting in which and through which they develop and the cultural context in which they develop and of which they form an inseparable part. Religious traditions continue *and* change also because of the faith of persons. The received religious tradition contributes to the nurturing of faith, but the expressions of faith can either transmit unaltered that tradition or change it radically; and similarly the failure to find one's faith nurtured by, or the failure to express one's faith by means of, and through, a religious tradition, could also contribute to the demise of that religious tradition.

There is, therefore, a dynamic relationship between faith and doctrines and rituals, a relationship that works in subtle ways. There is also a dynamic relationship between my faith, what I mean by faith, and faith. Is my faith limited by what I mean by faith, by what I understand faith to be? Is what I mean by faith consonant with the testimony of others who have expressed their faith through the forms of expression that I, too, endorse? Is my faith consistent within its own patterns of expression, integrative in its cohesive force working within this person that I am? Whether I fail to express my faith fully on a given occasion, tomorrow perhaps, or on an occasion last week, say, would depend upon what I understand faith to be, would depend, also, on whether I understand myself well enough to know wherein I have failed to express my faith authentically or adequately, would depend, further, on whether there is a quality of human life to which one might apply the term "faith."

Christians have had faith and they also have had doctrines of faith rich in their subtlety, impressive in scope, important in their historical development; doctrines not at all *given,* but hammered out in the course of decades, if not centuries, by persons who attempted to give expression of and for their self-understanding of this new quality of life that they had been enabled to discover in and through God's salvific act in Christ. We misunderstand those among us who are Christians if we interpret their faith as being synonymous with Christianity, if we interpret their faith as being placed in Christianity. Their faith has been placed in the heart of God as that heart has become manifested in the Christ-event. And their capacity to do this, to find that the expression of their faith discovers its fullness in responding to God's act in Jesus the Christ in this manner, their ability to discover a supportive orientation in living life, in living through life well, in receiving a point on which to stand that enables them to seek to heal our human wounds, has been interpreted and endorsed as the result of the initiative of God. This capacity or ability is not entirely our doing, so Christians have affirmed; it is the result of God's grace. The Christian doctrines of faith tend to function as a model *of* a person's self-understanding in his or her orientation to life in its broadest sense and also as a model *for* a personal response to God's act in Christ that introduces a person into a religious community. But these Christian doctrines of faith are themselves expressions of faith.

Others—Jews and Hindus, for example—can have faith, too, of course, certainly. They are able (shall I say, also, enabled?) to lead the kind of life that demonstrates for others of us the noblest that is within us, that blend of humility and humaneness, calm and steady courage, an alignment of thought, word, and deed, that indicate the presence of consistent balance within the human personality, which simultaneously integrates oneself and sets aside one's self-centeredness, providing a fulcrum for abiding relationships of faithfulness with others, in being supportive of others. They have been able (enabled?) through their faith to discover, to receive, and to endorse this quality of life. They have expressed their faith in a variety of ways, but they have also shown us this quality of life, this adamantine sturdiness, with the tender texture of the human heart, or at least they have shown us what the human heart can become.

In our study of our faith, globally considered, we can come to see the bewildering variety of the manifestations of our faith, in poetry and in song, in sculpture and in architecture, in scripture and in chants, in doctrines and in rituals, in myths and in pilgrimage, in cogency of the intellect and in faithfulness of the heart, in art and in institutions and in enduring friendships. We can learn more about these forms, and others, and their dynamic interrelationship with faith, in one's own lifetime and over the centuries. In this study we can come to learn more about the modes in which our faith, our human religious faith, has been and is made manifest. We would do well not to stampede over this patent variety of expressions of faith, not to run roughshod over them, with some glib notion that they are merely and superficially only varieties of expressions. On the contrary, these expressions are genuine expressions, and as such they inform one's faith as one's faith gives form to them. We will reach the creative edge of our colloquia at their best when we come to understand, as deeply as the sincere application of our thinking will allow, the quality of heart and mind, and the concomitant orientation to life in its broadest sense, that these expressions communicate. Therein might we come to find the extension of the horizons of our own understanding of our own lives in faith, of ourselves as religious men and women.

These manifestations are testimonies of what persons have been enabled to discern to be at the heart of what is true and real. Let me put it this way: *Messiah* is a Hebrew word, a human word, and *Christ* is derived from a Greek word; it, too, is a human word. The degree to which a person is willing to assume the designation of being a Christian and the degree to which he or she, on a much more subtle and engaging level, aspires to be Christian, depends mightily on what such person is enabled to discern in and through those words. The words are human words; the discernment is divine.

*Shinjin* is a human word. It, like the human word *Christ,* is not at all limited to a particular religious community. Some of us have found in and through the word *shinjin* more than what the two *kanji* forming the term might ordinarily mean to others. Some of us, it seems, have chosen, deliberately, as an expression of our faith, to use this human word, "*shinjin*" (信心), in a particular way to indicate the pervasive, penetrative merging of Salvific Truth in the hearts and minds of persons. This is a distinctive testimony in the religious history of humankind; this is a unique formulation, a cherished expression, one singularly worthy of a Jōdo Shinshū or Shin Buddhist's lifetime commitment, one that engenders respect from any reflective person who seriously becomes engaged with it.

For me to say that *shinjin* means for some Buddhists what "faith" means to me is, I think, to misunderstand Buddhists at the deepest level of their religious life. It seems that Buddhists have placed their faith in the abiding, compassionate means of Amida in causing to arise *shinjin* and the concurrent assurance of birth/enlightenment, as I have been enabled to place my faith in God through the salvific activity of God in Christ. Although we seek to understand faith, we would do well to preserve, and study, too, the modes in which we have expressed our faith, for in the dynamic interpenetration within the actuality of our lives in our aspirations for, responses to, and creative receptivity of Salvific Truth lies the hope for us all in the depths of our own personal lives and in the continued existence of our species on this earth. Between the personal response in faith and the insight into reality on which we have placed our hearts lies the dynamic of growth into becoming ever more genuinely human.

I think we have our work cut out for us; the task awaits our doing it—the response is ours, if we have the courage and the commitment, indeed, if we have the faith. For, it seems, every generation of religious thinkers that has had its eyes on the future has experienced the creative growing pains of bringing traditional learning into the present in preparation for tomorrow. We know too little to speak of a "mutual transformation" of something called "Buddhism" and something called "Christianity." We move cautiously and deliberately in weighty matters—and we have only just begun. Shall we, all of us, walk together into our future? Let us be prepared to lose our balance a bit, which, as we remember from our toddler days, is the way we learned to walk; but let us, all of us, do this together, just as, we can also readily acknowledge, none of us learned to walk alone.

# III

# Converging Affirmations from Different Perspectives

# 8

# "Relying Upon" or "Taking Refuge" as a Genuinely Human Activity

*A closer look at our religious traditions enables us to see more clearly massive assumptions uncritically held in our own cultural context. For example, individualism has become so pervasive in Europe and North America that affirming one's reliance upon or finding refuge in transcendence is readily interpreted as some kind of weakness, of a lack of self-assertiveness, cowing in the face of uncertainty rather than what it has been seen to be by the great majority of persons who have graced our human history—a centering of oneself in one's response to transcendence and in contributing to enduring community. We turn now to consider a religious orientation representative of one's becoming authentically human.*

Religious people, in the course of our human history, have participated in community, that is, they have established cohesive social organizations based on shared commitments to one another, to one's parents and to one's children, as well as to the parents and children of others. Religious people live in space and time that are undergirded with meaning, a weighty fact the full ramifications of which are difficult to imagine. For a religious person, one's own life is not like a solitary cipher tumbling in a chaotic eruption of disconnected events with no sense of inheritance from the past and no purpose for the future. Religious persons have found a point of orientation that provides insight into the meaning of life (which is more than merely a biological process), while simultaneously contributing to psychological stability by disclosing altruistic communal norms that enable one reliably to anticipate and consistently to evaluate human behavior both for the individual and society, and a sense of grounded acceptance that is not provisional, not conditional, not conventional, but unshakably established in reality. Happy is one who has this insight, discerns this psychological well-being, and gratefully acknowledges being accepted. Without an orientation, there is no sense of direction. And where there is no sense of direction a person has no recourse but to measure all things from the perspective of his or her own individual anchorage, where value is bestowed by an individual projecting private preferences rather than being discerned as both given and integrative, as is the experience of persons living in community.

Friedrich Schleiermacher (1768–1834) drew attention to the significance of an immediate awareness of a feeling of absolute dependence in religious living and indicated that this kind of awareness and living represents humanity at its fullest. For Schleiermacher, "in the feeling of absolute dependence, God is actually experienced in the only way open to us, and to be conscious of being absolutely dependent is to be conscious of being in relation to God."[1] Schleiermacher's notion of absolute dependence as being at the core of the religious life has come under criticism over the decades, but his contribution is still major. To the degree that I say that I am absolutely, ultimately dependent upon another who is alluringly above my capacity to manipulate conceptually, who is consistently behind my ability to think logically, who is supportively beneath my sequence of judgments about what is proper for my life, who is teleologically beyond the life span that is before me, who pervasively and compassionately informs human relationships at their noblest, to that degree am I grounded, established, settled, with insight, with psychological stability and with a realization of acceptance that brings liberation from indolence, freedom from loneliness, and profound gratitude.

This orientation to transcendence that is discerned as absolute dependence provides a protection from distress, a shelter from the onslaughts of difficulties, provides confidence based on experience, which can be depended upon, relied upon when all else seems awry. There is more to it than this, which might suggest merely an orientation that provides protection. This fundamental orientation in one's life also enables one to place the world into perspective, to have a point on which to stand that is more fundamental than the world itself, a point that gives one a foundation on the basis of which to put limits on the world, to define the world, a point from which to view the world, to find that the world has become salvificly intelligible.

We could turn to several strands in the religious history of humankind to begin a consideration of what one might call "taking refuge."[2] In this chapter, we will consider briefly contributions by the Theravāda Buddhist tradition, two theistic strands in the Hindu tradition before turning to a more sustained consideration of the Jōdo Shinshū tradition of Japan. We turn to India, to that great source of multifaceted influences that has significantly shaped our one global history.

## THERAVĀDA, ŚRĪVAIṢṆAVA, ŚAIVASIDDHĀNTA TESTIMONIES

Quite some time ago important words were said about the notion of refuge (P: *saraṇa*), and by finding this refuge secure men and women have become Buddhists.

Many for refuge go
To mountains and to forests,
To shrines that are groves or trees—
Humans who are threatened by fear.
    This is not a refuge secure,
    This refuge is not the highest.
    Having come to this refuge,
    One is not released from all misery.
But who to the Buddha, Dhamma,
And Saṅgha as refuge has gone,
Sees with full insight
The four noble truths;
    Misery, the arising of misery,
    And the transcending of misery,
    The noble Eightfold Path
    Leading to the allaying of misery
This, indeed, is a refuge secure.
This is the highest refuge.
Having come to this refuge,
One is released from all misery.[3]

Right at the center of the South Asian Buddhist experience with this notion of taking refuge was an awareness that the public act is not in itself synonymous with liberation. There can be a level of going for refuge that, although admirable, religious, impressive, is considered customary (*lokiyasaraṇagamana*). But there is another dimension, another level of going for refuge (*lokuttarasaraṇagamana*) which occurs at the moment of the arising of the path (*maggakhaṇa*)[4] and is the arising of insight-wisdom which transcends the world(s) (*lokuttarapaññā*), namely, insight into Salvific Truth. This is that refuge supreme, this refuge cannot be altered either by oneself or by another.[5]

Of considerable significance is the way this general notion of refuge has been readily endorsed by both early Indian Buddhists, including the Theravāda, and the rich theistic movements that have graced the Hindu tradition. These theistic traditions have seen the point of what has come to be called "the ultimate statement" uttered by Krishna:

Abandoning all that is expected of you (*dharma*s)
Come unto me as your sole refuge;
I shall release you from all sins,
Do not despair.[6]

One of the great theologians in India's past, and of our human heritage, was Rāmānuja (approximately 1017–1137) who contributed to the formation of the

Śrīvaiṣṇava movement.[7] Central in a consideration of refuge in the Śrīvaiṣṇava movement is a text entitled the *Śaraṇāgatigadya*. Although it is not established whether Rāmānuja actually wrote this text,[8] there is no question that within the Śrīvaiṣṇava heritage the centrality of the text is assured and the authorship by Rāmānuja is affirmed.

Rāmānuja, in those writings clearly established as his, urged that the discipline of loving devotion (*bhaktiyoga*) was the reliable means for attaining the grace of God, and indispensable for this was prostration or surrender (*prapatti*). In the *Śaraṇāgatigadya* the only way open for one is to prostrate oneself, to surrender, because one's evil actions and detrimental consequences are of such magnitude that one cannot even imagine beginning successfully to engage in any discipline whatsoever, even the discipline of loving devotion.[9]

We catch this theme again in another important text for the Śrīvaiṣṇava tradition, the *Śrīraṅgagadya*,

> Destitute of bhakti . . . right knowledge . . . and all spiritual qualities like goodness and faith . . . sunk in the endless and hard-to-pass-over ocean of . . . beginningless sins conducive to knowledge and action which are contrary to that [right knowledge and action] . . . seeing no other means . . . I resort to your two lotus-like feet as refuge, O Nārāyana. . . . [10]

The absence of any other means is an acknowledgment that the traditionally institutionalized paths or disciplines leading to salvation are no longer relevant because one is no longer able to launch oneself in those disciplines. What is left for one to do? Vasudha Narayanan puts it this way:

> The common denominator of all those who surrender (*prapanna*s) is expressed here: one comes for protection and throws oneself at the mercy of the Lord because one does not have the strength to adopt a scripturally sanctioned way (*upāya*) which will procure his [God's] grace.[11]

Kūraṭṭāḻvaṉ, a contemporary of Rāmānuja, aware of his own evil deeds, being depleted of any good quality, acknowledged the divine initiative when he uttered

> O Varada! Even these words of surrender could not have come outside your grace (*prasāda*); therefore, you are gracious (*prasāda*) toward me. Now I live. . . . [12]

This overwhelming sense of soteriological inadequacy following upon one's reflections upon oneself—one's actions, one's knowledge of one's inner motives—appears in another vibrant theistic movement in India, the Śaivasiddhānta, particularly in the writings of the *nāyanmār*s, "precursors" or "leaders," composers of engaging devotional hymns in the Tamil language celebrating the grace of Śiva.[13]

Maheswari Arulchelvam, in speaking about one of the great Tamil poets, Māṇikkavāçagar, notes his joy that "God, out of his great love and grace, has deigned to accept as his own such an unworthy creature." "One is filled with ecstasy, with unspeakable joy at God's graciousness. One cannot thank God enough for his graciousness because God has accepted someone so utterly unworthy of him. . . ."[14] Māṇikkavāçagar said

> Him none by hearing know; He knoweth no decay;
> He hath no kin; naught asking, heareth all!
> While people of the land beheld, here on this earth to me a cur,
> He gave a royal seat;
> To me, a dog, all things not shown before, He showed;
> All things not heard before, He caused to hear;
> And guarding me from future "birth," He made me His.
> Such is the wondrous work our Lord hath wrought for me![15]

Men and women who have been a part of the heritage of these two great theistic streams in the grand Hindu tradition would readily concur about the importance of having a fundamental religious orientation, of refuge, of surrender, of a self-analysis that sharply circumscribes the soteriological efficacy of one's own actions.[16]

I have mentioned these three significant expressions of religiousness in our global religious history—the Theravāda, the Śrīvaiṣṇava and the Śaivasiddhānta—not to suggest a kind of historical development in India that might have led through China into our contemporary experience in Japan today. On the contrary, I mention these three examples *because they continue to be a part of our contemporary experience* in our world today.

## THE INSIGHT OF SHINRAN AND JŌDO SHINSHŪ

We turn now to the Jōdo Shinshū tradition of Japan and to Shinran, another figure who has illumined our human religious history.[17] Naturally, one might anticipate our turning to the frequently emphasized notion of Other Power (*tariki*) and the total commitment to this espoused by the Jōdo Shinshū tradition as the prime example of a sense of absolute dependence at the foundation of the religious life. Of course, the notion of *shinjin* is featured majestically in the writings of Shinran, and one would be amiss not to see the interconnectedness of other key religious terms with the core notion of *shinjin*. The general notion of "refuge," to which we will now turn, is likewise, in the thought of Shinran, involved in that salvific matrix that is *shinjin*.[18]

In considering the terms that reflect a sense of "relying upon" or "taking refuge" in the writings of Shinran, we will explore one dimension of what several scholars writing in the English medium have noted as an interior dialectic, which exemplifies "a shifting of frames of reference—between two fundamental modes or models of apprehending true reality," an "interpersonal" over against a "teleological" dimension.[19] This interpersonal dimension represents also an attitude of personal engagement on the part of Shinran akin to his frequently expressed sense of indebtedness (*on*) with regard to Amida and Śākyamuni and the great predecessors in the Pure Land heritage.[20]

We again begin with *kimyō,* which we have considered to some extent in our chapter 1. With Shinran there is a clear association between the Sanskrit derived *namu* (Skt.: *namo/namas*) and the Chinese inherited *kanji* pronounced in Japanese as *kimyō*.[21] And Shinran appropriates the Pure Land heritage discerned as coming from India through China. He understands his legacy as stemming from the realization behind Nāgārjuna's reference to have taken refuge in Amida,[22] and Vasubandhu's affirmation, "I take refuge in the Tathagata of unhindered light,[which] means to follow the command of the Tathagata."[23] Shinran follows Shan-tao (J: Zendō, 613–681) who acknowledges that refuge "further signifies aspiration for birth and turning over the virtue,"[24] and Shinran records a further gloss: "*Namu* means 'to take refuge.'[25] 'To take refuge' is to respond to the command [*chokumei*] and follow the call [*meishi*] of the two honored ones, Śākyamuni and Amida."[26]

One of the more detailed interpretations of *kimyō* passed on from Shan-tao to Shinran is as follows:

> From these passages, we see that the word *namu* means "to take refuge." In the term "to take refuge" (*kimyo*) *ki* means "to arrive at." Further, it is used in compounds to mean "to yield joyfully to" (*kietsu*) and "to take shelter in" (*kisai*).[27] *Myo* means "to act," "to invite," "to command," "to teach," "path," "message," "to devise," "to summon." Thus, *kimyo* is the command of the Primal Vow calling to and summoning us.[28]

Although Shinran used *kimyō* liberally in the portion of the *Jōdo Wasan* dealing with praise of Amida Buddha,[29] it is difficult to say that it is a term particularly suited to convey the subtleties of his thinking. He more or less inherited the term from his received Pure Land tradition.

Of significance is what he did with it, that is, with the way he found it to form a part of what one might call a "*shinjin* cluster," to indicate an engaged relationship within nonduality. Often Shinran will utilize a sequential method of analogy by association, where, for example, he will say something like *A* is the same as *B*, and *B* is the same as *C*, and *C* is *D,* so *D* is the same as *A*. Shinran, in this way, indicates that to take refuge with the mind that is single (*isshin ni kimyō*) is true and genuine *shinjin*.[30] We also find *kimyō* used to indicate the orientation to both practice (*gyō*) and *shinjin* that enables beings to be "grasped never to be abandoned."[31] Even though there is surely a tone of formality in the use of *kimyō,* carrying overtones of reverently responding to one's lord (cf. *chokumei*), one finds semantic frames with other terms suggesting how *kimyō* is associated with ritual worship.[32] Shinran was aware of the old setting of the refuge formula. Consulting passages from rather old texts, he records references to taking refuge (*kie*) in the Buddha[33] as well as the standard formula for the three gems: refuge (*kimyō*) in the Buddha, refuge (*kimyō*) in Dharma, and refuge (*kimyō*) in the Saṅgha.[34]

It is not clear whether one is to infer that Shinran had already realized *shinjin* when he turned (*kisu*) to the Primal Vow and put aside sundry practices.[35] Perhaps there might be a thread of autobiographical reflection in his observation:

> When we reflect upon our cyclic transmigration, we find it difficult, even in the passage of infinite kalpas, to turn to the Buddha's Vow-Power for refuge [*butsuganriki ni kishi*] and enter the sea of absolute dependence. We should indeed lament it and deeply deplore it.[36]

Surely, as his life became more abundant Shinran sensed the authentically human experiences associated with this matter of taking refuge. He recorded passages indicating a *cohesive attitudinal field,* of bowing to and worshiping, of constantly thinking on Amida, in which the notion of *kimyō* also finds its place.[37] Moreover, in one of his more extensive textual comments, Shinran unambiguously associates taking refuge (*kimyō*) and worship (*raihai*), and with considerable insight he indicates refuge (*kimyō*) to be more fundamental. Having referred to the examples of Nāgārjuna and Vasubandhu, Shinran writes,

> For these reasons, we know that taking refuge manifests itself as worship. Worship itself, however, is only to pay homage and does not necessarily imply taking refuge; rather, taking refuge expresses itself in worship. From this we can infer that taking refuge is central.[38]

And he concludes his general observation, "The two terms, 'take refuge,' (*kimyō*) and 'worship,' (*raihai*) complement each other, revealing the basic meaning all the more clearly."[39] It would come as no surprise, therefore, to find "worship" or "bowing down in homage" (as translators might interpret customary ritual bowing in worship) appearing alternatingly, as it were, with *kimyō* in the *Jōdo Wasan.*[40]

Although the call of Amida and one's response are always central in this *coherent attitudinal field,* in the sense of taking refuge in or relying on, there are other key doctrinal formulations that are given their focal significance from the devotee's perspective by noting them as worthy of one's relying on them or taking refuge in them. So one reads of those who "rely (from *ki*) on the universal Vow" and that one can "Take refuge (*kimyō*) in the Great Mind Sea."[41] Shinran, in his hymns (*wasans*), mentions T'an-luan (J: Donran 476–542) who deeply, sincerely, profoundly took refuge in the Pure Land (*jōdo ni fukaku kiseshimeki*).[42] And in keeping with the discernment of Tao-ch'o (J: Dōsaku 562–645), Shinran notes that even while we are being driven by the winds and rains of detrimental behavior all Buddhas urge us to take refuge in the Pure Land (*susumete jōdo ni kiseshimeri*).[43] Further, these key terms enable one quickly also to see the importance of tradition as a source on which one can rely, indeed, even resort to as a kind of refuge. For example, as one can rely or depend on Amida,[44] one can "take refuge (*ki*) in the true words of the Great Sage."[45] So also the *sūtra*s can be relied or depended on (*yoru*),[46] and one can rely on (*shinzu beshi*) "the teachings of these venerable masters."[47]

There is another kindred term, both in meaning and in use, namely, *tanomu*, often utilized as an indigenous Japanese expression representing *kimyō* and *kie*. Although in Shinran's writings one notes the use of *tanomu* applied generally to persons who are committing themselves to religious pursuits, at issue was not whether persons were expressing the human religious activity communicated in the verb *tanomu*, but whether or not this quality of relying upon (*tanomu*) was in self-power (*jiriki o tanomu*) or Other Power (*tariki o tanomu*).[48] Shinran appropriated this human religious quality, *tanomu*, and found it adequately expressive of one's salvific relationship with compassionate reality. He understood Tao-ch'o to have done this.[49]

The relevant meaning of *tanomu* for our purposes is "to entrust [something] to someone," and in Jōdo Shinshū this "something" is one's life, and this basic sense as well as Shinran's masterful use of this word provide another example in a *coherent attitudinal field*: there is interlinkage. For example, the action in the verbal structure, "we should completely entrust ourselves" (*tanomu beshi*), is an action fully consonant with the arising of true, real, honest-authenticity of heart (*shinjitsu shinjin*).[50] We see this unambiguously stated with the use of another verb, *makaseru* ("to entrust," "trust [a person] with [something]"): "Simply give yourself up to Tathagata's Vow [*nyorai no seigan ni makase mairase tamōbeku*]; avoid calculating in any way."[51]

Another important notion within the *coherent attitudinal field* that indicates involvement with one's heritage and also an existential immediacy in one's realization of salvific reality is the activity of hearing (*mon*/*kiku*). Shinran elaborates: "'To hear' in the sūtra means that sentient beings hear the origin, cause, and effect of the Buddha's Vow and do not have doubt in them. This is described as 'to hear' [*mon*]."[52] We read another gloss, "'*To welcome*' means that Amida receives us, awaits us. Hearing the inconceivable selected Primal Vow and the holy Name of supreme wisdom without a single doubt is called true and real shinjin; it is also called the diamond-like heart."[53] And the point is explicitly made: "*Hear* is a word indicating shinjin [*mon wa kikutoiu, shinjin o arawasuminori nari*]."[54] And the association is maintained in phrases such as "When they hear and entrust."[55] Shinran himself indicated his joy upon receiving his heritage. He continued,

> Rare it is to hear them [scriptures and commentaries], but already I have been able to hear. Reverently entrusting myself to the teaching, practice, and realization that are the true essence of the Pure Land Way, I am especially aware of the profundity of the Tathagata's benevolence.[56]

We have seen the cluster forming within this *coherent attitudinal field*—*kimyō, kie, tanomu, makaseru,* and *mon/kiku*—and we know the focal point of coherence is in *shinjin.* Yet there is another integral dimension within this *coherent attitudinal field*: "change of heart" (*eshin*). This change of heart is not merely changing one's opinion, disposition, or point of view. It is a changing of the heart, the heart now is other than what it was. We are told by Yuien, in the second part of the *Tannishō,* that this change occurs only once[57] and that it is closely associated with entrusting to the Primal Vow, to aspiring for the Pure Land,[58] to saying the *nembutsu.*[59] Just as one was urged not to rely on self-power, so this turning about of mind or change of heart means to put aside the mind of self-power,[60] which act is inseparably a part of one's entering the ocean of true and real *shinjin.*[61] This sense of turning about of the heart, of the heart's changing and becoming new, is very much akin to the Christian Greek New Testament notion of *metanoia* (μετάνοια), a 180-degree change in direction and orientation, carrying with it a sense of remorse, of repentance.

We know the soteriological centrality of the Primal Vow (*hongan*), and we are also aware of the pivotal importance that *shinjin* has in the thinking of Shinran. The "keystone" or "cornerstone" notion, the notion that connects this Primal Vow, to which one is simply to give oneself, with the arising of *shinjin,* which represents salvation in this life, is *ekō,* the turning toward another that constitutes both the manifestation of compassion in the cosmos and our own true humanity.[62] But, we are told, sentient beings have neither an honest nor a pure mind for this turning toward another in an act of conveying to that other a transference of merit.[63] Shinran makes it clear that the Tathāgata's *ekō* brings enlightenment within one's horizon:

> If it were not for the Tathāgata's merit-transference,
> How could we ever attain realization in the Pure Land.[64]

Just as we have been told that persons should not rely on self-power, so also we are reminded again that reciting the *nembutsu* with a sense of self-power does not provide a basis for transferring merit to others.[65] The name of Amida has been turned over to us (*mida no ekō no mina*)[66] and, following Tan-l'uan, Shinran indicates the twofold activity of inclusive involvement (*ōsō-ekō,* transference while going forward, onward, and *gensō-ekō,* transference while returning, drawing near) engendered by Amida which is consequently brought within the reach of our awareness (*nyorai nishu no ekō o fukaku shinzuru hito wa*)[67] through the merit transference of Amida's Vow of wisdom (*mida chigan no ekō*).[68] Hence, we see that Shinran, particularly in his *Sōzōmatsu Wasan,* sets up the dilemma precisely:

> With my mind as deceitful as serpents and scorpions,
> I am incapable of accomplishing virtuous deeds of
> self-power.
> Unless I rely on the Tathāgata's merit-transference,
> [*nyorai no ekō o tanoma de wa*]
> I will end without shame or repentance.[69]

With care, Shinran draws upon the themes he has inherited in his tradition and weaves a fabric with overlapping patterns: the manifestation of the one mind (*isshin*) is a turning over of merit on the part of Amida,[70] a merit transference of going on and of returning (*ō-gen* [abbreviation for *ōsō* + *gensō-*] *no ekō*), which meets in *shinjin,* and originates in Other Power (*tariki*).[71] Ultimately, the sole cause for birth is the result of Amida's turning over of this virtue or transferring this merit.[72] Or, phrased differently, the twin realizations of Nirvāṇa in the realm of the Vow (*gando*) as well as the awakening of great compassion (*daihi*) are the result of Amida's *ekō.*[73]

Yuien leads us then to our final step in our survey of key terms forming a *coherent attitudinal field,* to the undercurrent of the compassionate cosmos, to *jinen.* We know that we are still involved with poor decisions, egocentric considerations, selfish pursuits, subtle possessiveness, and we know what might be involved in repentance and in change of heart. How are we, Yuien considers, to go on repenting and seeking to change our hearts with each detrimental act we commit. We need, he suggests, to trust the power of the Vow, to yield to its efficacy, and "gentleheartedness and forbearance will surely arise in us through the working of jinen."[74]

We tread lightly when we consider *jinen,* having been told on several occasions that *jinen* "is none other than being free of all calculation,"[75] and that we are attempting to handle "the mystery of the wisdom of Buddhas (*kore wa butsu chi no fushigi*)."[76] If the entirety of what has been collated and designated as the fifth letter was written by Shinran, we could say that he there located *jinen* as a profound soteriological notion, indicating the involvement which formless salvific reality has with human beings. And, further, Amida is the means by which we come to learn of this undergirding salvific naturalness that abides.[77] Shinran knew that this naturalness, arising from the efficacy of the Primal Vow and the concomitant arising of *shinjin,* could be relied upon without doubt, without calculation, and that it enables one to know with certainty that one is assured of attaining complete Nirvāṇa.[78] When one is in this supportive undercurrent of salvific naturalness one no longer has to worry about self-working, about whether one is good or bad, about motivation for uttering the *nembutsu.* One is being carried by the efficacy of the Primal Vow "to make us all attain the supreme Buddhahood."[79] Regularly, we read that the efficacy of the Vow and the certainty of one's attaining complete enlightenment is established naturally (*jinen*) and that the stage of non-retrogression arises of itself.[80] And the virtues that are directed by Amida to the person of *shinjin* are not sought but naturally arise for this person who is grasped never to be abandoned, who is the recipient of the diamond-like mind, free from all calculation.[81] For Shan-tao's (J: Zendō 613–681) use of "necessarily" or "inevitably" *hitsu,* Shinran provides a gloss with *jinen*: "'One necessarily attains birth' One is brought to the attainment of birth naturally, by *jinen*."[82] Again and again one reads of the person within *jinen* that there is no calculation, that one is not seeking anything. Even the "constant mindfulness of the Primal Vow" of such a person arises naturally.[83] One has entrusted one's life to the efficacy of the Vow and one's birth is settled, naturally.

Shinran explicitly connects the notion of *jinen* with a well-established Buddhist idea, namely, "having the quality of Dharma," when he provides notes on a passage from the *Larger Sūtra*:

> *Know that these people:* people realizing shinjin. *Acquire the great benefit*: they will realize the supreme nirvana; hence it is further stated, *and, as such, are furnished with the supreme virtues. As such* means immediately; it also means dharmicness [*hōsoku*]. In entrusting ourselves to the Tathagata's Primal Vow and saying the Name once, necessarily, without seeking it, we are made to receive the supreme virtues, and without knowing it, we acquire the great and vast benefit. This is dharmicness, by which one will immediately realize the various facts of enlightenment naturally [*jinen*]. "Dharmicness" means not brought about in any way by the practicer's calculation; from the very beginning one shares in the benefit that surpasses conception. It indicates the nature of *jinen*. "Dharmicness" expresses the natural working (*jinen*) in the life of the person who realizes shinjin and says the Name once.[84]

The soteriological zone covered by the notion of *jinen* is precisely the efficacy of the Primal Vow integrally related to the person of *shinjin*. If there is absolutely no calculation in *jinen,* if *jinen* is solely the efficacy of the Primal Vow, Other Power, one would not find it inconsistent for Shinran to write a *wasan,* based on Shan-tao's writings, in which he refers to the Pure Land of *jinen* (*jinen no jōdo*)[85] or to write the following:

> Since shinjin arises from the Vow,
> We attain Buddhahood through the nembutsu by the
> [Vow's] spontaneous working.
> The spontaneous working is itself the fulfilled land;
> Our realization of supreme nirvana is beyond doubt.[86]

And in another *wasan,* based on the teaching of the *Larger Sūtra,* Shinran mentions "the Pure Land that is naturalness (*jinen no jōdo*)," perhaps indicating the utter pervasiveness of the natural soteriological disposition of reality.[87] Moreover, of course, one infers, a person who has realized authentic, genuine *shinjin* knows this, since such person is born in the genuine fulfilled land.[88]

## RESOUNDING GOOD NEWS

The evidence adduced from four major religious movements—the Theravāda, Śrīvaiṣṇava, Śaivasiddhānta and Jōdo Shinshū—indicates that one of the most pressing problems of the contemporary world is to be found with us, not with the soteriological status of reality. In all the traditions mentioned there is the testimony that salvific reality arises within one in this life and is fully arisen or is fully attained, variously elaborated, upon death. In other words, the testimony of such incipient arising is something like a joyous affirmation: "*YES! for the meantime in which we do our living . . .*" Yes, reality is known as it really is, one's limitations *and* the limitless, the finite in the presence of the infinite, yielding a catalytic creativity in the context of a coherent wholeness. And yet, it seems we are not quite *it,* not quite there, to use spatial terms, unfortunately. We can see the world from a new perspective, see the way things really have become as they really are, see ourselves as we truly are (our past, which has shaped us and to a considerable degree our future possibilities, our aspirations), and yet we look upon this *from* a perspective, in the Jōdo Shinshū case, in the person that we are with the Buddha mind.

Echoes of past discussions within the Jōdo Shinshū tradition of learning reverberate around the notion of "birth," *ōjō.*[89] Is this "birth" into the Pure Land in this life or only at death? It seems to me that *shinjin is salvation,* ever so. Yet our individuality abides and it is this individuality, this *bonbu* particularity of ordinariness with which we are familiar, that generates a dynamic tension delicately adumbrated by Shinran and eloquently elaborated by some contemporary scholars writing for an English-reading public.[90] And the activity of such person who has undergone the transformational realization of authentic *shinjin* is not actually the giving of virtue, but the sharing of virtue given by Amida, discerned as "going" and as "returning." However, upon death, it seems to me, the dialectical tension subsides; one then *is* "going-*and*-returning" (because there is no longer that from which one leaves upon going and that to which one comes upon returning), one then *is* reality, *is* wisdom, *is* compassion, without individuality whatsoever.

It would seem, therefore, that the question whether there is *ōjō,* birth, in this life or upon death, or both in this life and upon death, needs to be approached with considerable circumspection and humility because the person who has realized the answer does not see the point of raising the question and the person who grapples with the question might not know the answer.

To my way of thinking, however, there remains another problem, and this problem seems to be with life in the world—both in the past and in the contemporary setting—not with salvation. The evidence we have adduced, with the Theravāda, with the Śrīvaiṣṇava, with the Śaivasiddhānta, and with the writings of Shinran, indicate that a Gospel message is being communicated by each, a resounding Good News, that there is *no problem* insofar as salvation itself is concerned. The problem—and we have known this all along—lies with *us*.

"We live in a time which suffers in the profoundest way from loneliness. . . ." M. Holmes Hartshorne writes,

> It is a world that has no concern for what concerns us most deeply: our hopes, our fears, our anxieties, our love, ourselves. In consequence our need of others intensifies; they must take the place of God. And so we try to get others to like us, because what is loneliness but the fate of being cut off from others and from life itself? We are cut off, because we fear that if another person really knew us as we are, he or she could not possibly love us. It is not simply that we are not loved; we are not loveable. This is the deepest anxiety, I think, with respect to loneliness. We know so much about ourselves, whom we do not really like, that the thought that anybody could love me as I am, if he or she knew me as I am, is unsupportable.[91]

This seems to be a fair description of our contemporary scene; loneliness at rush hour. Some might say that there is no exit from this condition. Others might say there are ways to exit. One way is by becoming an aesthete, seeking to fulfill one's culturally sanctioned desires and to become enraptured by one's self-sanctioned values, no longer to be bored with one's existence. Another supposed exit would be to construct with but a little bias one's own moral criteria and to live at ease within one's own self-righteousness. Søren Kierkegaard (1813–1855), attempting to let persons take note of their being enamored with Christendom in Denmark and their simultaneous failure to discern Jesus Christ, of their non-selfconscious choices of cultural elitism and moral smugness, wrote of only one way out, which "happens only by the grace of God in Jesus Christ. It is not something we do, not a higher rung on the ladder of spiritual achievement, not a higher stage of existence." Hartshorne explains Kierkegaard's attempt to help his contemporaries see themselves as indeed they were. Kierkegaard, according to Hartshorne, suggested

> that the cultivation and increase of the aesthetical elements in life only lead to cynicism and deeper despair . . . that moral self-righteousness, based on the illusion of being the absolute, leads not to moral integrity but to overweening pride coupled with banality. Thus would Kierkegaard try to nudge the Philistine reader to—to become a Christian? No, that he

> could not do. One does not become a Christian by reading a book, though one may perhaps take notice. One becomes a Christian only by the grace of God in Christ. Luther's confession lives on in Kierkegaard: salvation is by divine grace through faith in Jesus Christ.[92]

This seems to me to be the point: finding a point of orientation that provides meaning in life, psychological stability, and a sense of grounded acceptance has been the experience of religious men and women around the world. This grounded acceptance arises in one when the reality of one's inadequacies is matched by the reality of one's acceptance. It is upon becoming initially aware of our inadequacies that we build our walls of defensiveness, hoard our tidbit traces of possessiveness (whether regarding things or our distorted sense of our own importance), because we are aware of our inadequacies and we seek to defend ourselves. God's grace, for our theistic neighbors of India, accepts us, and the compassionate salvific quality of reality is fundamentally and reliably supporting for those of us who are Theravāda Buddhists, and embraces those of us who are Jōdo Shinshū Buddhists. This is difficult for us to accept—and there is no small amount of irony in this: we prefer not to accept what enables us to become genuinely human. This is difficult, and this, it seems to me, is the difficulty of liberation or salvation in the contemporary world and in every contemporary world in human history.

# 9

# Love and Compassion as Given

*Doctrinal structures and systems are important conceptual constructions made by persons of faith. In the course of decades, even centuries, those constructions have contributed to maintaining recognizable patterns of discourse. They have changed, too, through the centuries. Running through these formulations is a significant insight about religious persons: Jōdo Shinshū, Theravāda, and Christian. We find in the moments when authentic love and genuine compassion are expressed that the act that arises in those moments seems somehow not the result of our deliberate creation but a spontaneous response that we have been enabled at those moments to make.*

In attempting to understand religious men and women we see the remarkable variety in the modes of expressing the quality of faith. Religious traditions differ, of course, but persons who participate in these traditions demonstrate discernibly similar patterns of faith and response. We know an awareness of refuge is one response. Another is a profound sense of love and compassion.

Let us turn our attention to love and compassion in the experience of Christians and Buddhists—Theravāda and Jōdo Shinshū—to consider a remarkable dialectic in a profound awareness of one's receiving and responding. Were I to attempt to consider some of the key notions that relate to a topic such as "*agapē* (αγάπη) and compassion, their relation to insight or faith,"[1] and to discuss their ramifications within these three great traditions I would be faced with a restriction that would allow no more than a paragraph or so for each notion in the different contexts, leaving aside whether one might want to trace the notions through millennia.

There is a fundamental experiential dimension which one can infer from the manifestation of love (*agapē*) and/or compassion (*karuṇā*) among Theravāda Buddhists, Jōdo Shinshū Buddhists, and perhaps more than a few Christians. This experiential dimension suggests that love (*agapē*) and compassion (*karuṇā*) are, like salvific insight or faith, *given*; that when persons authentically manifest love (*agapē*) and compassion (*karuṇā*) they do so as an expression of salvific insight or faith; that the ideal paradigm for love (*agapē*) and compassion (*karuṇā*) is found in the *actions* of focal personages.

## *AGAPĒ*

By the time that some correspondence and a few accounts written in *koine* Greek that had to do with what we now tend to call "the early Christian community" began to appear and to circulate, later to form a part of the New Testament, verb and noun forms of *agapē* already had served for well over two centuries as a vehicle for expressing a sense of the quality of love. Regularly, the translators engaged in translating the Hebrew Scriptures into the Greek of the Septuagint (LXX) chose verb and noun forms of our word *agapē* (αγάπη) as translations for the Hebrew verb form *āhav*' and *āhe-v'* and *ahavāh'*. We find this use of *agapē* in contexts dealing with love for one's neighbor (Lev. 19:18), love of oneself (Lev. 19:34), love of God "with all one's heart" (Deut. 6:5), as well as with love toward one's wife (Ecc. 9:9), man toward man (Ps. 109:4–5 [LXX 108:4–5]), between man and woman (II Sam. 1:26 [LXX Regnorum II 1:26]).[2] Hence, one might want to modify slightly Anders Nygren's observation, "The New Testament uses this new word [that is, *agapē*] because it must communicate a message of a new kind, namely, God's love revealed through Jesus Christ, given through Jesus Christ."[3]

When we turn to the contextualization of *agapē* in the New Testament, we find the overwhelming theme to be the salvific activity of God in Jesus the Christ reconciling the world, demonstrating the love of God for humankind, and the consequent potentialities that are brought within the realm of possible human actions because of God's salvific activity, initiated from beyond the realm of possible human actions. The notion of *agapē* is set within this context in the Christian heritage: God's love for humankind, our love for each other in light of this divine love. This self-giving act of love on the part of God provides the core notion of *agapē*.

There is not sufficient space to go into a careful study of the New Testament evidence or to consider thoroughly the work of others. Much has been said about the New Testament sense of *agapē,* much written also about a Hellenistic sense of *erōs* (ἔρως) and the interplay these two great notions have had in the history of Christian thought.[4] One might want to argue that the task before us is to put aside *erōs* entirely and to reclaim the New Testament sense of *agapē,*[5] or one might want to side with Paul Tillich, perhaps, when he states, "No love is real without a unity of *erōs* and *agape*."[6]

Two beautiful passages occur in a letter written from the church in Rome to the church in Corinth in the last decade or so of the first century AD, a letter ascribed to a person named Clement (probably the third or fourth bishop of Rome), a letter that came to be referred to as First Clement ("I Clement"), a letter, nevertheless, written by a person not having had the opportunity of reading Nygren's *Agape and Eros* or Tillich's *Dynamics of Faith*. The first passage reads,

> Who is able to explain the bond of the love of God? Who is sufficient to tell the greatness of its beauty? The height to which love lifts us is not to be expressed. Love unites us to God.[7]

And one reads further,

> See, beloved, how great and wonderful is love, and that of its perfection there is no expression. Who is able to be found in it save those to whom God grants it? Let us then beg and pray of his mercy[8] that we may be found in love, without human partisanship, free from blame.[9]

These passages from this letter tell us that *agapē* cannot be measured by the human mind, cannot be made plain, explained. *Agapē* evokes from men and women a quality of perception in personal relationships that is genuinely human—what a modern would tell us is the overlapping of the categories of ethics and aesthetics. It engenders an awareness in one of a delicate sense of being taken up. With subtlety, the passages present the notion of *agapē* not as a mental state resulting from deliberation, not actually as an act of the will,[10] but as a state of awareness in which men and women whom God has deemed worthy find themselves to have entered.[11] These passages from I Clement have told us a great deal.

And, of course, there is more to the story. Ignatius, who achieved martyrdom under Trajan (AD 98–117) in Rome, has left a testimony about the interrelatedness of faith and love, not only addressing our theme immediately but indicating how faith (*pistis* πίστις) and *agapē* might provide a formal parallel teleological structure with salvific insight-wisdom (*paññā*) and compassion (*karuṇā*). Ignatius writes,

> None of these things are unknown to you if you possess perfect faith towards Jesus Christ, and love, which are the beginning and end of life; for the beginning is faith and the end is love, and when the two are joined together in unity it is God, and all other noble things follow after them.[12]

Perhaps there is no more succinct statement to indicate what some of the early Christian leaders thought the relation of faith and *agapē* to be.

### *KARUṆĀ*

In turning to the rich vocabulary in the Indian heritage of the Buddhist tradition, one need not cast about for long to determine concepts representing human dispositions akin to *agapē*. Although translators of the New Testament into Indian

Languages have preferred forms derived from the Sanskrit base of *prī/prīti/prema* as translations for *agapaō* (ἀγαπάω), the verb "to love," and *agapē,* "love,"[13] this Indian etymological base for and sense of "love" has not figured as prominently as have other notions in the Buddhist soteriological framework. I put aside all debates comparing *agapē* and the Latin notion of "tender caring," (*caritas,* as Augustine might have intended it) with "compassion" (*karuṇā*), "friendliness" (*mettā*), "sympathetic joy" (*muditā*), attempts that, having clearly differentiated *agapē* from "law" (*nomos*: νόμος), *erōs,* and *caritas* on the Western scene, seek to argue that *agapē* necessarily differs from the cluster of associated Buddhist terms. I have found—shall I say for all practical purposes—that a person pointed out to me as being characterized by *karuṇā* would be, in every case that I might conceive, a person living quite similarly to how I have been enabled to imagine a person manifesting *agapē* might live. Although my position on this point might be considered less than persuasive on the bases of etymology, structures of lexical items, or usage in semantic frames, however, on the basis of the patterns of the human heart in human behavior (the "by their fruits you shall know them" scale), I, in advancing this particular point based on my experiences over the years living among Buddhists, feel quite comfortable, to use that great Quaker phrase.

Certainly, space does not allow a detailed analysis of nuances of the several major terms derived from our Indian Buddhist heritage. Let me, therefore, focus on *karuṇā,* assuredly a jewel of a concept in the crown of our humanity. Basically, *karuṇā* means "compassion." We are told by an eminent Theravāda Buddhist commentator, Buddhaghosa, writing in Sri Lanka in the fifth century AD,

> It is compassion in the sense that when there is suffering among others it moves the heart of good people [literally, it makes the movement of the heart among the good ones]. Moreover, it is compassion in the sense that it slays the suffering of others, attacks it, destroys it. Furthermore, it is compassion in the sense that it is scattered among those who are suffering, it is extended to them by means of pervasion.[14]

Further, it is said,

> It is compassion because of the desire to remove misfortune and suffering in a manner beginning with "O let them be released from suffering!"[15]

*Karuṇā* implies a sense of sadness, of pity in response to the object which becomes the recipient of compassion. *Karuṇā* is not identical to *agapē* in meaning. Yet the cognitive and behavioral structures in which these two terms function are quite similar. One might agree with Nygren's observation that *agapē* "is the centre of Christianity, the Christian fundamental motif *par excellence,* the answer to both the religious and the ethical question"[16] and also make the point that customarily *agapē* has been interpreted to mean that kind of unconditioned love, unqualified love, love without qualification, that is directed toward the unlovely/unloved as well as to the lovely, the loved. Yet that great Greek term *eleos,* "mercy, compassion, pity," running through the LXX and New Testament, reminds one that while John 3:16 represents God's love (*agapē*), the act there mentioned is not at all devoid of God's compassion.

One would want to note also a peculiarly self-effacing quality that *karuṇā,* as in the case of a "compassionate one" (*karuṇāvant*), and *agapē,* as "one characterized by *agapē,*" convey. These are not terms that one would use to refer to oneself, of course. Their being so used would immediately make suspect the validity of the observation. They are terms to be used by one's neighbor about oneself. Within the Theravāda Buddhist heritage, *karuṇā* tends not to stand alone, as is also the case with *agapē* in the Christian case. Often *karuṇā* is listed along with the superior abodes of meditative-absorption (*brahmavihāras*).[17] The weighty companion concept of *karuṇā,* the one that makes clear to us the great significance Buddhists have found in *karuṇā,* is *paññā,* salvific insight-wisdom, that wisdom which on the highest level (*lokuttarapaññā*) brings with it simultaneously knowledge of the basis of reality and liberation—it is knowing Truth which sets one free. *Karuṇā,* according to the Buddhist testimony, is intimately related with this *paññā.* And one is reminded of the structural relation between faith (*pistis*) and *agapē* in the Christian witness.

Buddhaghosa gives some consideration to the epithets of the Buddha. Commenting on the phrase, "endowed with vision and [associated] conduct," Buddhaghosa writes,

> [The Buddha,] having known what is beneficial and detrimental for all beings because of his knowing everything, having led them aside from what is detrimental because of great compassionateness, urges them to the beneficial.[18]

The continuing commentarial tradition focuses on this passage and provides us with a more complete understanding of *karuṇā* in the context of *paññā.* The commentarial discussion, utilizing the categories of *paññā* and *karuṇā,* presents roughly *fourteen parallel observations* beginning in the first paragraph with the term *paññā,* followed by *karuṇā,* and utilizing just the reverse order in the second paragraph.

The key notion is found in the first sentence of the commentarial passage: "Here, the Teacher's being endowed with vision indicates the greatness of wisdom, being endowed with [associated] conduct, the greatness of compassion."[19] One notes the way the tradition maintained that the sense of vision, of seeing, discernment, insight, referred to wisdom, and the sense of action, tasks, accomplishments for others referred to the quality of compassion. It appears that *paññā* indicates how one is to understand reality; *karuṇā* indicates how one is to live within it. Moreover, the point seems to be that for those in whom *paññā* has arisen, *karuṇā* will be the natural expression that is authentically human in relationships with all living beings.

By turning one's attention to the Buddha as a glorious exemplar of compassion, *karuṇā,* one notes his compassion in, for example, (1) his dissemination of Dhamma, (2) his endurance of the misery of *saṃsāra,* the continuing whirl of rebirth and redeath, (3) his attempts to counteract the misery of others, (4) his attainment of Nibbāna, (5) the crossing over (the river of *saṃsāra*) of others, (6) fulfilling what is to be done by a Buddha, (7) while a Bodhisattva, a being for enlightenment (*bodhi*), keeping his face toward *saṃsāra,* (8) by the absence of violence toward others, (9) by protecting others and thereby protecting oneself, (10) not tormenting others, (11) by his (parent-like) guardianship (*nātha*) of the world, (12) humility, (13) assistance given to all beings, (14) this compassion is devoid of (merely) sentimental affection and sorrow.

Canonical accounts of the ministry of the Buddha provide the Theravāda heritage with an unsurpassed example of compassion. Were one to look for one point in the memory of the Buddhist heritage, one point that would demonstrate the core understanding of *karuṇā* (on analogy with *agapē* in John 3:16), one might turn to that momentous occasion reflected in a conversation between a chief god, Brahmā Sahampati, and the newly realized Awakened One (*buddha*), who is now to be known as the One of Great Compassion (*mahākaruṇāvant*) preeminently for the following decisive act to move from seclusion to teach Dhamma.

> Lost indeed, Sir, is the world; indeed destroyed, Sir, is the world since, alas, the mind of the Tathāgata, Worthy One, Perfectly Enlightened One inclines to inactivity and not to the teaching of Dhamma.
>
> Let the Bhagavan preach Dhamma; let the Sugata preach Dhamma. Beings there are who have little dust in their eyes, who might become knowers of Dhamma, who, from not hearing Dhamma, deteriorate.
>
> Open this door of the deathless; let them hear Dhamma awakened unto by the Spotless One.

To this the Buddha replied,

> Opened for them are the doors of the deathless. They who have ears to hear, let them disclose faith.[20]

The opening of the doors of the deathless, the giving of Dhamma that provides both contextuality for meaning in life and a path by means of which to live life well, thereby indicating that the fundamental truth of human life is manifestly more than mortality, was an *action* performed by a Spotless One, a person of great compassion, whose example abides engagingly even into our day and continues to engender a sense of deep relevance. Two of the most popular recent composer-vocalists in Sri Lanka have found sculptured representations of the

Buddha, of such a person, to be both alluring and capable of evoking deep religious sentiments. Victor Ratnayake has sung,

> Among a thousand fires of lamentations and sorrows,
> In the darkness of fires burning in my heart and mind,
> O Lord, by simply seeing your statue,
> They become completely extinguished—
> What is the mystery?

And W. D. Amaradeva has sung in response to a statue of the Buddha in Anurādhapura, Sri Lanka,

> Falling currents of loving kindness, gentleness, compassion
> Flowing from eyes half-closed. . . . [21]

What is it to live compassionately? Live as the Buddha lived. And one might want to note that the coming of Christ into the world was placed in the context of *agapē* as the sharing of Dhamma has been interpreted in the context of *karuṇā.*

## *JIHI*

The Buddhist tradition has not forgotten the twin dimensions of both fundamental reality and humanity at its comprehensive best: of wisdom (J: *hannya*;[22] so also *chie*) and compassion (J: *jihi*). Even in the institutional and doctrinal form that the tradition has taken in response to the creative insight of Shinran (1173–1262) and the Pure Land patriarchs who went before him, one finds this theme of compassion and wisdom; the "vast power of great compassion and all-embracing wisdom."[23] Whereas the Theravāda tradition has tended to hold that one is able to discern the paradigm for wisdom and compassion in the life and example of the Buddha, primarily that he was the model *for* wisdom and compassion, Jōdo Shinshū, the authentic teaching about the Pure Land, has tended to affirm that the life and example of Śākyamuni is a manifestation of wisdom and compassion, primarily that he was a model *of* wisdom and compassion.[24]

The theme of compassion, especially of Amida's compassion, runs throughout the writings of Shinran. Perhaps the most relevant passage remembered to have been spoken by Shinran, for our purposes here, is one found in the *Tannishō,* where it is recorded, concerning compassion, *jihi,*

> In the matter of compassion, the Path of Sages and the Pure Land path differ. Compassion in the Path of Sages is to pity, sympathize with, and care for beings. But the desire to save others from suffering is vastly difficult to fulfill.

> Compassion in the Pure Land path lies in saying the Name, quickly attaining Buddhahood, and freely benefitting sentient beings with a heart of great love and great compassion [*daiji-daihishin*]. In our present lives, it is hard to carry out the desire to aid others however much love and tenderness [*itooshi fubin to*] we may feel; hence such compassion always falls short of fulfillment. Only the saying of the Name manifests the heart of great compassion [*daijihishin*] that is replete and thoroughgoing.[25]

Shinran continually returns to the centrality of the compassion of Amida Buddha and its vast, pervasive, transformative efficacy.[26] One notes also that the arising of the threefold mind (*sanshin* or *sanjin*), a complex formulation of the beatific moment in the life of a Jōdo Shinshū Buddhist when the mind or heart that is sincere, deeply authentic, and which aspires to be born in the Pure Land, is directed toward beings by the mind of great compassion, the mind of Amida Buddha. On that occasion, this threefold mind, yet single, is the mind of great compassion,[27] the mind of Amida. Shinran is fully convinced that self-interest in the form of "calculation" (*hakarai*) is so pervasive that it is difficult to conceive, in the first place, that one actually could acquire merit that then might be transferred to others and, in the second place, that such transfer could be an authentic expression of one's genuine compassion for others. Everything that is soteriologically efficacious rests upon the initiative of Amida, which is grounded in reality that is compassionate. The focal point of all of this is the supreme Vow of great compassion.[28]

Rather recently Jōdo Shinshū has become more widely known in the United States, due ever increasingly to the work of the Institute of Buddhist Studies in Berkeley, California, and to a band of impressive translators working in two settings in Kyoto. Those translators have made a disciplined statement about the notion of compassion. Presenting their opinion in an extended quotation will bring to a close this segment on Jōdo Shinshū and will lay the foundation for the closing statement of this chapter. In a glossary entry one reads,

> *Great compassion* (*daihi* . . . ) According to *Webster's International Dictionary*, compassion means to bear with or suffer with another being: it is a "deep feeling for and understanding of misery or suffering and the concomitant desire to promote its alleviation; spiritual consciousness of the personal tragedy of another or others and selfless tenderness directed toward it." While this definition seems to convey the idea of Buddhist compassion, it is inadequate because it maintains the distinction between self and other, for in Buddhism compassion goes beyond any division or dichotomy between self and other into the world of complete identity. The basic meaning of "sorrow" in *daihi* or "lament" in the Sanskrit equivalent, *mahā-karuṇā,* attempts to show this selfsame identity wherein the misery, suffering, or personal tragedy of another is

> none other than one's very own. Such a non-dichotomous compassion is guided by *prajñā,* a wisdom that surpasses conventional thinking and feeling and moves in non-dichotomous perception (*nirvikalpajñāna*). This is the essence of the buddha of immeasurable life and light.[29]

We are told that this "spiritual consciousness of the personal tragedy of another or others and selfless tenderness directed toward it" is inadequate to communicate what Buddhists have discerned in and through compassion. We are informed that compassion has to be seen as non-dichotomous in order for "Buddhist [?] compassion" to be interpreted adequately.

## COMPASSION AS GIVEN

It is not necessarily the case that Christians of various persuasions and Buddhists of differing traditions, too, are in fundamental agreement about a dimension of personal awareness and action—communicated by means of three sub-terms: *agapē, karuṇā,* and *jihi*—to which the English words *love/compassion* point. However, it is also not necessarily the case that possible differences in interpretation must remain as barriers to more fundamental mutual understanding.

Our splendid Jōdo Shinshū scholars have stressed the necessity of understanding fully the pervasiveness of a non-dichotomous perception, which non-dichotomous structure is also present in insight-realization of fundamental reality. It just might be the case that greater understanding of *paññā/prajñā* (*hannya* and *chie*) might occur by means of an outsider's deeper reflection on "compassion" *karuṇā* (*jihi*). Speaking for those of us who participate in the Christian tradition in the West, it just might be the case that our Palestinian heart, our Jewish and Christian heart, is more closely attuned to sensitivities held by persons who have become Buddhists than our Greek/Roman "head" might readily seem to allow. Compassion might well be the mode by means of which most of us, persons all, discern non-dichotomous reality. For in *agapē,* especially in the sense of "the *agape* of the cross,"[30] one finds the self-emptying love/compassion that gives in totality, wherein one has one's first taste, perhaps, of freedom.

In *karuṇā,* when it is permeated by *paññā,* one loses all sense of self-estimation (cf. Skt./P., *māna*), which is a fetter that can hold one back from the arising of Nibbāna. This self-estimation arises among the childish, we are told—perhaps, embarrassingly so—and is to be discarded by perfected persons (*arahants*). The Theravāda heritage interprets this self-estimation to be ninefold:

> [1] I am better than my superior, [2] I am the same as my superior, [3] I am worse than my superior, [4] I am better than my equals, [5] I am the same as my equals, [6] I am worse than my equals, [7] I am better than my inferior, [8] I am the same as my inferior, [9] I am worse than my inferior.[31]

In *karuṇā,* when it is permeated by *paññā,* all barriers of differentiation are torn down.[32] And also in the sacramental act of uttering the name of Amida (the *nembutsu—namo Amida Butsu*), gratefulness for the great compassionate Vow is in one's heart, fills full one's heart, fulfills one's aspirations, is present but is not possessed.[33]

We find, consequently, that this quality of love or compassion, to which we have referred, is itself held before us as manifested in the Christ, in the Buddha, in Amida Buddha. There are differences in nuance in the content of the concept, it appears, but the perception of the relevance of the concept and the living activity of becoming engaged with the quality to which this concept points, are *given* to us as some Theravāda and Jōdo-shinshū and Christian men and women have averred. That is to say, each person is not left to his or her wits to think out a notion of love or compassion that is capable of transforming human personality with soteriological efficacy or to "hit upon" such notion as occasion might have it. The heritages that are ours have held before us an indication of how human life and reality converge: in truth and reality, in wisdom and love.

It becomes clearer that we might contribute more significantly to interreligious understanding were we to move our discussion from problems of time or questions of ontology or matters of emptiness (*śūnyatā/mu*) or issues of so-called "truth claims" to a serious and thorough study of religiously grounded notions of love and compassion. We welcome our theologians and philosophers who have joined our historians of religion and our philologists in the comparative study of our one global religious history. No longer remote is the day when our psychologists might find themselves prepared to come aboard.

# 10

# Toward an Understanding of What Is Inconceivable

*In the swirl of non-humanistic secular assumptions and the clamor for undeniable verification principles, religious affirmations are interpreted as metaphor at best and religious worldviews, as myth narrowly and inadequately defined. In learning of religious affirmations in the company of friends, one sees that the swirl and clamor are provincial and hardly self-conscious in light of our global religious and intellectual history. The term* transcendence *is becoming more and more helpful in religious discourse which talks about a life that is given orientation and meaning while seeking greater understanding of what transcends one's conceptuality.*

In our continuing attempt to understand the religious life of men and women who have found life more abundant in their becoming Buddhist, we see that, like all human endeavors, this enterprise, too, has had a history. There was a time when attempting to understand religious life as we are attempting was not even considered. Then there came a time when such effort was considered at best suspect, as involving on the part of a Christian, say, a kind of disloyalty to Christ. There was, as we will see in our chapter 13, dealing with the on-site case of Sri Lanka, a time of debate, and a century of growth into greater understanding. Christians now have come to see that the notion of Christ to which creative thinkers in earlier generations had been considered disloyal was itself a particular interpretation. Not only are institutions situated in history, as we have long known, but human thoughts are also children of the decades.

Of course our thinking changes, and this is due in large measure to our being led out from what we have known, the root sense of our word *education.* Upon meeting persons whom we have come to love, upon standing with them to share as best we can their view of our common life, their vision of what is behind our common life, of that toward which our common life might move, the horizons of our lives are mutually extended and we search for new ways to give expression to what we have been enabled to see. This might take place in translating the Bible, as we will consider in our chapter 16. It might give rise to our pausing quietly to marvel at the similarity in our celebrating the distinctive good fortune that is also a part of our lot as mortals: being enabled to manifest love and compassion.

In our study, so much of what we seek to understand exceeds our grasp. Recognizing this encourages us to work at our diligent best in seeking to understand another. Consequently, we attempt to gain as much information about a point under consideration as possible. We have mentioned a problem in the academic setting today, found in the way persons are willing to let themselves become intellectually tethered by a misplaced loyalty given solely to one particular discipline. Usually, more is demanded than merely deciding whether one is seeing trees or a forest. A materialist might look at the same thing and see neither trees nor a forest, but only wood. An enterprising person might look at both the trees and the forest and see houses to be built and jobs to be developed. One might look at the very same view of trees and a forest and see majestic beauty. A great deal of understanding is to be found in the response one makes to what is there before one.

## DISCERNING RELATIONSHIP WITH WHAT IS INCONCEIVABLE

Considering the title of this chapter, one might quibble that it seems far-fetched indeed to seek to understand what is inconceivable. This appears from the outset to be an impossibility. However, becoming aware of the *relationship* in which a human being is enabled to enter in response to what is for that person inconceivable is surely another matter entirely. Our movement nearer understanding, toward understanding, leads us to take the point of view of a person who speaks to us from the past and from a Japanese perspective on our human situation.

Shinran wrote,

> As I reverently contemplate the True Buddha and Land, (I realize that) the Buddha is the Tathāgata of Inconceivable Light and His Land is the Land of Immeasurable Light.[1]
>
> This Tathāgata is also known as *Namu-fukashigikō-butsu* (namu-Buddha of inconceivable light) and is the "dharmakaya as compassionate means."[2]

Western scholars of the Buddhist tradition have been familiar with confronting the new in the Buddhist heritage; dimensions of a worldview and sources of human self-understanding that tend not to fit readily into customary frames of reference formulated, nurtured, and passed on through Western culture. These scholars have met a notion known as *hōben* (Skt: *upāya*) before, have even found standard English equivalents such as "provisional means" or "expedient means." And Western scholars have had little difficulty in understanding Buddhist representatives, in the past and present, who have spoken about the efficacy of provisional means or expedients in bringing about the moment of the arising of Salvific Truth, enlightenment. Given the provisionality of the means and the justificatory consequences of the end, namely, enlightenment, Western interpreters have had little difficulty in discerning the compassionate quality of the means or expedients as well as the finality of and complete liberation involved in the end. And yet, one can detect a little disquiet among some Western scholars and Christian interpreters about an apparent provisionality or penultimacy of compassion, on the one hand, and, on the other, a disconcertedness among some Buddhists about the way interpreters tend to underrate the provisional, the expedient means.

The issue becomes sharply focused when we turn to the Jōdo Shinshū heritage and consider Amida, who is explicitly referred to as *hōben*. If Amida is merely a provisional means, we might anticipate our Western interpreters to say, one would need to move through that provisional means to the ultimate reality that somehow would be sensed to "stand behind" Amida, to be more real, the true source of final enlightenment.

*Hōben,* "provisional means" or "expedient means," is an extraordinarily difficult term to handle adequately in the Jōdo Shinshū heritage. We note that superlative translators handle the one term, *hōben,* differently in different contexts.[3] When *hōben* appears in a context considering modes of religious discipline that are based on the agency of the person (*jiriki*), a sense of expediency, provisionality, temporariness is found in the term. We find *hōben* used to designate the expedient gate and the provisional gate; they are *hōben* of the Pure Land (*jōdo no hōben*). They are provisional means of the Pure Land; they are not singularly genuine, directly authentic (*makoto*) means of attaining the Pure Land.[4] They are put into contrast with the basis of true and real piety or virtue (*shinjitsu kudoku*)—the Primal Vow.

We meet our term *hōben* in still another context. A "nembutsu-being" (*nembutsu shujō*), we are told, is a person "who has realized diamond-like *shinjin*" (*kongō no shinjin o etaru hito nari*).[5] A few lines farther we read that this great notion of *shinjin* is considered *hōben*; and the phrase enters into English as "through the compassionate means of shinjin" (*shinjin no hōben*).[6] Our translators have chosen another phrase for *hōben* in this context dealing with *shinjin.* Rather than "provisional means" and the like, one reads "compassionate means." In checking the "Glossary" to *Notes on Once-calling and Many-calling*, the text presently being considered, we do not find an entry under "Provisional" or "Expedient" or *hōben* (although other transliterated terms appear). We do find "Compassionate means (*hoben*)"[7] and infer that although *hōben* might have differing meanings or nuances, as faithfully noted in the glossary entry, the idea of "compassionate means" is the primary meaning that needs to be communicated in order for an English reader to begin to discern the Jōdo Shinshū heritage as those within it have come to see it.

We have found how modes of the religious life following alternative practices perceived to be "self-power" have been considered the result of *hōben,* how the arising of *shinjin* also is by means of *hōben,*[8] how, too, by means of *hōben* one comes really to hear the Vow.[9]

Amida as *dharmakāya* in form is also *hōben*. T'an-luan (J: Donran) introduced the intrinsic and integral twofold dimension of *dharmakāya*. He wrote,

> Buddhas and Bodhisattvas have two kinds of Dharma Bodies: firstly, the Dharma Body of Dharma-nature [*hosshō hosshin*], and, secondly, the Dharma Body of Expediency [*hōben hosshin*]. Depending on the Dharma Body of Dharma-nature, the Dharma Body of Expediency arises; depending on the Dharma Body of Expediency, the Dharma Body of Dharma-nature reveals itself. These two Dharma Bodies are distinct but not separate, one but not identical. [10]

Shinran maintains the notion of the three bodies of the Buddha, which he received through the heritage of his tradition,[11] and, at the same time, he stands fully in the wake of T'an-luan in holding to the discernible distinction yet indivisibility of *dharmakāya* (*hosshin*).[12] Shinran turns full face to the issue we are considering:

> "Compassionate means [*hōben*]" refers to manifesting form [*katachi*], revealing a name, and making itself known to sentient beings. It refers to Amida Buddha. This Tathagata is light. Light is none other than wisdom; wisdom is the form of light [*chie wa hikari no katachi nari*]. Wisdom is, in addition, formless [*chie mata katachi nakereba*]; hence this Tathāgata is the Buddha of inconceivable light [*fukashigikō butsu*].[13]

*Hōben* has many referents: to paths and practices, to "self-power" (*jiriki*), to "other-power" (*tariki*), insofar as *shinjin* arises through *hōben,* to form, to the Name, which is also the Primal Vow,[14] and to a distinctive yet fundamentally inseparable dimension of *dharmakāya* itself. And *hōben* involves something else—sentient beings. *Hōben* also is fundamentally *relational*; it provides the point of contact between the human mind or heart (*shin*/*kokoro*) and Salvific Truth. We come to see in the thought of Shinran that the cosmos is focused on the heart that can be enabled to manifest the sincere, serene joy (*shingyō*) of Salvific Truth, which inherently and inescapably avails itself to human discernment.[15]

Whereas the translation committee that has given us the Ryukoku Translation Series, (*RTS*) working at Ryukoku University in Kyoto, has tended toward uniformity in translating *hōben* in all contexts as "provisional means" or "expedient means," the committee responsible for the Shin Buddhism Translation Series (*SBTS*), working at Hongwanji International Center (sponsored by

Nishi-Hongwanji, which is also the founding institution of Ryukoku University), has preferred to provide a distinction in English between "provisional means" and "compassionate means," letting the former refer to alternative orientations in religious living and the latter to apperceptions of salvific awareness as expressed in Jōdo Shinshū.

Although one might well make the point that in every case where *hōben* appears one is to understand it as meaning "compassionate means," one, nevertheless, discerns, on the part of the committee providing the Shin Buddhism Translation Series, an attempt to *do something* with *hōben* when bringing it into the English medium in the context of the translations. Colleagues working to produce the Ryukoku Translation Series are aware of delicate dimensions in the notion of *hōben*; are aware, too, of the stumbling block that *hōben* has tended to be for Western scholars of the Buddhist heritage in Japan as they turn their attention to Jōdo Shinshū.[16]

There have been numerous Western scholars who have contributed significantly to our knowledge of the Buddhist heritage of Japan. The majority of these scholars have not focused their attention on the most popular form of expressing piety in that heritage in Japan, namely, Jōdo Shinshū. Even today, generally speaking and with only slight overstatement, Americans tend to be surprised to learn that not all Buddhists in Japan are Zen Buddhists. They are more surprised to find that Zen does not represent the most popular form of the Buddhist heritage in Japan.

In a consideration of Zen, Westerners tend to approach *hōben* with twin assumptions: the fundamental value of "being" (ontology), and the soteriological convergence of "being" and the "purposeful end" (teleology). There has been an admirable ability among Western interpreters to become self-conscious about these assumptions in a serious commitment to understand Zen Buddhists. These interpreters readily let the value commitment to "being" fall away, in an attempt to understand, before the notion of "emptiness" (*śūnyatā/mu*), which transcends both being and nonbeing. But we have not witnessed this development before *hōben* in considerations of the Jōdo Shinshū heritage. If it is *hōben,* it is asserted, it is not fundamentally real nor is it final—it is merely expedient, temporary, provisional.

Upon turning to the Jōdo Shinshū heritage, a Western interpreter might think that one is expected to "move through" *hōben,* that is, to move beyond the numerous practices endorsed by other strands of the Buddhist heritage in Japan, and also to move beyond the Name, the Vow, the means of the arising of *shinjin,* Dharmākara, Amida, beyond all of the elaborate schemes, whatever is provisional, to arrive at, attain, finally, the fundamental reality of *dharmakāya*-as-suchness, ultimate *dharmakāya*—a kind of Zen for the ordinary person living "in the meantime." But such interpretation would miss a lively dynamic expressed in the writings of Shinran and averred by sensitive men and women as a consequence of their engaged participation in the continuing Jōdo Shinshū tradition.

## RELATIONSHIP GROUNDED IN OTHER-POWER

How can one set about to uncover this dynamic that springs from a deep realization that within *hōben* one has found both the means of "self-power" (*jiriki*) and also the means of "other-power" (*tariki*), that *hōben* is authentically known when it is discerned as "other-power," an "other-power" that is discovered to have become present in one's life with a thoroughgoing, all-pervasive assurance that is grounded on the soteriological realizability of the fundamental order of reality—that this order of reality can be realized in the personal recesses of one's life, to be quietly, even gently, naturally absolutely supportive (*jinen hōni*)?

One recalls the insight of T'an-luan (J: Donran) of the intrinsic and integral dimensions of *dharmakāya*: *dharmakāya*-as-suchness and *dharmakāya*-as-compassion. One recalls, also, that Shinran confirmed this insight of his heritage; he saw the point of it and appropriated it. He also appropriated the profoundly subtle differentiation provided by the concepts "self-power" and "other power." The indirect, below-the-surface, devious, and difficult-to-discern operation of human calculation (*hakarai*) continues detrimentally in human acts with devastating subtlety. The only way open to men and women is the calculation, designing (*on-hakarai*) of Śākyamuni and Amida.[17]

We begin to nudge an interpretation of *hōben* that enables one to understand it to be just as real as the awareness of one's own calculation (*hakarai*), for the salvific designing (*on-hakarai*) that enables one to become free of one's own *hakarai* must be at least as real in its soteriological efficacy as one's own *hakarai* is in detrimental futility. Shinran was fully aware of the inadequacy of thinking that one must somehow go beyond Amida to fundamental reality, to penetrate behind Amida to ultimate realization of *dharmakāya,* because this way of thinking suggests that one must *do something,* assuming, of course, that one *can do something.* If one relinquishes the absolute necessity of "other-power," "self-power"/"calculation" (*jiriki/hakarai*) will arise with its characteristically persistent tendency toward distortion, especially in a life-setting that is found to be awry (*mappō*). We are moving to a subtle cutting edge in Shinran's thought, one sufficiently delicate that we turn to Shinran for guidance. Concerning "the mystery of the wisdom of Buddhas," it is recorded that Shinran said,

> As for *jinen* [自然], *ji* means "of itself"—it is not through the practicer's calculation [*hakarai*]; one is made to become so. *Nen* means "one is made to become so"—it is not through the practicer's calculation [*hakarai*]; it is through the working of the Vow of Tathagata [*nyorai no chikai*]. As for *hōni* [法爾], it means "one is made to become so through the working of the Vow of Tathagata [*nyorai no on-chikai*]." *Hōni* means that one is made to become so (*ni*) by virtue of this dharma (*hō*) [*kono hō no toku*], being the working of the Vow where there is no calculation [*hakarai*] on the part of the practicer. In short, there is no place at all

for the practicer's calculation [*hakarai*]. We are taught, therefore, that in Other Power no selfworking is true working [*kono yueni gi naki o gi tosutoshiru beshito nari*].

*Jinen* [自然] means that from the very beginning one is made to become so. Amida's Vow [*mida butsu no on-chikai*] is, from the very beginning, designed to have each person entrust himself [*tanomase*] in *namu-amida-butsu* and be received in the Buddha Land; none of this is through the practicer's calculation [*hakarai*]. Thus, there is no room for him to be concerned with his being good or bad. This is the meaning of *jinen* as I have learned it.

This Vow [*chikai*] is the Vow to make us all attain the supreme Buddhahood. The supreme Buddha is formless, and because of being formless is called *jinen*. When this Buddha is shown as being with form [*katachi*], it is not called the supreme nirvana (Buddha). In order to make us realize that the true Buddha is formless, it is expressly called Amida Buddha; so I have been taught. Amida Buddha is the medium [*ryō*] through which we are made to realize *jinen*. After we have realized that this is the way it is, we should not be forever talking about *jinen*. If one always talks about *jinen*, then the truth that Other Power is[18] no selfworking will again become a problem of selfworking. This is the mystery of the wisdom of Buddhas [*bucchi no fushigi*].[19]

*Jinen-hōni* represents the salvific stability of reality, the natural and normative, preexistent, underlying truth. The selfworking (*gi* in the Ryukoku Translation Series this word is taken as "reasoning") of a person who has entered the way—that is, one's attempting to determine what is proper to be done with a sense of self-agency in religious discipline, involving, regularly, one's own "counting up" or "measuring" (*hakarai*) the desired benefits from the formal observance of a rite considered to be proper in a customarily given situation—is to be offset by being set aside through the agency of "other-power." Assuredly, this passage indicates, there is to be no calculation on the part of the practicer.

An extraordinarily delicate passage is found in this extended quotation. In the third paragraph, two ways of referring to the supreme Buddha are mentioned: it is called *jinen* because it is formless. At the same time one reads that in order that one might realize this, "it is expressly called Amida Buddha." And one notes that Amida is considered to be form (*katachi*).

Further, there is the crucial point that "Amida Buddha is the medium [*ryō*: in the *RTS*, this word is taken as "source"] through which we are made to realize *jinen*." We would miss the force of the term *ryō*, here translated as "medium," if we take it to mean merely "means by which" or with a spatial sense of something standing in the "middle," between humankind, on the one hand, and fundamental formless reality that stands beyond or behind the "middle/medium." The force of *ryō* is that it is precisely the context *in which jinen*, that is, the formless supreme Buddha, is to be realized. *Ryō* is the surrounding and pervading environment in which one realizes *jinen*. There, in the midst of form, is the formless. At the moment of the complete demise of one's calculation one realizes *jinen*, the salvific stability of reality, the excellent reliability of Salvific Truth.

Take away Amida and one must exercise self-exertion, self-working, self-power, it is averred. Interpret Amida as intermediate and a problem arises: what is the proper way to interpret or to understand Amida in order to realize the ultimate of which Amida is seen to be the penultimate. But Amida, even though *hōben*, abides and is not penultimate. A comment shared with me on an occasion in Kyoto, "Amida is all that we have to be concerned about," tends to make sense.

## THE *ON*-RELATIONSHIP

But there is another dimension of the Jōdo Shinshū heritage to which one might turn to see more clearly an enhanced and real dynamic that Jōdo Shinshū Buddhists have tended to discover in the notion of *hōben*. *Hōben* is relational, we have mentioned. The reality quotient of *hōben* is not only rooted in essence, as an inseparable dimension of *dharmakāya* as doctrinally stated, but *in the existential reality of human life* in the here and now, in space and time. *Hōben* is as real as Shinran's own understanding of his own life.

We turn to consider briefly a term that is also relational, a weighty and important term in understanding the interpretations of persons who have seen the point of the Jōdo Shinshū heritage—the term is *on* (恩). *On*, in English, can mean "benevolence," "kindness," "generosity," "a favor," "goodness," and the like. But these qualities do not exist "out there," as it were, remote from persons. There must be a recipient of benevolence or kindness. The use of the term *on* not only communicates this relational reality but also heightens it. *On* indicates a participatory engagement in the benevolent act or act of kindness. To refer to the Buddha's benevolence (*on*) means not merely that by definition the Buddha is benevolent but that one has for oneself realized in the center of one's self-understanding the reality of the relationship in which the quality of *on* has become known—not primarily provisionally, not fundamentally expediently, but preeminently *personally*.

*On* is simultaneously a gracious and efficacious act expressed from one heart in a relationship and an act that affects the heart of another participating in this relationship. In a sense *on* is the causal activity that links hearts and minds. It is an expression from a heart that is moved, an expression that moves the heart of another. *On*, ideally, is affirmed by the recipient; were this not so, *on* would be merely a cultural norm that, like other cultural norms, could be manipulated by less scrupulous, certainly less caring, persons and, as merely a cultural norm having lost its linkage with a transcendent referent, *on* could be interpreted by a recipient as a burden, alas, one worth avoiding if possible.

*On* also is akin to "gratitude,"[20] a sense of obligation, a duty that is not discerned as being placed upon one from "outside," from something called "society," but a duty recognized by oneself, for oneself, for which one is deeply grateful. "Knowing what has been done" by another or others for oneself (Skt: *kṛtajña*; P: *kataññu*)—Buddhists have long been familiar with this—would tend to persuade a reflective person to understand that there is no "self-made man" or "self-made woman."

*On* means, then, "benevolence" *and* "gratitude." And, within the Jōdo Shinshū heritage, this great notion provides a creative edge that cuts away any theoretical projection that *dharmakāya*-as-compassion (*hōben hosshin*) is merely a provisional means or expedient means while it also undercuts a sense of estrangement. A glance at definitions provided in glossaries makes us alert that we are on to a weighty subject: for *on* we find "beneficial act or service, grace,"[21] and under the entry *button,* we find "Buddha's Benevolence, indebtedness to Buddha."[22] Turning to some of the writings of Shinran, one finds that *on* provides a context in which he understands himself to be; within a shared human experience with great Buddhist figures who preceded him[23] and within a relationship with Śākyamuni and Amida, more particularly Amida.[24]

Shinran, in anticipation of the possibility that readers who had not realized the insight attained by him would ridicule him, or perhaps do worse, writes, "Mindful solely of the depth and vastness of the Buddha's benevolence [*button*], I am unconcerned about being personally abused."[25] Further, Shinran says,

> Now that I have entered the Sea of the Vow once and for all, I deeply acknowledge the Buddha's Benevolence [*fukaku button o shireri*]. In order to repay my indebtedness to His Utmost Virtue [*shitoku o hōsha sen tame ni*], I have gleaned the essential passages of the True Teaching and always utter with recollection the Sea of the Inconceivable Virtue.[26]

And elsewhere he writes, "And knowing keenly that the Buddha's benevolence [*button*] is difficult to fathom, I seek to clarify it through this collection of passages on the Pure Land way."[27]

One sees clearly that Shinran interpreted his literary activity, his unusual patience in collecting and recording passages, character by character, his glosses, his painstaking efforts to assure that texts were intelligible to a wide reading public, as the kind of act a person does upon recognizing an *on*-relationship with Amida, with Śākyamuni, with the great masters of the past, including, of course, Hōnen, his own teacher. In short, Shinran shares his fundamental orientation to his own life and ministry, and he offers a glimpse of the point on which he was enabled to stand: "Reverently embracing the Tathagata's teaching, respond in gratitude to his benevolence [*on o hōji toku o sha seiyo*] and be thankful for his compassion."[28]

*On* is a relationship in which Shinran participated. And this relationship was one of great existential significance; a real relationship within which one's life takes on fundamental meaning—within this relationship one can conceive of one's life in no other way. We read,

> The Buddha's protection and testimony
> Are due to the accomplishment of the Compassionate Vow;
> Those who have attained Adamantine Mind
> Should try to repay Amida's Great Benevolence [*mida no daion hōzu beshi*].[29]

As it is with this "Adamantine Mind" or "diamond-like mind" (*kongō shin*), so it is with those who attain, in truth, sincere serenity (*shingyō*); "They desire to return in gratitude the Buddha's benevolence [*button hōzuru omoi ari*]."[30] And one reads,

> Only by entering the transcendent wisdom of faith,
> Can we become one who returns in gratitude the Buddha's benevolence.
> *Shinjin o chie ni iri te koso*
> *Button hōzuru mi to wa nare* [31]

In the final analysis, the realization of a soteriological transformation that terminates the human experience of customary, recurrent coursing through *saṃsāra* and simultaneously causes to arise an assurance of birth in the Pure Land, by enabling one to see wherein the limits of this world fall—and also simultaneously brings about an ability to move beyond the limits of inadequately self-imposed egocentrism in the quest to relieve the suffering of sentient beings—this realization and the concomitant assurance of "attaining the supreme *nirvāṇa,*" one learns, "Is due to the Tathāgata's twofold merit-transference [*ekō*]. Realizing gratitude for such benevolence [*ondoku*] is truly impossible."[32]

And yet one is not left without recourse, not isolated from a form for expressing this gratitude, privately and communally. It is in saying the name (the *nembutsu*: *namu amida butsu*) that one moves into the form suitable for expressing this gratitude. But this realization is more than merely saying the name, or pronouncing it or uttering it. Translators are casting around for a suitable English term (or for any term in human speech) to catch and to communicate this elusive yet riveting realization. It is, in a profound sense, hearing the name, really hearing the name in the moment of creative passivity, poised with creative receptivity, when the name is truly heard on one's human lips. It seems that the name becomes heard, arises in one's voice, without the "namer," the name is pronounced without the "pronouncer."

Part of the power of "other-power" (*tariki*) is that it informs one of "self-power" (*jiriki*), defines "self-power" in the classic sense of *definire,* "to limit," "to set a limit to." It is tempting to say that both "other-power" and "self-power" must somehow be transcended, that they are held in mutual negation. This may be so, but one wonders whether this way of considering the point is formulaic, is a whit too neat, might suggest something that one can get one's mind on, so to speak, something one somehow must do, might indicate *hakarai.* It appears that, in a dialectic of assumed opposites, one might say without "other-power" there is no "self-power," but it would be awry to claim that without "self-power" there is no "other-power." It appears that the point is "without self-power," *there, right there,* is "other-power." And a life without this particular kind of "self-power" is a life lived with gratitude abounding.[33]

One cannot reach the depths of the Buddha's benevolence, or measure it, or calculate an appropriate response, or determine precisely what one must do to repay this benevolence. There is no adequately grateful response, worthy of the name, to this benevolence if the response is associated with one's own volition. Although willing a grateful heart into existence is impressive, it is, nevertheless, inadequate.[34]

Indicating that a life lived within the Buddha's compassion expressed in the nineteenth and twentieth vows is a life supported by the "depth of the Buddha's benevolence [*button fukakini*]," Shinran concludes, "Thus the depth of the Buddha's benevolence is without bound." He continues, immediately, to say, "But how much more should we realize the benevolence of the Buddha with birth into the true and real land and attainment of the enlightenment of the supreme nirvana [*shinjitsu no hōdo e ōjōshite dainehan no satori*]."[35]

The *on*-relationship of which Shinran spoke, the realization of what others had done for him, the orientation to all that he found worthy of cherishing, seem to lie more deeply than the customary English word *gratitude* suggests—his life, as he came to see it, was given birth, his future was given purpose because of Amida's and Śākyamuni's *on,* because of the *on* of the great lights of his heritage. How is one to measure the *on* of the Buddha? One cannot, of course; at our wits' best such measuring remains *our* measuring (*hakarai*). Shinran seems to have provided a mode for appraising one's *on*-relationship with Amida. In glossing a passage written by Seikaku (1167–1235), Shinran indicated the pervasive reorientation of life in recognizing the *on* of one's teacher who leads one to see how Salvific Truth has been made available within one. The passage reads,

> We should realize, then, the vast and profound benevolence [*oshie no on*] of the great master's teaching. *Even by grinding your bones, then, should you repay it*; *even by crushing your body should it be returned*: Realizing the vastness of the benevolence of the great master's teaching, you should repay it [*oshie no ondoku*], even if you grind your bones to dust; return it [*ondoku*], even if you crush your body to nothing. Carefully study this teaching of Master Seikaku.[36]

In a more comprehensive perspective, Shinran penned, with profound human insight, the following *wasan*:

The benevolence of the Tathāgata's great compassion [*nyorai daihi no ondoku*],
Even if we must crush our bodies, should be returned in gratitude.
The benevolence of the masters and teachers,
Even if we must break our bones, should be returned in gratitude.[37]

If *on* means benevolence, it is the benevolence that is received in the "marrow of one's bones." If *on* is gratitude, it is the inestimable gratitude before which the value of one's own life itself pales.

If one's relationship with one's teacher is a marker of a real experience, carrying an undeniable reality quotient that is real, then even though Amida might be interpreted to be *hōben,* this Amida, and the ensuing *on*-relationship discerned by one who recognizes it, is as real as anything that can be felt, experienced, or conceived. And the reality so conceived—conceived this way—is not dissociated from fundamental and final reality. The *dharmakāya*-as-suchness is beyond comprehension, is inconceivable. This *dharmakāya*-as-compassionate-means (*hōben*) is perceivable, falls within form and discernment.

Is *hōben* real or is it only provisional or temporary, to return to the issue raised at the beginning of this chapter? It is as real as one's sense of *on.* Insofar as *hōben* can engender a sense of *on,* one can conclude that this *hōben* is as real in one's life as one's own awareness of oneself.

Whereas T'an-luan's insight into the intrinsic and integral quality of the *dharmakāya,* as being singular and yet of two dimensions, was a doctrinal formulation of the reality underpinning *hōben,* we find in Shinran an existential elaboration. Recognizing the pervasiveness of one's subtle calculations revolving around oneself, percolating even in the depths of an unseeing *id,* one recognizes simultaneously that reality takes on the form of compassion. An interpreter's saying, therefore, that the compassionate form, *hōben,* is not real involves an inadequate understanding of the pervasiveness of one's calculation (*hakarai*). Recognizing the comprehensiveness of one's sense of *on* concomitantly causes to arise a wholesome realization of one's destitute condition and a mature understanding of one's assurance of birth into the Pure Land. To say that *hōben* is not real would allow no room for the reality of the transformative realization that occurred in the life of Shinran.

An engaging dynamic is generated in the very act of one's discerning *on.* One can certainly recognize benevolence, and one can be grateful, but search as one might (*hakarai*) there is no duty the performance of which would constitute an adequate compensation, nothing that can be done by one fully to meet the obligation, no act that would be considered appropriate, either so considered by oneself or by others, no rite that customarily would be considered proper; in short, there is no self-working or reasoning (*gi*)—only a response of being deeply, profoundly, authentically, honestly grateful.

This *hōben-on* complex is at the heart of the soteriological process for men and women in the Jōdo Shinshū heritage. Moving into relation with this complex, that is, discerning that it is alluring, one manifests one's faith and participates in a religious heritage of impressive magnitude. Upon discovering this complex to be real, essentially and existentially, one meets an imperative. And at this point the religious problem of the great notion of *shinjin* arises—there is nothing, absolutely nothing, that one can do. *Shinjin* arises as the result of "other-power." So *hōben,* Amida as *inconceivable* light, wisdom that is perceivable but which also transcends conceptualization, instills in one the sense of *on,* which engenders an imperative to respond. And yet no response is fully adequate except, perhaps, to be truly grateful, sincerely, authentically, grateful for Amida, for *shinjin,* for the Pure Land. And yet, even at this deep dimension of human self-understanding, one realizes the inadequacy of one's response. Insofar as one is responding, it is, of course, one's response, and to that extent it is not *shinjin.*

Into the grateful heart (*shin/kokoro*) *shinjin* arises, and the sense of gratefulness that precedes the arising of *shinjin* is not subsequently negated or transformed, but deepened by one's realization of truth and reality, when the aspiration for what was hoped for, for what was not yet seen, becomes the gratefulness for what was to have been known and is now realized.

Amida is as real, one can say, as the truth of one's gratefulness. And one should think that full enlightenment would bring with it no need to reevaluate the case.

# 11

# The Arising of Salvific Realization as Buddhists and Christians Have Affirmed

*So often what initially appear to be fundamental differences in doctrinal formulations have tended to lead some not to discern wherein persons have provided testimony to foundational religious awareness but have developed different ways to represent it. We look not for the "essence of Buddhism," or "of Christianity," but to personal responses in the soteriological process. Our task, then, is not to comprehend transcendence but only to recognize where it begins.*

## FROM REIFIED SYSTEMS TO PERSONAL RESPONSES

We have moved beyond a matter of merely translating one Japanese word into one English word to find that a Japanese word carried with it a cluster of associated religious apperceptions that function in the religious life of Jōdo Shinshū Buddhists in a manner similar to the way another concept and satellite connotations function in the religious life of Christians. And we could continue in our considerations of key religious notions. One thinks, further, of the uninhibited pervasive force of the Primal Vow (*honganriki*) made by Amida as the Bodhisattva Dharmākara and the cosmic soteriological ramifications of the Christ-event, of *shinjin* and the notion of "Christ in me." In this chapter, we will consider another converging affirmation made by Buddhists and Christians about salvific realization, that transforming occurrence in one's response to transcendence.

Were we to look at reified systems, analogous frames of reference would hardly be seen. Even were we merely to have studied doctrines, the depth of impact of these notions could easily be overlooked. It is when we look to the persons responding to that to which the Buddhist and Christian traditions have pointed that we find a place at which to continue our enhanced understanding of each other. So again we return to two great wings within the Buddhist tradition. Because some of us have chosen to continue to participate in the religious heritage that has enabled persons, by means of their participation, to become Buddhists, we have around us today a glorious religious tradition and impressive men and women. Buddhists have graced this planet for centuries. With this most will agree.

At first glance, some have looked upon this tradition from some distance removed, as it were, seeing a "comprehensive something" of bewildering variety, multifarious strands, manifold modifications, and have concluded, grandly, broadly, that there is only one massive, static system, called "Buddhism." The subsequent tendency has been to attempt to disclose the "essence" of "Buddhism," or some "common core" of this variegated tradition, and to try to make the case that this represents what "Buddhism" was or was to have been or is or, put another way, this "common core" is the *sine qua non* of the Buddhist tradition. But the historical record makes this attempt not only difficult—the changes through the centuries and across cultures have been many—but also not very informative: the "essence" would tend to be so general, or the "common core" so rudimentary, that hardly anything would have been uncovered or stated. While making this closer inspection, one becomes more aware of the variety, the differences, the unique variations within strands or regional movements differing from century to century, from country to country, from culture to culture, within the Buddhist tradition. And the different manifestations of religiousness within the tradition over the centuries have been significant.

We note today the growing interest among some Jōdo Shinshū Buddhists and some Christian theologians in Buddhist-Christian dialogue. An implication of the theme of the third biennial conference of the International Association of Shin Buddhist Studies held at Berkeley in August 1987, "Shin Buddhism as a Member in the Global Communities of Faith," is that Jōdo Shinshū is to be seen as taking its place, as it were, among the religious communities of the world. And this acknowledgment one applauds, assuredly.

However, the Jōdo Shinshū and the Theravāda traditions tend to "pass in the dark," both hitherto being relatively unable to interpret meaningfully, from within their received traditions, the presence of the other. Jōdo Shinshū thinkers, if they were to consider the Theravāda of the twenty-first century, might write off their presence as merely a "holdover" of what has been called "*hīnayāna,*" the small vehicle, or the inferior way. Most Theravāda thinkers give no thought to Jōdo Shinshū. If they were to choose to consider Jōdo Shinshū they might consider it, at best, to be a late addendum in the history of the Buddhist tradition and, at worst, a corruption that allows for meat eating, beer and whisky drinking, cigarette smoking, even the presence of married "priests" posing as Buddhists. Our Southern friends also could be temporarily blinded by the external institutional glitter that suggests the apparent wealth of Jōdo Shinshū in Japan.

What are we to do? I propose to continue a consideration of Jōdo Shinshū or Shin Buddhists and Theravāda Buddhists not by attempting to disclose an "essence of Buddhism," to which both movements subscribe, or a "core" of the Buddhist tradition, to be found in both, or by considering doctrinal formulations and systems, but by trying to uncover a foundation for mutual understanding on the bases of shared insights into personal responses in the soteriological process.

## THERAVĀDA AND JŌDO SHINSHŪ: ONE DOES NOT LIBERATE ONESELF

Theravāda Buddhists have been in conversations with Christian representatives for well over a century. This is just about enough time for misunderstandings to become established, and also enough time for insights to begin to emerge. This sequence of conversations has led Theravāda writers, in their efforts either to posture against Christian thinkers or to communicate accurately with them, to presuppose assumptions on the part of their readers, to become preoccupied with Western readers, rather than to write creatively, authentically, from within the frame of reference of their own religious heritage. Such authors attempt to make it clear that the Buddha was *not* a God, is *not* a savior, that there is *no* soul, that "faith" is blind, that one must save oneself. Patient scholars know that this abrupt way of putting it is hardly adequate.

The stress on self-agency expressed in English by many Theravāda authors has led to gross misunderstanding among English-reading students of this tradition. It appears that a current and casual use of the English word *faith* has influenced some of our Theravāda English-writing authors more than the Pali word *saddhā* (Sinhala: *śraddhā*/verb *adahanavā*). "Faith," for these writers, has tended to mean trust in that which is incapable of being empirically verified, or a kind of "blind trust" or "blind faith," what a person takes to be the case when he or she does not know better; in any case, faith is not entirely bad, but hardly soteriologically efficacious either. Further, one is told repeatedly that one has to work out one's own salvation, which is treated as a corollary to the idea of there being no savior or savior God. This has been pounded into the English-reading audience to such extent that one has failed to see what Theravāda Buddhists have long known—in the final analysis one does *not* work out one's own salvation or liberation or release.

In the Theravāda vision, let me call it, one does not save or liberate oneself. Shall I merely note in passing that this ought to be obvious for those of us who are Theravāda Buddhists and who have found that fundamentally there is no enduring substantial self that could *do* the saving, or releasing, or bring about the liberation in the first place? One does not liberate oneself. Grasping this point fully is crucial for one attempting to understand both Theravāda Buddhists and life as Theravāda Buddhists have understood it—one does not liberate oneself. And in affirming this point, too, Jōdo Shinshū Buddhists step alongside Theravāda

Buddhists. Although the Japanese technical vocabulary of "self-power" (*jiriki*) and "other-power" (*tariki*) is foreign to the Theravāda tradition, some of the implications reflected in the terms are not. Theravāda sources do not place emphases on "other-power." Nor in considering the arising of salvific insight-wisdom is emphasis placed on "self-power." The testimony of the Theravāda indicates that the soteriological breakthrough occurs in a context that is neither the result of "self-power" nor "other-power." Certainly, it is not the result of "self-power," Theravāda Buddhists have known. On this Jōdo Shinshū and Theravāda Buddhists would agree. To say that this breakthrough is the result of "other-power" is, in the Theravāda frame of reference, to say too much, indeed, to tend to project too much.

The Theravāda tradition has maintained a basic distinction between that which is ordinary, customary, sometimes called "worldly" or "mundane" (*lokiya*) and that which is world-transcending, or supramundane (*lokuttara*). One notes this twofold distinction applied to salvific insight-wisdom (*paññā*),[1] and to modes of going for refuge (*lokiya/lokuttara-saraṇagamana*).[2]

Mahinda Palihawadana, in stressing the importance of the distinction between *lokiya* and *lokuttara*, has said that the Theravāda salvific process has in reality four aspects rather then three, viz.

> 1. *sīla*
> 2. *samādhi*
> 3. *lokiya paññā*
> 4. *lokuttara paññā*
>
> The Theravāda realm of possible action is constituted by 1, 2, and 3 above. The fourth is outside that realm.[3]

Palihawadana provides us with an insightful presentation of a discussion in the *Visuddhimagga* on the arising of the path (*magga*), considered in the Theravāda as the arising of the Path of Stream Attainment (*sotāpattimagga*). By means of meditative introspection (*vipassanā*) the mental synergies (*saṅkhāra*s) contemplate the *saṅkhāra*s and, seeing the inadequacies of all *saṅkhāra*s, the thought arises, as it were, "'Let me be quiet, wholly relaxed.'"[4] The *Visuddhimagga* tells us,

> For the one who repeats, cultivates, practices this equipoise with regard to the *saṅkhāra*s, firm faith (*saddhā*) becomes stronger, energy well fixed, mind well collected, more refined equipoise with regard to the *saṅkhāra*s arises.
>
> To that one the thought occurs, "Now the path (*magga*) will arise."[5]

Standing at the point of saying "Now the path will arise," one is in position for its arising but, of course, the path (*magga*) does not arise merely because one has had the thought of its arising. A magnificent shift occurs; one is enabled to say not only, "Now the path will arise," a statement made right at the limits of the realm of possible human action. One now realizes that a controlling force has arisen, a faculty has arisen (*indriya*—the controlling force or faculty "to say 'I will realize that which has not been realized' (*anaññātaññassāmītindriyam.*)."[6] The Theravāda commentarial tradition has maintained this awareness of the incipient turning, a kind of initial *metanoia,* associated with the arising of the path.[7]

There follows the arising of what has been called "conformity knowledge" (*anulomañāṇa*), the insight that enables one to see things as they really are and as they should be seen. What is impermanent, what arises and falls, what undergoes dissolution, what is fearful, what poses a danger, what is an object of dispassion, and so forth—all of these are known as they are to be known precisely in light of the way things are. This conformity knowledge enables a person to see the real state of affairs.[8] With the arising of this conformity knowledge, one nudges the limit of possible human action, one witnesses the falling away of calculation, the end of one's own attempts to do anything, even the cultivation of wholesome action (*kusalakamma*) that might "count," as it were, toward the attainment of the arising of the path (*magga*). It is said,

> Herein, there is nothing further that is to be done by one wishing for the attainment of the knowledge of the first path. What was to have been done by one has been done by means of the arising of the insight dwelling in conformity [knowledge].[9]

When in the early stages of writing this chapter on this particular point, I found myself using here the phrase, "the last movement," in speaking of the process of deepening insight that leads to emergence of the path that is called "Change-of-lineage-knowledge (*gotrabhūñāṇa*)."[10] "The last movement" is a legitimate translation of the Pali. But I sense that the point is even more delicate than I first thought. Movement, in this context, might suggest an agent doing the movement, while the Pali passage suggests that the activity is to be found *in the process that is the insight itself*—the insight that is the "Change-of-lineage-knowledge" *itself leads to the moment* of emergence, of arising.

So there is a further unfolding of the process, the "Change-of-lineage-knowledge." This "Change-of-lineage (*gotrabhū*)" is a relatively late technical term and has become very important in the development of the Theravāda as well as other strands of the Buddhist movement. According to the *Visuddhimagga*, when the "Culminating, irrevocable Change-of-lineage-knowledge, which is the irrevocable culminating apex of insight, arises,"[11] the mind becomes centered on Nibbāna and one is of the lineage of the Noble Ones.

> The conformity [knowledge] is able to dispel the darkness of the defilements that enveloped truth but is not able to become centered

on Nibbāna. Change-of-lineage (*gotrabhū*) is able to become centered solely on Nibbāna. It cannot dispel the darkness that enveloped truth.[12]

This "Change-of-lineage-knowledge" is called "turning toward the path"[13] in the sense of orientation with poised attentiveness to what has now come within the scope of awareness. While the faculty of being able to say, "I will know what has not been known," and the arising of "Change-of-lineage-knowledge" provide the initial shifting in orientation, in turning, the "metanoic" event is not complete without the arising of the path.

> Thus Change-of-lineage-knowledge is able only to see Nibbāna, not to dispel the defilements. Hence it is called "turning to the path."
>
> Although it [Change-of-lineage-knowledge] is not itself [this] turning, having been established in the position of this turning and, as if having given a sign to the path "Now arise!", it ceases. And having not abandoned that sign given by it [Change-of-lineage-knowledge], following upon that knowledge in uninterrupted continuity, the path (*magga*) arises, breaking through and exploding the mass of greed, the mass of hatred, the mass of delusion, not penetrated before, not exploded before.[14]
>
> And not only does this path cause the breaking through of the mass of greed, etc., but also indeed it dries up the ocean of misery of the whirl of this beginningless *saṃsāra,* closes all doors [leading to states] of woe, sets in one's presence the seven noble treasures, abandons the eightfold confused path, quietens all enmities and fears, leads to the state of a cherished son [lit. breast-son] of the Perfectly Enlightened One, and it conduces to the acquisition of many hundreds of other advantages.[15]

About this *magga* event, it has been said, "It is the true blessed event of the religious life of the Theravāda Buddhist."[16]

Palihawadana has also provided a splendid summary statement of the soteriological process from within the Theravāda frame or reference.

*a.* The operation of the law of "causal orderliness" (in its positive aspect and in its negative aspect) explains the events in the Buddhist salvific process: (i) "something done," etc., followed by "natural changes"; (ii) "absence of conditions" followed by "absence of consequences."

*b.* The final element in this procession of events is the brief cessation of *sankhāra* activity. This last event contains a new element: non-operation of will, of the "wanting-to-become-something." This amounts to the "absence of the conditions for defilement."

*c.* In the next events, there is the "discarding of defilement," which happens because the other factor necessary for it now takes place, namely, contact with the "reality-beyond-the-world" (*lokuttara dhamma*). But this contact is "not a production in one's being, but an encounter at first hand."[17]

This way of formulating the process would certainly find friendly the notion of the pervasiveness of one's own "calculation" (J: *hakarai*) in the religious life, of which Shinran wrote. Those self-centered calculations would represent defiling *saṅkhāra*s that would, in the nature of the case, merely continue giving rise to the presence of defilements.

In the Theravāda formulation, one finds that there is an initial discernment that a process has indeed begun, one that can be relied upon. There is firstly that awareness that one will know what has not been known before followed by the awareness that one is oneself undergoing a "change of lineage," that is, becoming significantly other than what one was. Then, with the arising of the path (*magga*), one is assured[18] that final and complete Enlightenment/Nibbāna will arise sometime in future, within the next seven life sequences among the realms of gods and humans.[19]

There is, then, absence of calculation (J: *hakarai*) and there is certainty of attaining Nibbāna. At the moment of the arising of the Path of Stream Attainment (*sotāpattimaggakkhaṇe*), proper view (*sammādiṭṭhi*) and the other seven factors of the eightfold path emerge from their opposites and related defilements and associated consequences. At the same time, not all of the fetters are broken. One can truly see with understanding the way things have become (*yathābhūtam*) while not being wholly other than what one was, that is, entirely free—a sentiment not entirely foreign to the notion of "deep mind" (J: *jinshin*) in Jōdo Shinshū thought.

Shinran's frustration with the procedures at Mt. Hiei indicates his recognition that precepts and ritual are hardly soteriologically adequate. Theravāda Buddhists would fully understand Shinran, recalling the old admonition not to become misled into thinking that precepts, ritual, liturgy, in themselves, lead one onward.[20] And with Shinran's struggle with the subtle, pervasive perversion of *hakarai,* calculation, a Theravāda Buddhist would understand the fundamental inability of a person to will this qualitative change, or of a psychic process to cleanse itself without the presence of a purification that arises free from the defilements of that very psychic process. With the arising of the path the three fetters of (1) preoccupying opinions about the reality of one's individuality (*sakkāyadiṭṭhi*), (2) skeptical, disorienting doubt (*vicikicchā*), and (3) doting on precepts and practices (*sīlabbataparāmāsa*), are completely destroyed.[21] They are destroyed by the vision of Nibbāna. "How is the Path of Stream Attainment a vision? Because [in it] there is the first vision of Nibbāna."[22]

It is remarkable that persons living within the Buddhist tradition in Japan and in Sri Lanka have affirmed that when the mind becomes uncluttered, poised, free from egocentric psychic processes, free from fetters, at that moment (and it has been called a "moment": P: *khaṇa,* J: *ichinen*) something extraordinary happens. It is certainly not "brain death," but, on the contrary, the arising of "the blessed event." How does one utilize language to refer to this moment, as it were, to talk about it? Talk about it we have; in different languages in different parts of the world. The relevant linguistic capability will probably arise as we launch our discussion in colloquia, in the future.

We have talked about this personal transformation: some of us have expressed it as the arising of *magga,* others of us have expressed it as the arising of *shinjin.* Such expressions are manifestations of faith of religious persons.

## A CHRISTIAN'S AFFIRMATION: ONE DOES NOT SAVE ONESELF

In turning now to mention key themes present in Christian considerations of what I have called salvific realization, I must point out quickly that when I was a young man and realized the presence of God disclosed to me through the agency of the Holy Spirit and made intelligible through the Christ-event I would not have conceptualized the experience as a "salvific realization." Hardly! There were considerable emotions swirling, a dynamic of sorts of intense singularity on my part but discerned in the buttressing presence of others. There was a calming, sobering sense arising not quite simultaneously but not without *uninterrupted continuity* either that brought with it a sense of being taken up, a sense of release and of ease.

The language we used at the time and the place to talk about this enormously complex and transformative experience was, "I took Jesus as my personal savior," or, more mundanely, "I joined the church," usually meaning, inadequately, a particular institution in town. One would be somewhat reluctant at the time to say, "I am saved," but not in replying "Yes" to the question, "Are you saved?" But what was the structure of what was going on at the time in the mind and heart of this young man? How might the older person which that young man has become speak of what occurred? More engagingly, perhaps, how might that person consider that occurrence now after nearly forty years of studying the great religious traditions of humankind?

What was going on in the mind and heart of that young man has been variously discussed under important theological headings: faith, salvation, redemption, atonement, forgiveness, repentance, revelation, and the like—magnificent notions these, each receiving weighty attention in the history of Christian thought. Although we cannot investigate these notions here we might offer a basic insight which they all address. The given situation in which persons find themselves in their ordinary reflections on questions of meaning and purpose in life, of their sense of humanity as presented to themselves by the model of their own lives with all their particularity, is fundamentally awry, inadequate because of the centripetal force of egocentrism and of the subtle and continuous drive of self-aggrandizement, of the delicate and persistent deceitful machinations of duplicitous rationalizations. In more customary theological language, this is sin. This is pride. This is at the heart of the self when it discovers that it is not and cannot be the ontological ground for its own worth, or of its own lastingness beyond four score years and ten. Along with this restlessness there is also reinforced by pride the existential recognition that to "be a man at all is to be involved in pain, loss, and estrangement—in short, to lead a precarious and even perilous existence. It means that one's very self is constantly menaced both from without and within by dark, destructive forces which are indicated by such words as sin, guilt, or death." Roger Hazelton, the author of these words, continues, "There is that in man's own condition against which he needs to be guarded, from which he needs to be preserved or freed, and of which he must be made aware, however painfully or reluctantly."[23] We are aware of ourselves; of our sin, our pride, and our existential condition. We are also aware that as one looks out on the affairs of humankind in search for incontrovertible evidence of God's presence, one will not be able to demonstrate it. One acknowledges oneself as one is and affirms God in spite of the evidence. John B. Carman catches this dialectic nicely in saying, "for Christians believe both *with* the evidence of human creatureliness and *against* the evidence of God's absence from the created universe."[24]

This might be difficult to explain through intellectualizations and through rational arguments, of course. But the crucial role of the imagination comes into play with significant impact for we cannot imagine ourselves without imagination. In this salvific realization of which Christians speak, this *fides salvifica,* imagination is the ingredient that enables one to interpret the *coincidentia* or simultaneity of an awakening of conscience with the conviction of sin. John Baillie has observed in this context,

> The new convert may long have known and believed all that the Church teaches about God and Christ, but somehow only now has the meaning of it all "come home" to him. He has never, we say, "taken it to himself" before. What is this "coming home", this "taking to oneself", which alone gives to faith a salvific power? It is, of course, something that God brings to pass in the soul; but perhaps it is more in the realm of the imagination that He brings it to pass than in the realm of the intellect.

John Baillie continues, "I have long been of opinion that the part played by the imagination in the soul's dealings with God, though it has always been understood by those skilled in the practice of the Christian cure of souls, has never been given proper place in Christian theology, which has too much been ruled by intellectualistic preconceptions."[25]

For a long time in the history of Christian thought there has been discussion about the degree to which there is radical discontinuity between a natural state of grace, as it were, and the saving grace effected by God through the Christ-event and the activity of the Holy Spirit. Some consider this conversion realization to be in a moment, others take it as possibly a process. This is the old "twice born" and "once born" discussion. John Baillie addresses this notion that one is either saved or not saved and notes, "It follows from this that the transition from the state of nature to the state of grace always takes place in a single moment, a mathematical point of time. This is explicitly insisted on by many old theologians, both Roman and Protestant."[26] But there is within the Christian heritage the point of view that one is able to grow into faith, which process is itself a gift of God. The evidence drawn from the New Testament does not substantiate an interpretation that this salvific realization is what Alan Richardson calls a "dateable process,"[27] or instantaneous moment, although this position has been developed in Christian thought and is widely held today. The main point to see is that Jesus, in his Galilean ministry, makes integral the combination of repentance and faith. Richardson says, "The encounter with Christ produced both these things in men's hearts . . . and both of them are God's gifts, not men's achievements."[28]

There is in all of this a paradox, a paradox of Grace. Donald M. Baillie, in introducing this paradox, provides this observation. "Never is human action more truly and fully personal, never does the agent feel more perfectly free, than in those moments of which he can say as a Christian that whatever good was in them was not his but God's."[29] D. M. Baillie avers that this paradoxical conviction "lies at the very heart of the Christian life."[30]

An old question within the Christian tradition has been, "Why did God become man? For what purpose did Christ come down from heaven?"[31] This question brings focal attention to the meaning of the Incarnation and the assurance of meaning for one's life. Melanchthon (1497–1560, whose original name was Philip Schwarzerd, author of the Augsburg Confession, an important interpreter of Luther's thinking) it was who said that "to know Christ is simply to know His benefits."[32] D. M. Baillie concludes from this a way to discern the meaning of the Incarnation:

> any knowledge of Christ, or any Christology, which cannot show how it makes a vital difference, and brings "saving benefits" to our human situation, must be more than suspect. The *Heidelberg Catechism* asks at one decisive point, "But what doth it help thee now, that thou believest all this?" This question of "saving benefits" may well be used, as in principle it has regularly been used since the days of the Fathers, to test any proposed interpretation of the Incarnation and to draw out its meaning. If your Christology is true, what difference does it make? How are we the better off, in the actual business of living, for having such a Christ?[33]

One benefit a Christian can discern lies in a newfound sense of freedom, freedom from the crippling effects of repression of former failures, freedom from a sublimated psychology of escapism that will surface crushingly in the midst of the massive pressures of life. Another benefit would be a realistic appraisal of ourselves, that we are not without sin, which appraisal brings with it an acknowledging of who and what we really are: sinners saved by the grace of God, deceivers who, on this point, are free from deceit, and glory in the taste of that freedom. And, of course, the benefits continue.

No longer will the sin of pride disorient one who has been enabled to find faith in God through Christ. D. M. Baillie summarizes for us the refreshment realized upon overcoming self-centeredness,

> which is the essence of sin, and even of the pride which is its most deadly form, because it will not accept the forgiveness of sins; the pride that makes us refuse "justification by faith" and choose "justification by works"? The Christian way is the very opposite. It sets us free for the service of God and man by delivering us from ourselves. And so its ultimate confession . . . is: Not I, but the grace of God.[34]

"*Not I*" the voices of men and women participating in our three great religious traditions have been saying for centuries. At the limit of possible human action, at the falling away of all calculation, entirely, at the moment of radical honesty, informed variously by the conceptualizations and customary practices passed down through traditions while simultaneously breaking through the form of those concepts at a moment of creative receptivity, one discerns where transcendence begins, which is a salvific realization. We speak of this occurrence as the arising of the path (*magga*), one's first glimpse of Nibbāna/Nirvāṇa, as the arising of *shinjin,* the Buddha-mind, as the presence of God: Spirit, Son, and Father.

Ask us to try to define transcendence and we, over centuries and around the world, will provide, argue for, even defend, the enormous variety of attempts, both in any one tradition and among the three. Ask us to articulate precisely the personal transformation involved and, even after massive delimiting categories are projected onto the realization—sociological, psychological, philosophical, theological, even a combination—many variegated extensive, complex analyses will be offered. But the fundamental formal structure abides and is divine. Responses to transcendence have been multiform and numerous. The discernment providing the foundation for the response is not foreign to Theravāda, Jōdo Shinshū, and Christian men and women. Our task is not to comprehend transcendence but only to recognize where it begins.

# 12

# Relationality in Religious Awareness

*We are involved with humanity, of that religious persons are assured, and although this involvement expresses itself variously in the different traditions persons have continued to bear witness to the relationality of human life: with each other and crucially with salvific truth without the abiding presence of which, it has been affirmed, human life would hardly become authentic, humane.*

Relationality is at the heart of what it means to be genuinely human. It is a quality in which one participates when one is not cut off from the past—an open past—or from others or from meaning or, for some, even from hope. Central in this relationality is response, particularly, as we have indicated, response to transcendence which provides a center of value and a mutually recognized basis of and for community. Without relationality, there is fragmentation, disintegration, even despair, certainly isolation and estrangement. Relationality stands behind our capacity to be intelligible, to have thoughts wherein differentiations and connections operate, distinctions and comparisons apply. If things and thoughts are unrelated and disconnected, personality dislocation occurs—or has already occurred. Part of the lament of younger generations arises from a sense of disconnectedness of life, one's own and others, of one academic discipline from others, of religious doctrines and environmental issues, of theological affirmations and self-understanding, of a human activity that we call science and a human activity that we call faithfulness. Without relationality, individuals remain isolated integers, failing to live fully as persons.

In this chapter, we direct our attention to religious paradigms that depict foundations for relationality, particularly between persons and transcendence, without which reality and without which personal responses, the Buddha, Amida Buddha, and the Christ lose their identity. We will not argue that these focal religious images are the same or that they are analogous. The point is that they are homologous, that is to say, they are demonstrative of how we human beings have found our way to, or have been enabled to, conceptualize, to represent in ideas, what has simultaneously transformed our lives, is not entirely of our own creation, and at the same time exceeds our grasp. That transcendence is beyond our ability to conceptualize it fully, that in responding to it we discover wherein we enter a process of transcending—transcending what we had thought, how we had lived—we are consequently aware that religious awareness, although highly significant in being supportive in its integrative quality, is not itself salvific. Ultimately, perhaps one might speak of a salvific immediacy of engagement in which dimensions necessary for relations to occur have themselves become transcended. That engagement is, it seems, salvific. But speaking and writing of that engagement tend readily also to exceed our grasp, our conceptuality, our language. However, relationality in religious awareness is nearer to hand, indeed, provides support for living life well and about this, it appears, religious persons have given us remarkable testimonies.

We begin with the way Theravāda Buddhists, because they have been able to become engaged with Salvific Truth (*Dhamma*) through the teachings (*dhamma*) of the Buddha, have represented the relationality of the Buddha with the Salvific Truth that he rediscovered *and* those teachings, which he gave to humanity, that lead to that Salvific Truth. Next we move to Jōdo Shinshū referring briefly to the contribution of T'an-luan and especially to the sense of relationality in Shinran's understanding of the disclosure of Salvific Truth. We will next move to the relationality involved in one's consideration of Jesus as the Christ in a key dimension of theological reflection that demonstrates his role in relationality as presented in the Christian theological affirmation of the Trinity. These inquiries will converge in our important theme of relationality, which persons have discovered in their religious lives, a triadic relationality of transcendence, modes of human apprehension, and the creative response of persons.

Persons familiar with the major contributions to religious studies by Wilfred Smith will detect my indebtedness to his way of approaching issues of religiousness and more importantly, in this chapter, to his dynamic sense of transcendence as process, as involving human beings. Transcendence, for Smith, is not static, something out there and beyond, as is inadequately often thought. One spots the dynamic process transcendence involves in Smith's observations:

> Central to an understanding of the universe, of humanity, and of transcendence itself as a principle, is that the three are interrelated, intimately—and dynamically. Characteristic of transcendence is its *process quality,* and its *involvement of us* in its process. Characteristic of the universe is that it *keeps transcending us*—us and our grasp, though not entirely. Characteristic of us is that *we are self-transcending* especially as we move through time, and that our awareness of the universe, of reality, of truth, though always partial, can, if we take proper steps, be

less partial today than it was yesterday, less partial tomorrow than it is today [emphasis added].[1]

## RELATIONALITY: THE BUDDHA

When one considers the Buddha, one meets a historical figure; in this case, a human being—but, in a sense, much more—and a focal figure in one of humankind's great religious traditions—and much more. From one point of view, "the Buddha" refers to a person who really lived, an objective referent in space and time. From another point of view, this person has been, and is, acclaimed as "the Awakened One," for centuries now, even today. Were this not to have been the case and to have continued to be a recorded and observable event, the Buddha would have been forgotten and, today, probably would be of little interest. This epithet *buddha,* "the Awakened One," has been extended to the Buddha because of what persons have found to be true in his teachings, passed down through the years, and in the collective memory of his life and testimonial accounts of that life. From the beginning, then, to speak of the Buddha is to speak in human terms, in terms, too, of relation, not merely between and among human beings but with the preexistent Salfivic Truth that he rediscovered, which rediscovery constitutes the basis for his being affirmed as the Awakened One, at the time he lived, and, importantly, subsequently, in the lives of men and women through the centuries and around the world. Persons do not affirm that he is the Awakened One merely because they were taught this—at least not if they are reflective persons. Nor do they propose it because everyone around them is doing the same. Both occasions are important, of course, in shaping a cumulative religious tradition. But both are not sufficiently foundational for the living of one's life in the world as one knows it to be.

A personal realization of abiding truth is required to anchor a reflective person's life. And, for centuries and through many cultures, men and women have had a realization that the truth made accessible through the Awakened One's teachings, is, indeed, salvific, does, certainly, enable life to be lived with dignity, purpose, and meaning to be found in one's own life and in relation with others, and the natural human physical process into death to be a noble human experience.

As one finds one's *identity* in relation, for example, as a man might be a son, a husband, a father, a friend, and so on, so, too, the Buddha's identity is found in relation: surely with Dhamma as Salvific Truth, but also as teacher of dhamma as the reliable expression in words that will lead one, if followed conscientiously, faithfully, to that Salvific Truth. And further, the Buddha's identity through the centuries is in relation with countless men and women who have averred that the Buddha is indeed the Awakened One because they have confirmed the availability of Salvific Truth in the living of their lives.

Of numerous possibilities that one might choose to investigate, or themes to pursue, one of the most engaging has to do with a delicate and profound shift in perspective metaphorically communicated by referring to a bodily activity, in this case, the act of seeing. Now, of course, the notion of seeing yields an immense field for interpretation: seeing, perceiving, discerning, realizing, knowing, and understanding, to name a few. Particularly interesting is the way a change—let us say, a change in fundamental orientation—occurs in the lives of persons that enables them to see with insight what otherwise they had only noticed. The pivoting on this delicate soteriological point is subtle and a consideration of a related dialectic will be instructive for persons seeking to understand a dimension in human religiousness. In Pali, one turns to the word *passati,* "one sees," with the implied meaning, "to know" or "to find."[2]

One of the most celebrated passages in the Theravāda canonical literature is an exchange between a bhikkhu named Vakkali and the Buddha.[3] Our story begins with the Auspicious One (*bhagavan*) living in a grove near Rājagaha. At that time, Venerable Vakkali was not at all well, in pain, considerably ill. Vakkali asked his attendants to go to the Buddha with a statement and a request. The statement and the request communicate what the tradition considers to be a quality of faith (P: *saddhā*). Vakkali asks his attendants,

> having approached the Bhagavan with my words, show obeisance with your heads at the feet of the Bhagavan, saying "the fellow monk Vakkali is not well, in pain and is very ill. He does obeisance at the feet of the Bhagavan." And say also, "it would be well, indeed, were the Bhagavan, out of compassion, to come to the fellow monk Vakkali."

Vakkali was sick and in considerable distress. He wanted to communicate this to the Buddha *and* he wanted the Buddha to come, to be present in person by his bedside, as an expression of the Buddha's sympathetic consciousness of Vakkali's poor condition and a desire to alleviate it. And note, too, the presence of the notion of showing obeisance (lit., pay homage with the head at the Bhagavan's feet) which is mentioned three times in the narrative before the Buddha signals, in his customary way of remaining silent, his agreement to visit Vakkali.

It appears that upon seeing the Buddha approaching from afar, Vakkali, out of anxiety about propriety in showing due respect for the presence of the Buddha, tossed about on his bed.[4] The text is already setting up an engaging dynamic with some degree of tension. A sick monk longs for the physical presence of the Buddha, seeking healing of his illness—all understandable, ordinary human wishes. His veneration of the Buddha is framed for us by ritual acts of obeisance and his aspiration is for improved physical health. The dramatic plants are in place and, with Vakkali perturbed about failing in hospitable deference, the conversation begins.

Advising Vakkali not to fret about not providing an appropriate seat, the Buddha takes an available seat and asks how Vakkali is fairing, whether he is improving, whether his aches and pains are decreasing. Vakkali replies that he is not managing very well and that his pains are, indeed, increasing. Then a somewhat surprising turn in the conversation occurs: there is no question about food and water, possible cause of the illness, whether attendants are rendering suitable care. The Buddha asks, rather, whether Vakkali has remorse, whether he has any regret. Vakkali replies that he is not troubled and has no remorse. The Buddha then asks whether Vakkali blames himself regarding his own moral virtue. To Vakkali's reply that he did not, the Buddha inquires again, this time whether some remorse and regret remain.

And then the dramatic issue emerges. Vakkali puts it this way: "For a long time, I have been desiring to approach the Bhagavan for a *darśana,* but there has not been enough strength in my body that I might approach the Bhagavan for a *darśana*."[5] The problem is that Vakkali, for a long time, really wanted to see the Buddha—this is ocular perception but not without a heightened sense of the significant presence of that looked upon—but had been too weak to make the journey.

It is at this point in the story that the Buddha speaks words that have echoed through the centuries.

> Pull yourself together, Vakkali! What is there for you with seeing this putrid body. Indeed, Vakkali, the one who sees Dhamma sees me. The one who sees me sees Dhamma. Indeed, Vakkali, the one seeing Dhamma sees me; the one seeing me sees Dhamma.[6]

The Buddha immediately turns Vakkali's attention to five aggregates that constitute the empirical individual and acknowledges Vakkali's recognition of their transitoriness, concluding, "Seeing it so, one knows that one does not go to such [current] state again." The Buddha then departs.

Vakkali is subsequently carried to a place for the night, in the very early morning of which two *devas* appear before the Buddha. One *deva* announces that Vakkali indeed aspires for release (*vimokkhāya ceteti*). The other *deva* says, "Surely he will attain release completely." At dawn, the Buddha requests that some bhikkhus go to Vakkali to inform him of the announcements by the *devas* and with words of profound consolation the Buddha adds, "Fear not, Vakkali, do not fear, Vakkali. Your dying will not be detrimental, your death will not be bad." When Vakkali hears all of this, he affirms, "have no doubt that there is no desire, passion, affection in me for that which is impermanent, painful, of the nature of change." Shortly thereafter, Vakkali takes up a knife and kills himself.[7] The story ends with metaphorical power. Dark clouds move here and there covering the sky in darkness. The tumbling, churning, dark clouds represent Māra searching for but not finding the consciousness of Vakkali, who has attained final Nibbāna (*parinibbuto*).

The paradigm shift provides a new context for understanding a sick bhikkhu's physical pains and his predominant disposition toward the efficacy of devotion in ritual acts. There is a more fundamental order of truth—not in contradiction, but in ever expanding and inclusive supportiveness. The body, as well as the other four aggregates that cluster to form an empirically discernible individual, is fleeting, is not stable, and will dissolve, decaying in the process—the jolting assertion the Buddha made when he referred *to his own body* as "putrid." The foundational truth is the reliability of this regular process of impermanence. Vakkali came to see this, but also much more. All that comes together to form an individual—physical form, feeling, perception, synergetic process, and consciousness—is fleeting and, because of this, it is awry and of the nature of withering. Upon seeing this point, obviously in the sense of understanding,[8] Vakkali gives a testimony that there was neither delight nor passion nor love for any of these aggregates nor doubt regarding this truth about these things. A change of orientation to the entire setting has now occurred. The longing of a sick man to see the body of the Buddha has become the acknowledgment by a wise man of the abidingness of Salvific Truth.

Let us turn to some important terms to catch a glimpse of subtle and profound affirmations of what Theravāda Buddhists have seen. And the sight is spectacular, like a majestic waterfall with both a cumulative force of tradition and the alluring quality of rainbows appearing now here, now there in the mist. The approach for, or procedure of, our reflections is not to trace upstream to find a tiny spring of origins, as it were, nor to trace the meanderings of brook, stream, and river, but to see the collective efforts of persons discerning, responding, and remembering the conceptual structure of what has been passed down and the truth thereby disclosed. Usually, interpreters of the Vakkali passage move quickly on with a passing comment that *rūpakāya* refers to the Buddha's material or physical body and *dhammakāya* means the body of teaching or doctrine. We shall reflect more carefully on this old and frequently repeated passage.

But much more is going on in the Vakkali story. To return to the "seeing" passage, the focus is on the relation of the physical presence of the Buddha and also the abiding Salvific Truth which his teachings have made accessible. This is no easy matter, for the relation is not posited as though it is an objective impersonal fact, but requires an engaged response on the part of persons to the truth of that relation. The tradition offers categories for understanding the truth of the relation: material or form body (*rūpakāya*), dhammabody (*dhammakāya*), one who has become Dhamma (*dhammabhūto*), who has become the best or the highest (*brahmabhūto*). The key point that is being underscored is the salvific continuity in the figure of the Buddha, a man among men and women, the paradigm for integrity, the illustrious one whose teaching (*dhamma*) converges consistently and reliably in his life with the Salvific Truth (*Dhamma*) which he rediscovered. Were there to be any distortion whatsoever between what he taught and the truth about which he spoke, there would remain at the core of the Theravāda tradition a soteriological gap, so to speak, that would have to be addressed, filled, for there to be clarity and continuity in doctrinal formulations about the possibility of personal realization of Salvific Truth in this very life.

What is the truth about the physical body that is being observed? What kind of seeing is taking place in the one who "sees Dhamma"? What is the relationship of this person and Dhamma, rather, the integral, contiguous completeness of the realization in his being wholly awake, his qualities as an auspicious exemplar, and the teachings? What is seen? What might be a few consequences of this seeing?

More than four decades ago I was inside the main inner hall of the Kelaniya temple in Sri Lanka at the beginning of the dramatic final evening of its extravagant *perahära*. The great doors were shut behind us and worship in sound (*śabdapūja*) began. The shrill, piercing sound of the *horäna* and the concussion felt from the sounding of many drums in the presence of a veiled Buddha image was a marvelous sight to behold. The cacophony of drums, the images and paintings lit by flickering torches, the smell of flowers and incense, the presence of other people all converged to provide a "feast for the *eyes*."

In Anurādhapura there is a statue of the Buddha in meditation posture (*Samādhi budu piḷimaya*). It is a serene place where, even on Posān Poya when the coming of Mahinda to Sri Lanka is commemorated, when many thousands of pilgrims arrive at the memorable sites at this ancient capital city, the area around this statue remains quiet. It is a place for calm, of peace. This, too, is a *sight* to behold.

How much more would be a sight of the Buddha in our midst! The ordinary, average person (*puthujjana*), so often mentioned in Theravāda literature, is not a simpleton! The ordinary sense of seeing is the customary mode by which average persons sort out visible objects in form and color, in movement and distance, and in spatial dimensions.[9] The ordinariness in this sense is placed in perspective by the extraordinariness of Salvific Truth and the profound change appropriating that truth has in the lives of persons. Seeing a physical body is by means of the ordinary "eye of flesh" (*maṃsacakkhu*), while seeing Dhamma involves the "eye of knowledge" (*ñāṇacakkhu*).[10]

What do the commentaries tell us about what is being seen in this and related passages? Certainly it is not "doctrine," although this term is often used in English interpretations of this matter. Nor is it "teaching." Doctrines and teachings do not transform persons. It is the activity of becoming engaged with that to which doctrines point, to that about which the teachings teach, that enables one to discern wherein and how one can become, or has become, other than what one was. Any interpretation less than this would fail to heed a Buddhist admonition to avoid clinging to views, that is, to doctrines, to teachings.

Having learned of Vakkali's desire to engage in acts of devotion, of his longing to see the Buddha, one's expectations are flanked by the Buddha's poignant comment about the true condition of the human body—Vakkali's as well as his own. The cumulative tradition preserves this story, replicated at numerous places. The story presents a lively dialectic in which one understands the true condition of all materiality in light of reality; *rūpakāya* in light of *dhammakāya*—the former is seen by discerning the latter, understood through a realization of the latter. The dialectic this coincidence of opposites initially provides moves through one's personal reflections and in the developing tradition toward correlation.

The adjective used by the Buddha to describe his physical body, the body that Vakkali longed to see, at the feet of which he wished to place his head in obeisance, is *pūti,* akin to the Latin base for the English word *pus.*[11] There is a radical shift here, a reorientation to the physical body *sub specie aeternitatis,* under the form of eternity, a recognition of the universal principle that defines the body—odious, offensive to the senses. Yet this is just the opposite of a standard description of the Bhagavan, the auspicious exemplar, the Lord, as represented in the Theravāda cumulative tradition. "And he has glory of each and every limb, perfect in every way, which is able to bring about a delicate sense of composure (*pasāda*) in the eyes of persons which are bedecked with a *darśana* of his physical body" (*Visuddhimagga* [*Harvard Oriental Series*] VII, 61, [*Pali Text Society*], I, 211).[12]

A splendid example of the complementarity and cumulative convergence of these two dimensions of the Buddha as they become integrally fulfilled in the life of a person of insightful faith is reflected in a passage in the commentary on the *Sutta-nipāta.*

> Then Dhaniyo, having seen the *dhammakāya* with the eye of wisdom, with thoroughly established faith, well-rooted and with unshakable serenity in the Tathāgata, having a heart reproved, thought "The bonds are severed. There is no re-entering a womb for me. Having put an end to Avīci [hell] and to whatever other limit of existence, who else other than the Bhagavan will roar the Lion's roar. My teacher has come." (*Sutta-Nipāta Commentary: Being Paramatthajotikā II,* I, 41[on *Sutta-Nipāta*, vs. 30])

The commentary continues,

> There, because Dhaniyo, with his wife and children, having seen by the world-transcending eye the *dhammakāya* through a penetration (attainment) of the noble path, having seen with the customary eye the *rūpakāya,* acquired the attainment of faith, and hence he said, "Indeed, it is no little gain for us that we have seen the Bhagavan." (*Sutta-Nipāta Commentary: Being Paramatthajotikā II,* I, 42 [on *Sutta-Nipāta,* vs. 31])

We see that the two bodies are held together in the figure of the Buddha/Tathāgata/Bhagavan, with the *dhammakāya,* without exception, being the primary, foundational element. When the focus is on the *rūpakāya* of men and women, in light of Dhamma, the reality of the material body's inherent nature of decay and passing away is seen—not in despair but in a calming, supportive sense. When the *rūpakāya* of the Buddha is seen, in light of *dhammakāya,* it is also celebrated for its beauty and attractiveness as a metaphorical example of virtuous living, that is, living completely in accordance with Dhamma.

In the several strands of the Vakkali narrative, all relate Vakkali's longing to see the Buddha, or wishing ever to remain in his presence, and the popular exchange between the two.[13]

The themes of our Vakkali passage also enable us to see an example of how the developing tradition addresses the relationship between the person of the Buddha and Salvific Truth. In our narrative, the focus shifts from the physical, a particular human being with stress placed on the form of a human being, to a particular person, the Buddha, with emphasis placed on a complex of distinguishing characteristics indicating identity in relation. Concerning the term *dhammakāya*, a commentary asks, "Why is the Tathāgata called *dhammakāya*?" The passage continues, "The Tathāgata, having reflected on the *tepiṭaka* Buddha-word [the three baskets of the collection of scripture] in his heart, sent it forth in words. Therefore his body is Dhamma because he himself consists of Dhamma" (*Sumaṅgalavilāsinī: Buddhaghosa's Commentary on the Dīgha-Nikāya,* III, 865 [on *Dīgha Nikāya,* III, 84]). The parallelism appears elsewhere.[14]

The sense of identity *in* relation, closer than identity *by* association, appears in a late utilization of our Vakkali passage, extending the sense in going to the Buddha as refuge by indicating that when one goes for refuge in the Bhagavan, one also goes to Dhamma as refuge (*Vaṃsatthapakāsinī: Commentary on the Mahāvaṃsa,* I, 45–46). And one who teaches Dhamma as it was heard, with the words "Thus I have heard" (*evaṃ me sutaṃ*), sees the dhamma-body (*dhammasarīra*) of the Bhagavan (*Sumaṅgalavilāsinī,* I, 34; *Săratthappakāsini,* I, 12).[15]

The later tradition inherited much that had gone before, providing both flashes of insight along the way and structured scholastic analyses. The quality of faith becoming fulfilled in Vakkali's attainment of Arahantship echoes in the words describing his "having an abundance of faith by means of [his seeing] the [Buddha's] incomparable physical body, having an abundance of insight-wisdom by means of [his seeing the] profound body of teachings." (*Mahābodhivaṃsa,* 83). The subsequent heritage reveals a continuity with what went before. Sinhala Buddhist writers provide several informative glosses for the term *dhammakāya.* It is the instruction in the teachings written in books (*Śrī Saddharmāvavāda Saṃgrahaya,* 263, 285), even as the entire three baskets of the canon which are also written down (ibid., 300), and which can be spoken and heard (ibid., 300, 302, 304). The distinction between *rūpakāya* and *dhammakāya* is maintained, with the *rūpakāya* considered in light of the exceptional physical qualities of the Buddha. When these qualities are expressed in the homiletical etymological elaboration of the word *bhagavan,* in the standard phrasing "*ti pi so bhagavan,*" the "body of Dhamma," *dhammakāya,* is utilized (*Saddharmālaṅkāraya,* 2).

Also, the interpretation of *dhammakāya* as that which was taught by the Buddha, particularly in the classic threefold analysis of that which is to be learned (the authoritative teaching), practice, and penetration or attainment, is maintained (*Śrī Saddharmāvavāda Saṃgrahaya,* 249). The wealth of the *dhammakāya,* we learn, as the tradition has continued, is attained by means of the eye of knowledge (*Saddharmālaṅkāraya,* 370).

The identity in relation of the Buddha and the body of Dhamma, *dhammakāya,* is expressed with an alluring metaphor. The Buddha, we learn, caused "the nectar of Dhamma true to overflow from the vessel of his body that was filled with the ambrosia of Dhamma just as honey in a filled bowl overflows and falls outside when there is no space inside" (*Pūjāvaliya,* 190).

Insofar as one today might consider the current English usage or sense of "believing," "to believe," suggests holding a position one is oneself incapable of persuasively demonstrating or, for one person, a position about which another person is not really certain,[16] *seeing,* in spite of the cliché, *is far more than believing.* In religious discourse, metaphors and analogies abound, levels of discourse operate. We see this in the metaphorical use of "eye" (*cakkhu*) to communicate insight, penetrative vision, and understanding. As pertaining to the Buddha, we see it designating his knowledge of everything that can be known in space and time, of all knowables (*sabbadhamma*), forming an epithet of the Buddha (*cakkhumant*), "one having vision" (*Sutta-Nipāta,* vv. 992–993). The received tradition is aware of the force of "eye" in the sense of insight. "'Eye of Dhamma' [*dhammacakkhu*] in the sense of eye [vision, insight] with regard to knowables, or eye made of, consisting of Dhamma. In other places [in the texts] it is a synonym for the three paths, but here just the path of stream entrance."[17] In offering this interpretation, the literary tradition is no doubt also fully aware that the texts, elsewhere, put into words what the insight of *dhammacakkhu* discloses: "Whatever has the inherent nature of arising, all that has the inherent nature of cessation." This phrasing regarding the Dhamma-eye occurs in canonical texts (*Majjhima-nikāya,* I, 380; *Vinaya,* I, 16; *Udāna,* vs. 49, for example), and one notes its applicability to the insight of Upāli, a householder.[18] There are alternative and complementary ways of illustrating the metaphorical eye, the eye of Dhamma. One reads, "'*Dhammacakkhu*' in the sense of vision of the Path of Stream Attainment or Entrance, which is the comprehensive acquisition of the teaching of the four [noble] truths."[19]

*Rūpakāya* and *dhammakāya,* when held together, bring into focus the life and ministry of the Buddha, the latter undergirding the majestic resplendence of the former. The pair, working together, provide a continuity between the religious practices of devotion through ritual and joy of faith *and* the religious attainment of salvific knowledge through insight yielding a clarity and a sense of composure. *Rūpakāya* enables one to visualize through metaphor the just desserts of a singularly virtuous life. *Dhammakāya* suggests the profound basis on which a virtuous life can be established. Both *rūpakāya* and *dhammakāya* bring together into a focal aperture an extremely broad perspective drawn from narratives from the past and stories of the present, teachings remembered and elaborated through the centuries and today. It is only *dhammakāya* that simultaneously and integrally relates Salvific Truth that abides with human words uttered from a perceptive, wise, and undivided heart in such a way that one's thorough penetration of the truth of the words is assured of being fully integrated with that abiding Salvific Truth. *Dhammakāya,* the body of teaching with which one can become engaged, is also that with which the Buddha himself became (*dhammabhūto*), having himself reflected on it in his heart.

There is some hesitance in the Theravāda tradition to append terms or designations for anything that might be sensed as having unchanging ontological reality, as truly, lastingly, statically existent. Having a hesitance in making this move, a quiet continuity in refraining from making it, is not the same as saying there *is* absolutely such an eternally existing, ontological something. It seems that as soon as one makes such an assertion, freedom is, to some degree, curtailed—so Theravāda Buddhists have known for centuries the salvific quality of this freedom to be. Nor is it the same as saying there *is not* a salvific givenness in the order of the universe, one that abides and is not apart from persons and that has become known, revealed. This delicate hesitance is based upon the affirmations of men and women that what was not known before has now become known, both in human history and in personal awareness, and in that knowledge a life-transforming realization has occurred. This is, of course, revelation.[20]

## RELATIONALITY: IN AMIDA BUDDHA

Because Buddhists were on the move sharing a message that enabled men and women to find a supportive orientation to life by introducing them into a context which provided meaning to their existence, arising from a past beyond recall and extending into an unseen future, the Buddhist tradition moved through central Asia along the trade routes into areas we now call China, arriving possibly as early as the first century BCE. As that religious tradition was appropriated by Chinese men and women, as Chinese entered the monastic institution, the tradition, in its cumulative process, changed. It did this because persons in particular life situations responded to that tradition with the creativity of their own minds, drawing upon their own particular life experiences, with the integrity of their own personalities. T'an-luan (476–542; J: Donran) was such a person.

The Jōdo Shinshū tradition holds T'an-luan, considered to have been from the north of China, in highest regard, acknowledging him as the first Chinese patriarch in the lineage of Pure Land masters, even as a revered Bodhisattva.[21] He and other Chinese at the time, it seems, were able to differentiate between the Daoist tradition (C: *dao-chiao*) and the Buddhist tradition (C: *fo-chiao*), or Buddhist learning (C: *fo-hsüeh*). It is said that T'an-luan, having studied with Bodhiruci, a learned master from India, subsequently burned his texts about the

Dao, which he had apparently studied for some years, and committed himself to the Pure Land way.[22]

One of T'an-luan's important contributions was his *Commentary on the Treatise on Birth,* a commentary on *Treatise on the Pure Land* considered a scripture written by one Vasubandhu (approximately 320–400 CE) in India.[23] This commentary, framed by the work attributed to Vasubandhu, has been of considerable influence in the unfolding of the Pure Land tradition in China and also in Japan.[24] It is not our concern here to consider the accuracy of this attribution of Vasubandhu's authorship, the legitimacy of the claim and the original source of the document. Rather, we look for the cumulative significance of this work and the way persons, particularly in the case of T'an-luan, received it, appropriated it, and became engaged in a process of transcending to some degree by means of it. Because T'an-luan was in position to do what he in fact did and, indeed, chose to do, he has contributed to the formation of the ongoing Pure Land tradition.[25] Because of the mode in which he chose to respond, by writing a commentary, and because of his soteriological astuteness—might one say his theological keenness—the Pure Land tradition became differentiated as a distinct Buddhist path in China.[26]

T'an-luan was fully aware of the limits of one's capabilities to apprehend reality completely with concepts forged in the process of ordinary discourse. This had been and continues to be a basic Buddhist insight. At the same time, he was hardly dismayed by this awareness. This orientation continues to be profoundly expressed by religious men and women. He moved constructively through a moment of discerning one's incapacity to comprehend transcendence and chose, instead of recoiling in the presence of transcendence, to respond creatively and, as Smith would suggest, to be enabled to transcend what he had been before. The heritage that he embraced gave him a way of contextualizing the dynamic he was experiencing and his faith led him to respond as he did: brilliantly, insightfully, profoundly, and with lasting consequence.

T'an-luan was well aware of the tradition of the Pure Land and of Amida Buddha, the presiding Buddha of that land. He affirmed that one can enter, be born in, that Pure Land at death. But T'an-luan did more. He carefully considered the Buddha of three-dimensional space-time (Śākyamuni), who lived a life capable of being documented, and the Buddha below and beyond—behind and above—space-time, Amida, both of whom were/are not beyond the possibility of contributing to a transformative realization by means of one's becoming engaged with them in meditation, in repeated reflection. Textual study and the religious imagination are pivotal, but not exhaustive in a consideration of T'an-luan's insight. He could, for example, comprehend the accounts of the life and teachings of Śākyamuni. He could also comprehend his own religious imagination with regard to Amida. But the impressiveness of those teachings and the life of that teacher and the integrative supportiveness of devotion to Amida Buddha were so reassuringly palpable that he realized they were true and real.

He sought to elaborate this relationship. It is to this point that we now turn, and on this point that we recall the Buddha as Theravāda Buddhists have remembered him, of his *identity in relation.* He was who he was, who he became, because of his relationship with, his embodiment of, Salvific Truth of which he taught, which his life demonstrated, and also he is remembered even today as the one who he became because of the relationship men and women have chosen (been enabled?) to have with this living memory and that to which this memory has enabled them to be introduced. With thoroughgoing ramifications Theravāda Buddhists have profoundly affirmed that this was not of their own creation; that the teachings, the mode of living, the realization of Salvific Truth available to them, the identity in relationality of the Buddha, are a gift. It has been revealed to them.

Again, with T'an-luan our key word is *dharmakāya,* a great human concept like others it has been our good fortune to develop in our many languages in our global history: "the truth," "the good," *logos*, faith, love, promise, *shinjin,* Torah, faithful submission (from the Arabic root *slm*: is*lām,* mus*lim*), *Ātman/ Brahman,* and *Dharma/Dhamma*, among others. When Buddhists in India began to search for a term in human speech to communicate the foundational principle that, they realized, stood simultaneously behind speech and extended beyond the reach of conceptuality expressed in human language, they chose brilliantly when they began to focus on a compound term: *dharma* and *kāya, "dharma-body,"* or "body of Dharma," as representing the truth, the fundamental absolute, the final reality, the inexpressible real. They had long known the force of the term *dharma* to refer to the infinitesimal insubstantial reals, to "knowables," as the underlying supportive "conceptuals" that bear, support, or carry (from the Skt: root *dhṛ* "to bear, support") characteristics or marks that the mind, perceptions, and sensations can recognize, which enable one to speak of a world of visibles and knowables that can be perceived and anticipated because of a regular causal process, without requiring a notion of static substantiality or underlying continuing substantial existence. They had also found the depth of meaning in Dharma as "Salvific Truth," as that unto which a young man in India became awakened and hence became worthy of the title of "Awakened One," "Buddha." Men and women became engaged with Salvific Truth by discovering the support (*dhṛ*) provided for their lives in their response to Dharma taught by the Buddha. We have seen the commitment made by persons participating in the Theravāda tradition to the reliable continuity maintained by the Buddha with that which he rediscovered and that which he spoke about his rediscovery, and the way that would lead conscientious persons to it. We saw there how *dharmakāya/dhammakāya* was used as a "bridge concept," as it were, to maintain this soteriological contiguity between the teaching (*dharma*) about Salvific Truth (*Dharma*) as fully rediscovered and as faithfully and adequately put into words by the Buddha.

Exactly when and where, in what century or in what area of India, the use of *dharmakāya* to represent the fundamental absolute reality first occurred is not known, but it became a more frequently utilized term and notion in the relatively early Mahāyāna literature. Certainly the notion was on the scene, discussed, and interrelated with other ideas in writings associated with the Yogacāra school in the fourth century CE. The *"body-notion," kāya,* as we have seen, was frequently applied to the Buddha, as "physical," or "material" body, *rūpakāya,* and, of course, as we have also seen, as *dhammakāya.* We recall the way Theravāda considerations of *dhammakāya* provided a context for analysis of five aggregates that cluster to form the evanescent individual man or woman and, at the same time, how it drew attention to the marvelous physical attributes indicative of the superlative moral virtues possessed by the Buddha. In time, as the centuries passed, reflections on the historical Buddha, the remarkable personage in space-time manifestation, led to his being seen as an apparitional body (Skt: *nirmāṇa-kāya*) of the fundamental salvific reality (*dharmakāya*) the preexistent availability of which enabled there to be a person who became awakened to it in the first place. In meditational exercises, initially espoused particularly in the Yogacāra school, one would aspire to meditative imaging of the glorified or reward or recompense body of the Buddha (Skt: *saṃbhogakāya*), a meaning variously explained as either the body assumed by one as a reward for magnificent virtuousness or a body that can be visualized and enjoyed by one as a reward in the stillness of focal trance-meditation. Again, we see clearly the soteriological continuity being maintained between Salvific Truth, which abides, the appearance of the Buddha in India, and the manifestation of the Buddha in meditative absorption. There were, and are, therefore three bodies of the Buddha (Skt: *tri-kāya*). The continuity is conceptualized not only as "out there," in the order of fundamental reality, but also in meditational awareness in the person himself or herself.

The salvific efficacy was immediate for T'an-luan and entirely sufficient. In order to provide some narrative indication of it, T'an-luan stood within his heritage and presented the relationship between the manifested Buddhas and Bodhisattvas together with the manifested Buddha Lands, all forming a part of the Mahāyāna Buddhist soteriological world view, and the inexpressible ultimate reality symbolized in the term *dharmakāya.* T'an-luan writes about interpenetration of the two dimensions of reality: *dharmakāya* as suchness (J: *hosshin*) and *dharmakāya* as compassionate means (J: *hōben hosshin*).[27] He introduces his comments in the context of analyzing the elaborate adornments of the Pure Land and the qualities of the Buddhas and Bodhisattvas and the relationship of this elaborateness with the fundamental reality. He notes that these two dimensions of Salvific Truth, the inexpressible incomprehensible suchness, various adornments of Buddhas, Bodhisattvas, and Buddha Lands, interpenetrate, that there is a reciprocal, interdependent mutuality. Why is this so? T'an-luan writes,

> Because all Buddhas and bodhisattvas have dharma-bodies of two dimensions:[28] dharma-body as suchness and dharma-body as compassionate means. Dharma-body as compassionate means arises from

> dharma-body as suchness,[29] and dharma-body as suchness emerges out of dharma-body as compassionate means.[30] These two dimensions of dharma-body differ but are not separable;[31] they are one,[32] but cannot be regarded as identical.[33] Thus, extensive and brief interpenetrate[34] and together are termed 'dharma.' If bodhisattvas do not realize that extensive and brief interpenetrate, they are incapable of self-benefit and benefiting others.[35]

Shinran (1173–1263), as we have seen, lived within a received tradition and responded creatively to his awareness of the truth which that tradition enabled him to apprehend. He also did not inherit an orientation to space-time-causal sequence, what the West tends to call history, that found in this notion the fundamental criterion for either establishing or arguing for reality; what others have stressed as "historical reality." This does not at all mean that Shinran was not engaged with what is true and real. He, like T'an-luan, was certain that he was so engaged, and the testimony through time indicates that he was. Shinran was concerned with what theologians from all religious traditions have been concerned; namely, how to give expression to the inexpressible, how symbolically to begin to conceptualize that which ultimately exceeds, extends beyond, all human concepts. At the same time, existentially, Shinran entertained the notion of *dharmakāya* with a qualitative discernment, an insight into the compassionate nature of reality as made known to him through the presence of Amida Buddha in his awareness. He discovered in his own life and in the order of the world around him the soteriological givenness in the order of things. He wrote of the *dharmakāya* that is characterized by its own nature (Skt: *dharmatā-dharmakāya*; J: *hosshō-hosshin*), *dharmakāya* that is the foundation for the patterned process of causality and consequentiality, that which enables things to be just-as-they-have-become-ness and also to be just-as-they-are-ness. This grand phrase, *dharmatā-dharmakāya*, is more customarily translated as "Dharma-body as suchness"[36] or as "Dharma-body of Dharma-nature."[37] This notion, of course, is considerably abstract and extraordinarily difficult to express adequately. But there is a dimension to all of this which is just as remarkable. *Dharmakāya,* which itself is without both form *and* formlessness, of itself manifests itself in form as Amida Buddha. In the form of Amida Buddha, this reality, this *dharmakāya* is called *dharmakāya* as compassionate means.

Shinran creatively appropriated T'an-luan's insight regarding the two kinds of *dharmakāya,* identifying Amida with the *dharmakāya* of compassionate means and affirming its inseparable mutual interpenetrationality with *dharmakāya* as suchness, the fundamental, true reality.[38] The Jōdo Shinshū tradition continues to maintain this insight into the salvific order of reality. We see this in the English introduction to *The Jōdo Wasan—The Hymns on the Pure Land* (*RTS*) where the translators comment on the bodies with which we began this segment noting that "The unmanifested, formless, personal embodiment of the Truth is 'Dharma-body' (*dharmakāya*), and the manifested embodiments are the 'Recompensed or Rewarded Body' (*saṃbhoghakāya*; also known as 'Enjoyment Body') *and* [emphasis added] the 'Transformed Body' (*nirmāṇakāya*)." These Buddhist scholars state, "The essential characteristic of the Pure Land is Dharma-nature itself (the Land of Dharma-nature), but it is often described in the sūtras as a land glorified with various meritorious adornments."[39] One sees clearly the parallelism with the Theravāda interpretation of the *dhammakāya* and the glorified body, a metaphorical example of virtuous living, the *rūpakāya*, of the Buddha.

Dennis Hirota provides a summation of the dynamic at work in Shinran's understanding of the relationship of true reality and Amida together with the Pure Land. The observation is sufficiently pivotal that I quote it at some length.

> Although Tathagata, or true reality, is said to pervade all beings, since it completely transcends the conceptualization of human intellect, ordinarily it lies beyond our awareness; its presence therefore holds no significance for our existence. As long as we remain ignorant of it, our delusional attachments bind us solely to samsaric life. Thus, the idea of immanence in the teleological structure is balanced by a movement toward beings, which is formulated as an interpersonal element of self-revelation.
>
> > "Dharma-body as suchness has neither color nor form; thus, the mind cannot grasp it nor words describe it. From this oneness was manifested form, called dharma-body as compassionate means. Taking this form, the Buddha announced the name Bhiksu Dharmakara and established the Forty-eight great Vows that surpass conceptual understanding" [Hirota is quoting from *Notes on Essentials* (*SBTS*)].
>
> Here, form emerges in self-revelatory activity directed to ignorant beings. It is through Amida's arising from formless reality and the self-revelation of Amida to beings that Buddha-nature can manifest itself in them as the entrusting of themselves to the Vow. Formless reality cannot simply unfold itself in beings; *its emergence takes place only through provision for an apprehension of itself as personal. Beings' attainment of shinjin, then, represents a movement of reality toward beings.* Further, while it is not beings' will to reach the transcendent, this attainment of shinjin harbors their natural and necessary movement towards awakening to reality. (emphasis added)[40]

Hirota has continued to elaborate the salvific engagement to which Shinran draws our attention. He writes of "Truth as Dialogic Event and Authentic Life in Shinran," and points out several dimensions involved in Shinran's understanding of truth: that truth is not primarily propositional, that truth is reality itself, and at the same time truth "does stand in relation to understanding and does take the form of words"; that truth as true reality arises from "the deepest samadhi, which is itself true reality—the 'dharma most rare and wondrous' or the 'abode of all buddhas'"; that truth is "not a matter of correspondence or coherence"; that truth does not rest on the authority of the Buddha, and that upon *shinjin* becoming established one is grounded in the reality which verbal expressions attempt to communicate.[41] Of course, one is reminded of so many parallels with Theravāda affirmations, with perhaps one difference: namely, that there the teachings are true in internal coherence and also in correspondence to the way things are, that is, to the way things have become. With the arising of the path realization, *magga,* one is established in the reality which verbal expressions attempt to communicate.[42] We see in Hirota's observation the integral relation of a salvific realization (*shinjin*) with the compassionate order of the universe inseparably grounded on/in ultimate reality. For Jōdo Shinshū men and women, Amida's identity is discovered in relationality in revelation; inseparably with ultimate reality and so also within the human heart.

In another study,[43] Hirota speaks of this revelation as "the emerging into form—into the realm of words and concepts—of the formless and timeless. In other words, it is event. In terms of language, it is clothed as narrative."[44] Following a suggestion by Karl Barth, Hirota makes an important contribution to our understanding of Shinran, and, in the context of this present study, of the Theravāda and Christian cases, too. Quoting Barth, "He unveils Himself as the one He is by veiling Himself in a form which He Himself is not," Hirota states with insight, "Perhaps the genuine hiddenness of the transcendent must rather be revealed to human beings, as an aspect of the unveiling itself."[45]

Hirota makes an advance on current limitations in mutual understanding among Jōdo Shinshū Buddhists and Christians who have drawn fundamental distinctions between reality quotients in myth and history, variously conceived. Hirota writes,

> Of course, it may be asserted that Śākyamuni and Jesus were historical while Dharmākara-Amida is from the beginning transhistorical (mythic), but surely what is most important for Buddhists and Christians is their double nature of comprehensibility and hiddenness.[46]

## RELATIONALITY: THE CHRIST

How does one establish conceptually the ineradicable soteriological continuity between the reality of one's religious realization and the salvific efficacy of engagement with transcendence? One can speak of the embodiment of Dharma in the *dharmakāya* of the historical Buddha Śākyamuni, as we have seen. One can affirm this confirmed contiguity as T'an-luan and Shinran did in their responses to the salvific activity of Amida Buddha as a compassionate, inseparable, interdependent dimension of absolute reality, as *dharmakāya* as compassionate means and *dharmakāya* as suchness. In the Christian cumulative tradition, the relatively early church fathers met a comparable issue.[47] Working with texts discovered to be scripture,[48] they sought diligently to give expression to teachings and testimonies recorded in the Bible, particularly in what came to be called the New Testament, in a way that was both inclusive and consistent. In all three religious communities in our considerations here, we see a similarity in structure rather than identity in statement. We need to see this clearly: our three communities were not affirming the same thing as much as demonstrating similar responses to a comparable issue—identity in soteriological relation.

Of course, were one to say that the Buddha was only a teacher who wandered in a relatively small area in India, that Amida is merely a myth, in an ill-informed sense of "myth," and that Jesus was deified by a marginalized cultic group in the eastern Mediterranean basin, one would be working with an extraordinarily narrow and entirely inadequate sense of how one is to understand the establishment of identity, especially of figures such as these. If one were to assert that one understood the identity of the Buddha, Amida Buddha, and the Christ, working solely with this narrow, restrictive, and reductive sense of identity, obviously one would not grasp the significance of the collective continuity of the memory of men and women over centuries nor would one understand the transformative quality of engagement with transcendence in the lives of men and women made possible by the Buddha, Amida Buddha, and the Christ. It is on this level, one more foundational and one also more inclusive, that we see clearly the way men and women participating in religious traditions affirm the soteriological relationality in the religious life both in the past and today.

Perhaps I should distinguish between my use of relationality and a notion of centrality. From a Christian perspective, in issues of religious pluralism one hears that one is to hold to the "centrality of Christ." This position is clear and, when held with humility, is impressive and from it we can learn a great deal. But it works with an inadequate spatial metaphor, that is to say, having all human issues, aspirations, hopes, in all cultures and languages, of all times, revolve around Christ—and hence we have a notion of the Christian fulfilment of human seeking, of inclusivist religious interpretations, even, among fewer and fewer perhaps, exclusivist interpretations. I find, rather, that Christ is relational, which is to say that for one who has somehow been enabled to view the world with the salvific activity of God in the Christ-event *at the center of one's life,* even today, one, again somehow, thereby is enabled to *relate* with insight and sympathy, with understanding and cheerful humaneness, to the presence of men and women of faith participating in other religious traditions around the globe and here at home.

Let us turn to the great lights, impressive theologians all, of the relatively early Christian Church, particularly, in the period we are considering, of the so-called Eastern Church, those who wrote in Greek, who hailed from places such as Alexandria, Jerusalem, Antioch, Nicaea, Chalcedon, Ephesus, Constantinople—all places not uninfluenced by the Roman Empire. These thinkers were aware of the contributions from Athens, and, of course, of Rome. I note, however, yet significantly, that these persons were unaware of Varanāsi (Benares), Nālanda, Anurādhapura, T'ien-t'ai, and other important places on our globe where religious thinkers were putting their minds to questions of religious truth in centers of cultural grandeur.

We will consider briefly the first three councils: Nicaea (Nicaea I, AD 325), Constantinople (Constantinople I, AD 381), and Chalcedon (AD 451).[49]

Some have said that Nicaea provides an example of the Hellenization of a simpler Jewish-influenced religious movement. The crosscurrents of the intellectual milieu and the multifaceted cultural impingements of the Greek-reading intelligentsia of the eastern Mediterranean area and also of the Latin-reading intelligentsia of the western Mediterranean area were so variegated, multileveled, complex, and intermingled in the third and fourth centuries that it is difficult to isolate something called "Hellenization" as influencing either positively or negatively the thinking of the theologians at Nicaea. If there is any interplay between Greek assumptions operating at the councils in considering New Testament records, the council of Nicaea represents more a *response* to customary Hellenic assumptions.[50] There are historical sociopolitical circumstances of the period contributing to the formation of these councils that, although of considerable importance in gaining a fuller understanding of what was developing at the time both theologically and institutionally, and the consequences through the history of the church, exceed the scope of our present concern.

The origin of the core of the creed later formed at Nicaea existed previously in Jerusalem and was also utilized in the baptismal formula of Caesarea.[51] The affirmation of faith as expressed by the Council of Nicaea (AD 325) reads,

> The profession of faith of the 318 fathers. We believe in one God the Father all powerful, maker of all things both seen and unseen. And in one Lord Jesus Christ, the Son of God, the only-begotten begotten from the Father, that is from the substance of the Father [*ek tēs ousias tou patros* / ἐκ τῆς οὐσίας τοὺ πατρός/*est de substantia patris*], God from God, light from light, true God from true God, begotten not made, consubstantial with the Father [*homoousion tō patri* / ὁμοούσιον τῷ πατρι/*unius substantiae cum patre (quod Graeci dicunt homousion)*], through whom all things came to be, both those in heaven and those on earth; for us humans and for our salvation he came down and became incarnate, became human [*sarxōthenta evanthrōpēsanta* / σαρχωθέντα, ἐνανθρωπήσαντα/*incarnatus est, homo factus est*], suffered and rose up on the third day, went up into the heavens, is coming to judge the living and the dead. And in the holy Spirit.[52]

In AD 381, at the Council of Constantinople, some revision of the earlier Nicaean creed was made, later to be adopted by the council at Chalcedon (AD

451). The relevant passages, for our purposes, from the formulation of the AD 381 creed read,

> We believe in one God the Father. . . . And in one Lord Jesus Christ, the only-begotten Son of God . . . consubstantial with the Father [*homoousion tō patri* / ὁμοούσιον τῷ πατρί / *hoc est eiusdem cum patre substantiae*] . . . became incarnate from the holy Spirit and the virgin Mary, became human. . . .[53]

We turn, finally, to the Council of Chalcedon (AD 451) with its extended formulation regarding Christ.

> So, following the saintly fathers, we all with one voice teach the confession of one and the same Son, our Lord Jesus Christ: the same perfect in divinity and perfect in humanity, the same truly God and truly man [*theon alēthōs kai anthrōpon alēthōs* / θεὸν ἀληθῶς χαί ανθρωπον ἀληθῶς / *Deum vere et hominem vere*], of a rational soul and body [*psuchēs logikēs kai sōmatos* / ψυχῆς λογιχῆς χαί σώματος / *anima rationali et corpore*] consubstantial with the Father [*homoousion tō patri* / ὁμοούσιον τῶ πατρί/*consubstantialem patri*] as regards his divinity, and the same consubstantial with us [*homoousion ēmin* / ὁμοούσιον *ἡμ ῖν/consubstantialem nobis*]; like us in all respects except for sin; begotten before the ages from the Father as regards his divinity, and in the last days the same for us and for our salvation from Mary, the virgin God-bearer, as regards his humanity [*anthrōpotēta* ἀνθρωπότητα / *humanitatem*]; one and the same Christ, Son, Lord, only-begotten, acknowledged in two natures which undergo no confusion, no change, no division, no separation [*en duo phusesin asugchutōs, atreptōs adiairetōs, achoristōs* / ἐν δύο φύσεσιν ἀσυγχύτως, ἀτρέπτως, ἀδιαιρέτως, ἀχωρίστως / *in duabus naturis inconfuse, immutabiliter, indivise, inseparabiliter*]; at no point was the difference between the natures taken away through the union, but rather the property of both natures is preserved and comes together into a single person and a single subsistent being [*hen prosōpon mian upostasin suntrechousēs* / ἕν πρόσωπον μίαν ὑπόστασιν συντρεχούσης / *in unam personam atque subsistentiam concurrente*]; he is not parted or divided into two persons, but is one and the same only-begotten Son, God, Word, Lord Jesus Christ, just as the prophets taught from the beginning.[54]

Given the not altogether consistent record of the Gospels, the various emphases in other New Testament records, the challenging theological task of integrating the heritage from the Old Testament and the Jewish witness, the pressing task of continuing the support of others in a developing community, the institutional adjustments in complex sociocultural and political settings, and the number of bright minds applying themselves with integrity[55] to the issue we are considering, the early councils preserve for us today the converging of faith and wisdom, of loyalty to a received tradition and faithfulness to a corporate witness to Jesus, the Christ. Indeed, it is not difficult to see the process leading to and from these early councils as cumulative: other thinkers on the scene at the time, now held by some as heretics, were also offering their opinions, which, though not accepted at the councils, nevertheless contributed to the shaping of the thinking of the participants of those councils in the formulation of their responses to those opinions, and consequently of the ongoing tradition.

The participants in these councils were struggling with a familiar problem of how to give expression to the extraordinary in ordinary language, how to bring into focus concepts beyond the range of language by the use of language forged in customary spatiotemporal discourse. The magnitude of scholarship that has addressed these councils, the currents that led up to them, and the subsequent streams of theological understanding that have come from them is truly formidable, much too massive even remotely to summarize in our consideration. A few observations might be offered, however.

*Relationality*; *Identity in Relation*; *Perichōrēsis*. These interrelated ideas run dramatically through the notion of the Trinity, as they do through so many other dimensions of human understanding—the importance of community in personal fulfillment, of becoming fully a person; the significance of the other who calls one out from oneself into who one truly is, in relationship; the sense of continuity so important in mental health and self-understanding whereby one's past is related to one's present and to one's future; the capacity for thought and for language.

Central in the understanding of Christ in the Trinity is the way this figure contributes to the formation of relationality of the Father and the Holy Sprit; how, too, this figure itself finds its identity in this relation and how, once formed, once seen, contributes to the interpenetrative relationality of the Trinity itself. That one can speak of the Trinity not only as a fourth- and fifth-century doctrine hammered out in a relatively small area of our globe, as an interpretation of God affirmed century by century not without significant contributions by impressive thinkers, such as Gregory Nazianzus in the fourth century and John of Damascus in the eighth century,[56] but also as a continuing response to transcendence cherished today by perhaps a quarter of the world's population, speaks of another crucial sense of relation, without which, of course, the notion of the Trinity might have long ago become forgotten. We see this in our time, for example, in the writing of the late Colin Gunton, a perceptive Christian theologian who addressed the dislocation and estrangement of a so-called postmodern world[57] with keen theological imagination by drawing attention to "a conception of God who is both one and three, whose being consists in a relationality that derives from the otherness-in-relation of Father, Son and Spirit."[58] Gunton introduced what he called "open transcendentals" into theological discourse because, he suggests, as "finite and fallible human beings, should we not rather seek for a concept of truth that is appropriate to our limits, both in capacity and in time and space? For something that can be believed short of absolute certainty?"[59] Gunton seeks, in his notion of an "open transcendental,"

> to find concepts which do succeed in some way or other in representing or echoing the universal marks of being. . . . [T]o find concepts whose value will be found not primarily in their clarity and certainty, but in their suggestiveness and potentiality for being deepened and enriched, during the continuing process of thought, from a wide range of sources in human life and cultures.[60]

Gunton finds in the idea of *perichōrēsis* one such "open transcendental." "The central point about the concept is that it enables theology to preserve both the one and the many in dynamic interrelation. It implies that the three persons of the Trinity exist only in reciprocal eternal relatedness. God is not God apart from the way in which Father, Son and Spirit in eternity give to and receive from each other what they essentially are."[61]

Thomas F. Torrance refers to *perichōrēsis* as "a refined form of thought which helps us to develop a careful theological way of interpreting the biblical teaching about the mutual indwelling of the Father and the Son and the Spirit and thus about the Communion of the Spirit." He continues,

> It indicates a sort of mutual containing or enveloping of realities, which we also speak of as *coinherence* or *coindwelling*. This concept in a verbal form was first used by Gregory Nazianzen to help express the way in which the divine and the human natures in the one Person of Christ coinhere in one another without the integrity of either being diminished by the presence of the other. It was then applied to speak of the way in which the three divine Persons mutually dwell in one another and coinhere or inexist in one another while nevertheless remaining other than one another and distinct from one another.[62]

Gunton builds on this perichoretic view of the Trinity and from this view offers an invitation to "begin to explore whether reality is on all its levels 'perichoretic', a dynamism of relatedness."[63] Gunton, with insight into a fundamental Christian theological perspective on life in the world, unwittingly offers a kind of ontologically based Christian complementarity to the grand insight of Buddhists, namely "dependent co-production," or "dependent-origination," *pratītyasamutpāda*. Gunton writes of perichoretic reciprocity,

> it also involves accepting gladly the limitations of being perichoretically bound up with other human beings and the non-personal universe.

> Such limitations are both spatial and temporal. There is not true freedom which does not also allow for the fact that we are passive as well as active in relation to others and the world: we are what we are in perichoretic reciprocity.[64]

## PERICHORETIC RELATIONALITY

We have considered three examples of how persons have sought to give expression to their awareness of soteriological realizations and the relationality of those realizations with transcendence, in their becoming engaged in the process of transcending, and in doing so have developed similar structures for conceptuality. Of particular interest has been the presence of the idea of relationality and of identity in relation. We have seen how one's relation to Salvific Truth is given focus through the relation of the Buddha with the Salvific Truth that he rediscovered, becoming so holistically engaged with that Salvific Truth that that relationship and his articulation of the supportive way leading to that Salvific Truth converge in one magnificent human life. We have found wherein one's relationship with Amida Buddha is grounded in *shinjin,* which is Amida's mind given to one, and which is not separable (cf. Grk: *achōristōs*) from fundamental, absolute, indescribable reality, becoming inseparably and soteriologically a part of one, just as one is. So also, one's relation with God in Christ is not dissociated from engagement with the Holy Spirit: Trinity.

*Perichōrēsis,* a Christian theological concept, initially formulated in the Greek Church becoming known farther west by the twelfth century or so, formulated by persons not at all aware of the scope of our consideration, suggestively developed by a contemporary theologian writing with singular focus on the West, with but few passages indicating an awareness that the Christian tradition remains a minority movement in our human history, can be a helpful way of carrying forward from our commonality of conceptual structures, which we have just reviewed among Theravāda, Jōdo Shinshū Buddhists, and Christians, to a consideration to the future of our global religious colloquia.

We can extend Gunton's observation about *perichōrēsis* for today, as it were. As we reflect upon ourselves as Buddhists and Christians living daily into our common future, we, like others before us, live our lives looking forward into what is to come but as yet remains unknown. Rather than standing flat-footed looking backward to isolated, separable strands of differentiated historical traditions, we will prepare ourselves best for the days ahead if we turn ourselves, intellectually shift our perspective, to building for our tomorrow. In doing so, we bring from our past our distinctiveness, of course, but recognizing that insofar as it is from our past it is from our one human past on this globe, and in so recognizing our common past we will be more keenly prepared to discover how our traditions have not been as neatly differentiated in their development as we first had thought.

Through our colloquia, which only the obstinate would choose to abandon—a consequence of bias, whether of religious intolerance or of intellectual assumptions gone awry in an unself-conscious claim of objectivity—we might all, Buddhist, Christian, Hindu, Muslim, Jewish, and others, enter an awareness of our religious *perichōrēsis*. We will become what we each will become as we realize our common religious history and the creative in-existence, dynamic co-inherence, insights from different yet human perspectives on engagement with transcendence, which contribute to greater understanding leading to the formation of community among persons around the world. To paraphrase Gunton, we will become what we will become in perichoretic reciprocity.

The idea of interreligious perichoretic reciprocity among persons of faith can provide a conceptual structure or paradigm by which we can move beyond the notion of religious pluralism, which notion tends to mean merely that there are many religious traditions around the world and so they are and will be. One might seek to construct a theology or worldview that incorporates religious pluralism in this sense and attempt to construct a coherent interpretation. But one wonders whether this does not itself represent one perspective only and will tend to move us forward to greater understanding only insofar as persons adopt this particular perspective. Is there an alternative, one that recognizes the variety of ways religious persons around the globe have expressed their religiousness and, at the same time, maintains an open future to be constructed by men and women participating in these different religious traditions with a degree of self-consciousness that would enable them to discern the commonality, in large measure, of the personal, genuinely human quality of faith?

Perichoretic reciprocity that recognizes in us all the role that relationality has had in our religious awareness—involvement with others whom we have come to respect and response to transcendence both beyond our lives and in our lives—can provide an orientation to oneself, to one's community, one's heritage, and others of us in different religious traditions in our one human history. Acknowledging the availability of Salvific Truth that abides and to which persons have responded variously by discovering the relationality of the modes of apprehension to that salvific reality, and simultaneously to the relationality of persons throughout the centuries and around the globe, and also acknowledging the role of relationality in one's finding one's identity, enables one to see clearly the role transcendence and other persons, past and present, have played in one's own life and in the lives of men and women through the centuries and around the world.

If one recognizes perichoretic relationality in one's own religious pilgrimage and celebrates the supportiveness this awareness provides, one has found the reason for extending this structure of interpretation to include persons who have perpetuated the great religious traditions, which have contributed enormously to humanity's understanding of itself. From this perspective one might say that the day will come when Buddhists and Christians, through colloquia, will participate in the religious heritage of each other (which to a considerable degree scholars in comparative studies are already doing to the extent that they make their work known to persons of the religious traditions being studied), contributing to an increasingly common future without losing the formative qualitative experiences they each have received through their own religious heritage.

Of course, doctrinal formulations, rituals, and worldviews differ. We would expect this, of course, as these great traditions have developed in different parts of the world. But the world in which they have developed is one world and the worldviews are nevertheless views of one world; it has always been so. We have just not seen it. And speaking metaphorically of "different worlds" has not helped the situation. It is possible that a Buddhist and a Christian can participate in each other's religious lives, as Buddhist and Christian, each helping the other to find new insights and greater understanding of himself or herself and of this world without ceasing to be a Buddhist or a Christian. Such relationality in perichoretic reciprocity would mean that assisting a Buddhist to become a better Buddhist would be a Christian thing to do. So also, assisting a Christian to become a better Christian would be a Buddhist thing to do. And the day might come when a co-inherence or co-indwelling of distinguishable but not fundamentally different religious traditions will occur because persons have come to discern the faith of persons, arisen in relation, which provides the enduring basis for a relationality of perichoretic reciprocity.

In the final analysis, "*Not I*" the voices of men and women participating in our three great religious movements have been saying for centuries. At the limit of possible human action, at the falling away of all calculation, entirely, at the moment of radical honesty, informed variously by the conceptualizations and customary practices passed down through traditions while simultaneously breaking through the form of those concepts at a moment of creative receptivity, one discerns where one becomes engaged in the process of transcending which is a salvific realization. We speak of this occurrence as arising of the path (*magga*), one's first glimpse of Nibbāna/Nirvāṇa, as the arising of *shinjin,* the Buddha-mind, as the presence of God: Spirit, Son, and Father.

To become aware of our mutual responses to transcendence in relationality of perichoretic reciprocity and to be supportive of each other in this religious awareness is not at all to say that the salvific realizations cherished by men and women of the different religious traditions are the same. Our task is much more modest in its focus on religious awareness and not on salvific realization itself. Yet even to continue in this task will require all the virtues we, all of us, have learned from these religious heritages and also from the academic tradition at its best: responses to Salvific Truth, certainly, and patience, intelligence, faithfulness, loyalty, truthfulness, and, of course, love.

# IV

# Building from Our Past into Our Common Future

# 13

# From Controversy to Understanding

## *More than a Century of Progress*

*From our more theoretical considerations we now move to an on-site test case, to an occasion that shows what we have done in Sri Lanka, how we have managed to move to greater interreligious understanding and to work together to move from misapprehensions of each other to an awareness of our mutually recognized religiousness. It has taken more than a century, but the process has been both steady and promising.*

The process whereby persons, at the depths of their religiousness, seek to understand other persons, also at the depths of their religiousness, is not an inevitable process in human history. It is under way today, happily one can report. In chapter 1 we drew attention to a Baptist speaking openly about matters of faith among Japanese Buddhists in recent years, and suggested that such would not have been likely a century earlier. Later, in our chapter 17, we will focus more precisely on Buddhists and Baptists, particularly with reference to Sri Lanka. The particular case of Sri Lanka over the last century until now is fascinating and highly instructive in helping us to become self-conscious of issues in our inquiry, of its recent nature, and of the exhilarating possibilities before us.

The month of August, the eight month of the year, the month so designated in honor of Augustus Caesar, has been an important month in the history of Sri Lanka. That we in Sri Lanka can today designate a period of time as "August," that the related system for structuring a calendar is accepted and in wide use in this country, is noteworthy in itself. However, that to which the "month of August" refers is also known as the fifth or sixth month of the year (*nikiṇi-masaya*: July-August or *binara-masaya*: August-September) for those of us who have been nurtured in the Sinhala heritage.

Calendars, concepts that represent consensus about a way to reckon time, can be divisive in human relationships. Though such a consensus has been a requirement for the formation of complex civilizations—indeed, as civilizations have intermeshed in the past so have calendars—calendars, in the intermeshing of civilizations, on occasion, have collided. The seasons have meant a great deal to us, their comings and goings—again and again. We have tried our hand at reckonings: the Babylonians and ancient Egyptians had their systems; so too have the Jews, the Christians,[1] and the Muslims; so, too, of course, Buddhists. And we have differed in our decisions about starting points in the reckoning of time.[2]

Although we have had some difficulty reaching precision in measuring what we call time, although starting points have varied, although we have calculated yearly sequences variously and have divided those units of time differently—some according to a solar year and some according to a lunar year—the units, we have come to learn, refer to one event: the orbiting of the earth and its satellite moon around the sun. The phenomenon, the appearance, has yielded itself to another interpretation, one familiar in human history, one not altogether placed aside—the period in which the sun apparently passes through the twelve signs of the zodiac, a period of reckoning reinforced by the recurrence of the seasons. We have seen "sunrise" and "sunset," and most of us would agree have been the better for it, although we know now that the sun neither rises nor sets. Yet, I suppose, we will not soon find alternative, more immediately communicative, ways of expressing these human experiences in English.

That we today classify the days, months, and years as we do in Sri Lanka is obviously not an automatic occurrence, is not inevitable. That we have two New Year observances—one according to the "Western calendar" and the other according to age-old custom—might strike a non-Jewish Westerner as a bit novel. Two ways of reckoning time have been adopted in Sri Lanka, without the one negating the other.[3] The earth revolves, time passes; we are born, we live, grow old, and die; we celebrate the process, the rains, the seasons, and we discern meaning in it all. We are earthlings all—yet through our various modes of appropriating meaning we are human also.

What has occurred in the "month of August"—a valid measure of time in Sri Lanka for all that—is significant in the history of this country, not primarily because of the colorful pageant of the *äsala perahära* in Kandy, although some have found this festive occasion to present afresh, annually, much that instills pride in the Sinhala cultural heritage. August has been a month in which events indicative of change, in some cases divisive, in some cases rejuvenative, incipiently discernible or manifestly, have occurred. It was in August 1750—the year in which Johann Sebastian Bach died—that a third delegation of Buddhists left for Thailand (Siam) successfully to arrange for the reestablishment of higher ordination (*upasampadā*) of what came to be known as the Siam monastic lineage, *Siam-nikāya* in Sri Lanka.[4] It was in August, too, and this time in 1812—a year that witnessed the United States and Great Britain at war, that saw Napoleon invade Russia—that the Colombo Auxiliary Bible Society, representing the British and Foreign Bible Society, was organized to revive a practice, begun in Sri Lanka by the Dutch, of printing Christian religious literature. And later other denominations came and established their presses producing publications that tended, unfortunately, to move from a concern to nurture the local Christian community to polemical triumphalism, to the launching of an assault against others.

In 1862, in August—a month after Abraham Lincoln read to his cabinet a draft of what came to be called the Emancipation Proclamation, one year before Karl Marx established in London the First International (his International Workingmen's Association), seven years before a major Vatican Council, less than ten years after Japan again became receptive to the West—a group of Buddhist monks, having received the higher ordination in Myanmar (Burma), arrived in Sri Lanka setting the scene for the later development of the *Rāmañña-nikāya,* Rāmañña monastic lineage, in this country.

This month has recorded periods of change through a little more than a century of our history: persons from Thailand (Siam), Myanmar (Burma), Holland, and Great Britain and elsewhere have been a part of the history of persons in Sri Lanka; and this interaction was occurring in a world filled with vision and blindness, with promise of human community and dignity of persons alongside military campaigns and polemics.

Still other significant events have occurred in August. Two are particularly instructive when placed in juxtaposition; two events of note, one well known, the other less so but no less instructive.

## AN EVENT IN AUGUST 1873: *VĀDAYA*—DEBATE; AN ISSUE OF CONTROVERSY

We humans have debated—there is little novel in this observation. We have engaged in discussions on controversial issues, have begun to move through a process of understanding called dialogue into an era of mutual understanding through colloquia. Rarely have debates, however, led beyond clarification of the major issues to resolution of fundamental problems of misunderstanding. Points are given, applause and cheers are received in debates; but it is colloquia, not debates, that render reflection and deepening discernment.

A little more than 139 years ago in Sri Lanka, persons were engaged in debate; excitedly involved, ironically as one today might judge, in arguing about which of two received traditions, the Christian or the Buddhist, expressed more convincingly messages of good news. Two magnificently impressive religious traditions had become catechisms, and catechisms collide. Religious heritages that espoused the gentleness and virtue of humility had become systems that made claims, and claims, especially those of superiority, conflict. Traditions that had been passed on from generation to generation because persons had found a liberating quality of human life in relinquishing inordinate desire, had become institutions, and institutions have vested interests. Some of us were aggressive, less than humanely sensitive, in those days. Others of us felt threatened, were defensive. Positions moved from being pastoral within the Christian and Buddhist communities to apologetic between the two, to polemical against each other. In polemics, poles are clearly drawn and set apart. And when people from separate camps engage in persistent argument tendentious tribalism tends to emerge.

Drawing our attention again to a time of debates a century or so ago might suggest that the period was one only of controversy, but as the historical record becomes more fully known, I should think, one will come to learn that the argumentativeness was not countrywide, that only sections within the leadership were primarily involved. The debates were indicative of a spirit of the times, however, among those who were active in the public arena in which attempts to shape popular opinion occurred.

The records unfold a decade of debate—through a written exchange of questions and response, point/counterpoint, at Baddēgama, in 1865; a debate in public forum at Udanviṭa, in 1866; at Gampola, in 1871, to the more frequently recalled debate at Pānadura, on August 26 and 28, 1873. In reading accounts of these debates, one is struck by the frequency of occurrence of militaristic language; phrases containing words such as "weapons," "strategy," "attack," and "enemy." Monolithic, reified, conceptualized giants had collided; something, as it were, called "Christianity" was challenging and being threatened by something called "Buddhism."[5] At Pānadura, persons spoke of the untrueness of Buddhism (*buddhāgamē asatyakama*). Others said that Christianity was a deceitful religion (*boru āgamak*), and they apparently did so with enthusiasm.[6]

Argumentative assaults were mounted, lines were drawn, defenses structured, counteroffenses designed—and a pattern became established; the mirror image of conflict, to become more like that which is thought to be the adversary. But the matter becomes more complicated when success becomes measured through conflict. The mirror image intentionally distorts, the purpose being to present an image that only apparently represents the case while searching behind the scene for another position, an unanticipated posture. Victorious military strategists excel in this, and, it would appear, not a few persons within some strands of the Christian community and a few among segments of the Buddhist community were becoming familiar with such tactics.

A great deal has happened in the years since the Pānadura debate of August 1873.

Gradually, not without disappointing setbacks ensuing from a spectrum of misdirected motivation, outright aggressiveness, fundamental misunderstanding, Christians no longer continued to build for the destruction of "Buddhism," and Buddhists no longer sensed a threatening, politically aligned institutional oppressiveness. Yes, things have changed since that event in Pānadura; political hegemony stemming from the European sociocultural ensembles of Holland and Great Britain have come and gone. Independence is in hand. Democratic socialist political ideology and political realism have provided the citizenry with legitimate modes of self-expression. Different programs for structuring the educational system of the country have been attempted; greater social mobility is noted in an increasing population. Major international events have been held in the country, and international organizations tend regularly to take seriously the opinions of the Sri Lankan political leadership. Major attempts have been made by the government, by private organizations and institutes, on large and small scales, to assist in the development of persons and infrastructures. Also in this interval we have witnessed bitter communalism, with periodic eruptions of unanticipated ferocity, staccato flashes of a disruptive insurgency with consequent wrenching pain and suffering.

Since the 1970s, the fighting in Sri Lanka has become steadily more widespread, more technologically sophisticated, more deadly. A prolonged and bewilderingly violent separatist movement that has relentlessly chafed sensibilities with daily accounts of death and destruction has led some to the borders of quiet despair and others to a functional callousness. Since the 1980s, a Tamil military force with tenacity and advanced weaponry maintained a vicious conflict with government troops and police, both Sinhalas and Tamils. People no longer had faces and names; they were labeled "Tigers" who sought for an independent "Tamil Homeland," Tamil Elaam, on the one hand, and "the Government," which sought to maintain the political integrity of one nation, on the other. Mothers and fathers know better than this; these men and women were sons and daughters with personal names, and their deaths brought great sadness not only to the persons who knew them. For nearly three decades, fighting continued. Massacres were perpetrated on both sides. Bodies of Tamil young people were found in cities and in jungle. Approximately one hundred and fifty people, mostly Sinhala, were massacred while visiting a sacred site in Anurādhapura. And the war continued, in jungle, in outlying cities, and in the capitol of Colombo. In the years since this fighting began, more than seven hundred thousand sons and daughters of Sri Lanka have been killed.

The assassination of a brilliant Tamil lawyer, a personal friend, a Hindu, with a law degree from Harvard and a fellowship awarded to Yale, a member of Parliament in Sri Lanka, a promising spokesman for Tamil aspirations and a beacon for Sinhala understanding, a husband and father, was deeply disturbing. No less disturbing, personally, was the assassination at a political rally of a very promising Sinhala politician, a Buddhist, a son of the Dean of Sanskrit learning in Sri Lanka, a marvelously thoughtful host. Suicide bombers have been on the scene in Sri Lanka for a long time.

From time to time there are cease-fire agreements and talks between the major parties involved. Men and women in Sri Lanka do not need to be told that this sorry state of affairs has gone on too long. They, too, are seeking ways leading to resolution. And one remains optimistic. There is too much piety, in the real sense of this term, in this homeland of four magnificent religious traditions—Buddhist, Hindu, Muslim, and Christian—and too much intelligence in this country with such a remarkably high literacy rate for a vortex of internal destruction to last indefinitely.

In all this change, only briefly adumbrated here, one theme can be discerned—and the movements and countermovements in this society are extraordinarily complex—namely, the fundamental humane conviction that this complex pluralistic society will somehow endure, will not become antagonistically fragmented, will remain, and will remain complex and pluralistic, and will be Sri Lankan.

Now in the interlinkage, reciprocal interpenetration of these currents of change and cumulative continuity, there has also been an exhilaratingly instructive development leading from a period of debate and controversy to a period marked by a widespread commitment to a development through understanding of a pluralistic community, a development quite counter to kinetic theorems in the physical world. In the past, a conceptually reified force called "Christianity" collided with a relatively stationary "something" called "Buddhism," and temporarily, as it were, knocked this "Buddhism" away and off-balance until this "Buddhism" returned with force to meet head-on this "Christianity," which swung back momentarily to move again decidedly in an impact course—a model of which might be an inelastic impact apparatus with the swinging and colliding balls demonstrating a part of Newton's third law of interaction. Yet this law no longer provides a parallel model for the process now under way.

There was a period in this recent past when it appeared that a model of elasticity would be desirable, that these two systems would have a resilience to resume their original conceptualized structure, institutional shape, once the pressure of the other was removed. It appears today, however, that a growing number of Buddhists and Christians are demonstrating a creative flexibility representing an ability not to break with noble religious heritages while simultaneously appropriating a common history of Sri Lanka and self-consciously participating in the shaping of a common future.

We have witnessed the beginning stages of a new process in Sri Lanka. We mentioned previously that not too long ago positions moved from being pastoral within the Christian and Buddhist communities to apologetic between the two, to polemical against each other. Something new is continuing to emerge from a reverse swing of the process—from polemics, through apologetics, through pastoral concerns within separate communities now to honest, truthful dialogue, even colloquia on issues related to the marriage of two persons from different religious communities, to supportive procedures in resettlement programs, and the topics for colloquia are still unfolding.

The situation has changed because persons have chosen to change it.

## AN EVENT IN AUGUST 1967: *ŚRADDHĀ*—FAITH

On August 13, 1967, a Catholic priest received a message from the Venerable Walagedera Somaloka Tissa Nayaka Thera, a patient at the Ayurvedic Hospital in Colombo. The Catholic priest went straightway

> to the hospital. After a pleasant conversation, when the Catholic priest stood to leave, the venerable Thera said to his friend: "Now bless me according to your faith, and I will bless you according to mine." This they did.[7]

I repeat, the situation has changed because persons have chosen to change it. But the process was not easy; certainly it was neither automatic nor inevitable. Creative flexibility allows for a foundation on which to stand while determining from an increasing number of alternatives that in which one will invest one's energy in the shaping of one's tomorrow.

Impressive thinkers have informed our understanding of humankind's religiousness, have attempted to propose methods of approach to this study that would contribute to understanding, and the list of significant contributions is steadily increasing. Persons who have described the work that they were doing as philological, or phenomenological, or philosophical, or historical, or theological, or sociological, or anthropological, or a combination of several, have proposed perspectives, sophisticated models, detailed analyses, and suggestive or plausible theories, not without considerable insight. A great deal has been said about context: the textual context, the context in which a phenomenon being studied or analyzed occurs, that is, appears, the historical context, and on and on.

One context not often adequately stressed, one that has regularly engendered greater understanding, is friendship. Perhaps an assumption that friendship entails unacceptable biases has led some, in the name of an impossible and detrimental ideal of objectivity, to refrain from exploring the potentially enormously productive context of friendship among persons of different religious communities seeking to understand themselves in their religiousness. Friendship, one should have thought, entails openness, honesty, integrity, veracity, a commitment to seek to understand, a willingness to be understood. This is a context that generates the activity of granting the benefit of the doubt that, on the one hand, holds in check a rapid drive to analysis and assertion of claims and, on the other hand, leads to further reflection and inquiry.

"The Venerable Thera said to his friend" our quotation reads; and one is led to the conclusion that what then transpired was due in grand measure to friendship, that friends were there.

In the blossoming of friendship with persons of other religious communities a complex, occasionally inchoate, incipiently inarticulate orientation evolves. Another person has now become a meaningful part of one's life; what happens to him or her in his or her life matters, really matters, to one. One's friends, if clarity and honesty of relationship are considered important, contribute to one's orientation in the religiously plural setting and that which obstructs this clarity, inhibits this depth, tends to impede, is, in some instances, disruptive of relationship, divisive of community and destructive of integrity. The meaning of one's life in the context of a particular religious tradition becomes deepened, more subtle, by the catalytic sincerity of friendship with persons of other religious traditions.

Defensive structures tend to become dismantled, barriers of closed systems disassembled; plate glass windows through which one can look out at others but which nevertheless separate persons are removed in the context of friendship.

Will such process in the context of friendship threaten the uniqueness of a given religious heritage? Will the particularity of one's received tradition be watered down, be lost, as it were, in a drive toward a nondescript universalism? Not necessarily, unless, of course, persons choose this. The Buddhist and Christian traditions have had universal messages, gospels capable of being appropriated by all reasonable persons, and yet the forms in which the messages have been structured, historically formulated, have been particular, have differed uniquely. Between the universal and the particular, which particularity also shapes significantly the form of the universal, a personal dialectic operates.

## A TIME FOR OPENNESS

In the process of participating self-consciously in these two traditions today in Sri Lanka, whether a Buddhist or a Christian, one is both translator and weaver, engaged in the not dissociated activities of, on the one hand, putting a received vocabulary into terms rich in personal relevance, and, on the other hand, dispersing strands of a received heritage in order to weave them oneself. But the dialectic functions on a deeper level when one interprets the activities; is the translator forgetting, the weaver unraveling? To what degree is one's loyalty primarily directed toward the past from which one's heritage derives or directed to the future into which one is moving moment by moment? A tradition is passed down from generation to generation because persons have found that tradition to be supportive of movement *into the future,* into the new. And so a translator might move away from searching for or utilizing a one-to-one correspondence in vocabulary, having discovered a deeper continuity in the convergence of broader, different, yet parallel semantic fields. A weaver might well form a strikingly new pattern based on abiding motifs without discarding received strands with which the work is being done.

Donald G. Dawe, a theologian in the Christian community, has suggested that careful consideration be given to the meaning that could be carried in the name of Jesus.

> [T]he "name of Jesus" is the disclosure of the structure of new being. It is the pattern of salvation. So the universality of Christianity is grounded in the translatability of the "name of Jesus," not in the imposition of particular formularies on others.[8]

There is openness in what Dawe is suggesting, allowing for encounter with others in the mutuality of salvific new being. Dawe certainly is not putting aside his Christian heritage; he is speaking from within his tradition and from his recognition, his celebration, his coming to know this "power of new being" through the particularity of Jesus of Nazareth, the Christ. It is because of the particularity of his heritage that he discerns the universality of the "power of new being" at different times and in different traditions.

In response to Dawe's statements, Eugene B. Borowitz, speaking self-consciously as a Jew, participating in not a dialogue but a colloquy, provided constructive remarks for Dawe's further consideration by noting some problems with what appeared to be a primary value orientation given by Dawe to a universalistic dimension of the Christian tradition and an apparent lower order value ascribed to what is particular. Borowitz sharply focused the paradox of a dynamic parallelism of particularity and universality by stating, "In any case, without a particularistic grounding for universalism, I do not see how it can arise." And he made the observation, "My point is that if universality is grounded in particular faith it would seem odd that universality could ever fundamentally negate the truth of particularity for in so doing it would destroy its own legitimation."[9]

Mahinda Palihawadana, a Sri Lankan Buddhist, has written of our setting:

> In religious forums across the globe Western religious leaders are crying out for a meeting of minds on the one hand on issues that seem to separate the great religions of the world and on the other on those that, more significantly, unite them. For quite understandable reasons, the initiative in this regard has so far come almost exclusively from the Christian world. Other religionists were at first rather cool to these overtures—perhaps not unjustifiably in view of the aggressive history of the Christian missionary enterprise, memories of which have not quite faded in Asia. But men of good will cannot continue to reject the invitation for dialogue, certainly not the Buddhists; nothing in their tradition could justify such a stand. This is a situation which demands from men of religiousness neither isolationism nor compromise but willingness to learn as much as to teach, to probe and to be probed, to be open and sensitive and to see beyond the superficial.[10]

It is time for openness; the stage is now set for it in Sri Lanka and elsewhere. This challenge of religious pluralism does not represent a "no-man's-land"—we have done away with militaristic jargon. The challenge is present for anyone who seeks to understand his or her neighbor, is there for anyone who wishes to know what most fundamentally contributes to meaning in the lives of others. The dimensions of this human inquiry are not without commonality, are not basically, inherently, foreign.

Wilfred Smith has proposed, on the basis of the evidence he has found, that faith is a generic human quality, a quality of life manifest yet not fully specified, a quality of insight and of response, deeply personal and orientationally pervasive; faith is "the fundamental religious category; even, the fundamental human category."[11] Smith speaks to our setting succinctly and with engaging relevance.

> There is no earthly reason why a Theravadin Buddhist, for example, should believe in God. For him not to understand the concept of God, on the other hand, as it has played a monumental role in Christian and Islamic and other world history, would be an intellectual shortcoming—minor, so long as he lived within his own community, but potentially more significant once he should come into the company of theists. By "understanding" here I intend his apprehending not what the term "God" means in his own worldview, where it refers to something that perhaps does not exist or is unworthy, but rather what it has meant to those who have used it to denote and to connote a great range of their life in the world, and the universally human reaching beyond the world: their perception both of empiricals and of ultimates.[12]

Faith and understanding are not bipolar, in fact they tend toward convergence. Smith's comments about our setting interrelate integrally faith and the intellectual pursuit of truth. Through his numerous writings, this scholar has moved our thinking beyond the older view of there being somewhere things called "great faiths" to a more illuminating view of there being faith in the minds and hearts of persons who, due to the depth and pervasiveness of faith, or lack of it, might have or might not have become great, distinguished by the quality of the life lived. Understanding the role terms such as *God* or *Dharma* have played in the lives of persons, as Smith put it, "their perception both of empiricals and of ultimates," can be an objective in a mode of inquiry that does not dissociate the intellectual, moral, and even theological, as Smith has also suggested.[13]

Complementing the cumulative persuasiveness in much of Smith's work is a confessional and invitational approach that tends to quicken religious sensitivity, an approach demonstrated by Raimundo Panikkar, a priest of the Catholic Church. Panikkar urges that religious dialogue *be religious.* "The principle is this: *The Religious encounter must be a truly religious one.* Anything short of this simply will not do."[14] For such encounter to occur, Panikkar stresses the need for *intrareligious* (a phrase he has coined) dialogue, that is,

> an inner dialogue within myself, an encounter in the depth of my personal religiousness, having met another religious experience on that very intimate level. In other words, if *interreligious* dialogue is to be real dialogue, an *intrareligious* dialogue must accompany it, i.e., it must begin with my questioning myself and the *relativity* of my beliefs (which does not mean their *relativism*), accepting the challenge of a change, a conversion and the risk of upsetting my traditional patterns.[15]

Complementing Smith's suggestion that the category of understanding might carry potential significance is Panikkar's suggestion of the category of growth. Of the ensuing intrareligious dialogue, Panikkar says,

> *Growth* is perhaps the most pertinent category to express this situation, which is more than simple development or explication. In growth there is continuity as well as novelty, development as well as real assimilation of something that was outside and is now incorporated, made one body. In growth, there is freedom.[16]

Recognizing the transformation from species-life into life that is genuinely human, whether this occurs in the life of one who is Buddhist or one who is Christian, becoming capable of recognizing this, or being so enabled, remembering that largely through one's religious heritage one has been introduced to this, one discerns faith in the lives of persons. Fortunate, too, is the one who enters into friendship with persons who know this quality of life, faith, who studies that which is different and finds that which is familiar because more about *us* has been learned, become known. And because one has learned, while seeking to understand, one has grown, one has become other than what one was, yet not in every way different.

"Now bless me according to your faith, and I will bless you according to mine," was spoken in August 1967, in Sri Lanka. Whether "according to Catholicism" or "according to Buddhism" was the intent of the exchange by the use of "your faith" and "mine," one might suggest that more was involved. The willingness of a Buddhist monk to be blessed and to offer a blessing for a Catholic priest demonstrates an at-homeness not so much with Christianity, but with the quality of life discerned in his friend. There is an openness here, "to probe and to be probed," as Palihawadana put it; indeed, there is more—an openness to bless and to be blessed.

Is it in our future in Sri Lanka and elsewhere for persons of one religious community to bless, to wish well, those of another religious community? This, of course, depends upon what we choose to do.

August has witnessed significant events in Sri Lanka, and one might not be branded an incorrigible optimist were one to note that in the course of a little more than a century, growth from anxious debate to friendship, from controversy to understanding, in Sri Lanka and elsewhere, has become a part of the record, and the faith of persons within different religious communities has been discerned.[17]

The new century seems to beckon.

# 14

# Religion and the Imperatives for Development

*Development is an increasingly popular notion in parts of the world and more often than not the notion is turned over solely to social and economic theorists to provide intellectual rationale, motivation and direction. More fundamental is the developmental mutual participation of persons that requires a center of value for and trust in each other. Religious reflections are germane and perhaps significantly consequential.*

## IN WHAT SENSE "DEVELOPMENT"?

The situation in which persons are living today in Sri Lanka is one of change. Change, of course, is built into the historical process *and* into the lives of persons. However, persons in Sri Lanka are met by a rapidity of change that, through its apparently relentlessly increasing pace, might tend to push one toward the borders of bewilderment. Further, this rapid process of change has been stimulated by trends and forces engendered within and extended from a variety of sources other than those that have developed from within the country's pluralistic heritage. This total fluid context manifest today in Sri Lanka has yet to find its meaning told by those who are familiar with the foundations for meaning that have been passed down through the religious traditions. It seems that the present situation in Sri Lanka represents a time neither conducive for timid thinking nor hospitable for inflexible dogmatism. It is a time that summons the best minds to interpret political, economic, and social developments by applying more than political, economic, and social theories, to provide a conceptual context in which these processes are given purpose fundamentally rooted in the total well-being of persons.[1]

On a wider scale in Sri Lanka, Buddhists, Hindus, Christians, and Muslims have had and will have their daily lives influenced by the

> decisions made by persons of different religious communities. This interdependent, intertwined pluralism has at times held firmly in this country's history, and at times it has unraveled in devastating disarray. These strands might be held together by political ideologies—we have seen the sequence: independence, national identity, development—and then again, perhaps not. Conceivably, coming to understand the religiousness of persons of other religious communities might provide a more cohesive bond in this religiously plural context than we might have imagined.[2]

These words, written thirty years ago, can be presented afresh today. Surely, we will agree, the observations contained in those words remain relevant to the case in this country now. We are not slow of learning in this island nation. One wonders why, therefore, we have not yet turned the flank on some of the problems that have been confronting us more recently.

Our topic is "Religion and the Imperatives for Development." I have found myself becoming more and more a personalist, increasingly so with each passing year of my life, as did Wilfred Smith. Being a personalist is not a regressive move, a kind of surrender in the face of the complexities of life, a retreat into subjectivism, a sign of intellectual atrophy, even, perhaps, of the setting in of old age. Hardly! Such position is grounded in the most rigorous examination of concepts and empirical realities.

Let us then consider our case at hand. We speak of development, and generally we know what we mean. Usually the point at issue is economic development. But from time to time we see our focus enlarged to include development in a much more comprehensive sense: economic, educational, infrastructural, legal, political, social, and on and on one might go. One point one would want to note early is the absence of something that is never included in such a listing. Have you ever heard of someone speaking in this context about the need for religious development? Of course not. When we focus on development studies, we tend to turn our eyes away from religious understanding. Other things need to be developed, it is assumed; religion will, more or less, have to take care of itself. Have we overlooked something? The topic we are considering is engaging. From one point of view, "Religion and the Imperatives for Development" might suggest that there *must be* development, *that development has its imperatives and, consequently, religion must come around to it,* that religion must be changed to become aligned with the imperatives for development. From another point of view, it could be rather just the opposite, *that religion presents the imperatives for development, provides the grounding, the foundations for development.* Resolutely do I hold to the long-range viability of the latter formulation, that religion provides the foundations for development.

Some of us in China have been following in accordance with the former formulation, that development has its imperatives and religion must come around to it. In *Religion under Socialism in China,*[3] Chinese scholars of the Shanghai Academy of Social Sciences note how, from their point of view, religion was used as a tool of suppression or an ideology of commiseration in what they call "Old China." It is apparent that for these Chinese social scientists, religion has become functionally viable on the basis of its social utility—a kind of All-China Patriotic Social Gospel Movement—that is, Buddhists, Daoists, and Christians contributing pragmatically, in fields and factories, to advance socialist social change.

Working with the assumption that religion is a compensatory ideology arising from ignorance or psychological and socioeconomic needs, these colleagues maintain that the "persistence of religion" is due to the yet unfulfilled social transformation of China. However, at the same time, and with some peculiar shortsightedness, it is affirmed that since religion flourishes in contemporary China believers should line up shoulder to shoulder to help build the ideal socialist society that, when finally arisen fully, will lead to the end of religion by alleviating the conditions that are said to give rise to religion in the first place.

Perhaps our first lesson is that one *uses* religion at one's own peril. When religion is used it is oppressive, it becomes merely one more utilitarian ideology. On the other hand, we certainly can use religious institutions. Indeed, when religious institutions are no longer relevant in responding constructively to human oppression and suffering, we do well to place them aside. We do this, however, not as a result of using religion but as a result of our being "used by religion," if you will, as a manifestation of our religiousness, of our faith.

We come back to where we began. When pressed, resolutely, what development studies are finally concerned with, that which is the ultimate goal of development programs, remains persons. Fundamentally, the reason for the continuing emphases on development remains the effort to cause to grow, to expand upon, to strengthen, to bring into activity, to unfold, to make more available, life abundant. And this, from a Christian's perspective, represents the heart of the purpose for God's coming to dwell, "to pitch a tent," among humankind—that there might be life abundant. It has been observed, for long, that humankind does not live by bread alone. Surely. Certainly, too, humankind does not live without bread.

## FAITH: TRUST, FAITHFULNESS, AND RESPONSIBILITY—IMPERATIVES FOR DEVELOPMENT

What then might one say about the imperatives that religion might bring to us in our attempts to aid in human development? Imperatives there are, aplenty. But space limitations push us to be succinct. What is *the imperative* for development? *That we have faith.* Before one recoils with the opinion that here is just another professional arguing for his particular ideological slant on things, let me say that what *I* mean by faith is not what I mean by *faith,* that is, my understanding of faith is limited. I do not know all there is to know about this quality of authentic human living. I think I have been enabled to glimpse a bit of it, however.

H. Richard Niebuhr, in a book edited posthumously by his son, *Faith on Earth: An Inquiry into the Structure of Human Faith,* reminds us of the Latin etymology of our English word *faith,* how this quality of life, this faith (*fides*) is to a great extent, and inseparably, grounded upon "the fundamental interaction of *fiducia* (trust) and *fidelitas* (loyalty or fidelity)."[4] He begins his book by saying, and I quote at length,

> Questions about faith arise in an urgent and tragic form as we view massive and petty breaches of faith—treasons, lying propaganda, the cultivation of mutual distrust as measures of party and national policy, the use of pretended loyalty in conspiracies against state and civilization, the enlistment of men as faithful followers of causes that depend for success on practices of deception. [In this situation a dark prospect opens before us as we reflect on the meaning of Jesus' question: "When the Son of man comes will he find faith on earth?" (Luke 18:8). He may have meant, "Will he find belief or trust in God?" But he may also have meant, "Will he find any faithfulness among men?"] The experiences of the twentieth century have brought into view the abyss of "faithlessness" into which men can fall. [We see this possibility—that human history will come to its end neither in a brotherhood of man nor in universal death under the blows of natural or man-made catastrophe, but in the gangrenous corruption of a social life in which every promise, contract, treaty, and "word of honor" is given and accepted in deception and distrust. If men no longer have faith in each other, can they exist as men?][5]

This faith, Niebuhr assures us, is triadic, is grounded in a triadic relation: (1) in oneself at the center of one's wholesome psychological core, (2) in relationship with others discovered to be one's companions, and (3) in a third dimension, in that which transcends. And running right the way through this triadic context is faith, in the sense both of depending on, trusting, and also in the sense of loyalty to, of responsibility.

There is no future worthy of our aspirations without promise keeping, without loyalty among persons, without responsibility among persons, without faith grounded in this kind of self-awareness, this kind of human relationship, this kind of response to transcendence. This trust among persons is at the core of religious living. And the religious person knows very well that we have within us the ability to deceive, to be untrustworthy, to be disloyal, to betray another. The religious person knows, existentially, at the center of his or her self-awareness the significance of trust in human understanding, one's own, and in understanding others.

How might one set about to give expression to this concern about the possible continuity of trust among persons from the perspective of our Buddhist heritage? One could do worse than to turn to a discussion of the qualities of human living that have to do with growth, increase, development (*aparihāniyā dhammā*).

One turns to the *Mahāparinibbāna Sutta*[6] and finds there a discussion well-known in Sri Lanka: Ajātasattu, king of Magadha, was bent on attacking and destroying the Vajjians, and sent his prime minister to the Buddha to inquire about his prediction of the outcome. With the prime minister seated in his presence, the Buddha turned to Ānanda and asked him whether seven qualities of humane living that are associated with growth were to be found among the Vajjians. When Ānanda related that indeed these qualities were to be found among the Vajjians, the Buddha concluded that the Vajjians would not decline, would not drift into ruin, would not waste away, but would prosper. The Buddha then told the prime minister that at one time while he was staying at Vesāli, at the Sārandada Cetiya, he it was who taught the Vajjians these qualities that continued to abide among them, that would contribute to their greater development.

And what are these qualities? Briefly, one might enumerate them as follows: (1) that many of them meet together frequently, (2) that they sit down together in concord and arise from their meeting in concord, and act in concord, (3) that they do not declare what has not been understood, they do not undercut what has been understood, they live according to what is fitting among the Vajjians, which has been known from of old, (4) that they honor, respect, pay heed to, revere the Vajjian elders and ponder what is to be heard from them, (5) that they do not cause to dwell with them, having taken them by force, women or daughters of the clan, (6) that they honor, respect, be attentive of, revere the Vajjian memorial mounds (*cetiyas*), near and remote, and do not neglect the fitting offerings as previously given, previously performed, and (7) that they provide fitting protection, shelter, and haven for the Arahants among the Vajjians, so that those Arahants who have not arrived, and those who have already come, can live at ease there.

We infer from this summation not primarily a sequence of customs from ancient times in *human history* as much as a continuing theme in *humane living*—that where there is trust, faithfulness, and responsibility within human relationships individuals can become persons, that when what has been learned from trusted persons has been enacted and has been found to have been indeed wise, a collection of individuals will become persons living in a community and that community will continue to develop.

So central is this theme of trust, faithfulness, and responsibility in this discourse about the Vajjians that the context led a redactor, apparently, to set there in the text also a long enumeration of over forty qualities of humane living associated with growth in both the Buddhist monastic and lay life.

## DEVELOPMENT: BECOMING EVER MORE AUTHENTICALLY HUMAN

What might we conclude? There is not much to conclude that we have not already known; that development rests on more than successful economic programs, that "what works" presupposes a shared assumption of *why* persons want something to work.

Within our religious traditions one finds an affirmation that compassion is at the heart of the cosmos. For those among us who are Jewish, one notes it was God who took the initiative to help mold a group into a people, a band into a community. For Christians, the coming of Jesus who is seen as the Christ is a manifestation of God's self-emptying love (*agapē*) for humankind. Those among us who are Muslim know well that God has enabled us to call upon him as "God the Merciful, the Compassionate." Those among us who have found that our lives have been salvaged by the inexplicable grace of Śiva realize fully the virtue of giving to others, having already received from God the gift of grace. And Theravāda Buddhists celebrate the Buddha's great decision to preach Dhamma (the foundation for humane living), that momentous occasion which undergirds his title as the Great Compassionate One (*Mahākaruṇāvant*). It should come as no surprise, then, to find that the Pure Land Buddhists of Japan, who recognize compassion at the core of existence, at the heart of Salvific Truth, are the ones who have worked with extraordinary commitment to uplift the outcasts in Japan over the centuries. These religious persons are also joined by other religious people, by this I intend those among us who are secular humanists in the grand and noble sense, who have given their lives to building a setting in which the dignity of being human can be given full expression, who are prepared to undergo great sacrifice in order to defend and preserve the dignity of the human personality.

The qualities that I have been attempting to illustrate do not represent something unusual, extraneous to the routine of customary living, are not qualities added to what constitutes a normal human being. Rather, it is just the opposite, it seems. These qualities suggests to us what it is like to become authentically human, truly human, to be a genuine human being. We see, therefore, that a genuine human being responds to the other, especially if that other is suffering or is in need of having his or her life enriched by being presented with enhanced alternatives for the future.

To attempt to state succinctly, by way of a tentative conclusion, what one might say about "Religion and the Imperatives for Development," one might put it like this: If you become what you aspire to be based upon the cumulative wisdom that trusted ones have shared with you, you will find yourself creatively contributing to an enhancement of trust and loyalty, to a deeper understanding of the dignity of the human personality, in yourself and toward those around you, thereby making more stable the foundations for humane development that is ever more inclusive and supportive of others. We have at our fingertips the testimony of religious persons through millennia about how this can be done.

15

# Getting First Things First

## *Some Reflections on a Response by Venerable Ananda Maitreya*

*In order to move away from unhelpful conceptualization of reified entities such as "Buddhism" and "Christianity" to find wherein we, all of us, are involved in the development of others of us, we listen carefully to what we are told. "Buddhism" is not at the heart of living life well. Rather it is "refraining from what is detrimental" and all that follows from this.*

For many years Ven. Balangoda Ananda Maitreya has been held in high regard among Buddhists and Western students of the Buddhist heritage. One of his writings, a chapter entitled "Buddhism in Theravāda Countries," appeared in a book widely used for a time in American colleges and universities.[1] Western students have also seen this outstanding representative of the Buddhist testimony in Sri Lanka in another medium of instruction, also widely used in the United States, a film, "Buddhism: Footprint of the Buddha."[2] In that film, an interlocutor, Ronald Eyre, asked Ven. Ananda Maitreya, "If I said to you 'Can you put Buddhism in a nutshell?' what would you do?" Unperturbed by the remarkably inept conceptualization of "Buddhism," whatever on earth (or in heaven, or beyond heaven) that might mean, unperplexed by a request utilizing a spatial category metaphorically to press for an essence of essences to represent more than two thousand years of a portion of our human saga known to Theravāda Buddhists as the Buddhist cumulative tradition, Ven. Ananda Maitreya chose to repeat words from of old. He replied,

> The Lord Buddha said,
> *sabbapāpassa akaraṇaṃ kusalassa upasampadā*
> *sacittapariyodapanaṃ etaṃ buddhāna sāsanaṃ*

These words, occurring in the *Dhammapada*, have been rendered into English by students of the next generation still continuing the international collaboration in which Ven. Ananda Maitreya played a stellar part:

Refraining from all that is detrimental,
The attainment of what is wholesome,
The purification of one's mind:
This is the instruction of Awakened Ones.[3]

This grand verse also appears in the *Mahāpadāna-suttanta* of the *Dīgha-nikāya*.[4] There, Vipassī, the first Buddha, is recorded as having uttered it in inaugurating the monastic precepts (*pāṭmokkha*). One misses the point entirely, it seems to me, when one attempts to put aside these mythical accounts as useless legend making. The myth of Vipassī informs us that human beings have affirmed that Dhamma, Salvific Truth, abides and with it human beings have become engaged, and thereby they have found it to be supportive since time immemorial. In fact, one notes that by means of these myths the distant past is being discerned to be replete with meaning because the past is not soteriologically dissociated from the present. Salvific Truth has not been apart from persons so that the hope that is available today, to put an end to *dukkha* and to realize Nibbāna, has been so also for persons of the distant past.

One is nearer the mark when one suggests, as has Sukumar Dutt, that "the verses of this hymn," as he puts it, "define what may be called the cardinal Buddhist virtues." He continues, "As described in the *Mahāpadāna,* the original Buddhist congregational service would seem to have been very closely akin to the *dhamma*-rehearsals of other sects in the wanderers' community. It represents the archaic practice among the Buddhists." Dutt provides a sound historical observation, "The substitution of a disciplinary code for a mere credo or a confession of faith is of much significance: *it evinces that the Sect has already become an Order*, recognizing now a common 'monastic discipline' (*Vinaya*) as its bond of union."[5]

In both locations, the verse forms a cluster with two other verses. While in the *Dīgha-nikāya* our verse appears in the middle of this cluster, in the *Dhammapada* our verse precedes the following two:

Forbearing patience is the highest austerity;
Nibbāna is supreme, the Awakened Ones say.
One who has gone forth is not one who hurts another,
No harasser of others is a recluse.
No faultfinding, no hurting, restraint in the *pātimokkha*,
Knowing the measure regarding food, solitary bed and chair,
Application, too, of higher perception:
This is the instruction of the Awakened Ones.

*khantī paramaṃ tapo titikkhā nibbānaṃ paramaṃ vadanti buddhā*
*na hi pabbajito parūpaghātī samaṇo hoti paraṃ viheṭhayanto.*
*anūpavādo anūpaghāto pātimokkhe ca saṃvaro*
*mattaññutā ca bhattasmiṃ pantaṃ ca sayanāsanaṃ*
*adhicitte ca āyogo etaṃ buddhāna sasanaṃ.*[6]

We can take this observation about the early formation of the Order a step further. These verses, especially our key verse, do not so much represent a substitution for "a mere credo or a confession of faith," in the sense of propositional assertions or doctrinal formulation, as they do a commitment to the efficacy of praxis. One notes primarily (1) a confidence in the natural capacity of a human being to discern, in the process of honest and sincere reflection undergirded by and arising from meditation, the alluring quality of a wholesome life and (2) an affirmation that a human being has the ability to respond in an integrative manner to that discernment, trusting that this living of a wholesome life is fully consonant with the fundamental order of all that can be known. Honest practice, rather than adherence to propositional statements or defending a kind of sophisticated empiricism, is at the heart of the Buddha's message and it appears that Ven. Ananda Maitreya demonstrated how one *gets first things first* when he placed this recognition to the front and at the center in his response to the "Can you put Buddhism in a nutshell?" query.

But more can be said about the insight of this splendid response. "Can you put Buddhism in a nutshell?" might represent for some a question such as, "What do Buddhists believe?" The response given by Ananda Maitreya indicates a Buddhist testimony that launching a religious life is not so much a matter of belief, what set of statements one is to believe, to what propositions one is to ascribe, as it is a matter of what one is *to do*,[7] wherein one is to set about to commit the living of one's life with integrity.[8]

Responding to a question, "Can you put Buddhism in a nutshell?" might lead one to reply by considering, "What makes one a Buddhist?" When wondering about this, one might begin to think in terms of a Buddhist catechism, as did Colonel Olcott[9] more than a century ago when defensive lines were being drawn between colossally conceptualized monolithic entities of "Buddhism," on the one hand, and "Christianity," on the other, as we noted in chapter 13. There is some irony in all of this, however, in that the verse under consideration is remarkably inclusive of key aspirations and dispositional orientations of religious persons around the globe and throughout human history.

There is no question whether Awakened Ones uttered these words or not. Surely they are the words of those who have seen through to what is involved in becoming fully human. However, it is highly unlikely that our verse was put forward as a *summation of doctrine*. No doctrine is mentioned; no explicit doctrinal connections are provided, nor systematic inferences made. Buddhists, in the course of time, have found this verse to be the splendid summation of much more than doctrine—more than "Buddhism" too, and more than can be put "in a nutshell" also. The verse has to do primarily *with life*. It is a verse that extends an invitation to live in accordance with it. It is also a verse that is a companion through one's life, against which one might check oneself in quiet moments of reflection. It is, moreover, a verse that can provide a *summation for one's life,* to lead one to consider whether one has been consistent with this wise and compassionate instruction. It surely is not far-fetched for one to suggest that the way one sets about to respond to this verse determines which path one is following. Once seen in this light, this marvelous verse does not play a divisive role in attempts to understand our religious pluralism, but an inclusive one. A person is a Buddhist not because he or she subscribes to this verse while other religious persons do not but because of the procedures he or she finds most supportive in leading him or her to discover for himself or herself the fulfillment of this arising of wholesome behavior and this purification of mind.

If this verse is seen as the "essence of Buddhism" or a summation of doctrine, the matter might consequently appear complicated. Mr. Eyre, our interlocutor in the film, replied to Ananda Maitreya's recitation of this verse, "Not easy." Ananda Maitreya responded, with a characteristic chuckle, "Well, it is if you understand it." This would suggest that Ananda Maitreya has found the convergence of the way of the Buddhas with this quality of wholesome living and purity of mind. It would seem that it is that "easiness," to which he refers, that would lead one to say not only that Ananda Maitreya is *a* Buddhist, but that he is also *Buddhist.*[10]

One of the obvious problems in using the concept "Buddhism" is that it in no way even remotely approaches a comprehensive representation of the scope of human involvement with transcendence affirmed by Buddhists in the course of more than 2,500 years in our global religious history. And one marvels at the enormously selective reification that would go on were one to try to compress this magnificent saga into one concept, "Buddhism," or to put it "in a nutshell." Of course, differentiation would be involved in this process, surely. To "put in a nutshell" seeks for succinct distinctiveness, reified differentiation, assumes that one is looking for nutshells and not seeing the tree that produced them. For some it would follow that holding to what has been placed, somehow, in that nutshell makes one a Buddhist.

The question of what makes one a Buddhist is not new, of course. Some have turned to the threefold refuge to indicate where one must look to determine what makes one a Buddhist. And, indeed, one detects early on in the Pali commentaries, an awareness of how a *customary,* yet admirable, commitment to the Buddha, Dhamma and the Saṅgha (*lokiyasaraṇagamana*) might be broken by following other teachers.[11] Olcott refers to these three magnificent objectives that provide supportive orientation for humane living, without spotting the subtle yet enormously consequential *world-transcending dimension* of this involvement (*lokuttarasaraṇagamana*), as "Who or what are the 'Three Guides' that a Buddhist is supposed to follow?" The shift in conceptualizing the matter is weighty. Using Olcott's phrasing, one might highlight this conceptual shift by nothing that the "three guides" for living life well have now become "three guides" for a Buddhist. In fact, one could put the matter this way: the question, "What must I do to become free, to live freely, to gain liberation?" has now become, "What must I do to be a Buddhist?" Of course the consequences of this shift are monumental. This threefold refuge, the three gems, a precious inheritance for living life well that parents would want to pass on to their children, has been rather recently introduced to children in Sri Lanka as "These are the three gems of Buddhism."[12] And one reads elsewhere, "It is by means of the moral precept of refuge that one becomes a Buddhist." Without that, one is told, "one is not a Buddhist."[13]

Certainly, one would want to make the point that there are Buddhist distinctives regarding how one might best live life well, how one might set about to seek a discipline that provides a kind of refreshing freedom. There are, of course, distinctive Buddhist doctrines, a particular view of the world, an understanding of how one is to understand oneself and one's context in life. Assuredly there is a special emphasis given by Buddhists to some aspects of religious living and there are particular religious rituals and institutions that readily enable one to distinguish the Buddhist cumulative tradition from others. However, this verse offered by Ven. Ananda Maitreya, a verse that has been a part of the Buddhist heritage for many centuries, provides a dialectic tension of sorts with the particularity of the Buddhist tradition by communicating the universal aspect of the vision and instruction of the Buddhas. By responding with this verse to the question, "Can you put Buddhism in a nutshell?" Ven. Ananda Maitreya indicated the way one can collapse a myriad of particulars that one has learned from one's heritage into a core perspective on how to live life well, integrate a multifaceted complex of memories gained in the course of one's life into a consistent pattern for living life well, structure a coherent undergirding objective for living into one's future a life that is lived well. A grand verse, this; and one with which religious persons from around the globe fully concur.

Did Ven. Ananda Maitreya put "Buddhism in a nutshell"? Some might see him as being successful in doing this. It is important to see that he did much more than this. He demonstrated how one sets about *getting first things first*—perceiving a context for interpreting a model for and a model of religious living. It might be said by some that this point is not easily apparent. Might one paraphrase Ven. Ananda Maitreya's words? "Well, it is if one understands it."

# 16

# Translational Theology

## *An Expression of the Faith of Christians in a Religiously Plural World*

*When Protestant missionaries arrived in Asia they quickly turned their attention to language study and translations of the Bible. Decisions about which terms in the host language would best represent Biblical ideas were weighty a century ago and more recently discussions about new translations have wide-ranging ramifications. Translations, too, involve personal faith.*

In the course of one's study, one's thinking on some issues changes. This particular study, over the years, is no unusual case to prove the exception. For example, when a draft of this chapter was first developed I used the phrase, "Christian Faith," in the title, and, indeed, so it stood when the chapter was first published[1] in a section entitled "Explorations," in *Christian Faith in a Religiously Plural World*. The editors introduced the chapter by stating,

> Professor Carman [in his address given at Washington and Lee University, in 1976, as a part of a symposium of the same title as the published volume] spoke of the Jewish and Christian willingness to translate their Scriptures as a witness to their conception of religion and that of human nature which underlies it. Translatability, he argues, is only possible if you assume there is a common humanity that lies behind the bewildering complexity of human religiousness. Translatability from one religious context to another presupposes there is some basis by which human beings may address one another in the name of their ultimate concern that transcends cultural and religious particularity. Such an overarching anthropological presupposition comes to the test when confronted by the

> difficult task of an actual translator struggling to make the message of his Scripture understandable to others.[2]

I, as a small part of the symposium at Washington and Lee University, explored attempts to translate key Biblical notions from Greek and English into a few South Asian languages, particularly Sanskrit, Hindi, and Sinhala. The paper, prepared for a study session of that symposium, was entitled, "Recent Issues in Biblical Interpretation: The New Testament in Asian Languages." The inquiry of this chapter grew out of that study session paper and in response to some of the issues raised in the course of the symposium. Yet, over the years, a significant difference in assumption has arisen: no longer is assuming "a common humanity" that lies "behind the bewildering complexity of human religiousness" quite adequate, although necessary. There is a movement toward clarity in probing what might be that "basis by which human beings may address one another in the name of their ultimate concern that transcends cultural and religious particularity." That basis is faith, as Wilfred Smith has since made evident.[3] That assumption is "anthropological" insofar as it has fundamentally to do with humanity. Faith hardly "comes to the test" so much as it becomes clearly manifested when we consider what is involved in translational theology.[4]

Christian Faith in a Religiously Plural World is an engaging topic—one that will probably continue to be with us for some time, and this on several levels. Several questions arise in grappling with such a topic. What is faith? How might it be discerned? What is its source? In what sense do we say "Christian faith" or "Christian" faith? Who is the "we" being envisioned when one says "In what sense do we say 'Christian faith' or 'Christian' faith?" What does it mean to speak of a plural world? What is required for one to understand the world to be religiously plural? Religiously? In what sense? Is there a place for Christian faith in a religiously plural world? If the evidence indicates that faith is the fundamental basis of our authentic humanity, in what sense then might one say the world is religiously plural? Does a recognition that this world is religiously plural suggest a failure, in some sense, of Christian faith, even the faith of Christians? Does the situation in which the Christian church finds itself today, one religious institution among others, give rise to disorienting uncertainty within the Christian community or rekindle a resolve to convert humankind even at the risk of renewing an attitudinal orientation called by some "Christian triumphalism?" Does the situation, rather, provide an exhilarating opportunity of participating with persons of other religious communities in building our common religious future?

Perhaps the easiest way to handle such questions might be to parry them or to ignore them and be lulled into a kind of laissez-faire theological solipsism: each person to his or her own experiences, each tradition to its own perspectives. Or perhaps these questions might be postponed, relegated for the time being to a kind of "back burner" consciousness, held there to be answered sometime in the future—probably by someone else. Christians have had faith sufficient to grapple with these and similar questions, and, as the symposium at Washington and Lee University demonstrated, have had the resolve to do this publicly and formally, in a manner that sharply focuses before university religion departments *and* the church the topic "Christian Faith in a Religiously Plural World," and as we would put it today, *the faith of Christians in our religiously plural world.*

Different theological positions have been presented by a number of theologians. Some have spoken of a discontinuity, of a tension, a "dynamic," a dialectic, when considering our religiously plural context. Recurrent interpretive themes have been frequent: special and general revelation, particularism, the particularity of Christ or the Christian tradition, as well as universalism, the universal message of the Christian faith, the universal soteriological process that God has engendered in the hearts of all religious persons. In most instances, Protestant theologians have aspired to formulate a position that is biblically based, although interpretations of what "biblically based" means are not always in accord.

During the Washington and Lee symposium, a lacuna in the considerations became apparent. What is the role of Christian Scripture in a consideration of the faith of Christians within a religiously plural world? Protestant theologians, especially in the context of religious pluralism, face the requirement of explicating the particularity of the Christ-event as God's saving activity to all religious persons *and* the particularity of the Bible for Christians as the primary written account of that saving activity. Some within the Christian community have attempted to develop a theological position from the Bible that would enable them to relate the Christian tradition to other traditions without theologically delimiting God's saving relationship to only one religious tradition of humankind and without being morally divisive between religious persons. Others within the Christian community have found in the Bible a charge to extend the Christian confession on this globe through conversion of the hearts and minds of all humankind and thereby to heal the cleavage between communities through discipleship under one Lord. There is a tension between these twin thrusts within the Christian tradition. This tension poses what Minor Lee Rogers called a *kōan* for some and an unresolvable dilemma for other Christians.[5] The situation in which Christians find themselves in a religiously plural world is one that provides a summons for all to engage in prayerful reflection.

During an open discussion period following a presentation at the symposium, John B. Carman was asked whether his position was based on the Bible. Immediately Carman replied, "I should hope so." Why, one might ask, was the reply given so readily? Why with such sober conviction? And, perhaps more germane to the concern here, why was the question raised in the first place? I should think it was a leading question designed either to establish a common premise or to terminate further discussion. Further, I should think the question and the response reflect a shared conviction that the task set for Christian theology in a religiously plural world must include a consideration of the significance of scripture for the Christian tradition as it has developed and for Christian thought and practice today.

Wilfred Smith, one of the speakers at the symposium, has written about the need to study the Bible in a relational and historical context: to study scripture as a phenomenon manifestly significant in the religious life of humankind; to study the Bible as scripture; to study how it arose, how it was adopted as scripture, how people have approached it, what they have done with it and have been enabled to do because of it through the centuries until today.[6] A subdivision implicit in Smith's more general concern, although not explicitly addressed by him, would be the study of processes of translating the Bible, not only into Western languages but also into other languages through which enormously influential religious apprehensions have been expressed for centuries by persons participating in the major religious traditions of Asia and elsewhere in the world. This would be a study not primarily of the dates and number of translations, but a study of attitudes toward the translating process itself, of theological issues raised in the translating process, and of ramifications of attitudes and issues in the history of humankind's religiousness and for the faith of Christians.

The history of Christian thought has been a history of communication and to no small extent has this history been one of translation, an activity of transferring concepts from one medium into another, the conveying of concepts from one language into another—a process, in the Christian context, having two inseparably intertwined strands: theology and language.

Donald G. Dawe, in his address at the symposium, noted the theological strand, to which we briefly referred in chapter 13, drawing our attention to the "name of Jesus" as the disclosure of the pattern of God's action in human salvation. As such, it is open to translation. This "name" may be translated or given fresh expression in differing times and places. It is not in the continuity of a verbalism but in faithfulness to its meaning that the saving power revealed in Jesus is actualized. This is true because, as Dawe puts it,

> the "name of Jesus" is the disclosure of the structure of new being. It is the pattern of salvation. So the universality of Christianity is grounded in the translatability of the "name of Jesus," not in the imposition of particular formularies on others. This power of new being operates throughout the world under the names of many religious traditions. It is recognized and celebrated by Christians because they know its pattern of meaning through Jesus of Nazareth.[7]

John Carman, in his consideration of the concept "religion," touched upon the twin strands, one concerning theology and the other language, in this process of translation.

> The concept of religion goes back to Western Christian translation language, and that, in turn, goes back to the Christian willingness to *translate* their sacred Scriptures into other languages, perhaps derived from the Hellenistic Jews' decision to translate the Hebrew Bible into Greek.

> The willingness to translate sacred words presupposes a confidence in a common element in human language and thus in human nature. A common element makes it possible for sacred truths to be expressed in another language. We are now so familiar with the process of translation as Christians that we may not understand how daring an undertaking was the Hellenistic Jews' translation of the Hebrew Bible, nor how important was their belief in the divine guidance of that translation. If we survey human religious practice, however, we see that translation or retranslation of sacred scriptures and liturgies has often been forbidden and very often, including in Christian circles, been viewed with deep suspicion.

I suggest that the human universal "religion" is by a circuitous route derived from early and later Christian confidence in the universal comprehensibility of the Christian message and the universal applicability of Christian piety. The divine Word can be expressed in differing human words because that divine Word is somehow behind every human being capable of uttering words.[8]

Dawe's notion of the "translatability of the 'name of Jesus'" and Carman's affirmation that the "divine Word can be expressed in differing human words because that divine Word is somehow behind every human being capable of uttering words" suggest a translational theology. Translational theology is the attempt to provide new form for traditional content, to give new expression to the salvific activity of God in Christ. The newness that translational theology seeks is not merely the novel. Rather, it is the fresh attempt to make relevant responses to the issues and questions raised by men and women within the Christian community *and* in other religious communities as they encounter one another in different times, in different places, and in different contexts. Translational theology is immensely complex. The notion of "translatability of the 'name of Jesus'" pivots on one's apperception of the Christ-event and one's interpretations of the testimony of scripture. An affirmation that "it is possible for sacred truths to be expressed in another language," that "the divine Word can be expressed in different human words," certainly represents the understanding endorsed by an impressive list of dedicated Christian biblical translators. But, in the process of translating, which human words in another language are to be used? Two levels of the process of translating sharply appear: on one level, a Christian translator might recognize the possibility "for sacred words to be expressed" through translation "in another language" and might discern that the "divine Word can be expressed" through translation "in different human words." Yet, on another level, a Christian translator might perceive sacred truths as *having been already expressed* and the divine Word *already communicated* through another language, in other religious traditions, in different human words.

Translational theology is *relational,* a sustained inquiry into the working of grammar and of God, an engaging study in matters of syntax and salvation, an investigation of possible connections between persons aspiring to live life religiously.

There is probably no occasion in the process of developing an authentic self-understanding of the faith of Christians in a religiously plural world on which the issue of particularity and universality within the Christian vision is more keenly sensed than the activity of translating the Bible into languages that have played an enormous role in the world's major religious traditions and cultural complexes. Technical terms abound, technical in the sense that the terms are peculiarly related to particular religious orientations expressed through doctrinal apperception and communal affirmations. When might a proper occasion arise, and what particular interpretation of God's revelatory activity in Christ would be requisite, for one to draw upon a weighty concept in another religious tradition and set that down as an approximate translation for a central biblical concept? What is an appropriate balance between the Bible as scripture, as canon, and one's discernment of Jesus in light of another of Dawe's observations: "In knowing Jesus, Christian faith is provided with the *canon*—the measuring stick—by which the activity of God may be discerned and confessed because it is Christ through whom this salvation is ultimately given"?[9] Of course, I do not wish to appear to be a biblicist tottering on the pinnacle of bibliolatry. Christians, gratefully, continue to stand in the wake of the writer of the Gospel according to John when he courageously chose *logos* (λόγος) to represent the preexisting Word of God that became "enfleshed." One wonders whether similar moves will be frequently met in the future of the Christian tradition or whether John's translational theology will largely remain a matter of the past.

John Carman, in preparing his major address, "Religion as a Problem for Christian Theology," and I, in preparing a paper for a study session, "Recent Issues in Biblical Interpretation: The New Testament in Asian Languages," independently found our way to a consideration of the Septuagint. This translation was a daring undertaking that was of considerable significance not only for Jews, as Carman has rightly noted, but also for Christians. It appears that Christians became aware of the legitimacy of the Septuagint and recognized in it a norm endorsed by Jewish scholars working in Alexandria—their predecessors by more than two centuries. This translation of the Hebrew scripture into Greek by learned Jewish men greatly facilitated the attempts by Christians to share their vision of the saving activity of God in Christ.[10]

Certainly, Jews and Christians utilized the Septuagint in different ways and for different purposes. Nevertheless, quite early Christians were working with sacred writings *in translation,* writings that came to be discerned as scripture, namely, the Old Testament. In the very early stages of the Christian movement one catches a glimpse of something quite extraordinary that, until recently, has not been frequently repeated. A situation occurred in which persons in one religious community were significantly assisted by the translation of scripture produced by persons in another religious community. Recently, this interpenetration of translational activity is becoming more noticeable. Some Hindus and Buddhists, for example, have been indebted to Christians who—working as indologists, Buddhologists, linguists, historians—have edited and translated Hindu and Buddhist scriptures. Persons in one community have been significantly assisted by the translation of scripture produced by persons of another religious community. One thinks of Mahatma Gandhi's personal discovery of the *Bhagavadgītā* in English translation and in London. Translational theology is *relational*. I wonder whether soon there might come a day when Hindus, Buddhists, and Muslims would provide for Christians significant and meaningful translations of the Bible.[11] Translational theology is *relational* and *personal*. It involves a continuing task to discover in oneself and in one's scripture a process of thinking that represents a continuity within the Christian tradition that is in accord with the deepest apprehensions of religious truth of men and women of other religious communities. No easy task, this! But wholesomely exhilarating, I should think, for Christians whose intellect is buttressed by the Holy Spirit.

In our lifetime, we are witnesses to a momentous event in translational theology. Sinhala Christians in Sri Lanka, who have been reared in a culture shaped by the Theravāda Buddhist tradition, have a mother tongue that is heavily weighted with religious insights handed down in prose and poetry, subtle argument and song by Buddhist men and women for centuries. They have chosen to take a concept from this context and to place it where the writer of the prologue to the Gospel according to John placed *logos*.[12]

Some Sinhala Christians, our brothers and sisters through discipleship in Christ, have listened carefully to the testimony of some Sinhala Buddhists, our brothers and sisters through the teachings of Christ, and have drawn upon their own religious experience to discern the magnificence of a Theravāda Buddhist concept, *Dharma/Dhamma*. (*Dhamma* is the Pali form of the word known to the Sinhalas through their Buddhist tradition, while *Dharma* is the Sanskrit form of the term, which is more frequently incorporated into the Sinhala language.) These Sinhala Christians have grappled intellectually with the concept within the Buddhist religious heritage. They have struggled with the moral issues of possible divisive reactions within and between the Buddhist and Christian communities in Sri Lanka and, perhaps, elsewhere. Assuredly, they have prayed for guidance in this demonstration of faith expressed through translational theology.

I first learned of the possibility of this development during a three-year period when my wife and I lived in Sri Lanka, 1968–1971. I was initially somewhat disquieted by the prospects. My doctoral dissertation was on Dharma as a religious concept within the Sinhala Theravāda and interpretations offered in the Western academic traditions,[13] and I was persuaded that the Sinhala Christian translators were misunderstanding what Buddhists were saying. I thought that they were not alert to the Sinhala Buddhists' affirmation that Dharma, on the highest level, transcends personalistic ascriptions. Further, to say that Dharma became "enfleshed" (as would be necessary in a translation of John 1:14) would tend to limit the notion for some Sinhala readers, bringing it to a *lower* order of consideration, much as a Greek of the time might have thought upon first reading John's usage of *logos*.[14] However, making such a judgment about the meaning of Dharma depends on personal understanding, attitudes and intentions. Wrestling with this kind of an interpretation illustrated to me how personal—not subjective—translational theology can be.

Linguistic proficiency and historical competence assist persons in their attempts to provide new translations such as this, but whether or not this particular translation will become widely accepted in Sri Lanka depends greatly upon what Christians do with it. Should the prevailing attitude be one of "one-upmanship" or competitiveness, if not confrontation, with Buddhists, the translation will foster a divisive tendency between communities. Nor will the translation, to speak of Dharma becoming "enfleshed," be widely accepted in Sri Lanka should the intent be to utilize this translation as a stratagem for conversion—this would be like telling a reflective Buddhist that eight transcends, is more than, ten. If this translation becomes widely accepted in Sri Lanka, of course by this I mean accepted widely by Buddhists and Christians, Christians will have demonstrated that they see more in Dharma-person (*dharmayānō*) than in Word-person (*vākyayānō*). They will have extended the horizon of their vision of Christ and will have deepened the bases of their self-understanding in Christ through the notion of Dharma-person. Buddhists will have found occasion to rest at ease knowing that Christians, in their different way, have also discerned the fundamental good news shared for centuries by Buddhists: Dharma/Dhamma, Salvific Truth, abides and it is not remote from, apart from, persons.

We will see very possibly developments in the use of the term *Dharma/Dhamma* by Sinhala Christian translators. Just as *logos,* as a term, can appear both in John 1:1 and in Acts 18:11, "And he settled down with them a year and a half teaching the word of God (*ton logon tou theou*: τὸν λόγον τοῦ Θεοῦ) among them," implying both a person and a true teaching, so also could the term *Dharma/Dhamma* be used in a variety of settings.[15] Similarly other terms with weighty Christian meaning will percolate through the Sanskrit, Hindi, and Sinhala languages, to mention but a few, the first two languages contributing to the Hindu tradition and the first and third to the Sinhala Theravāda Buddhist tradition. The Christian attempt to provide translations in East Asia will give rise to related theological issues of growing complexity.

Translation theology is *relational* because it deals with the relationship between, on the one hand, one's own experience in Christ, the witness of the Christian community, and the testimony of scripture, and, on the other hand, with the hopes and aspirations of persons participating in the other religious traditions. Translational theology is *personal* because a thorough, rigorous understanding and a humble attitude with a wholesome intention are crucial to probing, reflectively as a Christian, the thoughts and aspirations held most dearly by persons in other religious communities. Through this relational and personal activity one seeks to understand the religious insights of others in order to allow a two-way sharing. It makes the Christian affirmations more comprehensible to others, and enables Christians to discern more completely their life in Christ in a religiously plural world.

Whether or not *dharmayānō,* Dharma-person, continues in the Sinhala New Testament as a profoundly engaging translation of "the Word" (*ho logos*) depends not only upon the insights the term might enable Sinhala Christians to gain but to a considerable degree upon the response of Sinhala Buddhists. Christians would be ill-prepared for the future were we to think of this as only an isolated matter for a relatively few people halfway around the world. We must be alert to the possibility that this example of translational interaction might play an important part in sharing faithfully the Christian testimony of the saving activity of God in Christ and simultaneously deepening the faith of Christians in a religiously plural world.

Translational theology, of course, is also concerned with translating for the Christian community today the sacred truths of old. It is concerned with translating sacred truths communicated in one mode of discourse into a mode more comprehensible for persons in a secularized Western setting. But the Christian community is neither in isolation, nor is it limited to the West. The translational problems posed by the rise of modern Western secularity are appearing with greater impact in other areas on our globe.

Translational theology is *exploratory* and *explicatory.* It reflects the faith to doubt and to make a commitment to Christ. It requires a confidence in God sufficient to sustain an open-ended investigation into the religious history of humankind. Drawing upon what has been remembered by the Christian tradition and working with what one knows has enabled one to have faith, translational theology has the potential to reach out, to explore, and to extend the periphery of the Christian vision of humankind's religiousness. In this way it will help to disentangle from the extrinsic underbrush of human foibles and make clear the communal testimony, in tradition and in scripture, of the saving activity of Christ. In this process there arises a broadening perspective and a deepening understanding through faith of the expanding relationality of Christ in the faith of Christians in a religiously plural world.

The Washington and Lee symposium—the ten speakers, the other participants, and the conscientious organizers—began this gyroscopic rethinking of Christian self-understanding in our contemporary world and did so graciously. Although there have been some similar symposia since that occasion in 1976, some continuing discussions considering Buddhist and Christian understanding, some considerations launched by Roman Catholics, the great Protestant denominations in the United States have hardly seriously considered the issues. Much remains to be done and needs to be done with balance and perspective in a multidirectional and multidimensional way.

If financial exigence were of little moment one could readily envisage the form future symposia on the theme "The Faith of Christians in a Religiously Plural World" might take in order to continue moving us in the direction of greater understanding, to explore, to explicate, to discern relations, to check attitudes and review intent, to become personally engaged with the religious lives of persons in other religious communities, to translate sacred truths for Christians and for others. These are the present demanding challenges for Christian theology and a natural expression of the faith of Christians. These challenges set the task for translational theology that might lead us to a point where all of us on this globe begin to study soteriological overtones, in which study those of us who are Christian might see afresh our insights into Christian theology.

Should such symposia be in Europe and North America, sponsored by one of our great denominations, say, for example, our Baptists, five areas of scholarly competence and intellectual experience would need to be present:

1. Christian theologians from Europe and North America representing expertise in systematic theology, historical theology, and, perhaps, as some say, philosophical theology or liberation theology or feminist theology or womanist theology; they would be able to relate their probes to the intellectual spirit of the times and contemporary life situations of Christians in these cultural settings.
2. Leading Christian representatives from Asia and Africa—ministers, teachers, and translators—who are living in a context largely shaped by other major religious traditions; they would be in position to share the process of self-understanding developing within the Christian communities in the religiously plural setting of their parts of the world.
3. Christian biblical scholars who could assist in understanding the early Christian efforts to communicate the saving activity of God, the history of reflection on these accounts within the Church, as well as their interpretation of the Bible as scripture today; they would come to grips for the first time, perhaps, with the relevance of these developments for Christians and others in a religiously plural world.
4. Christian historians of religion, who have spent many years studying a religious tradition and community other than their own; they could contribute insights derived from their perspective of two religious traditions seen against the backdrop of humankind's complex religious history.
5. Representatives of other major religious traditions, persons knowledgeable of the Christian ministry and presence in Asia and Africa, or exposed to the Christian tradition in the West; they would, by their presence, keep sharply focused for Christians the reality of religious pluralism, and by their active participation they could provide a sympathetic view of the Christian tradition from the vantage point of a person living within another religious community. They could give a constructively critical view of the

misunderstandings held by Christians and could share with them perceptions of the religious life that would enable Christians to converse more congruously with others.

Conversation among persons of faith is an objective for Christians in the work of translational theology. The challenge is there and the task awaits one's doing it. Conversion and the transformation of human lives were never one's doing, never directly caused by one, in the first place. That remains in the domain of God.

17

# Buddhists and Baptists

## *In Conversation into Our Common Future*

*In the past fifty years or so Baptists have witnessed strands within the Southern Baptist Convention developing a fundamentalist strategy entirely foreign to foundational Baptist distinctives long cherished by Baptists in Europe and elsewhere in North America. Reflective Baptists have long held to the soteriological efficacy of the abiding presence of God, the freedom of conscience of all persons, and the dignity of the human personality. Buddhists and Baptists, in colloquia, will see common affirmations and orientations about living life religiously.*

### BECOMING INDEBTED TO ANOTHER IN THE PARTICULARITY OF OUR LIVES

Surely, one might say, the title of this chapter is awry! What in the world, or beyond the world, have Buddhists to do with Baptists, and vice versa? Has it not been the case that Baptists have sought to convert Buddhists, and this for well over a century, and that Buddhists have been somewhat less than kind to Baptists by asserting that they hold, at best, inadequate views? What on earth do Buddhists and Baptists (could one even say in our particular context, Southern Buddhists and Southern Baptists or Theravāda Buddhists and Texas Baptists) have in common that would even remotely suggest there might be a future for them in some sense *common,* other than, of course, one of mere temporal coexistence? And further, one would surmise that Buddhists, on the whole, know very little about Baptists, and Baptists are generally uninformed about Buddhists. Why then have I chosen this title and its implied topic?[1]

Let me say the subject of this chapter arises from *particularity* because a Buddhist became a Baptist's friend. I remember well meeting Professor O. H. de A. Wijesekera at the Center for the Study of World Religions at Harvard more than four decades ago. The occasion of our first meeting was one of failure on my part. It was my pleasant assignment to meet him at the train station in Boston, to bring him to the Center. I was there ahead of time, met the arriving train and waited for what I mistakenly took to be long enough. I returned to the Center and announced that he was not on the train, to be informed that he had, indeed, arrived and was on his way by taxi. Well, how does one extend an apology as a greeting? One of the first qualities I discerned in Professor Wijesekera, this Buddhist scholar and gentleman, was his *graciousness.* We were together at the Center for a semester, in the fall of 1965, my wife joining me in our delight in coming to know also Mabel Wijesekera.

We found our way to Sri Lanka in the fall of 1968, under the auspices of the Fulbright-Hayes Program, and it was not long before we were warmly welcomed in the Wijesekera home, by parents and children, on High Level Road just south of the Nugegoda intersection and north of the Gangodawila junction. Being received as friends when one is on the other side of the globe from one's home is no flippant event in one's life. We remain grateful for this reception. I recognized another quality in Professor and Mrs. Wijesekera—*hospitality.* In the fall of 1970, I was still in Sri Lanka under the auspices of the Fulbright-Hayes Program, slow learner that I am, while Professor Wijesekera was teaching two courses at Colgate University: one on Hinduism and one on Buddhism, as our records have it. He had been at Colgate, had taught there, before I had ever seen the place. And now Colgate has become an important part of my life, and this for very nearly forty years.

I warmly recall the hours spent with Professor Wijesekera in his home on High Level Road, working through portions of the Pali *Aṭṭhakavagga* of the *Sutta-nipāta.* A Buddhist and a Baptist were working together in an old Indian language, studying ancient words of wisdom, ever new and refreshing. A teacher was also being *patient* with an appreciative pupil. When I entered the house, he would always receive me warmly. Almost on every occasion during those afternoon sessions he would be in his sarong, cigar sometimes lit, sometimes not, ever enjoyed. Partially reclining in his chair, a leg comfortably raised and resting on a leg-brace swung from beneath his chair's right arm, we wandered through text and translation, grammar and syntax, concepts and customs, cheerful tales and laughter. It was during that time that I first learned the widespread Sri Lankan custom of reading aloud letters received to enable one's attendant friend to become a party to the correspondence and the communication—a wonderful custom greatly appreciated, one that we might have put aside in the United States to our loss.

It was with Professor Wijesekera that I first became aware of Colgate University. I had heard of it, somewhat remotely and indirectly, through the work of Kenneth W. Morgan and his sterling efforts to edit for English-reading students the scholarship of Buddhists, Hindus, and Muslims. I remember sharing with my wife then, in the fall of 1968, how it seemed that Colgate, or a setting like it, would be a splendid place to launch one's teaching ministry, let me call it. Little did I anticipate—I had absolutely no way of knowing—that four years later I would be teaching at Colgate, and from that institution would come once again to Sri Lanka, to celebrate the warm memory of this particular splendid man, one's teacher and friend, Oliver Hector de Alwis Wijesekera.

A Baptist was learning from a Buddhist, becoming ever more indebted to his kindness and for his scholarship, for his faithfulness, too, in sharing some of what he had learned over the years. In a sense, one can look back on those months in 1968, in Sri Lanka, to say that we were indeed building a common future, one that neither of us then were in position to anticipate fully. It was directly through the agency of Professor Wijesekera that I met Professor Mahinda Palihawadana, one of his former students, who was then teaching at Vidyodaya University. Since our first meeting in late 1968, Professor Palihawadana has come to Colgate on several occasions to teach two courses: we tend to call them now the Hindu Tradition and the Theravāda Buddhist Tradition. He, too, in a sense, has followed in the footsteps of his mentor. He, too, is a Buddhist who has worked closely over the years with a Baptist; most significantly, perhaps, as co-translator of a great Buddhist scripture, the *Dhammapada*.[2]

So perhaps one might say that our title and subject are *rooted in the particular,* in the meantime in which we do our living in empirical reality. I would suggest, moreover, that these relationships are rooted in reality that also extends beyond what is customarily taken to be the empirical. Generically, our subject concerns religious persons in our one, common, human religious history. Less universal, it deals with men and women aspiring to be better Buddhists and Christians. More particularly, it deals with Theravāda Buddhists and Baptists. So when I speak of Buddhists, I am referring here to Theravāda Buddhists of Sri Lanka, in general, and of Baptists, I have in mind Baptists in the United States.

## SOME BAPTIST DISTINCTIVES

Who are the Baptists? Let's look briefly at the meaning of the word before indicating some of the key ideas related to the notion and providing some comments about the people who endorse them. The word comes from Greek, *baptistēs* (*βαπτιστής*), "one who baptizes, a baptist," prominently used by Christian writers to refer to John the Baptist (also referred to as "the one baptizing" *ho baptizōn* [*ὁ βαπτίζων*] Mark 1:4), stemming from the verbal form *baptizō* (*βαπτιζω*), "to dip, immerse," and the noun, which is found only among Christian writers, *baptisma* (*βάπτισμα*), "immersion, baptism."

You will recall that Jesus was baptized by John and the use of the verb designating this activity occurs throughout the Gospels. The disciples of Jesus continued the rite in the formation of the early Christian community (as one notes in the New Testament book of Acts). In the writings of the Apostle Paul, the verb is used to indicate a metaphorical sharing in the death and resurrection of Christ.

> Do you not know that all of us who have been baptized into Christ Jesus (*ebaptisthēmen eis Christon Iēsoun* / *ἐβαπτίσθημεν εἰς Χριστὸν Ἰησοῦν*) were baptized into his death (*eis thanaton autou ebaptisthēmen* / *εἰς θάνατον αὐτοῦ ἐβαπτίσθημεν*)? We were buried therefore with him by baptism into death (*dia tou baptismatos eis ton thanaton* / *διὰ τοῦ βαπτίσματος εἰς τὸν θάνατον*), so that as Christ was raised from the dead by the glory of the Father, we too might walk in newness of life. (Romans 6:3–4)

One cannot provide a concise definition of what this "newness of life" (*kainotēs zōēs καινότης ζωῆς*) means except that it entails a newness that was not known before, that was not previously present, that is something remarkable. The context tells us that one who is so baptized has died, as it were, to sin and no longer is alive in sin. Should one become absolutely certain of what this newness of life entails, or were this newness of life no longer to be ever new, each day, perhaps, such life would become stale, commonplace, merely customary. *Newness of life.* We know that Paul used the image of baptism to reflect a newness of life transcending ethnic and socioeconomic identities:

> For by one Spirit we were all baptized into one body (*eis en sōma ebaptisthēmen* / *εἰς ἓν σῶμα ἐβαπτίσθημεν*)—Jews or Greeks, slaves or free—and all were made to drink of one Spirit. (I Corinthians 12:13)

Undoubtedly, the image Paul was working with, that of immersion, suggested death to sin, death to the old self, whether as seen in a participatory death with Christ in his crucifixion or with a death of one's sense of customary identity. *We die to self to rise anew.* The general notion of baptism is also, but far less frequently, used in the New Testament with regard to a baptism in, an immersion into, the Holy Spirit. In the experience of the early church, a sense of baptism also referred to the baptism of martyrdom.[3] So this rite of baptism, originally derived from a Jewish ritual washing, came, in the early formative Christian experience, to take on great metaphorical power representing a manifestation of a personal transformation and also a model for interpreting what constitutes newness of life. It is not difficult to understand a gradual development that occurred within the institutionalized Christian church to interpret the act or rite of baptism as a sacrament, as a sacred mystery, a means for the bestowal of grace.[4] However, Baptists have maintained that this rite is symbolic only, symbolic of a personal commitment, an outward manifestation of an inward transformation.

What is significant about Baptists? On a mundane level one would want to note that Baptists, in general, represent the largest Protestant perspective in the United States.[5] Basic to an understanding of Baptist distinctives is the fundamental conviction of and commitment to *religious freedom,* to the *freedom of conscience in matters of faith and practice,* or, put another way, to the dignity of the human personality in living the religious life. From this basic principle all other Baptist distinctives follow.

On the matter of *authority*: Baptists affirm the primacy of scripture as the means for illustrating the message of Jesus as the Christ and the early responses of his followers who came to constitute the Christian church. Scripture provides the means by which one measures one's life by the canon of Jesus the Christ and organizes one's religious community. It would follow, therefore, for Baptists, that the institutional church—as in the case of the Roman Catholic Church or any denomination with ranking authorities serving as priests, bishops, archbishops, cardinals, or popes, in council or out—does not and cannot have the final authority regarding one's life of faith and mode of practice. To be considered free in matters of religious living requires that one have the capacity to judge prudently, to evaluate carefully, to reflect maturely, to commit oneself responsibly. Baptists, in determining how to form a Christian church according to the early testimonies recorded in the New Testament, have followed the early Christian pattern of forming a group of "called-out ones" as a fellowship of men and women who have responded to the salvific activity of God in Christ and who have undergone the symbolic rite of baptism. A church, therefore, is a community of baptized believers.

Baptists baptize, and Baptists have long held that one is to know what is going on when one undergoes this rite, that is to say, one is to have placed one's heart on the salvific activity of God in Christ reconciling the world and to have committed oneself to the efficacy of this reconciling act in one's own new way of life. This emphasis that Baptists give to what has come to be called "*believer's baptism*" is based on a threefold foundation: (1) the testimony of scripture, that is, evidence drawn from the New Testament, (2) the non-sacramental quality of the rite of baptism, and (3) a doctrine of humankind. Believer's baptism assumes that the believer is old enough to be accountable or responsible for his or her actions both in reflecting upon them, and in turning from those actions that are to be left behind, and that the person is capable of understanding the symbolic meaning of the rite of baptism. Hence, infant baptism is not practiced by Baptists because it does not reflect the general practice recorded in the New Testament and also because an infant is not considered to be in a state of sin, resulting from original sin, from which to be assuaged, in varying degrees, by the rite of baptism considered to be sacramental. Baptists do not endorse the doctrine of original sin. Humankind, left to its own resources, is incorrigibly guileful, but this calculative cunning and its consequent despair is not the result of original sin, not the result of fundamental human depravity, but is the upshot of a propensity in human dispositions toward what is detrimental in human relationships, proclivities in human indulgence toward egocentricity, having no particular origin in space or time but regularly a part of the human experience.

This same sense of religious freedom, at the basis of the Baptist experience, has led to a Baptist affirmation of the "*priesthood of all believers*." This means that in matters of faith and practice, one is free to follow the dictates of one's heart in prayer, to have access, as it were, into the immediate presence of God, and to seek, as well as one might, to live freely in accordance with scripture and one's living relationship with God. There are no priests for Baptists, no one to serve as mediator between oneself and God, no authority to tell or advise one what to believe, to decide for one how to express one's faith, how to live a religious life. To say that such institutional authority is necessary contradicts that Baptist affirmation of freedom of conscience and religious liberty.

Then how are the churches governed? With Baptists, each local church is autonomous, each congregation freely reaches its own conclusions and makes its own decisions on matters of faith and practice and church polity. There is no higher authority in the guidance of a local church. These free agents who seek to relate with God in the immediacy of quiet prayer and who seek to find God's will in the manifestation of a life of faith voluntarily form a congregation, as was done in the very early church, to create fellowship and caring and to enhance that life of faith. This congregation can dismiss a pastor or invite a new one, manage the legal and fiscal affairs of the church, determine the form of worship, provide for the life of the congregation in the larger community, without required referral to any external institutional authority.

This sense of *religious freedom* replicated through these several distinctives has led Baptists to stand firmly for, what has been called in the United States, the *separation of church and state*. Roger Williams, persecuted by the Puritans of Boston, organized one of the first Baptist churches in America, in Providence, Rhode Island, around 1638. Another Baptist church was formed in Newport, Rhode Island, at about the same time. Williams was a leader in the cause of religious liberty and toleration, even having a guarantee to this effect written into the royal charter of Rhode Island in 1663 from Charles II. Although Williams was a Baptist for only a short time (he withdrew from the organized group of worshipers in Providence), nevertheless the principles he espoused in those years are the ones for which Baptists have been famous for more than three centuries. So firmly held was this commitment to religious freedom among the Baptists that Jewish men and women, seeking this same freedom, moved to Providence and to Rhode Island. And for this same reason Sabbatarians, later to be known as Seventh Day Adventists, built their first church in Providence. Thomas Jefferson, who was not a Baptist, celebrated this practice of religious freedom and toleration embedded in the principle of the separation of church and state. As one scholar puts it,

> Indeed, democratic America should be eternally grateful to the Baptists in colonial New England and Virginia, for it was their struggle for religious liberty which culminated victoriously in the exclusion of all religious tests and restrictions from the Constitution of the United States.[6]

Although these principles—religious freedom, the role of scripture, believer's baptism, freedom from ecclesiastical and civil authority, the autonomy of the local congregation, the priesthood of all believers, separation of church and state—were present to some degree throughout the history of Christianity, at various times, among different groups, the Baptists as a denomination emphasizing these principles began to take form in the seventeenth century in England. Although they there developed confessions of faith, they have subsequently held these confessions to provide guidelines, not at all to serve as authoritatively affirmed doctrines.

Now, do not get me wrong. Baptists are Christians, or should I say Baptists attempt to be Christian, to be Christ-like. And surely the testimony that Baptists bring to our colloquia about our global religious living differs from the testimony shared by those of us who are Buddhists. But surely Buddhists would be quick to see the common affirmations, the similar orientations, between themselves and Baptists about how one is to set about attempting to live a religious life in community.

## A BUDDHIST PRINCIPLE: CONTINUING INQUIRY

Would I have to labor the point that those of us who are reading this today and who are Buddhists understand fully the dynamics of these Baptist principles?[7] One scholar has put it this way:

> If there be any truth in the picture of the Lord, which the legends of the Pali canon assemble for us, an undoubted feature of it is that the founder of Buddhism is categorically against the claim of Authority in matters of religious faith and practice. In his reported dialogues and discourses, he insists, whenever the matter crops up, on individual realisation and conviction as the sole and sufficient criterion of "rightness" for every individual.[8]

Ānanda, restless with the prospects of the Buddha's *parinibbāna,* while being without clear pronouncements concerning the monastic institution (*Saṅgha*), was instructed by the Buddha,

> And whoever, O Ānanda, either right now or after me will dwell as one who has one's own lamp, as one who is a refuge unto oneself, as one who has refuge in no other, as one for whom Dhamma is a lamp, for whom Dhamma is a refuge, as one who has refuge in no other, they, bhikkhus, will be beyond [rebirth in] darkness, *they who have the desire to learn* (*ye keci sikkhā-kāmā*).[9]

This same theme appears again when the Buddha instructs Ānanda,

> This might occur among you, Ānanda, "The word of the teacher has passed away, our teacher is no more." But, Ānanda, it should not be

viewed this way. That Dhamma and *vinaya* which I have pointed out and made known, that is the teacher after I am gone.[10]

So even though the Buddhist tradition places emphasis on the individual's quest for understanding, that individual, whoever he or she might be, is not cut adrift, is not at a loss. The heritage signals that there is a teacher, as it were, namely the teaching and training with which one can become engaged and thereby attain Salvific Truth.

We find in the early quest for authority in the young Buddhist community, all the way through, on every occasion when a teaching is relayed—whether from one who heard it from the lips of the Buddha, or from a group of monks containing elders of considerable seniority residing at one monastic enclave (*āvāsa*), or from several elders who also were scholars of the canonical teachings, or from a single scholar—that teaching "is to be checked against the *sutta*s and is to be compared with the *vinaya*."[11] This practice of referral to the received teaching, interpreted as a means of understanding the Buddha's intention, is seen also on numerous occasions in the *Kathāvatthu*.

It appears that Buddhists, like Baptists, affirm the primacy of scripture, which, in the Buddhist case, is affirmed as the means for illustrating the message of the Buddha and also the early responses of his followers who came to constitute the community of the faithful (*Saṅgha*) or, more inclusively phrased, the fourfold assembly (*catu-parisā*: monks, nuns, laymen, and laywomen).

One notes also the presence of what surely is a commitment to religious liberty or freedom of conscience, although recently this commitment has been given a somewhat extraneous interpretation where the focus is moved from the relevance of the teachings in one's life context to a question of empirical verification of propositions. In a discourse, recently frequently cited, concerning the Kālāmas, the Buddha is recorded as having urged them carefully to consider and to endorse his words about greed, malice, delusion, illusion, and the like, when they know those words to be beneficial and *when they know those words to be so for themselves* (*yadā tumhe . . . attanā va jāneyyātha*).[12] The point is, of course, that one is not to be entirely on one's own to make one's way by one's own wits, to find release through one's own reflection, but, rather, that one is to consider in an engaged fashion what one has received, to accept it when persuaded, to place it aside when not.[13]

To return to the account of the Buddha's discourse with Ānanda during his final hours among his disciples, we have noted how he advised the disciples to let Dhamma and *vinaya* be their teacher. An engaging phrase occurs in the same discourse, and with a threefold repetition indicating its significance. The Buddha addressed the assembled bhikkhus saying, in effect, that the time might come when one or another of the bhikkhus might have doubt regarding the Buddha, about Dhamma, the Saṅgha, the salvific realization (*magga*), and the practice. He seems to have urged them not to reproach themselves with the thought that uncertainties on some issues arising later could have been avoided had they only asked the Buddha about those issues while he was living with them. The overriding concern of the Buddha is seen in his injunction, "Ask, O bhikkhus!" (*pucchatha bhikkhave*).[14]

## COMMON PRINCIPLES

"Truth is one! There is no second" (*ekam hi saccaṃ na dutīyam atthi*).[15] One might suggest that one way of speaking about the Buddha's awakening is that he realized the truth of this affirmation. Moreover, the Buddha was also concerned about the relationship of men and women to the truth that is one. It is a weighty matter to hold that truth is one, the ramifications of which in one's day-to-day evaluations are manifold and can be buttressingly profound.[16] It is of great significance that one might become existentially engaged with this truth that is one, to seek to orient one's life in terms of it, to seek for it in the hopes of finding it. The Buddha is recorded as having provided an evaluation of a situation that could very well apply to ours today: "For one's own dhamma some say is perfect; another's dhamma they say is inferior. Thus, disputing, they quarrel, each one's opinion they say is truth."[17]

Does this appear to represent the encounter between "Buddhism" and "Christianity" over the past century? Certainly a confrontational posture could be detected among some Baptists vis-à-vis Buddhists in Colombo not too long ago. But what do we make of it today? I am not talking about Buddhism and Christianity but about *Buddhists* and *Baptists*. More adequately formulated, I am referring to those of us who seek to follow the teachings of the Buddha in the hopes of attaining that to which he awoke, to those of us who seek to follow the teachings of the Christ in the hopes of attaining that for the purpose of which he spoke and lived.

Truth is one. Are we, who have discerned different visions, therefore, to argue? We often hear people speak of "truth-claims," and have heard it said that Buddhists and Christians make "conflicting 'truth-claims.'" Wilfred Smith, a person whom Professor Wijesekera knew well and much admired, wrote,

> I take the problem of religious diversity with the utmost earnestness and, I like to feel, with deliberate realism. My contention is that the problem can be perceived in more than one way; and that to perceive it in terms of truth-claims that conflict is not necessary, and not necessarily helpful.[18]

Smith has suggested several alternative ways of conceptualizing the process of our colloquia: rather than considering conflicting truth-claims, he queries, why not "divergent witness-bearing" or "the diversity of good news among religious groups," or "varying truth reports."[19] Smith moves to his conclusion by observing,

"To see difference as conflict is a decision—whether taken consciously or unconsciously." He continues,

> With a different prior orientation, however, it is both theoretically and practically possible to see two differing statements as an invitation to synthesis rather than a challenge to confrontation.[20]

Smith concludes, inadvertently and profoundly touching upon the motto of my university, a motto formulated by Baptists,

> And to conclude: may we not perhaps come nearer the truth—who is God [the motto is: *deo ac veritati*: for God, indeed, for Truth]—if we do not claim it, but recognize rather, in humility, that we are claimed by it, and are inspired by it, so as to strive onwards towards constantly closer approximations, excited and delighted that nowadays our intellectual apprehensions are being enlarged and deepened in the dialectic of our broadening and tantalizingly variegated community?[21]

What might be this truth that is one to which the passage in the *Sutta-nipāta* refers? Does it represent an abstract assertion about a theoretical objective truth that first must be subsumed into Western philosophical categories and then analytically debated? The *Mahāniddesa,* an old commentary considered to be canonical, commenting on this phrase "Truth is one! There is no second," notes,

> The cessation of *dukkha, nibbāna,* is called "one truth"; that which is the calming of all clustering synergistic impulses [*saṅkhārā*], the putting away of all substrata [*upadhi*], the destruction of craving [*taṅhā*], the absence of passion [*virāga*], cessation [*nirodha*], Nibbāna. Or "one truth" means the truth that is the path [*maggasacca*], the truth that is release [*niyyānasacca*], the practice [*paṭipadā*] going to the cessation of *dukkha,* the noble eight-fold way.[22]

Now, let me try to demonstrate how the Theravāda tradition has plaited the strands of this commentarial heritage with stellar fidelity. The *Paramatthajotikā,* which is a later commentary on the *Sutta-nipāta,* says "One truth means cessation or *magga*[-event]."[2] And the *Saddhamma-pajjotikā,* the commentary on the *Mahāniddesa,* maintains this same interpretation.[24] We find Buddhaghosa also stating this clearly in his *Visuddhimagga,* when he says of the word *truth,* it is used "both with regard to Nibbāna, truth in the highest sense [*paramatthasacca*], as well as *magga* in such passages as 'One Truth! There is no second.'"[25] And the subcommentary (*ṭīkā*) on the *Visuddhimagga* makes the same affirmation, that Nibbāna is not empty, not vain, is known in truth and that the knowing and penetration that brings this about is also not empty, not vain, is known in truth.

Although stated as being two—Nibbāna and the realization of Nibbāna—there is no contradiction and we are reminded of our original passage, "One truth! . . ."[26]

This truth, Nibbāna and its realization, is the heart of Dhamma unto which the Buddha awoke. This is not a truth that Buddhists go about claiming. Such activity would be embarrassingly inappropriate.[27] This is the truth, to paraphrase Wilfred Smith, that leads one, rather, into humility, to be claimed by it, inspired by it.

A passage often presented by Christians, including some Baptists, of course, in an exclusive way, considered by some to represent the central statement of a "Christian truth-claim," is found only in the fourteenth chapter of the Gospel according to John.[28] Grand notions such as God as Father, the "sentness," the coming of Jesus as the Son, verbal senses of coming and going in general, light and truth are favorite themes with this Gospel writer and they appear in our selected passage. We have long discerned a sensitivity to Greek thought in this Gospel. More recently, we have recognized its Jewish setting, its general affinity with the Dead Sea Scrolls,[29] and at the same time the fact that this Gospel is "profoundly anti-Jewish."[30] At least two factors provide a context for our passage: the one indicating the historical context of a gradually forming Christian community within and from a complex of religious trends and orientations, and the other pointing to a personal engagement with a soteriological message.[31]

There are grounds for finding a sense of exclusiveness in this passage. An early Christian community nurturing, preserving, coalescing around the very early Johannine literary corpus, even prior to AD 50,[32] was attempting to gain its balance, as it were, in response to a dialectic of initial interpretive judgments of the other offered by some Jews toward this early Christian group and by these Christians toward those Jews. One sees clearly a pattern of "us" (these Christians) against "them" (those Jews and other outsiders).[33]

On the level of a personal engagement with a soteriological message, the context has Peter saying to Jesus, "I will lay down this my life (*psuchēn ψυχήν*) for you." And Thomas has just asked, "Lord, we know not where you are going; how do we know the way (*hodon ὁδόν*)?" According to the Revised Standard Version of the Bible, Jesus replied to Thomas,

> I am the way, and the truth, and the life; no one comes to the Father, but by me. If you had known me, you would have known my Father also; henceforth you know him and have seen him. (John 14:6–7)

It would be a mistake to read this passage as providing a propositional formulation of a kind of soteriological syllogism. Charles H. Talbert is right when he notes our passage as forming a record of a "farewell speech" given by Jesus involving a prediction, an exhortation, and assurance,[34] a record being itself a kind of "meditation of Jesus' departure."[35]

In my judgment, English translations of this passage tend to underscore a sharply drawn exclusiveness that was developing in the early Johannine community but may not be so deeply etched in the original Greek. Let me give you a translation that I think is closer to the original.

> I myself am (that) *way* (*hodos ὁδὸς*), and (that) *truth* (*alētheia ἀλήθεια*), and (that) *life* (*zōē ζωή*); no one comes before (*erxetai pros ἔρχεται πρὸς*) [i.e., deeply understands, enters a living relationship now and always with, God as] the *Father* except through (*di'[a] δι '*) me. If you had known me, you would also have known my Father. From now on you know him and have seen him.[36]

I offer this interpretation because of the dramatic dual levels operating in the setting of the passage: a spatial reference suggested by a verb of motion, and a soteriological insight also suggested by a verb of motion. Verbs of motion, for example "to go, to come," in Greek, in Sanskrit and in Pali, are also used to indicate an activity of understanding. We might benefit from Buddhaghosa's observation,

> Whatever [philological] roots convey the meaning of "going" convey also the meaning of "knowing" (*buddhi*). Hence, for this [expression] "I go" the meaning "I know, I understand" is expressed.[37]

Joachim Jeremias and others have shown that Jesus emphasized God as Father,[38] in fact this was the core of his ministry: to see God as Father is to perceive the mission and ministry of Christ.[39] Surely, God was known to the hearers of Jesus as a God who acts in human history, as the God who led the children of Israel out of Egypt, as the author of Torah, as the father of his children, Israel, but this sense of "Father" is not central or consistently featured in the Hebrew scriptures and in Palestinian Jewish sources as a metaphor for understanding God.

The truth to which Christians are bearing witness in recording and cherishing this passage is that those of us who seek to know what God is like, to discover that God is Father, would want to become deeply, personally engaged with the way that Jesus demonstrated, the truth with which he was wholly identified and of which he spoke, and the quality of life that he made abundantly clear.[40] Becoming claimed by this truth, as Smith would put it, being inspired by it, would lead one to discern what it is like to discover God as Father. That is the message of our passage.

It should have been clear to those of us who attempt to be Christian that the question of truth is not a matter restricted to an impersonal, objective, ratiocinative process of analysis and debate. Much more is required in the process of understanding. The starting point is honesty, sincerity of discipleship, with the affirmation that truth can be known and that when it becomes known the situation is no longer conceptualized as one in which a person possesses the truth, hardly as one in which "truth-claims" are proffered. Rather, the Gospel according to John tells us that this truth which can be known, when known, sets us free.

Jesus, speaking to those Jews who were disclosing their newly discerned fidelity in him, said,

> If you continue (*meinēte* μείνητε)[41] in this word of mine, truly (*alēthōs* ἀληθῶς) you are my disciples, and you will know (*gnōsesthe* γνώσεσθε) *truth* (*tēn alētheian* τὴν ἀλήθειαν) and *truth* (*hē alētheia* ἡ ἀλήθεια) will free you. (John 8:31–32)

His hearers thought this statement referred to freedom from slavery. How could this be so for persons who were not slaves? Jesus replied that this freedom is freedom from the state of slavery to sin, and again he refers to his ministry as Son with reference to God as Father. Although this passage indicates an anti-Jewish posture being drawn by the Gospel writer,[42] the deeper sense of the availability of truth with which one can become personally engaged is clear. This truth which can be known, when known, enables something to occur. One becomes free from, finds a way out from, an involuntary state of incorrigible detrimental behavior and the inevitable disorienting consequences of that behavior.

Buddhists are aware of truth (*Dhamma*) that can be known, and have averred that when it becomes known truly, something remarkable happens.

> Dhamma, indeed, protects one who lives Dhamma.
> Dhamma well lived brings ease.
> This is the blessing when Dhamma is well lived,
> One who lives Dhamma goes not to a miserable existence.[43]

Although Theravāda Buddhists would not speak of "Priesthood of all believers," the *guru*, nevertheless, has been put aside. Although Theravāda Buddhists would caution against a practice of tenaciously interpreting scriptures literally—this would amount to grasping views, namely the views of the past—one is, nevertheless, to consult the text, carefully, bringing to bear the aids of recent scholarship, as the efforts of Professor Wijesekera so clearly made manifest. With this approach to scripture, Baptists should concur.

Buddhists have not held a notion comparable to original sin. The approach has been, rather, one of describing the state of affairs as presented in the context of our living. There are, of course, latent tendencies and hindrances that regularly erupt to lead the mind into disorientation and into a sense of bondage. These latent tendencies have been present insofar as one realizes that one is in *saṃsāra*. But the matter of origin of all this is put aside, "O monks, of incalculable beginning is *saṃsāra*; the point of origin is not apparent, of beings fettered by ignorance, bound by craving, who are running around, coming again and again."[44] Buddhists, therefore, would agree with Baptists in saying that our human predicament is not the result of a primal cause, is not a consequence of our fundamentally depraved nature, or of original sin, but is the result of our detrimental proclivities, inclinations, and tendencies, which are contributive to our human setting as we find it to be.[45]

Buddhists and Baptists have made it clear that they stand for religious freedom, freedom of conscience, religious toleration, although here and there along the way they have failed firmly so to stand. Further, both positions are committed to the continuation of inquiry, the process of seeking to know the truth for oneself (*cf.* P: *yadā tumhe . . . attanā va jāneyyātha*). Buddhists and Baptists, moreover, are fully aware of the advantage of refraining from affectation that regularly seems to arise from doting on precepts and rituals (P: *sīlabbataparāmāsa*) since, from both perspectives, liturgical acts, indeed, even good works, do not in themselves liberate one from oneself, do not bring salvation. Baptists have been enabled to testify that *one does not save oneself.* Buddhists have received from the tradition the witness that *Salvific Truth arises to one* who lives the religious life (*brahmacariya/dhammacārin*). Of course, Baptists are bearers of good news,[46] of God's reconciling act in Christ, affirming that salvation is by faith through grace and not of works. Buddhists have tended to be more reluctant to provide exhaustive elaborations about that moment of transformation when salvific insight-wisdom (*lokuttara-paññā*) arises. This much we can say: the arising of the path (*magga*) and the first glimpse of Nibbāna have not been classified as the fruit of one's action (*kammaphala*). Further, when reality is seen, where is the individuated, agential self that has brought this about, that has caused it?[47] And lastly, but fundamentally, the *magga*-event, the arising of the path, arises as a natural process expressive of the natural order of reality.[48]

The sociopolitical contexts in which the Buddhist tradition has evolved has, of course, not given rise to a consistent call for a "separation of 'church' and state," for a separation of the practices, rites, beliefs, institutions of a religious community and the state. The heritage of Buddhists, the commitment to freedom of inquiry and religious expression, would tend to lead to careful scrutiny of all attempts to develop either state sponsorship or repression of any religious tradition.

The act of taking refuge (*saraṇagamana*) is akin to the way Baptists interpret baptism. The customary procedure of taking refuge (*lokiyasaraṇagamana*), like baptism, is a ritual expression of faith enabling one to participate in a fellowship. The world-transcending going for refuge (*lokuttarasaraṇagamana*) is akin to the Pauline image of baptism, of one's dying with Christ in the passion of Christ, being buried with him, to rise in newness of life. We seek to die to self to rise anew.

Buddhists and Baptists, who both affirm the authority of scripture, know that the messages in their scripture differ, know well, too, that the doctrinal formulations created to carry the deep-meaning of human realizations recorded in those texts differ. But Buddhists and Baptists who are desirous of learning (P: *ye keci sikkhā-kāmā*), who continue to inquire (recall, P: *pucchatha bhikkhave*) in the context of freedom of conscience and religious liberty are uniquely poised to meet as religious persons of open minds and receptive hearts, to go with each other where the conversation leads—into our common future. There is already so very much that Buddhists and Baptists share as being at the very center of the religious life that one wonders why this has not been seen long before.

Buddhists and Baptists endorse these common principles of how religious living is to be grounded in a person's life and carried out in community. There is, therefore, no need to speak of universals, as it were, or monolithic concepts such as "building bridges of understanding" between Buddhism and Christianity, or describing how "Buddhism meets Christianity," or seeking for a "transformation of Buddhism and Christianity," or presenting Buddhism and Christianity as "rivals and allies." We begin afresh where we human beings have always begun—with the *particulars,* in the details, in the bedrock of our individual experiences and personal realizations. Truth also lies in the particular—as it did in a study and living room in a home on High Level Road just south of the Nugegoda intersection and north of the Gangodawila junction in Sri Lanka, as it does afresh today.

V

# The Challenge of Our Future

# 18

# Will There Be Faith on Earth?

*We cannot fail to recognize the moral demand which requires persons of different religious traditions to work together in the hope of forming community in the face of interpersonal fragmentation and international war. We can begin to meet the corrosive effect of radical secular individualism by considering afresh what it means to be human, which the Christian and Buddhist witness affirm involves faith.*

Mutual understanding of religious persons—Theravāda and Jōdo Shinshū Buddhists, Christians, and others—is a pressing requirement for our times, of course. There are numerous crises in our world today: wars, bloody skirmishes, terrorism, more than fifty million political and economic refugees, the AIDS epidemic, widespread starvation, global warming, the environment—deforestation, air and water pollution—the genuinely helpless state of some of our huge population centers with the breakdown of infrastructure—whether in Calcutta or Lagos, and one could certainly continue with this list.

A subtle, consequential crisis that confronts Buddhists and Christians today is the result of changes that have taken place in the broader context of our societies, in Europe, North America, Japan, and Sri Lanka, in which men and women aspire to live a religious life. This crisis is the result of a growing lack of faith, which has given rise to a movement toward radical individualism, coupled with an uninspired secularism, and a marginalization of the religious life. This crisis has arisen because, now more than ever, there seems to be a lack of faith: faith among persons, faith in a common cause, in a center of value, faith in reason, and faith in transcendence and the enriching experience of becoming engaged in the process of transcending. I will attempt to address this crisis by turning again to insights offered by H. Richard Niebuhr and Wilfred Smith, whom we have considered previously and whose thinking is rarely drawn upon in a contemporary complementarity. I will offer a tentative conclusion regarding compassion, wisdom, and faith.

I turn again to the opening paragraph of a work published posthumously, in which H. Richard Niebuhr parenthetically, but with alarming relevance, quotes a question recorded as being asked by Jesus: "'When the Son of man comes will he find faith on earth?' (Luke 18:8)." Acknowledging that Jesus might have meant faith in God, Niebuhr suggests, "he may also have meant, 'Will he find any faithfulness among men?'"[1] Noting the depths into which faithfulness among us fell in the twentieth century, Niebuhr proposes another possibility for the end-time of our future: not the brotherhood reflected in the "Ode to Joy" of Beethoven's Ninth Symphony nor nuclear holocaust adumbrated by our horrible experiences at Hiroshima and Nagasaki nor cataclysmic natural calamities, but a fourth possibility—as he puts it, "the gangrenous corruption of a social life in which every promise, contract, treaty and 'word of honor' is given and accepted in deception and distrust. If men no longer have faith in each other, can they exist as men?"[2] Niebuhr was well aware that we are promise keepers, but we are deceivers, too.

## THE CRISIS OF INDIFFERENT INDIVIDUALISM

Individualism, often championed in the United States, having, for the most part, become cut off from its noble humanistic heritage, has floundered in an era when values are no longer shared, when cultural norms have lost their relevance. Individualism, set adrift without a compass, has no anchor, no interweaving nexus that can continue to support it as a governing ideology other than a sheer drive for individual achievement and career success. Individualism, without a centripetal core of shared values of a society, has become centrifugally connected in tangential pursuits for one's own objectives. The modus operandi of this dislocated individualism is to succeed in any way whatever the cost. And the first consequential disposition that arises among persons is deception and the drive for self-aggrandizement. One no longer runs the risk of trusting another. Loss of responsibility for another is a correlative of failure to trust. The other person no longer matters unless that person has an immediate relationship to what is in one's own interest. We see this in our politicians, trapped in a loss of public trust. They are fully aware of this, are made uncomfortable by it, yet to perpetuate their place in office find it more and more difficult to become responsible and innovative thinkers. "Newspeak," the deceptive use of the language to manipulate the opinions of others, is commonplace in politics today. It is an uncomfortable business. We witness this in our litigious society which also demonstrates our lack of faith and responsibility. We cushion the impact of our nostalgia for former and more civil times by using humor to create so many jokes about lawyers. We laugh and mask our melancholy.[3]

H. Richard Niebuhr, long before *Star Trek* made popular the term *triangulation* on American television, introduced an idea of "triadic relation," which we have mentioned before: an interrelation between one person and another or others, and an integrative common cause, a center of value, a focal orientation, that represents a third and completing connection which is at the foundation of life that is lived in community. There is not much difficulty in understanding how faith—as trust in, loyalty and responsibility to—is operative among persons when community is formed and lives are lived with purpose. The social, interpersonal basis of our knowledge is fundamental, Niebuhr continued to stress.[4] Without this trust in others we would not have been able to learn much at all about anything. But the trust operating when we acquired our language and knowledge from and with others does not guarantee that we will act with responsibility to others, does not guarantee that we will not break this faith that we have had in others.

This faith, this confidence in and fidelity to others, can be grounded in a common cause, according to Niebuhr. But we need to keep a careful eye on this common cause. Niebuhr introduced theistic terms in order to clarify the disparate and multileveled forms in which persons can relate to these common causes. "Polytheism" represents the state in which a diffuse self gives multiple and limited loyalties to a number of centers of value, a faith that is expressed variously in one's own and variegated interests. "Henotheism," the practice of being loyal to one "god" among others, can be seen when one expresses loyalty to one's community, or one's nation, a kind of closed social faith. Over against these two forms of faith, Niebuhr introduced "radical monotheism," whose

> value-center is neither closed society nor the principle of such a society but the principle of being itself; its reference is to no one reality among the many but to the One beyond all the many, whence all the many derive their being, and by participation in which they exist. As faith, it is reliance on the source of all being for the significance of the self and of all that exists. It is the assurance that because I am, I am valued, and because you are, you are beloved, and because whatever is has being, therefore it is worthy of love. It is the confidence that whatever is, is good, because it exists as one thing among the many which all have their origin and their being, in the One—the principle of being which is also the principle of value.[5]

The human crises today arise from this lack of trust or confidence in and fidelity or responsibility to a common cause of such magnitude and transcendence, of such fundamental value and worth, that it provides value to us. Once we have broken through solipsistic concerns of self-aggrandizement, we still seem to stop short of becoming engaged with the process of transcending, of recognizing where transcendence begins and in responding in that recognition. Rather, our cause becomes our club or organization, our school or our family. We might press beyond this to think our cause is our district, region, province, or state, even our country. How slow we have been to learn that placing our loyalty in the nation as our ultimate cause—the ultimate for which life and death are meaningful—ends in devastating fragmentation of humanity if not ultimately ruin.

Niebuhr and Paul Tillich have introduced what is called the "Protestant principle" in such matters. It is the principle that consistently protests against the practice of holding the penultimate as ultimate, stopping short with the *idea* of God for *God,* halting prematurely the investigation of the mind and the devotion of the heart. The "Protestant principle" is iconoclastic of things made by humanity—concepts and liturgies—that inhibit one's encounter with the True and Merciful God, indeed, when pressed far enough, that inhibit one's encounter with God above God, with God beyond our concept of God.

Niebuhr and other Protestant Christian theologians would urge that we keep probing for ever more inclusive and comprehensive integrative causes until we reach the One. He called this One "the principle of being" and "the principle of value." In Buddhist-Christian conversations one might say, perhaps too quickly, that for Buddhists "emptiness" transcends both being and nonbeing, so, therefore, "principle of being" is not sufficiently final or ultimate. For Niebuhr, obviously, the "principle of being" is more fundamental than being. What it is in itself one finds difficult further to elaborate. We recall that it is, for Niebuhr, "the nameless ultimate Transcendent and Circumambient."[6] If Niebuhr had read in Buddhist Studies, he would have said, I am convinced, that the activity of his referring to the One—the personal disposition, the sense of trust and fidelity involved—is not unlike the activity others of us have been enabled to discern when we have spoken of Dharma in the highest sense, of *hosshin,* often translated as "*dharmakāya* as suchness."

## THE CRISIS OF NIHILISTIC SECULARISM

Wilfred Smith made his significant contributions to scholarship among the generation of scholars that followed Niebuhr. What Niebuhr touched upon from his faithful yet critical religious perspective from within the Christian heritage, Smith elaborated, persuasively, from his faithful Christian yet self-conscious perspective from within the religious heritage of humankind. As we have seen, their fundamental orientations to matters of religiousness are strikingly similar. Niebuhr's stress on the social nexus of human understanding, of values and worth, of meaning and commitment, of the key significance of selves in relationship, Smith underscored with his emphasis given to the significance of persons. Niebuhr's "Protestant principle" led him to speak ultimately of transcendence as the principle of being, the One, while Smith, a religious intellectual in a religiously plural world, also reiterated and frequently addressed the notion of "Transcendence." Both theologians were constructive critics of the society and culture in which they lived. Both were aware of the setting in history in which we live and do our thinking: how our ideas are historically dependent as well as culturally specific—as are and have been all human ideas.

Smith's remarkable insights are due to a considerable degree to his ability to reflect upon unchallenged assumptions, to his self-consciousness, to his turning with new searchlights to consider afresh his own heritage in light of what he had learned from others of us on this globe; other persons and other traditions, initially the Islamic witness, then others. And so he warns us of a nihilistic secularism that seems to be pervasively present today, a secularism based on a peculiar and relatively recent view that commonplace man-the-convenient is the measure of all things, man-the-ordinary, the biologically given species, is finally normative. Today, the religious life is widely interpreted, whether in department stores, on the streets, or in colleges far and wide, as something added to what is normative, as an addendum, as Smith has noted. This sense is widespread in the United States: to be religious, it is assumed, is to be unusual. One wonders whether this sense is becoming today more prevalent in South and Southeast Asia and Japan also.

Developing right along with this debased form of secular humanism, which is not representative of our noble humanistic heritage largely developed in the West, evolving more subtly and perniciously, is the assumption that both the activity of entrusting and that to which religious people entrust themselves, hold dear, give their hearts, are suspect, deemed unusual, certainly dubious orientations to life replete with opinion but not knowledge. Smith has spotted this cultural shift and has argued convincingly that the English verb "to believe," and the noun "belief," have, over recent centuries, come to mean, or to refer to, something which the person who believes cannot verify, and that the affirmations proposed as beliefs are propositions incapable of being verified, are positions about which one cannot be certain.[7] This drift, which is now the established assumption, is a demonstration writ large of the marginalization of the religious life. And this is another dimension of the human crisis that confronts religious men and women today. The crisis indicates a fundamental difference in understanding what it is to be human. So part of the human crisis today is the failure regularly to engage the question of what it is to be genuinely human.

We have also seen in the past seventy-five years the establishment of what have been called disciplines in the academy, restricted methods of approach to so-called fields that persons can cover or work in to demonstrate their mastery. The notion of disciplines has become so ingrained in our thinking that they have been called "ways of knowing," rather than modes of analyses, as though the human mind must function with alternative and disconnected means of knowing a subject. The intellectual stands firmly against this fragmentation of the mind's rigorous process of understanding, involving accumulation of facts, assimilation of materials, and acquisition of interrelations moving toward convergence, accurate and humanely adequate interpretation, to integrative understanding. It appears that many have chosen to follow Francis Bacon's notion that "Knowledge is power," finding the acquisition of knowledge, the control of information, especially in this technological age, to be the means to achieve success, to better one's life by achieving convenience, comfort, fame, and financial security. It seems that the commitment to reason leading to liberation and freedom is no longer pervasive today. There is no Truth the process of discovery of which leads to greater inclusiveness, to greater encompassing convergence. There are only truths substantiated by the different disciplines utilizing different and distinct methods. Disciplines are championed because they, as methods, yield anticipated and desired results. Emphasis is placed on methods: follow them well and the results are guaranteed. Does this appear akin to magic, and this at the core of what is called, for example, social *science*?

For a long time in the West and elsewhere the commitment by men and women to the activity of reason, in a universe not without consistent intelligibility in which human reason is grounded, involves faith, both confidence in the reliability of reason and fidelity to what this procedure requires of us: a character that is consistent, a mind that is committed to the pursuit of Truth, a refined patience to reflect thoroughly, to speak cogently, to act in a manner entirely congruous with order and the intelligibility of the universe. This commitment to truth, this confidence in truth and fidelity to truth, is through and through religious.

Our crisis in this case is that we have forgotten how this human quality of reason, readily seen among our noble humanists but also clearly discerned among religious intellectuals, is religious. Through reason one rises to the qualitative level of being genuinely human, participating in the inherent intelligibility of the cosmos, participating in Truth as one simultaneously is true oneself in this process of discovering truth. Faith in reason is confidence in reason, as well as fidelity to reason. However, now reason is often viewed on our college campuses as the means of arbitration exercised by persons who call themselves philosophers to adjudicate rival or conflicting claims made by different religions. That assumption is one of our human crises for religious persons today. Beliefs are in need of verification. Truth-claims, so-called, are in need of adjudication. In both cases, in the arena of modern negatively secular humankind, religious persons have to make a case, are expected to defend their unusualness.

## ON BECOMING GENUINELY HUMAN IN THE COMPANY OF FRIENDS

So, if we lack faith in each other, if we have no common cause that receives our allegiance, if we no longer put our trust in reason and in its guidance, and, in the final analysis, if we no longer have faith in the principle of transcendence, and the process its principle involves, is there any hope for us? Succinctly phrased, the answer is "No!" We will surely enter that period of degeneration that Niebuhr characterized as that "gangrenous corruption in a social life . . . in deception and distrust."

Whether we respond creatively and constructively to this crisis of faith is itself a crisis for us. If we have the heart and the mind to seek for that which is most inclusive in our discernment of the religious life, we might develop a workable response that could give us hope for the future. If we can celebrate compassion as a primal outpouring into the field of our discernment of the principle of being or the principle of reality, we might discern a viable foundation for faith. If transcendence is of such quality that upon our apprehending it we find compassion arising, we might therein find a cause worthy of our loyalty. In giving your loyalty to compassion, it gives value to you, yourself, and to me, also, and I to it, and we—you and I—to each other as we realize this compassion. We would not want to say that this compassion comprehends transcendence, because, obviously, we ourselves cannot comprehend transcendence. But this compassion that is apprehended is not apart from transcendence nor will it fail to reconfirm the continuity of our first apprehension of transcendence and subsequent explorations of the depth, height, and breadth of transcendence.

If compassion, which we have found to be given to us, becomes our grounded center of value in living, we are thereby enabled to form community with each other. And in that community, so grounded by a center of value, we find our own value and our selves no longer remain fragmented within themselves and among themselves but become integrated selves among ourselves.[8] Insofar as we are enabled to learn of this compassion, by aligning our faces in the same direction, we bring our attention to this center of value, and we become capable of trusting each other, of placing our faith in each other, and also we become enabled to be recipients of each other's faith as both fidelity and responsibility to each other.

If we can also celebrate wisdom as a primal outpouring into the field of our discernment of the principle of being or the principle of reality, we might thereby have been enabled to receive another viable, entirely complementary, foundation for faith. Just as we, in attempting to become fully human, have learned from and with others how to express compassion, so we also have learned with and from others the process of rationality in a life-context that is intelligible. We have learned from trusted others how to become engaged with reason, to perceive the interconnectedness of an integrated mind thinking coherently in an intelligible universe and to find in this interconnectedness a placement of our selves among other selves in a rational order of existence. We cannot say that reason comprehends transcendence because, as we said with regard to compassion, we ourselves cannot comprehend transcendence. We are enabled to have faith that reason is not apart from transcendence, is not in opposition to it, in the final analysis is not in defiance of it, but is fully in accord with transcendence. With faith in reason, one is not alone, desolate, for reason exists in intelligibility and in such sphere one's mind operates coherently and converges toward Truth, which, at the initial process of convergence, is one's first glimpse of transcendence, and surely such Truth will be realized when transcendence is attained. When one through reason understands persons and things and how they have come to be in the situation in which they are now, one realizes wisdom, a phrase used to characterize the state of a person who has manifest faith in reason.

Because of the Christ-event, the abiding quality of Salvific Truth (*Dharma*), and the Arising of the Vow, and their re-occurrence in the lives of persons, we have been enabled to discern where transcendence begins. If we are enabled, further, to perceive wherein compassion and wisdom begin to converge, we can apprehend where a life of freedom begins. A compassionate person is also wise and such person is worthy of trust and in such person we have faith. It is through keeping faith with such person, even though we ourselves often are deceitful, that we can come to understand the vision of transcendence that person celebrates and thereby come to understand more profoundly that person.

Will there be faith on earth? The answer to this question depends upon what we decide to do. If we can or are enabled to discern wherein there is convergence of compassion and wisdom within the person, convergence of God and Truth in Transcendence, we will have discovered wherein we have a common cause for which to live, persons in whom we have faith, and a reality in which we can live authentically. To be persons of faith, then, is not unusual, not an abnormality. Niebuhr has made the point that we cannot live as men and women without faith.[9] Smith has put it this way, "Standard man is man of faith. Faith . . . is normal in human life and normative."[10] So, put another way, the human crisis that confronts us is whether we will do or be enabled to do what is required of us to be genuinely human. And, men and women today, whether Christian or Buddhist or humanist, cannot be genuinely human alone, in isolation from each other, within our closed groups or societies or religious institutions and traditions.

As we consider ourselves the global religious history of our race, we acknowledge magnificent faith and shockingly cunning foibles, beautiful responses in caring, troubling pettiness, healing acts, and brutal wars. If we manage the crises confronting us today, in this culture and around the world, and if we gain our footing to provide intelligent and flexible responses arising as we enter our common future, we will be at our best upon recognizing that we have been, are, and can be in the company of friends.

# Notes

## FOREWORD

1. This is a major theme, of course, of Wilfred Cantwell Smith's manifesto for the comparative study of religions: "Comparative Religion: Whither—and Why?," in *The History of Religions: Essays in Methodology*, ed. Mircea Eliade and Joseph M. Kitagawa (Chicago: University of Chicago Press, 1959), 31–58. Smith's essay was published a half-century ago but its challenges are still fresh, and most of its lesson still to be learned.

2. Scholarship, of course, is one only example of "the activity of understanding," which is one of the overt themes of this collection, albeit Carter thematizes it here as an activity in religiousness itself (see his opening statement in Introductory Note: This is "a collection of a series of reflections that attempts to explore two fundamental dimensions of human religiousness: faith and the activity of understanding.") In this foreword, however, I direct our attention to the activity of understanding in scholarship and especially to friendship as part of the activity of scholarly understanding.

3. For some of many calls to turn scholarly self-consciousness to larger questions of the "moral formation" of the scholar, see the provocative, as well as very different works by Wilfred Cantwell Smith, "Methodology and the Study of Religion: Some Misgivings," in *Methodological Issues in Religious Studies*, ed. Robert D. Baird (Chico, CA: New Horizons Press, 1975), 1–30; Edward Said, *Humanism and Democratic Criticism* (New York: Columbia University Press, 2004); and Paul J. Griffiths, *The Vice of Curiosity: An Essay on Intellectual Appetite* (The 2005 J. J. Thiessen Lectures) (Winnipeg, Manitoba: CMU Press, 2005).

4. Paul Ricoeur, *The Symbolism of Evil* (Boston: Beacon Press, 1967), 348.

5. It is worthwhile to consider the suggestive choice of the preposition *into* here, as opposed to something such as "In conversation *about* our common future."

6. Page XXX.

7. Page XXX.

8. Page XXX.

9. John Ross Carter, *On Understanding Buddhists: Essays on the Therāvada Tradition in Sri Lanka* (Albany: State University of New York Press, 1993), ix.

10. Specifying the appearance of this relationship should not be taken lightly, of course. See *Suttasangahaṭṭhakathā*, ed. Baddegama Piyaratana (Simon Hewavitarne Bequest, Vol 25) (Colombo: Tripitaka Publication Press, 1985), 19: "'Ananda, there is a person because of a person.' That is to say, it is because of, or on account of, one person who is a teacher, that there is another person who is a student. 'I say that requital is not easy.'" Translation by Maria Heim.

11. Page XXX.

12. See Wilfred Cantwell Smith, *What is Scripture?,* 35.

13. Page XXX; emphasis added.

14. Carter, *On Understanding Buddhists,* ix.

15. Page XXX.

16. Page XXX.

17. Page XXX.

18. David Burrell, C.S., *Friendship and Ways to Truth* (South Bend: University of Notre Dame Press, 2000), 2.

19. Wilfred Cantwell Smith, "Methodology and the Study of Religion," 23.

## ACKNOWLEDGMENTS

1. Two companion volumes that give evidence to the significance of a religious heritage for providing orientation in one's attempt to live life well are now available. They arose from study tours conducted by Colgate undergraduates in Japan and on three occasions in Sri Lanka. They are John Ross Carter, ed., *The Religious Heritage of Japan: Foundations for cross-cultural understanding in a religiously plural world* (Portland, OR: Book East, 1999), and John Ross Carter, ed., *On Living Life Well: Echoes of the Words of the Buddha from the Theravāda Tradition* (Onalaska, WA: Pariyatti Press, 2010).

## INTRODUCTORY NOTE

1. One wishing to gain an overview of the Buddhist tradition in Asia, generally, and through its historical development, would want to consult Joseph M. Kitagawa and Mark D. Cummings, eds., *Buddhism and Asian History: Religion, History, and Culture—Readings from the Encyclopedia of Religion*, Mircea Eliade, ed. in chief (New York: MacMillan, 1989). A good place to start in a study of the tradition in South Asia, with a primary focus on Theravāda, would be Rupert Gethin, *The Foundations of Buddhism* (Oxford: Oxford University Press, 1998). For a firm foundation regarding Shinran and his significant life and thought, one would want to read Yoshifumi Ueda and Dennis Hirota, *Shinran: An Introduction to His Thought—With Selections from the Shin Buddhism Translation Series* (Kyoto: Hongwanji International Center, 1989).

2. So the Revised Standard Version of the Bible (*RSV*). I follow the Hebrew text of *Biblia Hebraica,* ed. Rud. Kittel (Stuttgart: Württenbergische Bibelanstalt for the American Bible Society, 1937).

3. So *RSV.* I follow here the Greek Text of *Novum Testamentum Graece,* cum apparatu critico curavit Eberhard Nestle (Stuttgart: Privileg. Württ. Bibelanstalt for the American Bible Society, n.d.).

4. Reference is to xlii.53 in A. Yusuf Ali, *The Holy Qur'ān: Text, Translation, and Commentary* (U.S.: McGregor and Werner,1946). On the "straight path," see Arthur J. Arberry, *The Koran Interpreted* (New York: Macmillan, 1955), 198; W. Montgomery Watt, *Companion to the Qur'ān: Based on the Arberry Translation* (London: George Allen and Unwin, 1967), 13; and Mahmoud Ayoub, *The Qur'an and Its Interpreters,* vol. I (Albany: State University of New York Press, 1984), 48–49.

5. H. A. R. Gibb and J. H. Kramers, eds., *The Shorter Encyclopaedia of Islam,* edited on behalf of the Royal Netherlands Academy (Ithaca: Cornell University Press, n.d.), 524a.

## CHAPTER 1. ON UNDERSTANDING RELIGIOUS MEN AND WOMEN

1. I am grateful to Professor Minoru Tada who gave the assignment, "Speak to us about what you are doing." Professor Tada, a scholar of American English literature, who seems never to lose patience with others, nor to refrain from extending a helping hand, brought distinction to Otani University prior to his retirement from teaching and now is President Emeritus of Obihiro-Otani Junior College of Hokkaido, Japan.

2. This church is considered "the Mother Church of Colgate University," being the institution that initiated the movement by the Baptist Education Society of the State of New York to launch the Hamilton Literary and Theological Institution in 1819, which became Madison University and later Colgate University. From this institution, between the years of its founding until roughly the mid-twentieth century, well over 125 Christian missionaries went to Asia alone while still others went to Africa, the eastern Mediterranean, Europe, and to the then western frontier of North America.

3. See the engaging chapter, "Christian—Noun, or Adjective?" in Wilfred Cantwell Smith, *Questions of Religious Truth* (New York: Charles Scribner's Sons, 1967), 99–123.

4. This study of Sri Lankan Buddhists, I am delighted to note, was published in Japan as *Dhamma: Western Academic and Sinhalese Buddhist Interpretations—A Study of a Religious Concept* (Tokyo: Hokuseido Press, 1979), in a series sponsored by The Eastern Institute under the direction of Hajime Nakamura, and, happily, has been translated into Sinhala by W. S. Karunatillake, as *Dhamma—aparadiga śāstrajña-saha siṃhala bauddha artha kathana āgamika saṃkalpayak piḷibaňda adhyayanayak* (Colombo: M. D. Gunasena, 1985, repr., 1999).

5. I have written on the Theravāda Buddhist tradition, on Dhamma, on "refuge" (*saraṇa*), being reminded by my colleague Mr. N. Kashiwahara that perhaps we need to give more thought to what might be the best English word to represent *saraṇa*. I have written a little about rites and rituals, on ethical appraisals, even on the recent and Western concept "Buddhism" and the yet more recent, later concept, "Early Buddhism." I have worked in translations, too; a major translation effort on the *Dhammapada* and its commentarial heritage, co-authored with Mahinda Palihawadana, has been published. I have studied a fair amount, have learned a good deal, but am aware that my understanding of the religious life of men and women remains incomplete. Yet, the search for this understanding continues, of course.

6. In 1973, I was a short-term researcher at Kokugakuin University in Tokyo. During 1985–86, I was a Visiting Research Associate in the Division of Cultural Anthropology at the National Museum of Ethnology in Osaka, at the invitation of Professor

Mikiharu Itoh, trying, as time allowed, to learn more about what has been called "religion and society" in Japan, and learning in the process that the English concepts "religion" and "society" are no longer adequate to support my inquiry. During this sabbatical year, I was also a Visiting Research Associate at Ryukoku University, being allowed to be a member of the Ryukoku Translation Center. I also had the opportunity of being a Visiting Research Associate at Kyoto Women's University. In 1993 I was a Visiting Research Associate at the Shin Buddhist Comprehensive Research Institute of Otani University. More recently, in 2006, I had the good fortune to hold a short-term Numata fellowship at Ryukoku and in the summer of 2009 to serve as a Numata visiting professor at Ryukoku. Persons in these three fine Buddhist institutions of higher learning in Kyoto have kindly given of their time to introduce me into the currents of religious living as men and women who are Jōdo Shinshū Buddhists have discerned them.

## CHAPTER 2. TRUTH AND HISTORY IN INTERRELIGIOUS UNDERSTANDING

1. H. Richard Niebuhr, "Preface," in *The Meaning of Revelation* (New York: Macmillan, 1946), viii–ix.

2. Wilfred Cantwell Smith, *The Meaning and End of Religion: A New Approach to the Religious Traditions of Mankind* (New York: Macmillan, 1962), 320, n.4 to chap. 7 (reference to p. 177). This work was published in paperback as "A Mentor Book" (New York: New American Library, 1964); and in paperback through Harper and Row (San Francisco: Harper and Row, 1978); more recently in paperback, and without the subtitle (Minneapolis: Fortress Press, 1991).

3. Wilfred Cantwell Smith, *Questions of Religious Truth,* 84. Smith, here, is considering the statement that the Qur'ān is the word of God. He writes, "What is a Christian, as Christian, to do with the statement that the Qur'an is the word of God? What is he to make of it? I see three levels at which the matter might be explored. The first is absolute and historical, the second is theological and communal, the third is personalist and existential." Ibid.

4. Wilfred Cantwell Smith, *Towards a World Theology: Faith and the Comparative History of Religion* (Philadelphia: The Westminster Press, 1981), 192–93.

5. His was a time of great European discovery: Diaz navigates around the Cape of Good Hope, 1486; Columbus reaches America, 1492; John Cabot reaches the mainland of North America, 1497; Da Gama reaches India around the Cape of Good Hope, 1498; Balboa looks upon the Pacific Ocean at the Isthmus of Panama, 1513; and Magellan circumnavigates the globe, 1519–1522. St. Ignatius might have known something about these events, but we, today, can gauge the impact of these activities in a way not available to him at the time he lived.

6. Indeed, it sometimes appears that Wilfred Smith, fully aware of the inadequacy of a reified concept "religion," nevertheless could be read as working with a somewhat reified concept of "history."

7. Of course, one might say that from a biological perspective of life-forms, the dinosaurs, because of the enormous longevity of their life-form on this planet, provide far more convincing evidence of biological survival capability than the human species. And, related to this, one could argue that the evolutionary process in its causal sequence is of fundamental significance in history. It remains the person who is doing this reasoning,

reflecting, arguing, and, finally, introducing the notion of "history." This observation, obviously, indicates my judgment that meaning in history is grounded in persons.

8. No doubt much of the general Western notion of history is derived from the vision of ancient Israelites, incorporated in the subsequent Jewish perspective. Throughout this cumulative process the notion of "peoplehood" became more central and crucial. In subsequent interpretations, this sense of divine activity and peoplehood was extended by Christians through the notion of the Church into a broader contextual frame; namely, a divine activity working broadly through all historical events, of persons and things. And, of course, Muslims, too, bear witness to this divine activity.

9. H. Richard Niebuhr, *Faith on Earth: An Inquiry into the Structure of Human Faith,* ed. Richard R. Niebuhr (New Haven and London: Yale University Press, 1989), 84.

10. Niebuhr, *The Meaning of Revelation,* 17–18.

11. Ibid., 22.

12. Niebuhr puts it this way: "When the evangelists of the New Testament and their successors pointed to history as the starting point of their faith and of their understanding of the world it was internal history that they indicated. They did not speak of events, as impersonally apprehended, but rather of what had happened to them in their community." And this insightful writer continues: "The inspiration of Christianity has been derived from history, it is true, but not from history as seen by a spectator; the constant reference is to subjective events, that is to events in the lives of subjects. What distinguishes such historic recall from the private histories of mystics is that it refers to communal events, remembered by a community and in a community." Ibid., 72. Today, in the attempts by Christians to establish mutual understanding with Buddhists, one does well to be alert to the percolation of fundamental assumptions in an affirmation that Jesus the Christ lived and taught in historical *reality* or in *real* history. The point is that the figure Jesus might have done so, even did so, one might aver, but the Christ of that event springs from a committed heart making that affirmation.

13. Smith, *Towards a World Theology,* 175. Smith provides a similar observation elsewhere: "Just as there can be no revelation that is not a revelation of something (or someone), so there can be none that is not a revelation *to* someone. There is no revelation of God except to particular persons." Smith, *Questions of Religious Truth,* 92.

14. Wilfred Cantwell Smith, *What is Scripture?: A Comparative Approach* (Minneapolis: Fortress Press, 1993), 239. Smith's use of *engagement* of course carries its English meaning, but with an overtone of the French for this bilingual Canadian: commitment, to carry out, observe obligations, a pledging and promissory involvement.

15. Aptly, for the conference held at Loyola Marymount, Smith observes, "This inescapable first step [the careful objective study of a religious tradition] is, however, only the first step: the one who takes it is an historian of a religious tradition, not yet an historian of religion. For this is *human* history. The faith of a Buddhist does not lie in the data of the Buddhist tradition. To apprehend it, one must know where to look. *The locus of faith is persons* [emphasis added]." Wilfred Cantwell Smith, "Objectivity and the Humane Sciences: A New Proposal," in *Modern Culture from A Comparative Perspective,* ed. John W. Burbidge (Albany: State University of New York Press, 1997), 133.

16. Wilfred Cantwell Smith, *Questions of Religious Truth*, 67. Smith reiterates this point with only slight modification elsewhere, in introducing his brilliant piece, "A Human View of Truth": "Let me begin with a statement of the thesis in highly summary form. Briefly, my suggestion is that the locus of truth is persons. Or, if not 'the'

locus, at least a central locus: of considerably greater importance and primacy than is now usually recognized." Wilfred Cantwell Smith, "A Human View of Truth," in *Modern Culture from a Comparative Perspective*, ed. John W. Burbidge (Albany: State University of New York Press, 1997), 99.

17. At the midpoint of the conference at Loyola Marymount University of Los Angeles, we witnessed the devastating criminal tragedy of September 11, 2001. With great dignity the university did that which was appropriate with impressive naturalness providing an uncontrived shift in perspective that reminded us all of the buttressing presence of tradition and meaning in a time of perplexity and despair. In the afternoon, the Buddhist and Christian conferees were ushered to specially designated seats at a magnificent Mass, made so not by pomp and circumstance, but by beautiful voices, by a student body familiar with words sung and chanted, filling the sanctuary to overflowing, and a ritual combining the reassuring testimony from the past into the immediately discerned presence of transcendence. Buddhists and Christians, in the midst of the impact of that September day of infamy, saw a response that brought distinction to Loyola Marymount University of Los Angeles, and to religious men and women.

18. It was T'an-luan (J: Donran, 476–542) who had the profound religious insight of *dharmakāya,* ultimate Truth and also ultimate Reality (*hosshō hosshin*), of itself and entirely consistent with itself, becoming apprehended by the human heart and mind as Amida Buddha, *dharmakāya* as compassion (*hōben hosshin*), by means of which persons can grasp with understanding the abiding truth that compassion is the foundation of all that can be known. I have attempted to address this magnificent discernment of the compassionate and salvific quality of reality in the thought of Shinran in our chapter 10, "Toward an Understanding of What Is Inconceivable." See the important passage at *Shinshū Shōgyō Zensho* (Kyoto: Ōyagi Kōbundō, 1984), 2:615.1–15. Henceforth this work will be noted as *SSZ*. This passage has been translated into English in *Notes on "Essentials of Faith Alone": A Translation of Shinran's Yuishinshō-monī,* Shin Buddhism Translation Series (*SBTS*), general ed. Yoshifumi Ueda (Kyoto: Hongwanji International Center, 1979), 42–43. This work also appears in *The Collected Works of Shinran,* vol. 1, *The Writings,* trans., with intro., glossaries and reading aids, Dennis Hirota (head trans.), Hisao Inagaki, Michio Tokunaga, and Ryushin Uryuzu, *SBTS* (Kyoto: Jōdo Shinshū Hongwanji-ha, 1997), 460–61.

T'an-luan seems to have found himself in a position not entirely unlike some theologians at the Council of Chalcedon (451), to which we will return in our chapter 12, who were attempting to articulate their understanding of the two natures of Christ: " . . . TWO NATURES, WITHOUT CONFUSION, WITHOUT CHANGE, WITHOUT DIVISION, WITHOUT SEPARATION. . . ." *Documents of the Christian Church,* selected and edited by Henry Bettenson (London: Oxford University Press, 1959 [of the work first published in Oxford's "The World's Classics" in 1943]), 73. I refer to T'an-luan's observation: "Depending on the Dharma Body of Dharma-nature, the Dharma Body of Expediency arises; depending on the Dharma Body of Expediency, the Dharma Body of Dharma-nature reveals itself. These two Dharma Bodies are distinct but not separate, one but not identical." *The Tanni Shō: Notes Lamenting Differences,* Ryukoku Translation Series (*RTS*), 4th ed. (of the first, 1962; Kyoto: Ryukoku Translation Center, Ryukoku University), 2:101 n. 24. Reference is made to the *Ōjō Ron Chū* as occurring in *SSZ* 1:336–7.

19. Wilfred Cantwell Smith, *Questions of Religious Truth,* 85.

## CHAPTER 3. INTERRELIGIOUS UNDERSTANDING AS A RELIGIOUS QUEST

This initial exploration of interreligious understanding was first offered in response to an invitation to write for a memorial volume dedicated to Godwin Samararatne of Sri Lanka whose quest for understanding I have appreciated throughout our nearly four decades of friendship. In his inquiry into the activity of the mind, into human relationships, into cross-cultural and interreligious understanding, Godwin was faithful to a Buddhist principle: "don't get stuck." Ever open to the new, continuingly and creatively receptive of others, never judgmental of theological affirmations, Godwin demonstrated to students at Colgate University, in a course on Buddhist meditation, and to Colgate students on three occasions at his meditation center at Nilambe, Sri Lanka, the integrative orientation to the truth by which he lived his life and the moral commitment by which he sought to understand others and the world in which we live.

1. One might agree with David Hume that fundamentally cognition is a combination of impressions arising from sensations and reflection on those sensations, yielding simple ideas that can become more complex either as a response to complex sensations or to the activity of the human imagination rearranging those ideas. According to this view, knowledge arises when resemblances between and among ideas are arranged and categorized. (This conceptualization of the process reflects, of course, the system-structuring of categories prevalent in Western scientific procedures.) Whatever might be a process of greater abstraction beyond these restructuring of resemblances of ideas, as this particular interpretation puts it, is due to habit or custom, a frequency of recurring usages only, not at all demonstrable from the empirically given. It is this habit or custom that leads one to propose a similarity in causes yielding particular effects, but such cannot either be inferred with reliability or demonstrated with precision. (One notes some of the points about habit or custom in the foundation of morals suggested by Hume's contemporary, Edmund Burke, 1729–1797.) If it were not to appear arrogant or flippant, one could say in response to Hume and of this line of inquiry, "Well, of course." We are, indeed, so constituted that sense perception and sense impressions are fundamental, without question, as building blocks with which our distinctive reflection, even imagination, set about to structure experiences upon which the mind can reflect in its cognitive processes, which are primary, without, of course, denying other forms of human experience. One recalls the words of the *Dhammapada*,

> Preceded by perception are mental states,
> For them is perception supreme,
> From perception have they sprung. . . .

See the opening two verses of "The Pairs" (Yamaka-vaggo) of the *Dhammapada: A New English Translation with the Pali Text and the First English Translation of the Commentary's Explanation of the Verses With Notes Translated from Sinhala Sources and Critical Textual Comments,* by John Ross Carter and Mahinda Palihawadana (New York: Oxford University Press, 1987), 89. (This work was first issued as an Oxford University Press paperback in 1998. The English translation with new explanatory notes appeared in the "Oxford World's Classics" series in 2000.)

2. The case has been made, convincingly, by Wilfred Cantwell Smith in his now classic work, *The Meaning and End of Religion.*

3. Occasionally in considering the "exclusivistic case" expressions such as "my Jesus," or "my God," are written off as a kind of *genitive of possession,* suggesting an inadequate theological awareness that one is attempting to possess Jesus, God, in one's own conceptualization. But could not this be interpreted as a *genitive of engagement or relevance* whereby one is giving testimony to the abiding presence of God in Christ in one's life?

4. Jonathan Lear, *Aristotle: The Desire to Understand* (Cambridge: Cambridge University Press, 1999 [of the work republished numerous times since 1988]), 6. Twin strands that have shaped mightily the religious heritage of the West, as often noted stemming from Palestinian and Greco-Roman complexes, have largely, though not exclusively, developed from the Greek language. The writers of the *koinē* Greek New Testament demonstrate a clear preference for two Greek terms, and their derivatives, to communicate knowledge/understanding: *oida* (οἶδα) and *ginōskō* (γινώσκω, a later form of γιγνώσκω), with much less predilection for the Greek word from which has derived the much more popular key term in philosophical discourse today: *epistēmē* (ἐπιστήμη). One finds *epistamai* "understand something, know," or "be acquainted with," prevalent in Acts, particularly in indirect discourse, and as participle in I Timothy and Mark, and *epistēmon,* "expert, learned, understanding," as noted in James. In fact, *epistēmē* itself appears only as a variant reading at Philippians 4:8.

5. Ibid., 8.

6. Ibid., 9.

7. Ibid., 14.

8. Ibid., 316–17.

9. H. Richard Niebuhr, *Faith on Earth*, 24.

10. H. Richard Niebuhr, *Radical Monotheism and Western Culture; with supplementary essays* (Louisville: Westminster/John Knox Press, 1960), 105 n.1. This work was first published in 1943 and often thereafter, and as a Harper Torchbook, with an introduction by James M. Gustafson, in 1970.

11. Niebuhr, *Faith on Earth,* 83.

12. Ibid.

13. Ibid., 84.

14. Ibid., 85.

15. Ibid., 84.

16. Wilfred Cantwell Smith, *Faith and Belief* (Princeton: Princeton University Press, 1979), 146. This work has been reissued with a new subtitle, *Faith and Belief: The Difference Between Them* (Oxford: Oneworld, 1998). Our new approach would be no longer to place primary emphasis on what Theravāda or Jōdo Shinshū Buddhists or Christians *believe* but on what these religious men and women *understand.*

17. This would suggest that one not *stop* one's inquiry by arguing for a kind of "comparative theology" in which one takes similarities of ideas and symbols found in another tradition and uses them to draw attention to fresh currents of thought and practice in one's own religious tradition. One runs the risk of missing the profundity of those ideas and symbols for others in manipulating them to extrapolate insights within the frame of reference of one's own, different religious heritage.

18. Wilfred Cantwell Smith, *Faith and Belief*, 147. We included this observation as part of an extended quotation from Smith below in our chapter 13, "From Controversy to Understanding: More than a Century of Progress" dealing with the particular setting of Sri Lanka.

19. Ibid., 170.

## CHAPTER 4. *SAṂVEGA* AND THE INCIPIENT PHASE OF FAITH

1. William Dwight Whitney, *The Roots, Verb-forms, and Primary Derivatives of the Sanskrit Language*, "American Oriental Series" (New Haven: American Oriental Society, 1945 [as a supplement to his *Sanskrit Grammar*, London: Trübner, 1885]), 159, *sv. vij* "tremble."

2. T. W. Rhys Davids and William Stede, eds., *The Pali Text Society's Pali-English Dictionary* (London: Luzac for the Pali Text Society [an edition of the work first published in fascicles, 1921–25], 1966). Hereafter noted as *PTSD.*

3. Buddhadatta Mahāthera, A. P., *Concise Pāli-English Dictionary* (Colombo: The Colombo Apothecaries' Co., 1968), 277b, *sv. saṃvega.*

4. Nyanatiloka, *Buddhist Dictionary: Manual of Buddhist Terms and Doctrines,* edited by Nyanaponika, 3rd ed. (Colombo: Frewin, 1972), 161, sv. *saṃvega-vatthu* and *saṃvejanīya-ṭṭhāna.*

5. Ananda K. Coomaraswamy, "*Saṃvega,* 'Aesthetic Shock,'" *Harvard Journal of Asiatic Studies* 7, no. 3 (February, 1943), 174.

6. Franklin Edgerton, *Buddhist Hybrid Sanskrit Grammar and Dictionary,* vol. 2, *Dictionary* (New Haven: Yale University Press, 1953), 541b, sv. *saṃvega.*

7. T. W. Rhys Davids and J. Estlin Carpenter, eds., *The Dīgha Nikāya* (London: Luzac for the Pali Text Society, 1949), 1:49–50. Unless otherwise indicated, all Pali references are to the editions published by the Pali Text Society (*PTS*).

8. Rhys Davids and Carpenter, eds., *The Dīgha Nikāya* (London: Oxford University Press for the Pali Text Society by Geoffrey Cumberlege, 1947 [of the work first published in 1903]), 2:240.

9. M. Léon Feer, ed., *The Saṃyutta-nikāya,* pts. 1–5 (London: Luzac for the Pali Text Society, 1960), 4:290.

10 *Saṃyutta-nikāya,* 5:270.

11. V. Trenckner, ed., *Majjhima-nikāya* (London: Luzac for the Pali Text Society, 1964), 1:253–54.

12. C. A. F. Rhys Davids, *The Visuddhi-magga of Buddhaghosa* (London: Oxford University Press for the Pali Text Society by Humphrey Milford, 1920), 107. In the broader context of this passage this disposition, placed alongside others pertaining to a person characterized as *buddhicarita,* follows an enumeration of dispositions applicable to a person characterized as *saddhācarita,* having a faithful temperament or being characterized by faith.

13. *The Path of Purification (Visuddhimagga) by Bhadantācariya Buddhaghosa*, trans. Bhikkhu Ñyāṇamoli (Colombo: M. D. Gunasena, 1964), 258.

14. *The Mahāvaṃsa*, chap. 23, vv. 62–63. Wilhelm Geiger catches the force nicely when he translates "With heart strongly moved," but his note fails to indicate a psychologically dynamic complementarity involved when he says, "the conception of

*saṃvega* is the negative side to the positive *pasāda*." *The Mahāvaṃsa or The Great Chronicle of Ceylon,* translated by Wilhelm Geiger with the assistance of Mabel Haynes Bode (Colombo: Ceylon Government Information Department, 1960 [of the work first published in 1912]), 160 n. 1.

15. On this notion see *Iti-vuttaka*, ed. Ernst Windisch (London: Oxford University Press for the Pali Text Society by Geoffrey Cumberlege, 1948), 30. *The Aṅguttara-nikāya*, pt. 2, edited by the Rev. Richard Morris (London: Luzac for the Pali Text Society, 1955), 115. *Visuddhimagga (PTS*), 107.

16. *The Vinaya Piṭakam,* vols. 1–5, ed. Hermann Oldenberg (London: Luzac for the Pali Text Society, 1964), 1:32.

17. *Saṃyutta-nikāya,* 1:197.

18. *Sutta-Nipāta,* new edition by Dines Andersen and Helmer Smith (London: Oxford University Press for the Pali Text Society by Geoffrey Cumberlege, 1948), vv. 935ff.

19. See the detailed fourfold illustration recorded in *Aṅguttara-nikāya,* 2:115.

20. *The Aṅguttara-nikāya,* pt. 1, edited by the Rev. Richard Morris, 2nd ed., revised by A. K. Warder (London: Luzac for the Pali Text Society, 1961), 43.

21. *Saṃyutta-nikāya,* 5:133–34.

22. So, *Aṅguttara-nikā*ya, 2:33.

23. As *Aṅguttara-nikāya*, 2:33, continues. There is repetition about impermanence, instability, and evanescence found at *Saṃyutta-nikāya,* 3:85.

24. Upon seeing one who had gone forth, the fourth omen, the Bodhisattva became delighted (*ruci*). *The Jātaka: Together with Its Commentary*, vols. 1–6, ed. V. Fausbøll (London: Luzac for the Pali Text Society, vol. 1, 1962; vols. 2–4, 1963; vol. 5, 1964), 1:59.

25. *The Milindapañho: Being Dialogues Between King Milinda and the Buddhist Sage Nāgasena,* ed. V. Trenckner (London: Luzac for the Pali Text Society, 1962), 236.

26. *Saṃyutta-nikāya,* 5:130.

27. *Visuddhimagga (PTS),* 135.

28. *Jātaka,* 1:137–38.

29. *Visuddhimagga (PTS),* 415.

30. *Mahāvaṃsa,* v. 24.

31. *Mahāvaṃsa,* chap. 1, vv. 3–4. The terms *pasāda* and *saṃvega* occur throughout in the postscripts following each individual chapter as, for example, "The first chapter called 'the arrival of the Tathāgata' in the *Mahāvaṃsa* made for the serenity and *saṃvega* of good persons." *Mahāvaṃsa,* 11. Wilhelm Geiger writes, "*Pasāda* signifies the feeling of blissfulness, joy and satisfaction in the doctrine of the Buddha, *saṃvega* the feeling of horror and recoil from the world and its misery." Op. cit., 1 n. 1.

32. *Dīgha Nikāya,* 2:214.

33. *Aṅguttara-nikāya,* 2:120.

34. *Dīgha Nikāya*, 2:140. This was said in Colombo, in 1968, of a Sri Lankan Buddhist man who passed away while on a *caitya* pilgrimage in India.

35. *Visuddhimagga (PTS),* 135.

36. Ven. Pandit W. Sorata Nayaka Thera, *Śri Sumaṅgalaśabdakoṣaya*: *A Sinhalese-Sinhalese Dictionary* (Colombo: Anula Press, 1963), sv. *dhammasaṃvega,* pt. 1, 482a. Reference in this work is to *Dhampiyā-aṭuvā-gāṭapadaya.*

## CHAPTER 5. *SHINJIN*: MORE THAN "FAITH"?

1. Morris Augustine, in his PhD dissertation entitled "The Buddhist Notion of Faith," provides a comprehensive study of the general sweep of the Buddhist tradition and brings together a great deal of information. However, he starts his discussion of *shinjin* without raising the question that I am here attempting to raise. *Shinjin* for Morris Augustine, means "faith" with no further discussion. I refer to Morris Jerome Augustine, "The Buddhist Notion of Faith," a dissertation presented to the Faculty of the Graduate Theological Union in partial fulfillment of the requirements for the degree of Doctor of Philosophy, Berkeley, California, May 1978 (Ann Arbor: University Microfilms International), printed by microfilm/xerography in 1982. See especially his chapter 4, "The Notion of Faith in Shinran's *Kyōgyōshinshō*," 175–225.

2. It should no longer come as a surprise in Buddhist Studies, in studies about Buddhists as religious men and women, to recognize that it is rather easy to talk about the "difficult path" (*nangyōdo*) but much more difficult to speak about the "easy path" (*igyōdo*). My own presentation in this chapter might appear in need of a *definition* of "faith." In many cases, one might expect this: provide a definition of faith and argue wherein a notion might be the same, similar, or different. Matters are not always so easy. If I will have demonstrated that we need to continue our discussions of *shinjin* and faith, then, to a considerable extent, the point of the chapter has been made. If *shinjin* is somehow "more than faith," then how would we—all of us—set about to discuss what we mean by *shinjin* and by faith?

3. In an unpublished lecture entitled "The 'Non-Self' Aspect in Shinran's Concept of 'Faith'" given at the Second Biennial Conference of the International Association of Shin Buddhist Studies, Honolulu, Hawaii, on August 3, 1985, 7, Michio Tokunaga has suggested "Shinran's 'faith' is nothing but the negation of self-power mind." Perhaps this is where *shinjin* arises in one's religious life, with the negation of "self-power mind." It would seem, however, that faith is already manifest in one's commitment to strive for the arising of *shinjin* knowing fully that one's striving, one's self-power, can never negate "self-power." One quickly detects wherein there might be a difference between "faith" and *shinjin*.

4. Our colleagues at the Ryukoku Translation Center of Ryukoku University have thoughtfully compiled textual references to a list of twenty related terms appearing in the *Kyōgyōshinshō*, a list that is probably not exhaustive. See *The Kyō Gyō Shin Shō (Ken Jōdo Shinjitsu Kyōgyōshō Monrui): The Teaching, Practice, Faith, and Enlightenment: A Collection of Passages Revealing The True Teaching, Practice, and Enlightenment of Pure Land Buddhism,* trans. Hisao Inagaki, Kosho Yukawa, and Thomas R. Okano, under the direction of Mitsuyuki Ishida, *RTS* (Kyoto: Ryukoku Univ., 1983), 5:122–24 and 122ff. n.1, providing elaborations.

5. Ibid., 101, 103. See also the important passage at ibid., 175–76.

6. See ibid., 112. We read also that "This mind or heart (*shin*) arises from the Wisdom of Infinite Light." Ibid., 124.

7. Ibid., 20.

8. Ibid. See also *The True Teaching, Practice and Realization of the Pure Land Way: A Translation of Shinran's Kyōgyōshinshō, SBTS,* general ed. Yoshifumi Ueda (Kyoto: Hongwanji International Center, 1983), 57.

9. See ibid., 156. *SSZ* 2: 41.10.

10. *Kyō Gyō Shin Shō, RTS*, 111. There are at least ten benefits accruing to a person with diamond-like heart or mind, but paramount is the actual realization that one "transcends crosswise the Five Evil Realms and the Eight Hindrances"; ibid., 120. On the Primal Vow, see below, our note 28 to chapter 9.

11. *The Kōsō Wasan: The Hymns of the Patriarchs, RTS* (Kyoto: Ryukoku Translation Center, Ryukoku Univ., 1974), 39, Column 6, *wasan* #19.

12. As, for example, at *Kyō Gyō Shin Shō, RTS*, 106–108.

13. I have attempted to avoid translating *shin* (transliterated identically but representing here two different words indicated in Japanese by two different *kanji* (心信), although no doubt difficult to follow in English, to some degree, but have otherwise followed the English translation provided at *Kyō Gyō Shin Shō, RTS,* 108.

14. The texts contrast *shin* (真) with *ke,* translated as "temporary," and *jitsu* we find contrasted with *gon,* translated as "expedient." *The Jōdo Wasan: The Hymns On the Pure Land,* translated and annotated by Ryukyo Fujimoto, Hisao Inagaki, and Leslie S. Kawamura, "Ryukoku Translation Series"(*RTS*) (Kyoto: Ryukoku University, 1984), 103, *wasan* # 71. Elsewhere, in speaking of *shin* as used in the expression "true disciples of Buddha," *shin* is contrasted both with *gi,* translated as "false" and *ke* again translated as "temporary." *Kyō Gyō Shin Shō, RTS*, 129. Taking a glance at *ke,* "temporary," and *gi,* "false," we find the following: "'Temporary' refers to the various beings in the Path of Sages and the beings who practice the meditative and non-meditative good deeds of the Pure Land Path." Further, "'False' refers to the sixty-two and ninety-five wrong views." Ibid., 131–32. I was surprised to read in a footnote about *gi*, "'False' refers to non-Buddhists." Ibid., 132 n. 1. Perhaps this note will be revised in a future edition of this important work.

15. When *shinjin* arises, a person is definitely assured of attaining birth in the Pure Land, never to regress, becomes firmly rooted in Salvific Truth, soteriological reality. Great care is taken to stress that this birth, this attainment, occurs immediately. *Notes on 'Essentials of Faith Alone': A Translation of Shinran's Yuishinshō-mon'i*, "Shin Buddhism Translation Series" (*SBTS*), general ed. Yoshifumi Ueda (Kyoto: Hongwanji International Center, 1979), 34–35; *Collected Works,* 1:454–55. See also *Jōdo Wasan, RTS*, 91, *wasan* #59. Some might want to see this immediacy primarily in terms of "clock-time," but it appears that it indicates, however, the immediacy of the salvific occurrence, that *there is no gap*. If there were a temporal gap, so to speak, there would have to be another stage, another agent, some other means to close it. From "our side," in human terms, we have tended to express the nonexistence of that "gap" by turning our attention to the most infinitesimal instant of time, to look there for the moment when time itself is pressed to its limits and collapses. The moment is so infinitesimal that our human reactions cannot get involved. This moment (*ichinen*) is in time but not of time.

The important work by Oscar Cullman, *Christ and Time: The Primitive Christian Conception of Time and History,* translated from the German by Floyd V. Filson (Philadelphia: Westminster Press, 1950), provides an interpretation of a sense of "fullness of time" (Grk: *kairos*) in the more linear process of time (Grk: *chronos*) that might prove engaging in a comparative analysis of *ichinen* in the context of *shinjin.*

16. *The True Teaching, Practice and Realization of the Pure Land Way, SBTS,* 1:139–40; *Collected Works,* 1:55–56. Cf. *SSZ,* 2:34.9–11.

17. One notes that this phrase, *makotoni shinnu,* was not translated "One knows in faith," a provocative point suggesting the issue at hand, whether *shinjin* is best

translated by "faith." This translation, ibid., was by the Shin Buddhism Translation staff. The Ryukoku Translation Center staff has similarly translated *makotoni shinnu* at *Kyō Gyō Shin Shō, RTS,* 106, 112, for example.

18. *The True Teaching, Practice and Realization of the Pure Land Way, SBTS,* 1:139–40; *Collected Works,* 1:55–56. Cf. *SSZ,* 2:34.9–11.

19. So Shinran glosses *chō* and *mon* at *SSZ,* 2:8.3. See *The True Teaching, Practice and Realization of the Pure Land Way, SBTS,* 1:77, where the phrase "will joyfully listen to" seems not to communicate the subtlety that Shinran discerned. *Collected Works,* 1:16–17.

20. *Notes on 'Essentials of Faith Alone,' SBTS,* 37; *Collected Works,* 1:456–57. Cf. *SSZ,* 2:626.7.

21. *Notes on the Inscriptions on Sacred Scrolls: A Translation of Shinran's Songō shinzō meimon,* "Shin Buddhism Translation Series" (*SBTS*), general ed. Yoshifumi Ueda (Kyoto: Hongwanji International Center, 1979), 45; *Collected Works,* 1:502. Cf. *SSZ*, 2:484.11.

22. Ibid., 51; *Collected Works,* 1:504–505. Cf. *SSZ,* 2:488.6–7. The passage of Shan-tao's that provides a basis for Shinran's gloss occurs here and also in *Kyō Gyō Shin Shō, RTS,* 46, and *The True Teaching, Practice and Realization, SBTS,* 109. Cf. *SSZ,* 2:21.13.

23. *Notes on 'Essentials of Faith Alone'* (*SBTS*), 39; *Collected Works,* 1:458–59. Michio Tokunaga has mentioned that the Shin Buddhism Translation staff also found that *shinjin* when associated with *jiriki* and used in a negative sense seemed awkward, and hence their translation of *jiriki no shin* (自力の信) as "self-willed conviction." But, I note again, *shin* (信) + *jin* (心) does not so occur. Cf. *SSZ,* 2:627.11.

24. See *Letters of Shinran: A Translation of Mattōshō,* "Shin Buddhism Translation Series" (*SBTS*), ed. Yoshifumi Ueda (Kyoto: Hongwanji International Center, 1978), 20; *Collected Works,* 1:52.

325. From another angle, one might point out how, in the face of a general and dominant Western orientation to individualism, a familiar strand of a dimension of faith is seen in those interpretations that highlight its role in the formation of foundations for community—loyalty, a sense of propriety, courtesy, reliability—which characteristics often *already* represent the case in the supportiveness of Japanese social and community life.

26. By introducing the term *dialectic* I do not wish to make matters more complicated or complex than they are. I use the term to underscore an "interplay" between dimensions of one holistic discernment. By no means do I intend to introduce a Hegelian framework of thesis/antithesis/sublation into a new thesis yielding another thesis/antithesis process. It would be tempting to apply such schema, but to do so would superimpose a remarkable paradigm of calculation onto a subject that is not designed to bear it. Nor do I use "dialectic" to refer primarily to proper reasoning, although this is a straightforward sense of the word. I use "dialectic" here to refer to a creative process of dynamic interrelationship of dimensions that work through each other while operating on each other. I interpret this notion to include a sense of communication into deepening understanding in the interplay of the dimensions, a process involving intelligibility based on a mutually interpenetrating fundamental principle. Consequently, one would discern in *logos* not only "word" or "speech" but primarily the classic Greek notion of *logos* itself. Suggestive in this usage would be the homologous relationship of *logos* and *jinen hōni.*

27. Paul Tillich has written about faith having to do with "Ultimate Concern" and this is an important contribution, one certainly worth noting. But one senses behind Tillich's notion a German sense of *Angst,* a deep, anxious, concern. I note this here because this notion of "concern" seems not quite to fit *shinjin* or the salvific insight attained by other Buddhists. Tillich's sense of "dynamics of faith" is somewhat akin to my use of "dialectic" in this chapter, but Tillich's frame of reference suggests that he found that dynamic to be between his Greek heritage and his Palestinian heritage, as these have contributed to the formation of his expression of faith. This is seen in the so-called "faith and reason" discussions. Tillich's notion of "the courage to be" seems to be an attempt at resolving the tension he sensed between faith and ontology, as it were, between God and Father of our Lord Jesus Christ and the Absolute. As significant as this great thinker's contributions have been, they seem unwieldy as reference points in Buddhist-Christian discussions.

28. Wilfred Cantwell Smith, *Questions of Religious Truth,* 99–123. This insightful thinker, although not working with materials drawn from the Jōdo Shinshū tradition, has demonstrated points of convergence in other cases that have provided theoretical structure for some of my considerations in this chapter. I note his important piece, "A Human View of Truth," in *Modern Culture from a Comparative Perspective,* ed. John W. Burbidge (Albany: State University of New York Press, 1997), 99–119. This work appeared in *Studies in Religion/Sciences Religieuses* (1971), 1.1:6–24; reprinted in *Truth and Dialogue: The Relationship between World Religions,* ed. John Hick (London: Sheldon Press, 1974); and *Truth and Dialogue in World Religions: Conflicting Truth Claims* (London: Sheldon Press, 1974).

## CHAPTER 6. CELEBRATING OUR FAITH

1. Joachim Jeremias, *The Prayers of Jesus* (Philadelphia: Fortress Press, 1984); the first chapter, "Abba," was translated by John Bowden with a copyright of 1967 by SCM Press.

2. So James Barr has argued in "Abba Isn't 'Daddy'," *Journal of Theological Studies* 39 (1988): 28–47; and "'Abba, Father' and the Familiarity of Jesus' Speech," *Theology* 91, no. 741 (1988): 173–79.

3. Too much remains not fully understood when we refer to this or that idea or concept, sign or object, sound or color as a religious symbol, although we have said something worth saying. But consider, for example, an American farmer who, at daybreak, enters his field and says, "Good morning, Lord." What do we make of that? We could say that this man was speaking symbolically, that he was expressing a greeting—not a proposition—and hence was providing us with linguistic evidence for inferring only the presence of an attitude. We might say that he was engaging in religious discourse, a different mode of speech and communication. But the farmer probably thought he was saying "Good morning" to Jesus the Christ. We could call his use of "Lord" a utilization of a gender-specific religious symbol derived from an outdated political-social order, and dispense with the matter. But an intellectual wants to understand *also* what this particular farmer meant when he said "Good morning, Lord." In seeking to understand *him* we cannot rule out from our considerations the possibility that he was not addressing a religious symbol that morning, at least that he at that time did not think that he was.

4. *Notes on 'Essentials of Faith Alone', SBTS,* 42–43; *Collected Works,* 1:460–61; see *SSZ,* 2:630.12–15. See also *Notes on Once-Calling and Many-Calling: A Translation of Shinran's Ichinen-tanen mon'i, SBTS,* general ed. Yoshifumi Ueda (Kyoto: Hongwanji International Center, 1981), 46; *Collected Works,* 1:486–87; and *SSZ,* 2:616.1–4.

5. Wilfred Smith has pointed the way for us in our comparative study of the religious traditions of humankind that leads us into our more fundamental study of ourselves as religious persons in human history. Like most creative thinkers, Smith's vision has been seen by some, misunderstood by others, found to be overly challenging by still others, and has been resoundingly applauded by many, too. Although his work has been criticized by some, it has not been challenged in a sustained study presented by any scholar through a series of works. What is difficult for those of us who are Canadian or American scholars to admit, and for those of us who are European scholars, too, is the situation in which we find ourselves: there has not yet appeared a scholar in position to bring to bear on his or her scholarship the depth and scope necessary to challenge the theses proposed and insights shared by Smith. In the course of my studies, I have found that Smith's approach in utilizing the historical method, his orientation to the significance of persons as also a locus of truth, his insight into the dynamic of faith and cumulative religious traditions, including, of course, community, his disciplined self-consciousness of his Christian heritage, his own faith as a Christian, his rigorous commitment to reason in the pursuit of truth *is* holding, is allowing the material accumulated for research to be seen in a new and more comprehensive way, is bringing critical scholarship into sensitive and humane colloquia, and this is occurring around the world. The problem that some might have with Smith's approach could be in its implicit iconoclasm, in the breakup and possible breakdown, of reified certainties as a result of discerning the fluidity of the human intellectual heritage within the historical process, in the tentativeness of our current thinking and writing, in the open-endedness of our future, which has tended to be, in fact, the ongoing process that most of us have experienced in the course of our human lives through the centuries of human history.

6. I note an engaging point that Shinran repeated in different contexts over the years:

> Know that shinjin is the true intent of the Pure Land teaching [*shinjin o jōdo shū no shō ī* ]. When one has understood this, then as our teacher Master Hōnen declared, "Other Power means that no selfworking is true working." [Perhaps one might render this as follows: "With regard to *tariki,* no sense of what is proper *is* what is proper" for *tariki ni wa gi no naki o mote gi to su*]. "Selfworking [*gi*]" is the calculating [*hakarai*] heart and mind [*kokoro*] of each practicer [*gyōja*]. As long as one possesses a calculating mind, then, one endeavors in self-power [*jiriki*]. You must understand fully the working of self-power [*yoku yoku kono jiriki no yō o kokoro ubeshi to nari*].

*Notes on the Inscriptions on Sacred Scrolls, SBTS,* 73; *Collected Works,* 1:519–20; *SSZ,* 2:602.14–603.2. See also an alternative formulation in *Letters, SBTS,* 29, Letter #5; *SSZ,* 2:663.10–11. See further the phrasing *gi naki o gi to su* in *Shōzōmatsu Wasan, RTS,* 55, 115 (on the latter page, *tariki* is also mentioned in contrast, of course), and 118.

7. *Notes on 'Essentials of Faith Alone,'* 48; *Collected Works,* 1:465; *SSZ,* 2:635.4.

8. The motto of Colgate University, where it is my privilege to teach, is *deo ac veritati,* "For God indeed for Truth," as I briefly mentioned previously and will

reintroduce in our chapter 17. The force of *ac* suggests that the noun that follows is intimately associated with the noun that precedes, more than *et* could communicate. The dative case indicates the dative of purpose, the purpose for which the institution was founded in 1819 and the purpose for which the students were to have pursued their studies. Alas, as is often the case among American colleges and universities, we have lost the perspective of our founders, and one finds a historian today with no greater motivational foundation for his or her work than that we can learn from history or that we are to train historians for graduate schools or that we are to develop educated citizens, and one finds a philosopher who defines philosophy as "what philosophers are doing," also alas.

9. Long ago, a group of Christians in Galatia circulated a letter received from Paul in which he demonstrated his faith by acknowledging, "I have been crucified with Christ [lit. co-crucified]; and I myself no longer live, but Christ is living in me; and the life I now live in the flesh I live by faith in the Son of God, who loved me and gave himself for me" (Galatians 2:20).

10. My faith does not save me. It is God in Christ that saves me. My faith, insofar as it is *my* faith, is the only faith that I know personally, in the depths of my heart, and is, at the same time, not sufficiently reliable to perform the kind of salvaging necessary to complete the task that needs to be done with regard to this particular life. Some of my Christian friends might urge that I increase my faith, might suggest that I do not have enough faith. And this might be so, of course. Christians might also suggest that I am being confusingly circuitous because the phrasing "my faith does not save me. It is God in Christ that saves me" is an expression of my faith, indicating thereby that I, too, am to be counted among the fold, happily, because, in spite of what I have said, I am still saved by faith.

Some Christians have held a doctrine of faith that tries to get at the core of this dynamic and sparkling dimension of self-understanding. In effect, this doctrine states, "We are saved by faith through grace and not by works alone" (Ephesians 2:4–10). The point is obviously that we cannot save ourselves. Further, the point is that faith does not do the saving, it is a necessary but certainly not a sufficient cause through which the salvific occurrence arises, it is *by means of faith*; faith is not the source of the salvific realization. The salvific activity is God's act in Christ, the free gift, *the gift* which has occurred through God's unconditioned grace, and it is this grace of God that enables one to put one's heart on God's act in Christ, that enables one, through the Holy Spirit, to respond by receiving and affirming this act, to attempt to find what one's life might become in light of this act. It is, in the final analysis, God who saves.

## CHAPTER 7. COLLOQUIA IN FAITH

1. Some time ago I looked at a syllabus for a seminar on "Buddhist-Christian Dialogue." The structure of the course seemed to be on dialogue between something called Buddhism and something called Christianity. It was interesting to note, in the Buddhist case, what appeared to be discrete units: Theravāda, Tibetan, something called "The Kyoto School," and Jōdo Shinshū. Perhaps there was only an attempt to present, in an American academic setting, a kind of conceptual running dialogue between Christianity and representative positions within the Buddhist case, positions whose Buddhist authors had given little attention to a need for dialogue among

themselves. Such seminar would tend to achieve at its conclusion nothing more than a series of alternative perspectives on the life-context and propositional formulations pertaining to reality that some persons in Asia, in different countries and in different centuries, have proposed—not for or to Christians or others, but to persons within their respective positions—and to consider the possible challenges these alternative proposals might pose for systematic Christian theology. This seminar would appear not even to have achieved the level of dialogue in its basic sense of communication.

2. There is a lacuna continuing to develop within Christian Studies in the United States. We have a number of young Buddhologists and Historians of Religion completing their graduate programs in leading universities. In most cases these young men and women achieve appointments in our colleges and universities. But we are not finding enough young men and women who have studied deeply the Buddhist and Christian traditions or the History of Religion to move into our denominational seminaries. We have not seen many appointments in these seminaries of persons capable of moving our thought, and the thought of the great and numerous Protestant groups, into the subject of interreligious understanding, not to mention the particularity of Buddhist-Christian understanding. The Roman Catholics are doing well enough; Protestants seem to be lagging behind.

3. At our most comprehensive level we are already beyond the dialogue phase, although I, too, am interested in Buddhist-Christian dialogue and will continue to be. But we are beyond this. Well over three decades ago Wilfred Smith suggested that "dialogue" was already dated and he proposed that we become engaged in "colloquia," where we talk among ourselves about ourselves as religious persons. I have been waiting for this sense of colloquia to arrive, for religious groups to move from dialogue to colloquia in major and significant ways. But this sense of colloquia has not arrived with institutional endorsement—although the reality of our religiously plural context is obvious everywhere around us—and religious groups and institutions still prefer to hold dialogue with others. Smith seems to have been hoping that scholars and theologians would rise to his sense of colloquia, that religious organizations would endorse it. Smith was right. Although he spoke from within empirical actuality and historical reality, he was, surprisingly, far ahead of the times and also far ahead of most scholars of our subject. It takes time for most of us to study two or more religious traditions with enough depth and scholarly acumen to see the point of holding colloquia. I suppose it takes three decades for most of us to reach the level from which Smith was writing when he made that suggestion—and once there, we resoundingly agree with him. At its best, dialogue is a preparation for colloquia.

4. Our hypothetical conference committee has its work cut out for it. We are to hold conferences among ourselves, as Jōdo Shinshū Buddhists, let us say, to discuss why we might want to have conferences, whether with other Buddhist groups and/or persons of other religious traditions. Then we are to set about to begin a series of dialogue conferences with persons of other religious traditions, keeping in mind, surely, that we are building for a series of colloquia with religious thinkers from the great religious traditions of our world.

5. See Wilfred Cantwell Smith, *What is Scripture? A Comparative Approach,* which we have previously noted. Smith's thorough study has shown us how scripture provides an example of commonality in our religious traditions rather than bases for argumentative differentiation.

6. One would want to establish as required reading a superb article, previously noted, by Wilfred Cantwell Smith, "A Human View of Truth," in Burbidge, op. cit.

## CHAPTER 8. "RELYING UPON" OR "TAKING REFUGE" AS A GENUINELY HUMAN ACTIVITY

This chapter developed from a presentation in response to an invitation to participate in Plenary Panel 1, "Ojo: The Problem of Salvation in the Contemporary World," as part of the proceedings of the International Association of Shin Buddhist Studies Convention, Tuesday, August 3, 1993.

If there is such a problem in our world today one might note that one's sense of what constitutes a problem or difficulty (J: *nan*) might be relative and that a great deal depends upon how the alleged problem is given focus. Consider the following:

> More difficult even than trust in the teachings of Śākyamuni's lifetime
> Is the true entrusting of the universal Vow [*gugan no shingyō nao katashi*];
> The sutra teaches that it is "the most difficult of all difficulties,"
> That "nothing surpasses this difficulty."

*Hymns of the Pure Land: A Translation of Shinran's Jōdo wasan, SBTS,* general ed. Yoshifumi Ueda (Kyoto: Hongwanji International Center, 1991), 61; also *Collected Works,* 1:344.

1. B. A. Gerrish on Friedrich Schleiermacher in *The Encyclopedia of Religion,* ed. in chief Mircea Eliade (New York: Macmillan, 1987), 13:111.

2. The topic of refuge as a religious category readily exceeds the limits of this chapter. With regard to the Jewish and Christian traditions, one might note there are several Hebrew words that communicate the sense of refuge which resound throughout the Hebrew Bible. It is very interesting, however, that the notions of "refuge" or "taking refuge" or stressing that God is "one's refuge," although of importance as the Christian tradition developed, do not appear in the Christian Greek New Testament.

3. *The Dhammapada*, vv. 188–192. The commentary's explanation, ibid., 248–249, although long, is worth noting here.

> *Mountains, forests*: Various persons, threatened by various kinds of fear and wishing to be free of fear or desiring to obtain sons, and so forth, go for "refuge" to mountain [shrines] here and there . . . to garden [shrines] . . . and so forth; to tree [shrines] . . . and so on. . . . *This is not a refuge*: All such "refuge" is insecure; it is not the highest [refuge]. And on account of it, not one among beings that are subject to birth, and so forth, is freed from [this] totality of suffering such as birth and the like. *But who*: Having indicated this refuge, which is insecure and not supreme, [the next line] has begun, [with the words] "But who . . ." to indicate [what then is] the secure and supreme refuge. [This is] what it means: the one who, lay person or recluse, *To the Buddha, Dhamma, and Saṅgha as refuge has gone*: Has gone to the Buddha, Dhamma, and Saṅgha as the best [refuge], resorting to the "topic of meditation" known as "calling to mind [the virtues of] Buddha, Dhamma, and Saṅgha" [in the formulas beginning with "So is that Blessed One the Worthy Being, the Fully Enlightened One" (endowed with knowledge and

noble conduct, the well-gone, knower of the worlds, incomparable trainer of human beings who are amenable to be trained, teacher of men and gods, the Blessed Awakened One)] and so forth [Well proclaimed by the Blessed One is Dhamma that is visible, timeless, characterized by (the imperatives) "Come! Look!", leading on, to be known personally by the wise. Well set out (on the Path) is the community of the Blessed One's disciples, directly set out is the community of the Blessed One's disciples, properly set out is the community of the Blessed One's disciples, fully set out is the community of the Blessed One's disciples—that is to say, the four pairs of persons, the eight persons (i.e., those who have attained the four Paths and the four Fruits). This community of the Blessed One's disciples is to be given offerings, is to be welcomed, is to be given gifts, is to be honored, is an incomparable field of merit for the world] even in this case, the "seeking of refuge" falls away and is [liable to be] disturbed by such [acts] as worshiping other *titthiyas* [precursors], and so on. [The stanza] proclaiming solely the refuge that is derived from the Path, in order to show its undisturbability, declares: *Sees with full insight the four noble truths*: The one who has gone for refuge to these [i.e., the world-transcending going for refuge because doubt and wrong knowledge with regard to the objects such as the Buddha, etc., are put aside by the knowledge accompanying the Paths. The person endowed with these Paths is one who has gone for refuge by way of this knowledge] [noble] truths by way of realizing them—this "going for refuge" is secure and supreme. That person is freed from the total misery of the whirl on account of this refuge. Hence it is said: *This, indeed, is a refuge secure.*

4. See the discussion of "The Arising of Salvific Realization as Buddhists and Christians Have Affirmed," in chapter 11, below.

5. See the discussion in my *On Understanding Buddhists: Essays on the Theravāda Tradition in Sri Lanka* (Albany: State University of New York Press, 1993), 55–70.

6. *Bhagavadgītā* 18:66 has come to be referred to as the *caramaśloka* and called "the last word." It reads,

> sarvadharmān parityajya māmekam. śaraṇaṃ vraja
> ahaṃ tvā sarvapāpebhyo mokṣayiṣyāmi mā śucaḥ

*Śrīmadbhagavadgītā Śrīśaṅkarabagavatpādācāryaviracitena bhāṣyeṇa sahitā: The Bhagavad-gītā with the Commentary of Śrī Śaṅkarācārya,* critically edited by Dinkar Vishnu Gokhale, Poona Oriental Series, no. 1 (Poona: Oriental Book Agency, 1950).

7. While keeping our focus on the notion of refuge, one would want to note, at least, that Rāmānuja also presents an insightful analysis of God's inaccessibility and compassionate manifestation, clearly akin to *hosshin* and *hosshin no hōben,* as T'an-luan and Shinran discerned it. We will consider these notions in our chapter 10, "Toward an Understanding of What Is Inconceivable."

Rāmānuja wrote:

> This Nārāyaṇa, the Supreme Person . . . when He created the entire universe of everything from the god Brahmā to motionless stones, remains with His same essential nature [*svena-rūpeṇa*] and is inaccessible even by such means as the meditation and worship of men or of gods like Brahmā.

> But being a shoreless ocean of compassion, gracious condescension, forgiving love . . . while still not losing His own inherent nature and attributes, He has assumed His own bodily form . . . has descended again and again . . . has granted them whatever they prayed for . . .

From Rāmānuja's *Gītābhāṣya*, p. 1, in the edition appearing in P. B. Annagarācārya, ed., *Śrī-Bhagavad-Rāmānuja-Granthamālā*. Complete works in Sanskrit (Kāñcīpuram: Granthamālā Office, 1956), as translated by John Braisted Carman and appearing in his *The Theology of Rāmānuja: An Essay in Interreligious Understanding* (New Haven: Yale University Press, 1974), 78.

8. Robert C. Lester, in "Rāmānuja and Śrī-vaiṣṇavism: The Concept of Prapatti or Śaraṇāgati," *History of Religions* (University of Chicago) 5 (Winter 1966), 5:266–82, follows Pandit Agnihothram in arguing that Rāmānuja did not write this work. Carman, op. cit., 63–64, suggests that on the matter of the question of authorship, the evidence is still out.

9. One is struck by the clarity of an observation, and its similarity to some of the ideas held in Jōdo Shinshū, provided in a commentary:

> In fact, the helpless Prapanna [person who has surrendered] is unable to perform the three Yogas on account of his sinful karmas and hence he has to give them up on account of his inability (to do it even in future). These sinful karmas which are enemies of salvation are so heinous in character that he has lost all hopes of being able to perform the Yogas at any time in future.

*Sri Bhagavad-Ramanuja's Saranaagati Gadya with English Translation of the Text and Its Commentary,* by Sri Srutaprakaasika Acharya, prepared under the guidance of Abhinava Desika Sri Uttamur Viraraghavacharya Swami by K. Bashyam, 3rd ed. (Madras: Visishtadavaita Pracharini Sabha, 1970), 43 (1st, 1959; 2nd, 1964).

10. The translation is by Lester, op. cit., 278.

11. Vasudha Narayanan, "*Karma, Bhaktiyoga,* and Grace in the Śrīvaiṣṇava Tradition: Rāmānuja and Kāraṭṭāḷvāṉ," in *Of Human Bondage and Divine Grace: A Global Testimony*, ed. John Ross Carter (La Salle, IL: Open Court, 1992), 65.

12. Ibid., 68, and translated by Vasudha Narayanan. The Śrīvaiṣṇava heritage, not long after the death of Rāmānuja, split into two branches. Among several causes for this split one had to do with a theological issue: the degree of self-agency involved in the granting of divine grace. The so-called Northern school (Vaṭakalai/Vaḍagalai), or "the monkey-hold school," held that one must at least be actively involved in seeking divine grace, taking the initiative to surrender, holding on tightly like a baby monkey holds tightly to its mother in order to be carried away. The Southern school (Teṅkalai/Teṅgalai), or the "cat-hold school," placed emphasis on one's passive receptivity of divine grace, in which one, like a kitten, is picked up and carried away by its mother.

13. Maheswari M. Arulchelvam writes,

> The hymns of the saints are rapturous outpourings of praise, of the power and majesty of God. Words are inadequate to convey all his greatness and his goodness. The devotee often recalls the many gracious acts God has done in times past, giving his love and grace to those who seek him. In the presence of this majestic God the devotee is struck with the feeling of great

unworthiness. Māṇikkavāçagar compares himself to a dog, unworthy, like a dog, in bondage to birth and decay.

Maheswari M. Arulchelvam, "The Gift Immutable," in *Of Human Bondage and Divine Grace: A Global Testimony,* ed. John Ross Carter (La Salle, IL: Open Court, 1992), 52.

14. Ibid., 53.

15. *Tiruvāçagam*, xv, 28, in *The Tiruvāçagam: The Tamil Text of the Fifty-one Poems,* trans. Rev. G. U. Pope (Oxford: Clarendon Press, 1900), 56, as quoted by M. M. Arulchelvam, op. cit., 53.

16. Professor V. A. Devasenapathi, former director of the S. Radhakrishnan Institute for the Advanced Study of Philosophy of the University of Madras, drew attention to an expression among some of the Tamil Poet-saints: that one seeks to be like an inanimate object when it comes to the granting of God's grace—"absolutely still, without any movement whatsoever." In a conversation in Chennai (Madras), March 1, 1993.

17. Shinran has not *become* an important figure in our global religious history solely because associations such as the International Association of Shin Buddhist Studies have been holding international conferences. It is also the other way around: that persons from all over the world are attending these conferences is due to our *finally coming to see* what has always been the case. Shinran has been an important figure in our global human religious history—we are only just recently beginning to see this.

18. We have seen, in chapter 5, "*Shinjin*: More Than 'Faith'?" a characteristic running through the writings of Shinran, namely both the importance of the notion of *shinjin* and the way many terms become associated with this one central notion.

19. So Dennis Hirota structures an insightful inquiry utilizing terms introduced by Gordon Kaufman. Dennis Hirota, "Breaking the Darkness: Images of Reality in the Shin Buddhist Path," *Japanese Religions* 16, no. 3 (January 1991): 18. This work has now also appeared as "Images of Reality in the Shin Buddhist Path: A Hermeneutical Approach," in *Toward a Contemporary Understanding of Pure Land Buddhism: Creating a Shin Buddhist Theology in a Religiously Plural World,* ed. Dennis Hirota (Albany: State University of New York Press, 2000), 23–72.

20. See below, our chapter 10, "Toward an Understanding of What Is Inconceivable."

21. We see this working both ways, as it were. Briefly glossing Vasubandhu, Shinran notes *kimyō = namu*: "*Take refuge in the Tathagata of unhindered light filling the ten quarters:* Take refuge [*kimyō*] translates *namu.* It means to follow the command of the Tathagata." *Notes on the Inscriptions on Sacred Scrolls,* 45; also *Collected Works,* 1:501. See *SSZ,* 2:584.11. Moreover, we see it phrased the other way around when Shinran provides a gloss on a passage of Shan-tao's, *namu = kimyō*: "Master Shan-tao states: '*Namu* means to take refuge [*kimyō*]'" and then continues with a gloss, "*Namu* means 'to take refuge' [*kimyō*). 'To take refuge' (*kimyō*) is to respond to the command and follow the call of the two honored ones, Śākyamuni and Amida. Thus, Shan-tao explains, *Namu means to take refuge.*" *Notes on Inscriptions, SBTS,* 51; also *Collected Works,* 1:505; *SSZ,* 2:588.6–7. We see this same gloss provided at *The True Teaching, Practice, and Realization of the Pure Land Way,* vol. 1, 109; also *Collected Works,* 1:37; *SSZ,* 2:21.13.

It appears that *kimyō* is somewhat of a formal technical term in the writings of Shinran, not very often used. However, it is worthy of note that "Of the seven surviving altar writings bearing Shinran's calligraphy, five hold the ten-character Name [*ki-m yō-jin-jip-pō-mu-ge-kō-nyo-rai*]." *Notes on Inscriptions, SBTS,* "Introduction,"15. It is said that Rennyo developed the practice of using only the name of six characters (*na-mu-a-mi-da-butsu*). Ibid., 15–16.

22. *Notes on Inscriptions,* 43; see also *Collected Works,* 1:499–500; *SSZ,* 2:13. "*For this reason I take refuge in Amida*: Bodhisattva Nāgārjuna constantly takes refuge [*kimyō*] in Amida Tathagata."

23. *Notes on Inscriptions,* 45; and *Collected Works,* 1:501; *SSZ,* 2:584.11. See also "Introduction," *The Jōdo Wasan,* 12–13.

24. Ibid., 51; *SSZ,* 2:588.5–6.3.

25. The two Chinese ideographs representing the sound *namu* from the Sanskrit *namo*/*namas* were not used in the customary fashion of communicating both meaning and sound but merely to preserve the original Sanskrit-derived sound. As they stand, the two *kanji* have no independent meaning. This indicates, of course, that we do not have a translation of *namu,* rather a preservation of the sound.

Another remarkable case of this sound preservation in religious contexts, and they are numerous, is the case with the Hebrew-derived *amen* in the Christian Church. The Hebrew word was preserved in the Greek New Testament and made its way through European languages into contemporary English. One hears it today in Japanese Christian worship services. *Amen* has literally gone around the world. It is derived from the Hebrew word *'emunā,* representing a verbal affirmation, a manifestation of faith in the Hebrew heritage. In its ritual use, *amen* means "let it be so."

26. *Notes on Inscriptions,* 51, and *Collected Works,* I, 504–505; *SSZ,* 2:588.5–6.

27. Our translators of this passage provide a note: "The same character, read both *etsu* and *sai* in these compounds, means 'to tell,' 'to state,' 'to declare one's thoughts' (Shinran's note)." *The True Teaching, Practice, and Realization, SBTS,* 111 n. 20; see also *Collected Works,* 1:38.

28. Ibid. *SSZ,* 2:22.9–10. We are told, "*Kimyō* . . . : 'Namas' in Skt: the term means 'taking refuge in'. 'Kimyō' means 'to follow the command'. To follow Amida Buddha's 'calling' is to have faith in His Saving Power." *The Shōshin Ge: The Gāthā of True Faith in the Nembutsu,* translated and annotated under the direction of Fugen Daien, *RTS* (Kyoto: Ryukoku Translation Center, Ryukoku University, 1984 [5th ed. of the work first published in 1961]), 17 n. 3.

29. *Kimyō* occurs twenty-one times, as a refrain, in the first fifty *wasan* hymns and only once in the remaining sixty-eight. I have consulted *Hymns of the Pure Land.* In another contribution in Japanese *wasan* style, the *Kōsō wasan,* our word *kimyō* occurs only once. See *Hymns of the Pure Land Masters: A Translation of Shinran's Kōsō wasan, SBTS,* general ed. Yoshifumi Ueda (Kyoto: Hongwanji International Center, 1992). See also *Collected Works,* 1:359–93.

30. Shinran puts it as follows:

To take refuge, with the mind that is single,
In the Buddha of unhindered light filling the ten quarters
Is, in the words of Vasubandhu, author of the Treatise,
The mind that aspires to attain Buddhahood.
The mind that aspires to attain Buddhahood
Is the mind to save all sentient beings;

The mind to save all sentient beings
Is true and real shinjin, which is Amida's benefitting of others.

*Hymns of the Pure Land Masters, wasans* number 17–18, pp. 14–15, and *Collected Works,* 1:365.

31. *The True Teaching, Practice, and Realization, SBTS,* passage # 71, 1:137, and *Collected Works,* 1:54; *SSZ,* 2:33.11.

32. Shinran quotes Genshin's use of "I take refuge in and worship" (*kimyō rei*) on six occasions in listing six kinds of virtue. *The True Teaching, Practice, and Realization, SBTS,* passage #64, 1:134–35, and *Collected Works,* 1:52; *SSZ,* 2:32.5–6.

33. From the *Nehan-gyō,* the *Nirvana Sutra,* "If one has taken refuge (*kie*) in the Buddha, one must not further take refuge (*kie*) in various gods." *The True Teaching, Practice, and Realization, SBTS,* passage #82, 4:555, and *Collected Works,* 1:255. See *SSZ,* 2:175.1–2.

34. From the *Hanju zammai kyō* or *Sutra of the Samadhi of All Buddhas' Presence, The True Teaching, Practice, and Realization, SBTS,* passage #83, 4:556, and *Collected Works,* 1:255. In one of the appendixes, 4:636, this text is noted as "One of the earliest sutras to treat practice centering on Amida." See *SSZ,* 2:175.3. On this passage and the one mentioned in the immediately preceding note, see also *Kyō Gyō Shin Shō,* 204.

35. Reference is to an event in Shinran's life, when he was twenty-nine years old in the year that he became a disciple of Hōnen in 1201. The key phrase in this passage is *hongan ni kisu,* "took refuge in the Primal Vow." *Kyō Gyō Shin Shō, RTS,* 208.

36. *Kyō Gyō Shin Shō, RTS,* 196. I have taken the liberty of changing the wording found in the original for *daishinkai* as "Sea of Great Faith" to "sea of absolute dependence."

37. So he quotes from *Hōgatsu-dōji shomon gyō,* noted as no longer extant, but quoted in Nāgārjuna's *Commentary on the Ten Bodhisattva Stages,* in one of the appendixes, "Names and Titles Cited," in *The True Teaching, Practice, and Realization, SBTS,* 1:197.

38. *The True Teaching, Practice, and Realization, SBTS,* 93, and *Collected Works,* 1:27. See *SSZ,* 2:14.11–15.1. The word for refuge used throughout is *kimyō.*

39. Ibid. One should note also that Genshin is quoted by Shinran using the same phrasing *kimyōrai* at *The True Teaching, Practice, and Realization, SBTS,* passage #64, 1:134–35; *Collected Works,* 1:52; *SSZ,* 2:32.5–6.

40. As, for example in *The Hymns of the Pure Land, RTS,* at *wasan* # 35, 30–35; #41, 36–37; and #49, 40–41.

41. So one notes in *The Hymns of the Pure Land, RTS, wasan* # 18, 45–46. One notes also *Hymns of the Pure Land,* 18–19, and *wasan* #18, the force of *ki* as "turning to," and "relying on" the Primal Vow in *hongan guzei ni kiseshimuru.*

42. *Hymns of the Pure Land Masters, RTS, wasan* #21, 18–19. We note also reference to Genshin, who took refuge (*kishi*) "in the Land of Serene Sustenance," *Shosin Ge, RTS,* 41; see also *The True Teaching, Practice, and Realization, SBTS,* 1:166, and *Collected Works,* 1:73; *SSZ,* 2:44.13c. So also did T'an-luan, *The True Teaching,* 1:164, and *Collected Works,* 1:72; *SSZ,* 2:45.5a, see *Shoshin Ge, RTS,* 34.

43. *Hymns of the Pure Land Masters, SBTS, wasan* #59, 44–45, and *Collected Works,* 1:376.

44. Shinran quotes Tao-ch'o's *Passages on the Land of Happiness,* here referring to a *gātha* on the Larger Sutra. *The True Teaching, Practice, and Realization, SBTS,* 1:100. See *Collected Works,* 1:31–32.

45. So *The True Teaching, Practice, and Realization, SBTS,* 1:160, and *Collected Works,* 1:69; *SSZ,* 2:43.7.

46. So *The True Teaching, Practice, and Realization, SBTS,* 1:163; *Collected Works,* 1:71; *SSZ,* 2:44.14c. Following Vasubandhu, one can rely (*yoru*) on the *sūtra. The True Teaching, Practice, and Realization,* 1:95–96, and *Collected Works,* 1:28–29.

47. Ibid., 1:166–67, and *Collected Works,* 1:73; *SSZ,* 2:46.5c.

48. *Notes on Once-Calling and Many-Calling,* 43–44, and *Collected Works,* 1:484. See also *SSZ,* 2:613.15–614.1. See also *Shōzōmatsu Wasan: Shinran's Hymns on the Last Age,* translated and annotated in The Ryukoku University Translation Center, *RTS* (Kyoto: Ryukoku University Press, 1980), 116 n. 2.

49. Tao-ch'o is remembered as having entrusted himself in the Other Power of the Primal Vow (*hongan tariki o tanomi tsutsu*). *Hymns of the Pure Land Masters, wasan* #56, 42–43; *Collected Works,* 1:43. See also *The Kōsō Wasan, RTS* (Kyoto: Ryukoku University, 1974), 79.

50. Shinran makes the centrality of this orientation clear:

> Since we have been given this Vow by the Tathagata, we can take any occasion in daily life for saying the Name and need not wait to recite it at the very end of life; we should simply *give ourselves up totally to the entrusting* [*tanomu beshi*] [emphasis added] with sincere mind of the Tathagata. When a person realizes this true and real shinjin [*shinjitsu shinjin*], he enters completely into the compassionate light that grasps, never to abandon, and hence becomes established in the stage of the truly settled.

See *Notes on Inscriptions, SBTS,* 34, and *Collected Works,* 1:494, and *SSZ,* 2:578.3–4. Shinran also utilizes the verbal sense of *tanomu* in *namo amida butsu. Letters,* 29. See *SSZ,* 2:663.13.

51. *Letters, SBTS,* Letter #10, 39. See *SSZ,* 2:671.8. The verbal derivative of *makaseru* appears also in Letter #9, ibid., 37; *SSZ,* 2:670.5.

52. *Kyō Gyō Shin Shō,, RTS,* 119.

53. *Notes on "Essentials of Faith Alone," SBTS,* 34; *Collected Works,* 2:454–55. On this page, at note 3, the translators write, "We have followed the autograph version in this sentence. Our basic text has: 'Hearing the revered Name of the inconceivable selected Primal Vow—the shinjin of supreme wisdom—and being without a single doubt is called true and real shinjin.'"

54. *Notes on Essentials,* 37; *Collected Works,* 1:456–57. *SSZ,* 2:626.7. "*Hear* is to entrust oneself." *Notes on Inscriptions,* 35; *Collected Works,* 1:495; *SSZ,* 2:578.15.

55. *The True Teaching, Practice, and Realization, SBTS,* 1:162; *Collected Works,* 1:70; *SSZ,* 2:44.6b. The relationship of hearing and trusting (*kiki shinzuru*) is applicable also to learning and understanding one's inherited teachings. *NEFA,* 38; *SSZ,* 2:627.5.

56. *The True Teaching, Practice and Realization, SBTS,* 1:59; *Collected Works,* 1:68.

57. If not, perhaps anxiety would plague us until we are finished. But see *Tannishō: A Primer—A Record of the Words of Shinran Set Down in Lamentation over*

*Departures from His Teaching,* trans. Dennis Hirota, intro. Tokunaga Michio (Kyoto: Ryukoku University, 1982), passage 16, 39, and the text on p. 112.

> For the person of wholehearted, single practice of the nembutsu, change of heart and mind occurs only once. A person who has been ignorant of the true significance of the Other Power of the Primal Vow comes to realize, through receiving Amida's wisdom, that he cannot attain birth by means of the thoughts and feelings he has harbored up to then, so he abandons his former heart and mind and entrusts himself to the Primal Vow. This is "change of heart."

58. On this latter point, see *The True Teaching, Practice, and Realization, SBTS,* 1:117; *Collected Works,* 1:41; *SSZ,* 2:25.5.

59. *The True Teaching, Practice, and Realization, SBTS,* 1:118; *Collected Works,* 1:42; *SSZ,* 25.8, on analogy of rubble becoming changed into gold.

60. Commenting on Seikaku's text, Shinran writes, "*Solely making beings turn about* instructs us, Singleheartedly make your heart turn about! *Turn about* means to overturn and discard the mind of self-power." *Notes on Essentials, SBTS,* 39; *Collected Works,* 1:459; *SSZ,* 2:628.6.

61. *Notes on Inscriptions,* 72; *Collected Works,* 1:519; *SSZ,* 2:601–13–14: *eshin shinjitsu shinjin gai ni kui.*

62. "Literally 'turning toward another' or 'redirecting'; often rendered 'merit-transference'" and defined under "Directing virtue" in the "Glossary" of *Passages on the Pure Land Way,* 79. "Skt: *pariṇāma* meaning 'alteration', 'transformation'. Literally, 'turning and moving towards', that is, to transfer merit which one has accumulated to another being for the sake of attaining Buddhahood." *Shōzōmatsu Wasan, RTS,* 21 n. 2.

63. *Kyō Gyō Shin Shō, RTS,* 109: *shinjitsu no ekōshin nashi, shōjō no ekōshin nashi.*

64. *Shōzōmatsu Wasan, RTS, wasan* #52, 52.

65. Ibid., *wasan* #39, 39. In fact, such self-power activity is called *fuekō,* "non-*ekō.*" See ibid., 39 n. 1. Shinran is recorded to have said that it was beyond his capacity to say the *nembutsu* under his own motivation and to transfer the virtue or direct the merit (*ekō*) to his departed ancestors. *Tannishō,* passage 5, 25; *Tanni Shō, RTS,* 27.

66. *Shōzōmatsu Wasan, wasan* #97, 97.

67. Ibid., *wasan* #24, 24. So also at *Hymns of the Pure Land Masters,* #34, 27; *Kōsō Wasan,* 56. *Wasans* #35–36 read:

> The directing of virtue for our going forth is such
> That when Amida's active means toward us reaches fulfillment
> We realize the shinjin and practice of the compassionate Vow;
> Then birth-and-death is itself nirvana.
> The directing of virtue for our return to this world is such
> That we attain the resultant state of benefiting and guiding others;
> Immediately reentering the world of beings,
> We perform the compassionate activity that is the virtue of
> Samantabhadra.

*Hymns of the Pure Land Masters,* 28–29.

68. *Shōzōmatsu Wasan, wasan* #25, 25.

69. Ibid., *wasan* #99, 99.

70. *Shoshin Ge, RTS,* 32.

71. Ibid., 35. The *Notes on Inscriptions,* 70; *Collected Works,* 1:518; *SSZ,* 2:600.9–10, notes *mida nyorai ekō no shinjitsu shinjin nari,* "true and real shinjin, which is given by Amida Tathagata."

72. *Kyō Gyō Shin Shō, RTS,* 101, 143.

73. *Hymns of the Pure Land Masters,* #20, 16–17; *Kōsō Wasan, RTS,* 40.

74. *Tannishō: A Primer,* passage #17, 40.

75. *Tannishō: A Primer,* passage #16, 40. See also *Notes on Essentials,* 32–33, "Since there is no contriving in any way to gain such virtues, it is called *jinen.*" See *Collected Works,* 1:451–55; *SSZ,* 2:623.8 and 11. See also *Notes on Inscriptions,* 38; *Collected Works,* 1:497, "*Jinen* means that there is no calculating on the part of the practicer." *SSZ,* 2:581.4; *Notes on Inscriptions,* 51; *Collected Works,* 1:505, "*Jinen* means that one does not calculate in any way whatever." *SSZ,* 2:588.13. See also *Notes on Inscriptions,* 35–36; *Collected Works,* 1:494–95. See further, *Letters* # 5, 29, *SSZ,* 2:663.9–11.

76. *Letters,* #5, 30; *SSZ,* 2:664.7–8.

77. So *Letters,* #5, 30; *SSZ,* 2:664.2–6. It is said that Shinran "realized this formlessness and on the basis of his experience called it 'jinen' . . . for the first time." *Letters,* "Introduction," 14–15.

78. *Shōshin Ge,* 30. See also note 2, this page. See also *Letters,* #5, 29; *SSZ,* 2:663.7–8.

79. *Letters,* #5, 29–30.

80. So *True Teaching, Practice, and Realization, SBTS,* 1:73, 121, 163, 182. See also *Notes on Inscriptions,* 35–37. At *Notes on Inscriptions,* 35–36, we read: "*Of itself* [*ji*] means that the calculation [*hakarai*] of sentient beings is not involved at all; it being made to become so, one is brought to attainment of the stage of non-retrogression. 'Of itself' expresses *jinen.*"

81. *Notes on Essentials,* 32–33; *Collected Works,* 1:453–54.

82. *Notes on Inscriptions,* 38, *SSZ,* 2:581.3–4; *Notes on Inscriptions,* 51, *SSZ,* 2:58.12–13.

83. *Notes on Essentials,* 33; *SSZ,* 2:623, 13–14. At *Notes on Once Calling,* 40; *Collected Works,* 1:481, we read: "In entrusting ourselves to the Tathagata's Primal Vow and saying the Name once, necessarily, without seeking it, we are made to receive the supreme virtues, and without knowing it, we acquire the great and vast benefit."

84. *Notes on Once Calling,* 40; *SSZ,* 2:611.7–11.

85. *Kōsō Wasan, wasan* #76, *RTS,* 101; *SBTS,* 58–59.

86. *Hymns of the Pure Land Masters, wasan* #82, 62–63. The *RTS* translation appearing in *Kōsō Wasan,* 107, has the last three lines reading:

> Becoming a Buddha through the Nembutsu is natural,
> And Naturalness itself is the Land of the Fulfilled Vow,—
> The Enlightenment of Supreme Nirvāṇa is certain.

87. The Greek term, *logos* (λόγος), by means of which our thoughts, speech, and actions are given orderly purpose, is similar, at points, with the notion of *jinen,* perhaps more so in the Johannine usage of *logos* in the Christian New Testament. And in the testimony of the Theravāda tradition, one might reconsider, in light of *jinen,* the

compound *dhammasudhammatā,* "the excellent reliability of Salvific Truth," which occurs in standard phrases in the Pali canon (*Saṃyutta-nikāya*, 2:99, following the *svākhyāto* [*svākkhāto*] formula, and *Theragātha,* 1, vv. 24, 220, 270, 286, in association with attaining the threefold knowledge and in fulfilling the *sāsana*).

88. *Notes on Essentials,* 39; *Collected Works,* 1:458–59; *SSZ,* 2:628.3–4, *shinjitsu shinjin o ureba jitsu hōdō ni mumaruto o shibetamaberu o jōdō shinshū to sutoshiru beshi.*

89. Not only in Shinshū Studies (*shinshūgaku*) is the matter complex, it is not made simpler by common Japanese parlance which utilizes *ōjō* to mean "death" rather than either "to go to be born" or "birth." There remains for further analysis that testy little linguistic peculiarity, *ōjōsuru,* "to be at one's wits' end," "to be at a loss." Further, the problem is not made easier when one notes that the majority of Jōdo Shinshū Buddhists mean by *ōjō* "to go to be born" at the time of death into the Pure Land rather than a birth into a new person of enlightenment which arises with the dawning of *shinjin* in this very life.

Perhaps there might be strands in the Christian New Testament that could speak to this context. Consider references that speak of "eternal life" that is already under way, as it were, in the life of a Christian. John 5:24, "Truly, truly [Grk: *amēn* ἀμὴν—this form is derived from the Hebrew *'emunā* mentioned above in note 25 of this chapter], I say to you, the one hearing my word and entrusting (*ho . . . pisteuōn* / ὁ . . . πιστεῦων) the one having sent me has life eternal (*achei zōēn aiōnion* / ἄχει ζωὴν αἰώνιον), and does not come into judgment but has passed over beyond death into this life." There is also John 6:47, "Truly, truly, I say to you, the one who is entrusting has life eternal." See also John 6:54; 17:3. In 1 John 5:11, one reads, "and this is the witness, that God gave us life eternal, and this life is in his Son." See also 1 John 5:20.

Now the internal dialect can be discerned when one takes these so-called Johannine passages and reflects on some of the observations of Paul. Consider 1 Corinthians 13:12, "Yet we are seeing through a mirror in a riddle (*en ainigmati* / ἐν αἰνίγματι) but then I shall fully know even as I also have been fully known." Paul writes at Romans 7:15, "I do not understand my own actions. For I practice what I do not wish and what I wish I do not do." And at 7:18, he continues, "For I know that that which is good (*agathon* / ἀγαθόν) does not dwell in me, that is in my flesh. The will is present in me but to enact what is right is not."

90. I refer to writings by Yoshifumi Ueda, Dennis Hirota, and Michio Tokunaga, Nobuo Nomura, to mention but a few. See Ueda, "The Mahāyāna Mode of Thought," and "The Structure of Shinran's Thought," appearing as chapters 2 and 4 respectively in *Shinran: An Introduction to His Thought.* See Dennis Hirota, in the aforementioned work and in "Breaking the Darkness: Images of Reality in the Shin Buddhist Path." See also his "Shinran's View of Language: A Buddhist Hermeneutics of Faith," *The Eastern Buddhist* 26, no. 1 (Spring 1993): 50–93. See further Michio Tokunaga, "The Dialectic of *Shinjin,*" in *The Religious Heritage of Japan,* 133–43, and his "Other Power and Social Ethics: The Bifurcation of Shinran's Teaching," ibid., 145–56. See Nobuo Nomura, "Shinran's View True Religion—From Amida Worship to the True and Real Religion," ibid., 117–31.

91. M. Holmes Hartshorne, "Of Human Bondage and Divine Grace," in *Of Human Bondage and Divine Grace: A Global Testimony*, ed. John Ross Carter (La Salle, IL: Open Court, 1992), 288.

92. M. Holmes Hartshorne, *Kierkegaard Godly Deceiver: The Nature and Meaning of His Pseudonymous Writings* (New York: Columbia University Press, 1990), 27.

CHAPTER 9. LOVE AND COMPASSION AS GIVEN

1. Of numerous possibilities, one thinks of *agapē, karuṇā, jihi* under which entry one notes in *A Dictionary of Chinese Buddhist Terms,* compiled by William Edward Soothill and Lewis Hodous (Taipei: Ch'eng Wen Publishing Co., 1970 [originally published by Kegan Paul, Trench, Trübner, and Co.]), 371b, *karuṇā,* which is defined as "Sympathy, pity for another in distress and the desire to help him, sad", *paññā/prajñā* (J: *hannya, chie*), and *saddhā/śraddhā, pistis* (πίστις), *credo, shin* (which, in *A Dictionary of Chinese Buddhist Terms,* 296a, is noted as representing the Sanskrit *śraddhā*), possibly even *shinjin,* not to mention *shinkō.*

2. *Biblia Hebraica*; *Septuaginta id est vestus testamentum graece uxta LXX interpretes,* ed. Alfred Rahlfs, vol. 2, editio sexta, for the American Bible Society (New York, Stuttgart: Privileg. Württ. Bibelanstalt, n.d.).

There is an interesting occurrence at Ps. 18:1(2) (LXX 17:2)—the only such occurrence with which I am familiar—where the root *rā'ham* (רחם), tending to be translated in the *kal* as "love," yet in the *piel* more often as "mercy," "compassion," is translated in the LXX in the *kal*-future as *agapēsō* (ἀγαπήσω). Elsewhere, however, in the LXX the noun or verb forms of *agapē* seem not to be regularly utilized for this Hebrew word.

The great Hebrew word *'hesed* (חסד), meaning "loving kindness," seems rather regularly translated in the LXX by *eleos* (ἔλεος), tending to mean there and in the New Testament "pity," "mercy," "compassion." It would be an interesting study in itself to look for possible shifts in meaning or significant continuity in sense that might have been occurring in the Old Testament through the Septuagint and into the New Testament with *āhav'* becoming *agapē* and *'hesed* becoming *eleos* so that our question "*agapē* and compassion" would suggest, if not require, also a study of *agapē* and *eleos.*

3. Anders Nygren, "Eros and Agape," trans. Werner Rode, *A Handbook of Christian Theology: Definition Essays on Concepts and Movements of Thought in Contemporary Protestantism* (New York: Meridian Books, 1958), 97.

4. Anders Nygren has provided the classic study in *Agape and Eros,* trans. Philip S. Watson (Philadelphia: Westminster Press, n.d. [1953?], of the work first published in an English translation in Great Britain by the S.P.C.K. House: pt. 1, 1932; pt. 2, vol. 1, 1938; pt. 2, vol. 2, 1939).

5. Anders Nygren, "Eros and Agape," 101, writes,

> The way is cleared thereby for a new ethics, an ethics in the Christian sense of the word, ruled by love which "does not seek its own," but gives itself freely, ready, if it should come to pass, to be "a love lost." With this, love has regained its New Testament meaning and has become "the *agape* of the cross" or—to use Luther's expressive phrase—it has become "*amor crucis ex cruce natus*"—the love of the cross born of the cross.

6. Paul Tillich, *Dynamics of Faith* (New York: Harper and Brothers, 1958), 114–15. Have we seen all of this before? Nygren, *Agape and Eros,* 391, writes, "Thus,

in Origen, for the first time in the history of the Christian idea of love, we find *a real synthesis between the Christian [agapē] and the Hellenistic [eros] views of love.* No later attempt at such a synthesis has gone beyond Origen in principle."

7. 1 Clement XLIX. 2–5, *The Apostolic Fathers: With and English Translation,* by Kirsopp Lake, vol. 1, The Loeb Classical Library (Cambridge: Harvard University Press, 1952), 93. It is possible, although not noted by Lake, that Clement here, in using "the bond" (*ton desmon* τὸν δεσμὸν), is indirectly recalling Col. 3:14, "And above all these put on love, which is the bond (*sudesmos* σύνδεσμος) of completeness." Lake provides references to 1 Pet. 4:8 and 1 Cor. 13:47 as sources from which Clement was drawing in this passage.

8. *Eleos.* This was the Greek term chosen to represent *'hesed* in the Hebrew Scriptures, and perhaps we should marvel how this sensitivity to deity or this interpretation of God's relationship to humankind, one of "loving-kindness," was passed on from those of us who were Jews to those of us who were Christians.

9. *Apostolic Fathers,* 1, 1 Clement, L.1–2, 95. Nygren, in *Agape and Eros,* 359–68, draws attention to the writings of Clement of Alexandria and argues that the sense there given to *agapē* is heavily influenced by the Hellenistic notion of *eros.* Kirsopp Lake, op. cit., 6–7, writes,

> It is noteworthy that I. Clement appears to be treated by Clement of Alexandria as Scripture, and this, especially in connection with its position in the codex Alexandrinus and in the Strassburg Coptic Ms., where it is directly joined on to the canonical books, suggests that at an early period in Alexandria and Egypt I. Clement was regarded as part of the New Testament.

10. I base this conclusion on the use of the passive forms, *eurethēnai* (εὑρεθῆναι), "be found," and *eurethōmen* (εὑρεθῶμεν), "we may be found" of the verb *euriskō* (εὑρίσκω), "to find."

11. Nygren writes, "We can never imagine on our own what *agape* is, because *agape* does not fall into the framework of human possibilities. *Agape* is the love which God proved to us by giving His only Son (John 3:16). If that had not happened, we never would have heard anything about *agape.*" Nygren, "Eros and Agape," *A Handbook of Christian Theology,* 97.

12. "The Epistles of Saint Ignatius: I—Ignatius to the Ephesians," 14, 1, *Apostolic Fathers; With An English Translation,* by Kirsopp Lake, vol. 1, The Loeb Classical Library (Cambridge: Harvard University Press, 1952), 189. Nygren, *Agape and Eros,* 261, observes that Ignatius "comes nearer the primitive Christian Agape motif than any other of the Apostolic Fathers." Nygren there draws attention to this passage and glosses it awkwardly, "In Faith and Love he [Ignatius] finds the whole content of Christianity; Faith is the beginning of Christian life, Love its end." Ignatius, rather, speaks not of Christianity but of Jesus Christ, not of Christian life, but of life itself. This distinction is of crucial significance.

13. See *Greek New Testament Terms in Indian Languages,* compiled by J. S. M. Hooper (Bangalore: The Bible Society of India and Ceylon, 1957), 2–4.

14. *Visuddhimagga of Buddhaghosācariya, HOS,* 9, 92, 263. See also the translation in *The Path of Purification by Bhadantācariya Buddhaghosa,* 343–44. The *Aṭṭakathāsūci,* pt. 3, ed. Pandita Kosgoda Sirisumedha Thero, rev. Pandita Dhammavaṃsa Thero (Colombo: M. D. Gunasena, 1969), 673b, indicates that this

passage is to be found in the *Aṭṭhasālinī,* the commentary on the *Dhammasaṅgaṇi.* See the English translation of that passage in *The Expositor,* vol. 1, trans. Pe Maung Tin, ed. and rev. Mrs. Rhys Davids (London: Published for the Pali Text Society by Luzac, 1958 [of the work first published in 1920]), 258.

15. *Visuddhajanavilāsinī nāma Apadānaṭṭhakathā,* ed. C. E. Godakumbura (London: Published for the Pali Text Society by Luzac, 1954), 200. See the *Aṭṭhakathāsūci,* 3, 673b, for a reference to the Hewavitarne editions published in Sinhala script (the slight and insignificant variant readings noted in the *Aṭṭhakathāsūci* are indicated in the notes to the Pali Text Society edition here cited).

16. Nygren, "Agape and Eros," *A Handbook of Christian Theology,* 48.

17. The standard listing, in Pali, is *mettā* (friendliness, heartfelt tenderness, loving-kindness), *muditā* (sympathetic joy, attuned sympathetic gladness), *karuṇā,* and *upekkhā* (equanimity, the condition of having no barriers whatsoever).

18. *Visuddhimagga, HOS,* 7:32, 167.

19. *Paramatthamañjūsā of Bhadantācariya Dhammapāla Thera: Or The Commentary of the Visuddhimagga,* ed. Morontuḍuwē Dhammānanda Thera (Colombo: Mahabodhi Press, 1928), 192–93.

20. *Majjhima-nikāya,* 1:168–69. For a treatment of this setting in the context of the disclosure of Dhamma, see my work, *Dhamma,* 70–74.

21. I have discussed the role of music in the religious life of Theravāda Buddhists in a chapter, "Music in the Theravāda Buddhist Heritage: In Chant, in Song, in Sri Lanka," in *On Understanding Buddhists,* 133–52.

22. See Soothill, *A Dictionary of Chinese Buddhist Terms,* 337b; *Matthews' Chinese-English Dictionary,* Revised American Edition (Cambridge: Harvard University Press, n.d. [1943?] of the work first published in 1931]), #4881, 675c; and Andrew Nathaniel Nelson, *The Modern Reader's Japanese-English Character Dictionary,* 2nd Revised Edition (Rutland, VT: Charles E. Tuttle, 1985), #3865, 763a.

23. One of numerous such passages noted here as an example: so *Passages on the Pure Land Way: A Translation of Shinran's Jōdo monrui jushō,* general ed. Yoshifumi Ueda, *SBTS* (Kyoto: Hongwanji International Center, 1982), 34. The original will be found at *SSZ,* 2:445; *Collected Works,* 1:299.

24. These two suggested functions of the notion of "model" are noted by Clifford Geertz, in "Religion as a Cultural System," *Anthropological Approaches to the Study of Religion,* ed. Michael Banton (New York: Praeger, 1966), 1–46, especially 7–8.

25. *Tannishō: A Primer,* 24. The Japanese text will be found, with Roman transliterations, on 62; *Collected Works,* 1:663. See *SSZ,* 2:775.

26. See, for example, the entries provided in the Japanese Index to *The Kyō Gyō Shin Shō, RTS,* 217.

27. *Passages on the Pure Land Way, SBTS,* 52; *Collected Works,* 1:313; *SSZ,* 2:452.

28. See, for example, *Passages on the Pure Land Way, SBTS,* 33, 34, 38, 41; *Collected Works,* 1:296ff.; and *SSZ,* 2:444, 445, 446, 447. In the Glossary to *Notes on Once-calling and Many-calling,* 66, the translation staff of the work enters under "Eighteenth Vow,"

> Among the forty-eight Vows of Amida Buddha found in the *Larger Sutra of Immeasurable Life,* revered by Pure Land Buddhists, the most significant is the Eighteenth Vow, because it manifests the working of true compassion

committed to the enlightenment of every being. Hōnen called it the King of the Vows. It reads: "If, when I attain Buddhahood, sentient beings throughout the ten quarters, realizing sincere mind, joyful faith, and aspiration to be born in my land and saying my Name even ten times, do not attain birth, may I not attain the supreme enlightenment; excluded are those who have slandered the dharma and committed the five grave offenses." Based upon the passage which testifies to the fulfillment of this Vow, Shinran interpreted sincere mind, joyful faith, and aspiration for birth not as necessary requirements to be prepared by the practicer, but rather as the compassionate working of the Primal Vow reaching down to man.

29. "Glossary of Shin Buddhist Terms" in *Notes on Once-calling and Many-calling, SBTS,* 72. This passage occurs in glossaries in subsequent translations in this series.

30. Nygren, "Eros and Agape," *A Handbook of Christian Theology,* 101.

31. *The Dhammapada,* v. 94 and pp. 158, 219, and note 39, p. 449 where the quotation appears as translated from the *Dhammapada Vivaraṇaya,* by Morogallē Siri Ñāṇobhāsa Tissa (Colombo: M. D. Gunasena, 1962), 191.

32. The Buddha, as the paradigm of one whose compassion is permeated by insight-wisdom, represents a pattern of human relationship that is more complete, more inclusive, than a current sense of self-sacrifice might suggest. He "perfected the state of the fourth person," as it is written in *Paramatthamañjūsā,* 1:193, recalling the categories "[1] One who pursues neither one's own benefit nor the benefit of another; [2] one who pursues the benefit of others but not the benefit of oneself; [3] one who pursues the benefit of oneself but not the benefits of others; [4] one who pursues both the benefit of oneself and the benefit of others" as noted in *Aṅguttara-nikāya,* 1:95–99. See, further, the extended treatment on *karuṇā* as a phase of meditative-absorption noted in the *Visuddhimagga, HOS,* 9:77–83.

33. It is recorded that Shinran said,

> Thus, a lifetime of saying the nembutsu with the thought, "If it were not for this compassionate Vow, how could such wretched evildoers as ourselves gain emancipation from birth-and-death?" is to be recognized as entirely an expression of gratitude for the benevolence of Amida's great compassion (*nyorai daihi no on*), of thankfulness for the Buddha's virtuous working.

*Tannishō: A Primer,* 36. The Japanese is noted on 102; *Collected Works,* 1:673. See also *SSZ,* 2:785.

## CHAPTER 10. TOWARD AN UNDERSTANDING OF WHAT IS INCONCEIVABLE

1. The patient work in translating the writings of Shinran into English by the members of the Ryukoku Translation Center, Ryukoku University, and the committee members of the Shin Buddhism Translation Series, Hongwanji International Center, Kyoto, reflects fully Shinran's commitment to share through intelligible human words a vision neither restricted by the level of one's linguistic competence nor limited to the sphere of human experience that can be readily communicated through human speech or the written word.

The passage quoted is from *Kyō Gyō Shin Shō, RTS,* 151. Yoichi Aizawa, my colleague at Colgate, assisted in checking my romanji transliterations of the original passages related to this chapter.

2. *Notes on Once-calling and Many-calling, SBTS,* 46.

3. For example, one reads, "The eighty-four thousand dharma-gates are all good practices of the provisional means of the Pure Land teaching [*jōdo no hōben*]; they are known as the Essential or Provisional Gate." No doubt the translation of "provisional means" for *hōben* in this passage is determined by the complex of "Essential [gate] (*yō mon*)" and "Provisional Gate," (*ke mon*) in the immediate context. Further, in this passage Shinran writes a marginal note: "*Provisional* [Gate—*ke mon*]: temporary; not true and real." (The passage under consideration is as follows: *hachi man shi sen no ho mon wa, mina kore jōdo o hōben no zen nari. kore o yō mon to iu, kore o ke mon to nazuke nari.* The passage is found in *Shinshū Shōgyō Zensho, SSZ,* 2:615.7–10). The phrase *jōdo no hōben,* taken in this translation as "the provisional means of the Pure Land teaching," provides an example of *hōben* interpreted to mean "provisional means" in the sense of a temporary expedient.

Keeping our attention on this passage, we begin to sense that the translation committee was struggling with unusually delicate issues. The passage continues, "his gate consists of the good practices, meditative and non-meditative, taught in the *Sutra of Meditation on Amida Buddha.*" And, after briefly summarizing the meditative and non-meditative good practices, the passage continues,

> These all belong to the Essential Gate, which is the provisional means of the Pure Land teaching [*kore mina jōdo hōben no yō mon nari*]; it is also called the Provisional Gate [*kore o ke mon to mo iu*]. Encouraging and guiding all sentient beings with various means [the phrase "with various means" has been added by the translators for the sake of clarity] through this Essential or Provisional Gate [*yō mon ke mon*], the Buddha teaches and encourages them to enter "the great treasure ocean of true and real virtue—the Primal Vow, perfect and unhindered, which is the one vehicle." Hence, all good acts of self-power are called provisional ways [*yoruzu no jiriki no zen gō oba hōben no mon to mōsu nari*].

*Notes on Once-calling and Many-calling,* 45; *Collected Works,* 1:486. See *SSZ,* 2:615.10–12, for the original passage.

Our key notion, *hōben*, appears in a context with an extending cluster of important concepts including the highly significant idea of "self-power" (*jiriki*), together with "Essential Gate" (*yō mon*) and "Provisional Gate" (*ke mon*).

4. One is not sure whether Shinran's marginal note, explicitly written on *ke mon,* is to be interpreted as applying also to *yō mon.*

5. *Notes on Once-calling,* 36; *Collected Works,* 1:477–78; *SSZ,* 2:608.4–5.

6. Ibid., 37; *Collected Works,* 1:477–478; *SSZ,* 2:608.5.

7. Ibid., 63. See also the entry, "Essential Gate and Provisional Gate (*yōmon, kemon*)," ibid., 69.

8. For example, one notes *Letters,* letter # 2, *SBTS,* 25; *Collected Works,* 1:527; *SSZ,* 2:660.9, "You should know that this shinjin is bestowed through the compassionate means [*on-hōben*] of Sakyamuni, Amida, and all the Buddhas in the [ten] quarters." Shinran also writes,

> . . . Sakyamuni and Amida [*shaka nyorai mida butsu*] are our parents of great compassion; using many and various compassionate means [*hōben*], they awaken the supreme shinjin [*mujō no shinjin*]. Thus the settling of true shinjin [*makoto no shinjin*] is the working [*on-hakarai*] of Sakyamuni and Amida.

*Letters,* letter #13, *SBTS,* 42; *Collected Works,* 1:540; *SSZ,* 2:673.14–674.2. Shinran mentions Shan-tao's *Hymn of Meditation on the Presence of the Buddha* in making this observation. In *The Kōsō Wasan, wasan* #74, 99, Shinran writes,

> Śākya and Amida are Compassion's parents;
> Using all means they skillfully [*hōben*] lead us
> And in us the supreme Faith [*mujō no shinjin*]
> Do they awaken.

At this place, p. 99, the Ryukoku Translation Center provides, in footnote 1, the passage by Shan-tao (J: Zendō), wherein both *hōben* and *shinjin* appear. This passage is translated, by the Ryukoku Translation Center staff,

> Tathāgata Śākyamuni is truly the parent of Compassion.
> Through various skillful means [*hōben*],
> He awakens the highest Faith in us.

9. And further, Shinran writes,

> There was a time for each of you when you knew nothing of Amida's Vow and did not say the Name of Amida Buddha, but now, guided by the compassionate means [*hōben*] of Sakyamuni and Amida, you have begun to hear the Vow.

*Letters,* letter #20, 60; *Collected Works,* 1:552–53; *SSZ,* 2:690.89.

10. Note 24 in "Supplementary Notes," *The Tanni Shō: Notes Lamenting Differences, RTS,* 101.

11. From *Letters,* letter #8, 35; *Collected Works,* 1:534–35; *SSZ,* 2:668.8, one reads,

> The three bodies are: first, the dharma-body [*hosshin*]; second, the fulfilled body [*hōjin*]; third, the personified body [*ōjin*]. The present 'Amida Tathagata' is a Tathagata of fulfilled body [*ima kono mida nyorai wa hōjin nyorai nari*].

12. From *Notes on Once-calling,* 46; *Collected Works,* 1:486–87; *SSZ,* 2:616.3–7, one reads,

> From this treasure ocean of oneness form [*katachi*] was manifested, taking the name of Bodhisattva Dharmākara, who, through establishing the unhindered Vow as the cause, became Amida Buddha. For this reason Amida is the "Tathagata of Fulfilled body [*hōjin nyorai*]." He has been called "Buddha of unhindered light filling the ten quarters." This Tathagata is also known as *Namu-fukashigikō-butsu* (namu-Buddha of inconceivable light) and is the "dharmakaya as compassionate means [*hōben hosshin*]."

13. *Notes on Once-calling,* 46; *Collected Works,* 1:486–87; *SSZ,* 2:616.7–10.

14. Shinran provides a gloss on the passage quoted above in note 3, from *Notes on Once-calling,* 45. For "the great treasure ocean of true and real virtue—the Primal

Vow, perfect and unhindered, which is the one vehicle," he notes, "'Unhindered' means that it cannot be obstructed or destroyed by blind passion and karmic evil. 'True and real virtue' is the Name. Since the wondrous principle of true reality or suchness has reached its perfection in the Primal Vow, this Vow is likened to a great treasure ocean." Ibid., 46; *Collected Works,* 1:486–87. See *SSZ,* 2:615.14–616.1.

15. In a very important passage, Shinran demonstrates the soteriological involvement of *hōben* with life in its broadest sense.

> Nirvana is called . . . true reality, dharmakaya, dharma-nature, suchness, oneness, and Buddha-nature. Buddha-nature is none other than Tathagata. This Tathagata pervades the countless worlds; it *fills the hearts and minds* (*shin/kokoro*) [emphases added] of the ocean of all beings. Thus, plants, trees, and land all attain Buddhahood.
>
> Since it is *with the heart and mind* [*shin/kokoro*] of all sentient beings that they *entrust themselves* to the Vow of the dharmakaya-as-compassion [*hōben hosshin no seigan o shingyōzuru*], *this shinjin* [emphasis added] is none other than Buddha-nature [*kono shinjin sunawachi busshō nari*]. This Buddha-nature is dharma-nature. Dharma-nature is the dharmakaya. *For this reason* there are two kinds of dharmakaya in regard to the Buddha. The first is called dharmakaya-as-suchness [*hoshō hosshin*] and the second, dharmakaya-as-compassion [*hōben hosshin*]. Dharmakaya-as-suchness has neither color nor form; thus, the mind [*kokoro*] cannot grasp it nor words describe it. From this oneness was manifested form [*katachi*], called dharmakaya-as-compassion [*hōben hosshin*]. Taking this form, the Buddha proclaimed his name as Bhikṣu Dharmākara and established the forty-eight great Vows *that surpass conceptual understanding* [emphases added].

*Notes on 'Essentials of Faith Alone,' SBTS,* 42–43; *Collected Works,* 1:460–62; *SSZ,* 2:630.1–15.

16. I should note that some colleagues serve on both translation committees, a sterling opportunity that was mine during a sabbatical year, 1985–86.

17. The old misunderstanding that one finds in Buddhist texts, representing a perspective of what has come to be called the Mahāyāna, that the way of the *Arahant* is somehow to be interpreted as "selfish," would not be in accord with the insight shared by Shinran: "other-power" is radically dissociated from "self-power"—there is not to be found the slightest trace of "calculation" (*hakarai*) in the person who has realized *shinjin.* Surely, the absence of this calculation (*hakarai*) would be a quality attributable to an *Arahant.* How then would an *Arahant* be considered "selfish" from this perspective?

18. The translators have added the phrase "the truth that Other Power is" for the sake of clarity.

19. *Letters,* letter #5, 29–30. The editor/translators mention in the introductory note, p. 29, "'On Jinen-hōni' is a direct record of Shinran's words made by Kenchi in 1258." *Collected Works,* 1:530. The passage is at *SSZ,* 2:663.6–664.8.

Another translation of this extended passage, "On Jinen-hōni," is found in *Shōzōmatsu Wasan, RTS,* 115–17. This translation is based on the "Bunmei (1466–1487) text, which Rennyo included in the *Sanjō Wasan,*" ibid., note 1, 114. See *SSZ,* 2:530–31.

20. See Minor L. Rogers, "Shin Buddhist Piety as Gratitude," in *Spoken and Unspoken Thanks: Some Comparative Soundings,* ed. John B. Carman and Frederick J: Streng (Center for the Study of World Religions, Harvard University, and Center for World Thanksgiving, Dallas, Texas, 1989), 93–111.

21. *The Shōshin Ge, RTS,* 55.

22. *The Jōdo Wasan, RTS,* 169.

23. Shinran writes regarding Nāgārjuna, "We should express our gratitude for the Great Compassionate Vow [*daihi guzei no on o hōzu beshi*]. (Thus Nāgārjuna said.)" *Shōshin Ge, RTS,* 30. Shinran sees himself standing with Vasubandhu when he writes of himself, "Hereupon, acknowledging the (Buddha's) benevolence and wishing to repay it [*chion hōtoku*], I open a master's commentary [T'an-luan's (J: Donran's) *Ojō Ron Chū,* commenting on the received text of the *Jōdo Ron* by Vasubandhu]. . . ." *Kyō Gyō Shin Shō, RTS,* 80. See also note 1 on p. 80. And of Vasubandhu, he writes, "Now he acknowledges the (Buddha's) benevolence and wishes to repay it [*on o shitte toku o hōzu*]." Ibid. Shinran demonstrates his awareness of Shan-tao's (J: Zendō's) orientation by quoting the Chinese master: "These people do not feel grateful for the Buddha's Benevolence [*kano button o nempō suru koto nashi*]." Ibid., 195.

Shinran also demonstrates his sense of the presence of *on* undergirding his self-understanding within the heritage of the master. He expresses this with regard to Hōnen, but also, indirectly, to the great masters who participated in the tradition; "I deeply acknowledge the Tathāgata's Compassion and sincerely appreciate the master's benevolence in instructing me [*makotoni shikyō no onkō aogu*]." Ibid., 211. At note 4, this page, it is mentioned that the comment by Shinran "refers particularly to Hōnen, but it also refers to the other Patriarchs." And, again regarding Hōnen, and indirectly Shan-tao, Shinran comments on a phrase written by Seikaku, another disciple of Hōnen: "'Reflecting on the master's teaching, it is one with Amida's compassionate Vow.' We should realize, then, the vast and profound benevolence [*oshie on*] of the great master's teaching." *Notes on the Inscriptions on Sacred Scrolls, SBTS,* 68; *Collected Works,* 1:516; *SSZ,* 2:599.14.

24. Further, one finds consistency in Shinran's sense of contextuality within the *on*-relationship with Śākyamuni, with Amida, and with the masters, by noting Shinran's motivation for writing. One reads,

> Reverently entrusting myself to the teaching, practice, and realization that are the true essence of the Pure Land way, I am especially aware of the profundity of the Tathagata's benevolence [*kotoni nyorai no ondoku fukaki koto oshinnu*]. Here I rejoice in what I have heard and extol what I have attained.

*The True Teaching, Practice, and Realization of the Pure Land Way, SBTS,* 1:59. This passage also occurs at *Kyō Gyō Shin Shō, RTS,* 26. See *SSZ,* 2:1.10–11. The *RTS* translation, loc. cit., provides an extended note:

> Ondoku . . . : Lit. "virtue of benevolence"; also simply "on." Originally, it is one of the three virtues of Buddhahood, the other two being "chitoku" . . . "virtue of wisdom", and "dantoku" . . . "virtue of destroying (defilements and ignorance)"; benevolence is a Buddha's intrinsic virtue out of which He has compassion for all sentient beings, makes a vow to save them, and actively engages in delivering them from Saṃsāra. In broader usage, the

term is applied to any kind action done to or for one by another person; particularly, a Buddha's or a teacher's kind instructions and painstaking efforts in enlightening us are referred to. Sanskrit equivalents are "upakāra", "upakaraṇa", "kṛita", and "sukṛita", meaning "service done", "kind action", and "benefit".

Again one reads,

Thus, taking refuge in the true words of the Great Sage and turning to the commentaries of the revered patriarchs, I realize the depth and vastness of the Buddha's benevolence [*button*] and compose the following hymn [Hymn of True Shinjin and the Nembutsu].

*The True Teaching, Practice, and Realization of the Pure Land Way, SBTS,* 1:160; *Collected Works,* 1:69. The passage also appears at *The Kyō Gyō Shin Shō, RTS,* 81. See *SSZ,* 2:43.7.

25. *The True Teaching, Practice, and Realization of the Pure Land Way, SBTS,* 2:202. *SSZ,* 2:47.5. See also *Kyō Gyō Shin Shō, RTS,* 85. This general orientation appears again when Shinran writes, "Hereupon, I have collected the essentials of the True Teaching, and have gleaned the important passages of Pure Land Buddhism [*Jōdo no*]. I only think of the Buddha's deep Benevolence [*tada button no fukaki koto o nenji te*], and do not care about people's abuse." *Kyō Gyō Shin Shō, RTS,* 211.

26. *Kyō Gyō Shin Shō, RTS,* 198.

27. *Passages on the Pure Land Way, SBTS,* 29. *SSZ,* 2:443.5–6.

28. Ibid., 29. *SSZ,* 2:443.4–5.

29. *Jōdo Wasan, RTS, wasan* #85, 117.

30. *Shōzōmatsu Wasan, RTS,* 30; *SSZ,* 2:519.5–10. See Rogers, "Shin Buddhist Piety as Gratitude," 11; 101 (1989).

31. *Shōzōmatsu Wasan, RTS,* 34. *SSZ,* 2:521.11–12. In the immediately following *wasan* (#35), one reads that "[w]ithout the transcendent wisdom of faith [*shinjin no chie*], / How could we ever realize nirvana [*ikade ka nehan o satora mashi*]?" Ibid., 35.

32. Ibid., 49. *SSZ,* 2:521.11–12.

33. Thus, a lifetime of saying the nembutsu with the thought, "If it were not for this compassionate Vow, how could such wretched evildoers as ourselves gain emancipation from birth-and-death?" is to be recognized as entirely an expression of gratitude for the benevolence of Amida's great compassion [*nyorai daihi no on*], of thankfulness for the Buddha's virtuous working. *Tannishō: A Primer,* 36. See also the section entitled "Text" of this volume, 14.6 on p. 102; *Collected Works,* 1:673; also *SSZ,* 2:785.12–14. See also Rogers, "Shin Buddhist Piety as Gratitude," 12; 102 (1989).

34. Because one doubts the inconceivable Buddha-wisdom
And prefers to pronounce the nembutsu through self-power,
One stops in the border land, the realm of sloth and complacency:
There is no gratitude for Buddha's benevolence [button hōzuru kokoro nashi].

*Shōzōmatsu Wasan, RTS,* 61. *SSZ,* 523.1–4. See also Rogers, "Shin Buddhist Piety as Gratitude," 11; 102 (1989).

35. *Letters,* letter #2, *SBTS,* 25; *Collected Works,* 1:527; *SSZ,* 2:660.15–661.1. A note is provided in the English translation of *Letters,* 25: "It is said that this letter was

copied from Shinran Shōnin's own draft, found among the remains of the venerable Shōshin-bō and circulated among the followers."

36. *Notes on the Inscriptions on Sacred Scrolls, SBTS,* 68; *Collected Works,* 1:516; *SSZ,* 2:599.14–600.2.

37. *Shōzōmatsu Wasan, RTS,* 59; *SSZ,* 2:523.1–4.

## CHAPTER 11. THE ARISING OF SALVIFIC REALIZATION AS BUDDHISTS AND CHRISTIANS HAVE AFFIRMED

1. To the question "How many kinds of *paññā*?" of several responses one is "twofold in the sense of customary and world-transcending (*lokiya-lokuttaravasena duvidhā*)." So *Visuddhimagga of Buddhaghosācariya, HOS,* chap. 14, par. 8, 370.

2. I have remarked on this in a chapter entitled, "The Notion of Refuge (*saraṇa*)" in *On Understanding Buddhists,* 55–70.

3. Mahinda Palihawadana, "Is There a Theravada Buddhist Idea of Grace?" in *Christian Faith in a Religiously Plural World,* 187. Caroline A. F. Rhys Davids, drawing from the *Atthasālinī,* provides the following note: "*Lokiyā* = bound down to, forming a part of, the circle (of existence), which for its dissolving and crumbling away (*lujjana palujjana*) is called *loko.* To have got beyond the world, to be a non-conforming feature in it—in it, but not of it—is to be *lokuttaro.*" *A Buddhist Manual of Psychological Ethics [Dhamma-saṅgaṇī]* (London: Published by the Pali Text Society and distributed by Routledge and Kegan Paul, 1974 [originally published by the Royal Asiatic Society in 1900]), 266 n. 3.

See also *The Nettipakaraṇa,* ed. E. Hardy (London: Luzac, 1961), 189–91, for a schematic presentation of the ways *lokiya* and *lokuttara* can be applied to *sutta.* I might also note a brief inquiry entitled, "Faith in the Wake of the *Dhammapada,*" where *saddhā* is noted as being both *lokiya* and *lokuttara.* See my *On Understanding Buddhists,* 105–14.

One can see how these two key terms, *lokiya* and *lokuttara,* indicate a structural correspondence with *jiriki* and *tariki*:

*lokuttara* || *tariki*
*lokiya* || *jiriki*

Consequently, insofar as *jiriki* is understood as "self-power," *lokiya,* which would include *sīla, samādhi,* and to a certain degree, *paññā,* too, applies to *jiriki* as that "realm of possible [human] action."

4. Palihawadana, "Is There a Theravada Buddhist Idea of Grace?" in *Christian Faith in a Religiously Plural World,* 189.

5. *Visuddhimagga, HOS,* 21, par. 128–29, p. 575. Compare Palihawadana, as cited in the immediately preceding note. Ñyāṇamoli translates "equanimity about formations" rather than my "equipoise with regard to mental synergies *saṅkhāras*" for the important notion *saṅkhārupekkhā. The Path of Purification,* 782. Palihawadana does not include the compound in his excerpts.

6. Palihawadana, "Is There a Theravada Buddhist Idea of Grace?" in *Christian Faith in a Religiously Plural World,* 190, draws our attention to this compound. The context of his presentation suggests that this occurrence falls within the category of *lokiya,* since he writes immediately following this point, "This is the end of our pilgrim's

operation in the field of possible action." But perhaps I have not fully understood what, indeed, might be an even more abstract subtlety in Palihawadana's presentation.

The *Visuddhimagga* discusses the faculties in chapter 16, *HOS,* noting *anaññātaññassāmītindriya* and mentions that with its arising three fetters are abandoned (*anaññātaññassāmītindriyassa saññojanattayappahānaṃ*), indicating thereby that this is an incipient phase of the Stream-Attainment-Path-Realization, *Visuddhimagga, HOS,* 16, par. 10, 419. The point is made clearer when this text notes that "[t]he remaining three [faculties/*indriyas* of which the one presently under discussion is the first] are world-transcending only (*Avasāne tīṇi lokuttarān'evā ti*)." *Visuddhimagga, HOS,* 16, par. 11, 419.

One of the earlier passages containing this compound associates it with a line of verse, "immovable is my release" (*akkuppā me vimuttīti*), and puts it into a category of three formally structured faculties (*tīṇi indriyāni*). *Iti-vuttaka,* 53.

7. So one notes in the *Aṭṭhakathāsūci,* 112b. For example, one finds commentarial passages such as the following: "This is a term for the knowledge of the Path of Stream Attainment." "The faculty that arises previously for one who enters into the thought 'I will know the attainment of that which has not been known with regard to this beginningless *saṃsāra*.'" "[It is] the faculty of one established in the first path who enters into the thought 'I will know, realize, that which has not been known, not penetrated, Dhamma of the four truths and the deathless state.'"

8. See *Visuddhimagga, HOS,* 21, paragraphs 128–33, 575–76.

9. *Visuddhimagga, HOS,* 22, par. 3, 577.

10. So *Visuddhimagga, HOS,* 21, par. 134, 576. *Sabbena sabbaṃ pana gotrabhūñāṇaṃ vuṭṭānagāminiyā vipassanāya pariyosānaṃ.*

11. *Visuddhimagga, HOS,* 22, par. 5, 577: *vipassanāya muddhabhūtam. apunarāvaṭṭakaṃ uppajjati gotrabhūñāṇaṃ.*

12. *Visuddhimagga, HOS,* 21, par. 7, 578.

13. *Visuddhimagga, HOS,* 21, par. 10, 579: *taṃ maggassa āvajjanan ti vuccati.*

14. *Visuddhimagga, HOS,* 22, par. 10–11, 579.

15. *Visuddhimagga, HOS,* 22, par. 14, 579.

16. Palihawadana, "Is There a Theravāda Buddhist Idea of Grace?" in *Christian Faith in a Religiously Plural World,* 191.

17. Ibid., 192.

18. A passage in the *Dīgha-nikāya* reads, "Now, Mahāli, a bhikkhu, by the complete destruction of three fetters, is one who has attained the stream (*sotāpanna*), having the inherent quality (*dhamma*) of not falling, assured, having enlightenment (*sambodiparāyano*) as final goal." *The Dīgha Nikāya,* 1:156. See also my *Dhamma,* 123–25.

19. See *Visuddhimagga, HOS,* 22, par. 18, 589.

20. See, for example, from one of the earliest strata of the Pali Canon, *Sutta-Nipāta,* vv. 790, 797.

21. See my *Dhamma,* 123 n. 33.

22. *Papañcasūdanī Majjhimanikāyaṭṭhakathā of Buddhaghosācariya*, pt. 1, eds. J. H. Woods and D. Kosambi (London: Published for the Pali Text Society by the Oxford University Press, 1922), 74: *Kasmā sotāpattimaggo dassanaṃ? Paṭhamaṃ nibbānadassanato.* See also my *Dhamma,* 124 n. 39.

23. Roger Hazelton, "Salvation," in *A Handbook of Christian Theology: Definition Essays on Concepts and Movements of Thought in Contemporary Protestantism,*

ed. Marvin Halverson and Arthur A. Cohen (New York: Living Age Books, published by Meridian Books, 1958), 336–37.

24. John B. Carman, *Majesty and Meekness: A Comparative Study of Contrast and Harmony in the Concept of God* (Grand Rapids: Eerdmans, 1994), 160.

25. John Baillie, *Our Knowledge of God* (New York: Charles Scirbner's Sons, 1939), 77.

26. Ibid., 85–86.

27. Alan Richardson, "Repent, Repentance, Convert, Conversion, Turn, Return," in *A Theological Word Book of the Bible,* ed. Alan Richardson (New York: MacMillan, 1951), 192.

28. Ibid., 191.

29. D. M. Baillie, *God Was in Christ: An Essay on Incarnation and Atonement* (New York: Charles Scribner's Sons, 1948).

30. Ibid., 115.

31. Ibid., 158. D. M. Baillie provides the Latin original: *Cur Deus Homo? Ad quid Christus descendebat*?

32. Ibid., 159.

33. Ibid. One notes the engaging discussion by Dennis Hirota about how a person is enabled to indicate the significance of wholly entrusting in and simultaneously being embraced by Amida Buddha by considering "'benefits in the present life.'" Dennis Hirota, "Religious Transformation in Shinran and Shōkū," *The Pure Land* (New Series), no. 4, 64–65.

34. Ibid., 170.

## CHAPTER 12. RELATIONALITY IN RELIGIOUS AWARENESS

1. Wilfred Cantwell Smith, "Thoughts on Transcendence," a paper read as "The Ingersoll Lecture" at Harvard Divinity School, March 10, 1988 (original title: "Transcendence"), 36. Republished from the *Harvard Divinity Bulletin* 18, no. 3 (Fall 1988): 10–15.

2. Grammatically, this form is the weak present tense of *dassati,* also "to see," which is the dominant form for non-present tense primarily meaning "saw," "to be seen," "to point out," "showed," and there is the notion of looking at something (*pekkhati*), "one looks at,' a less frequently occurring etymological form.

3. *Saṃyutta-nikāya,* 3:120, see also *Itivuttaka,* 91, and my *Dhamma,* 93, and related notes.

4. The *Sāratthappakāsini, Sārattha-ppakāsini: Buddhaghosa's Commentary on the Saṃyutta-nikāya,* ed. F. L. Woodward (London: Published for the Pali Text Society by Humphrey Milford, Oxford University Press, 1929–1937), on this passage, interprets the tossing about as due to Vakkali's deep concern about not rising to salute the Buddha and providing an appropriate seat. The Pali phrasing, *addas . . . dūrato āgacchantam*, the Venerable Vakkali "saw the Bhagavan coming from afar," is parallel to *addamsu kho pañcavaggiyā bhikkhū bhagavantam dūrato 'va āgacchantam . . .*" Vinaya, 1:10, where the ensuing discussion among the group of five mendicants was whether to offer a seat to the newly Awakened One.

5. *Saṃyutta-nikāya,* 3:120. It is unlikely that the more familiar notion of *darśana/darśan* in Hindu theistic traditions, where one is uplifted joyously and/or with

awe upon viewing the deity and also gratefully receives the gracious gaze of the deity, was at play during the time reflected in the Pali canon. It is likely that the term in the particular semantic frame here (*bhavantam dassanāya upasankam°*), and, as will be mentioned later in this chapter in the context of *pasāda* with reference to *Visuddhimagga, HOS,* 7:61, is not totally without some convergence in meaning. Utilizing the activity of the senses in acts of devotion—seeing, hearing, smelling, touching—has been long a part of Indian religiousness such that keeping *darśana* in our translation tends to underscore the depth and quality of the activity of the eyes in religious acts. This is hardly an act of "looking at" or of merely noticing.

6. *Saṃyutta-nikāya,* 3:120. Carter, *Dhamma,* 93.

7. Vakkali is well known in canonical and commentarial literature. His final demise is variously recorded, whether in apparent suicide as the *Saṃyutta-nikāya* account presents it, or while arising into the air at the instruction of the Buddha, according to the commentaries on the *Theragātha* and the *Dhammapada.* See Malalasekera, *Dictionary of Pali Proper Names,* 2:799–800, and F. L. Woodward, *The Book of the Kindred Sayings,* 3, note 4, 103–104. Woodward refers to the commentary on our passage and says that it was at the point of dying that Vakkali was able to attain release. The commentary on the *Aṅguttara-nikāya* notes that Vakkali jumped down from a considerable height but alighted safely in the presence of the Buddha. Vakkali is held as an exemplar of a person who is characterized as being devoted through faith. See our note 12 below.

8. *Papañcasūdanī Majjhimanikāyaṭṭhakathā,* 1:22 (on *Majjhima-nikāya,*1:1) draws a contrast between *cakhunā dassanam* and *ñāṇena dassanam* and quotes our key passage from *Saṃyutta-nikāya,* 3:120. The ordinary person puts emphasis on the customary activity of the eyes and seeks for the physical presence of the Buddha, while the person of admirable bearing sees with insight. The *Majjhima-nikāya* commentarial reference is considering the case of an average person (*puthujjana*). *Paramattha-Dīpanī Udānaṭṭhakathā (Udāna Commentary) of Dhammapālācariya,* ed. F. L. Woodward (London: Published for the Pali Text Society by the Oxford University Press, 1926), 310–11 (on *Udāna,* ed. Paul Steinthal [London: Published for the Pali Text Society by Geoffrey Cumberlege, Oxford University Press, 1948], 58), draws attention to Soṇa, who, as an average person, longed for the presence of the Buddha that he might be seen directly.

9. The human eye is a remarkable organ in its own right, and for some Christian theologians, conservative and liberal, on both sides of the Atlantic, in the past fifty or so years, the development of the organ of the eye has become a focal point for inferring divine intervention in the erstwhile natural evolutionary process.

10. *Paramattha-Dīpanī: Iti-Vuttakaṭṭhakathā (Iti-Vuttaka Commentary) of Dhammapālācariya,* 2:116 (*on Itivuttaka,* 90–91), where reference to *Saṃyutta-nikāya* 3:120 is included. The *Majjhima-nikāya* commentary, 1:22 (on *Majjhima-nikāya,* 1:19), notes the distinction between seeing (*dassanam*) with the eyes (*cakkhunā*) and with knowledge (*ñāṇena*), also referring to the account recorded at *Saṃyutta-nikāya,* 3:120.

11. *Sv. pūti* in *The Pali Text Society's Pali-English Dictionary.*

12. In order to facilitate ready reference to sources for quotations and comments in the text for the remainder of this section of chapter 12, I have inserted references in the text. Parallel and extended observations and elaborations will appear in the related notes. The *Visuddhimagga,* that great scholastic compilation of the literary heritage

by Buddhaghosa in fifth-century Sri Lanka, provides interpretations of *rūpakāya* that cluster around commentarial glosses for the epithet *bhagavan,* "fortunate one," "auspicious examplar," "Lord." In doing this, he shows the pair, *rūpakāka* and *dhammakāya,* in correlation rather than in contrast.

> By his state of fortunateness (*bhāgyavatā*) is illustrated the prosperity of his material body which bears a hundred [auspicious] marks of virtuous achievement (*puñña*: merit), and because of [his] state of having defects destroyed [is depicted] the prosperity of [his] *dhammakāya*. (*Visuddhimagga*, *HOS*, 7:60; *PTS,* 1:211)

The *Paramatthamañjūsā,* commenting on this passage in the *Visuddhimagga,* elaborates,

> "The prosperity of his material body," because of the fact that it is the root and the basis for bearing fruit on the part of those [others mentioned in the text]. "The prosperity of his *dhammakāya*" [is so because of the fact that it is the root and the basis] for the attainment of knowledge (*ñāṇa*) and so forth, because of the fact that it is preceded by the attainment of illumination (*pahāna*).

*Paramathamañjūsa,* commentary on the *Visuddhimagga,* 210 (on *Visuddhimagga, HOS,* 7:60; *PTS,* 1:211). The received tradition regarding this gloss is drawn from the *Lakkhaṇa-sutta* of the *Dīgha Nikāya,* 3:142–79, with its magnificent poetic depictions of an ideal life and its metaphorical casting of marks of an auspiciously great person. See also *Majjhima-nikāya,* vol. 2, ed. Robert Chalmers (London: Published for the Pali Text Society, 1960 [of the first edition, 1898]), 133–46, and the engaging exchange with the *brahmaṇa* Brahmāyu.

When the *Visuddhimagga* considers that great and persistent human issue of death, in its extended discussion about mindfulness on death, namely, that death, indeed, will come, *rūpakāya* and *dhammakāya* appear. There, the Buddha's physical body is described as being adorned with eighty minor marks and thirty-two marks of a great person. The passage says of the *dhammakāya,* "[his] magnificent *dhammakāya* [is] by means of precious gem-like qualities of the group of moral virtue, etc. [concentration, insight-wisdom, release, and knowledge combined with wisdom], made pure in every way" (*Visuddhimagga, HOS,* 7:23; *PTS,* 1:234). The commentary on this passage adds, "and because he has destroyed all defilements together with [their] mental traces." *Paramathamañjūsa,* commentary on the *Visuddhimagga,* 239 (on *Visuddhimagga HOS,* 8:23; *PTS,* 1:234). The commentator indicates that in this case, the Buddha, having such *dhamma*body, will not return to existence as we know it. All defilements are entirely destroyed as well as all of their *saṃsāric*-oriented traces or impressions.

Elsewhere the pair of terms appears with *rūpakāya* interpreted in light of the thirty major and eighty minor marks of a great person while his *dhammakāya* is glossed as being adorned with ten powers and four confidences. *Paramattha-Dipānī Theragāthā Aṭṭhakathā: The Commentary of Dhammapālācariya,* vol. 2, ed. F. L. Woodward (London: Published for the Pali Text Society by Luzac, 1952), 121–22 (on the *Thera- and Therī-gathā,* v. 288). The four confidences, presented at *Majjhima-nikāya,* 1:71–72, are (1) being fully awakened to all that there is to know, (2) knowledge that for him all defilements are destroyed, (3) the confidence of having described accurately obstacles that hinder one in religious living, and (4) that Dhamma as he taught it leads reliably to the destruction of *dukkha.*

Elsewhere, a commentary explains "the glory of Sakyaputta" as being due to the splendor of both the *rūpakāya* and the *dhammakāya* (*Paramatthadīpanī Theragāthā-Aṭṭhakathā*: 1:106, on *Theragāthā,* v. 94). The commentary on the *Khuddakapāṭha* offers considerable insight into the dynamic of an identity in relation. A complementary parallelism is maintained, in an extended gloss on *bhagavan,* when, on the one hand, the Buddha's *rūpakāya* is designated by "one hundred marks of merit (*puñña*)" while his *dhammakāya* demonstrates his destruction of defects (*The Khuddakapāt.ha: Together with Its Commentary Paramatthajotikā I,* 1:108; cf. *Sutta-Nipāta*, v. 258).

And further, in considering the customary beginning of discourses, "Thus have I heard," or "Thus it has been heard by me" (*evaṃ me sutaṃ*), one makes apparent the *dhamma*-[relic?]body (*dhamma-sarīra*) of the Bhagavan and causes to be resolved the disappointment people have in not seeing him. When one teaches Dhamma as it was heard, the heritage avers, "'This is not the proclamation of a departed teacher. This, indeed, is your teacher.'" (*Sutta-Nipāta Commentary,* 1:110 (cf. *Sutta-Nipāta,* v. 258). See also *Sutta-Nipāta Commentary,* 1:12; *Manorathapūraṇī*: *Buddhaghosa's Commentary on the Aṅguttara Nikāya,* vol. 1, ed. Max Walleser (London: Published for the Pali Text Society by Oxford University Press, 1924), 14; cf. *Sumaṅgala-vilāsinī: Buddhaghosa's Commentary on the Dīgha-Nikāya,* pt. 1, eds. T. W. Rhys Davids and J. Estlin Carpenter (London: Published for the Pali Text Society by Henry Frowde, Oxford University Press, 1886), 34. It is likely that in the context of considering the case of the Buddha's no longer being present in his ordinary body (*kāya*) that *sarīra* might have carried the added sense of relic-body, i.e., the *dhamma*body of one no longer with us in one sense and very much with us in another.

In considering another standard introductory phrase to the discourses, "At one time the Bhagavan . . . ," the *Paramatthajotikā* draws attention to the Bhagavan's not being present at the time and notes that this indicates the complete extinction of his *rūpakāya* (*rūpakāyaparinibbānam*). Even the Bhagavan, teacher of the noble Dhamma, whose body carried the ten powers and was like a cluster of diamonds, became fully extinct (*parinibbuta*), so how is it that one, with this knowledge, would engender a desire for life. So he causes somber emotion in those people intoxicated with life and he engenders effort regarding Dhamma true (*Paramatthajotikā I,* 1:110 [cf. *Sutta-Nipāta,* v. 258]).

13. These narrative strands differ in the subsequent development of the story. One account (*Iti-vuttaka,* 91) has Vakkali achieving Arahantship upon rising in the air. Another (*Manoratthapūraṇī: Buddhaghosa's Commentary on the Aṅguttara-nikāya,* 1:140ff. [on *Aṅguttara-nikāya,* 2:465ff.]) has him jumping down safely from a considerable height. Still in another (*Paramatthadīpani Theragāthā-Aṭṭhakathā,* 1:420) he attains Arahantship upon the visit of the Buddha. The use of the knife in our *Saṃyutta-nikāya* account provides, for Vakkali, the occasion for great pain which brought him to the point of recognizing his ordinary situation (*puthujjana*) and, with considerable focal concentration, of acknowledging his transformation into the condition of Arahantship. Vakkali, the tradition avers, is remembered as being preeminent among those who are zealous in faith (*saddhādhimutta*). See Malalasekera, loc. cit.

14. In dealing with this delicate theme of integral relationship of the person of the Buddha and Salvific Truth, a parallel expression was found to be useful: *dhammakāya, brahmakāya*; *dhammabhūta, brahmabhūta,*

> because he himself consists of Dhamma so is he *brahmakāya*. Dhamma is called Brahmā here in the sense of "best." He has become Dhamma (*dhammabhūta*) in the sense of being one who has Dhamma as inherent nature. He has become Brahmā in the sense that he himself is the best. (*Sumaṅgalavilāsinī,* 3:865 [on *Dīgha Nīkāya,* 3:84])

The parallelism appears elsewhere. Wilhelm and Magdalene Geiger have made an impressive but incomplete study of Dhamma restricting their work particularly to the canonical texts, with occasional interpretations provided by a few Pali commentaries. They were fully aware of some of the significance of the meaning of Dhamma in the highest sense. They wrote, "*Mit voller Absicht hat der Buddha den Begriff dhamma an die Stelle von brahman gesetzt*, an die Stelle der ewigen unveränderlichen Weltseele die Idee des ewigen Enstehens und Vergehens, an die Stelle der Vorstellung von der Substanz die von der Nichtsubstanz." Magdalene and Wilhelm Geiger, *Pāli Dhamma,* 7. It is doubtful whether the Buddha himself interpreted his activity as deliberately placing a concept in a particular parallel systematic position.

> He has become Dhamma because of setting in motion Dhamma that is to be learned [the authoritative teaching] without distortion or in the sense that he, having reflected in his heart, consists of Dhamma that was expressed in words. He has become Brahmā in the sense of "the best."

*Papañcasūdanī Majjhimanikāyaṭṭhakathā of Buddhaghosācariya,* pt. 2, 76 (on *Majjhima-nikāya,* 1:111). One should note that *-maya,* "made of," "consisting of," used in the commentaries, is the suffix most closely rendering a sense of identity.

One meets the standard phrasing, *dhammabhūta* and *brahmabhūta* again with one suggestive but unelaborated addition:

> become Dhamma, in the sense of one whose condition is not unfavorable (*aviparīta-bhāva'aṭṭhena*) or consists of Dhamma that was expressed in words or because of setting in motion Dhamma to be learned [the authoritative teaching] having reflected on it in his heart. *Brahmabhūta,* in the sense of "the best."

*Sāratha-ppakāsini: Buddhaghosa's Commentary on the Saṃyutta-nikāya,* 2:389 (on *Saṃyutta-nikāya,* 4:94). *Saddhamma-ppajotikā: The Commentary on the Mahā-niddesa I,* ed. A. P. Buddhadatta (London: Published for the Pali Text Society by Humphrey Milford, Oxford University Press, 1931), 2:295 (on *Neddesa I: Mahāniddesa,* 1:178 [on *Sutta-Nipāta,* v. 834]) reads *aviparītasabhāvatthena,* "one whose inherent nature is not unfavorable," or "one whose inherent nature is not distorted or perverted."

And elsewhere the integral identity in relation is communicated as "the one who has become Dhamma," which means "the one who has Dhamma as inherent or essential nature" (*dhammasabhāva*). *Brahmabhūta* is glossed, in parallel, as "the one who has the best (or the highest) as inherent or essential nature." *Manorathapūraṇī: Commentary on the Aṅguttara Nikāya,* vol. 5, with indexes to vols. 1–5, ed. Hermann Kopp (London: Published for the Pali Text Society by Luzac, 1956), 72 (on *Aṅguttara-nikāya*, 5:226). The parallelism appears numerously throughout the canon. One notes, for example, *Majjhima-nikāya,* 1:111 (cf. *Papañcasūdanī,* 2:76, on this), 3:195; *Aṅguttara-nikāya,* 5:226 (cf. *Manorathapūraṇī,* 5:72). Another set of parallels is *dhammajāla,* "net of

Dhamma," and *brahmajāla* (*Dīgha Nikāya,* 1:46). The commentary takes the former in the sense of "the teachings spoken in many strands." *Brahmajāla* here refers to the analysis of knowledge of omniscience in the sense of its being "superior" or "the best." (*Sumaṅgalavilāsinī,* 1:129). We find *dhammayāna*, "dhamma-vehicle," and *brahmayāna*, "best vehicle," both referring to "the noble eightfold path." *Saṃyutta-nikāya*, 5:5 (cf. *Sārattha-ppakāsini,* 3:121). Regularly *brahma*° in compounds is taken as "best" or "highest" or "superior," as in *brahmadeyya,* "best gift" (*Papañcasūdanī,* 3:415 [on *Majjhima-nikāya,* 2:164]), as "best" or "highest" world or realm, *brahmaloka* (*Sumaṅgala-vilāsīnī: Buddhaghosa's Commentary on the Dīgha Nikāya,* pt. 2, ed. W. Stede (London: Published for the Pali Text Society by Humphrey Milford, Oxford University Press, 1931), 663 [on *Dīgha Nikāya,* 2:240]). *Brahmabhūta,* "who has attained the highest or the best," can stand alone as a synonym for one who has realized the extinction of all defilements, who has realized the ease of meditative absorption (*jhāna*), paths, fruits, and Nibbāna (so *Papañcasūdanī,* 3:10 [on *Mijjhamanikāya,* 1:341]). And one living the higher life (*brahmacārin*) refers to one living the noble path in the best sense unendingly (cf. *Sumaṅgalavilāsinī,* 3:737 [on *Dīgha Nikāya,* 2:283]). Interesting variations appear at *Papañcasūdanī,* 3:418 (on *Majjhima-nikāya*, 2:165), where *brahmavaṇṇin* is glossed by "one having the best color—the meaning is one endowed with the best golden color among the pure castes." Also here one finds *brahmavaccasin* glossed by "one endowed with a body like the body of Mahābrahmā."

15. Different formulations of the teachings are offered for Dhamma in the compound, *dhammakāya.* The entire collection of utterances by the Awakened One(s) is frequently noted (*Sumaṅgalavilāsinī,* 3:865 [on *Dīgha Nikāya*, 3:84]) as is the spectrum of Salvific Truth presented as the authoritative teaching (*Papañcasūdanī,* 2:76 [on *Majjhima-nikāya,* 1:11]; *Sāratthappakāsini,* 2:389 [on *Samyutta-nikāya,* 4:94]; *Saddhammappajotikā,* 2:295 [on *Niddesa 1: Mahāniddesa,* 1:78 on *Sutta-Nipāta,* v. 834]), and also as the ninefold world-transcending Dhamma (*Paramatthadīpani Theragāthā-Aṭṭhakathā,* 2:20 [on *Theragāthā,* v. 49]; *Paramatthadīpanī: Itivuttakaṭṭhakathā,* 1:116 [on *Itivuttaka,* vv. 90–91]), or phrased as paths, fruits, and Nibbāna (*Paramatthadīpanī: Itivuttakaṭṭhakathā,* 3:164 [on *Theragāthā,* v. 1174]). The commentary on the *Udāna* utilizes the exchange as recorded in the *Saṃyutta-nikāya* and glosses Dhamma with "noble truths" (*Paramatthadīpanī Udānaṭṭhakathā,* 311 [on *Udāna,* v. 58]).

16. See Wilfred Cantwell Smith, *Faith and Belief.*

17. *Sumaṅgalavilāsinī,* 1:237 (on *Dīgha Nikāya,* 1:86). The same specificity of reference occurs at *Sumaṅgalavilāsinī,* 1:278 (on *Dīgha Nikāya,* 1:110). At *Sumaṅgalavilāsinī,* 2:467 (on *Dīgha Nikāya,* 2:38) reference is made to the knowledge of the three paths. However, *Sārattha-ppakāsini,* 2:392, no doubt led by the context of *Saṃyutta-nikāya,* 4:107, takes *dhammacakkhu* as referring to the four paths and the four fruits.

18. *Majjhima-nikāya,* 1:380. The commentary here makes a similar observation, drawing attention to another *sutta* where *dhammacakkhu* refers to the destruction of the "outflows" (*āsava*) related to the three paths, but here, at this place, it refers only to the path of stream entrance. See also *Paramattha-Dīpani Udānaṭṭhakathā,* 283 (on *Udāna,* 49) and *Dhammapāla's Paramattha-Dīpanī,* pt. 4, Being the Commentary on the *Vimāna-Vatthu*, ed. E. Hardy (London: Published for the Pali Text Society by Henry Frowde, Oxford University Press, 1901), 327, where it is stated succinctly, "*dhammacakkhu ti sotāpattimaggam.*"

19. *Manorathapūraṇī: Buddhaghosa's Commentary on the Aṅguttara-nikāya,* vol. 2, 356 (on *Aṅguttara-nikāya,* 1:242). *Papañcasūdanī,* 3:92 (on *Majjhima-nikāya,* 1:380), commenting on *diṭṭhidhamma*, in association with *dhammacakkhu*, takes the former to refer to the four noble truths, and the latter to understanding the arising and cessation of all things.

20. Wilfred Smith writes,

> The good news is not that God did something centuries ago in Palestine, however big that bang; but that He can and may do something, and something salvific, however small our capacity, for you and me today. *The locus of revelation is always the present, and always the person* [emphasis added]. The channel of revelation in the Christian case, Christ, is a figure in history. But history, I have insisted, moves forward, and is the process by which He comes to us; is not something to be studied backwards, as the process by which we try to recapture Him.

Wilfred Cantwell Smith, *Towards A World Theology,* 175. Smith, some years earlier, provided a similar observation. "Just as there can be no revelation that is not a revelation of something (or someone), so there can be none that is not a revelation *to* someone. There is no revelation of God except to particular persons." Wilfred Cantwell Smith, *Questions of Religious Truth* (New York: Charles Scribner's Sons, 1967), 92.

21. See the list given in the collection of *Hymns of the Pure Land Masters, SBTS,* and also in *Collected Works,* 1:367–93. Brief biographical points about T'an-luan are provided in "Notes on the Inscriptions on Sacred Scrolls," in *Collected Works,* 1:502–503. Hisao Inagaki, in his "Chapter 2 T'an-luan's life and work," provides an analysis of several biographies of T'an-luan: Hisao Inagaki, *T'an-luan's Commentary on Vasubandhu's Discourse on the Pure Land* (kyoto [*sic*]: Nagata Bunshodo, 1998), 17–37.

22. References can be found at "The True Teaching, Practice, and Realization," in *Collected Works, 1:72;* in "Passage on the Pure Land Way," in *Collected Works,* 1:307; and "Notes on the Inscriptions on Sacred Scrolls," *Collected Works,* 1:503.

23. It is not clear whether this Vasubandhu is the brother of Asaṅga, both focal figures in the rise of the Yogacāra school, and/or whether this is the same Vasubandhu who was considered the author of the *Abhidharmakośa.* Within the cumulative tradition that developed into the heritage of Jōdo Shinshū, Vasubandhu stands as the second Indian patriarch in the wake of Nāgārjuna and, ultimately, of Śākyamuni Buddha.

24. *Land of Bliss: The Paradise of the Buddha of Measureless Light,* Sanskrit and Chinese Versions of the Sukhāvatīvyūha Sutras, Introductions and English Translations by Luis O. Gómez (Honolulu: University of Hawai'i Press, 1996), 120.

25. See the succinct comments by Gómez, ibid., 134.

26. Yoshifumi Ueda and Dennis Hirota, *Shinran,* 133.

27. The force of *hōben* here, representing as we have seen the Sanskrit *upāya,* "means," "expediency," reflecting the soteriological efficacy in a compassionate cosmos, in a mythological or historical teacher, is difficult to grasp, especially for English readers as we have noted above in chapter10.

28. The Chinese reads *chung,* J: *shu,* with the sense, also, of "kinds."

29. Literally, "Depending on (J: *yotte,* because of, due to) *dharmakāya* of *dharma*-nature the *dharmakāya* of compassionate means arises" (J: *shōzu*) with the

sense of being given birth, produced, brought into existence, brought about, engendered, created.

30. Literally, as previously, "Depending on the dharma-body of compassionate means the dharma-body of suchness arises" (J: *idasu*) carrying also the sense of being born from, of appearing, extending, going out from.

31. Not with difference (C:, J: *i*), with indivisibility, without differentiation (C: *bun,* J: *wakatzu*).

32. One in unity (C: *i*, J: *itsu*).

33. The same, equal, uniform (C: *t'ung*, J: *dō*).

34. There is reciprocal, interdependent mutuality (C: *hsiang, siang*, J: *sō*).

35. Ueda and Hirota, *Shinran,* 308–309. They provide a version of an original text of this passage as entry #42 on p. 329. I have also consulted the text in *SSZ,* 2:336. I note another English translation of this important passage: "The reason is that Buddhas and Bodhisattvas have two Dharmakāyas: (1) Dharmakāya of Dharma-nature and (2) Dharmakāya of Expediency. From Dharmakāya of Dharma-nature originates the Dharmakāya of Expediency; through the Dharmakāya of Expediency the Dharmakāya of Dharma-nature is revealed. These two Dharmakāyas are different but inseparable; they are one but not the same." Inagaki, *T'an-luan's Commentary*, 264–65. See also Roger Jonathan Corless, *T'an-luan's Commentary on the Pure Land Discourse: An Annotated Translation and Soteriological Analysis of the Wang-Shêng-lun Chu* (Ann Arbor: University Microfilms, 1973, a PhD dissertation in Religion, University of Wisconsin, 1973), 297.

36. So Dennis Hirota in his chapter, "Images of Reality in the Shin Buddhist Path: A Hermeneutical Approach," in *Towards a Contemporary Understanding of Pure Land Buddhism,* 54.

37. So Hisao Inagaki in *The Three Pure Land Sutras: A Study and Translation from Chinese,* by Hisao Inagaki in collaboration with Harold Stewart (Kyoto: Nagata Bunshodo, 1994), 88–89, as it is also found translated at *Tannishō, RTS,* supplementary note 24, p. 101, and at *Jōdo Wasan, RTS,* 11.

38. Shinran indicates this by recording in the *Kyōgyōshinshō* a passage from T'an-luan, "[T]he Tathagata is the body of true reality and, further, the body for the sake of beings." *The True Teaching, Practice, and Realization, SBTS,* 3:209, also in *Collected Works,* 1:82.

39. *The Jōdo Wasan, RTS,* 10.

40. Dennis Hirota, "Images of Reality," in *Towards a Contemporary Understanding,* 55.

41. Dennis Hirota, "Truth as Dialogic Event and Authentic Life in Shinran," *Shinshūgaku* (March 2006), 7–9.

42. See the discussion of the arising of *Magga* and *Shinjin* above in our chapter 11.

43. Dennis Hirota, "Revelation as Sacrament in Shinran and Karl Barth," *Across the Pacific with Love,* "Leroy Seat Commemorative Book" (Fukuoka, Japan: Touka Shobo, 2006), 137–54.

44. Ibid., 143.

45. The quotation from Barth is at ibid., 144, and Hirota's insightful observation is found at ibid., 145.

46. Ibid., 145. H. Richard Niebuhr observes, "The inspiration of Christianity has been derived from history, it is true, but not from history as seen by a spectator; the

constant reference is to subjective events, that is to events in the lives of subjects." *The Meaning of Revelation,* 72.

47. Thomas F. Torrance demonstrates this particular point in the fourth-century Christian case when he writes,

> It had also become evident in the prolonged debates throughout the fourth century that the king-pin of the Nicene-Constantinopolitan Creed was the *homoousion*—the affirmation of oneness in being between the Son—and indeed the incarnate Son—and the Father. Without that ontic unity there is no Mediator between God and man and the identity of Jesus Christ has nothing to do with any *self*-giving or *self*-revealing on the part of the eternal God, in which event the whole structure not only of the Creed but of the Gospel itself would disintegrate and collapse.

T. F. Torrance, "Introduction," *The Incarnation: Ecumenical Studies in the Nicene-Constantinopolitan Creed A.D. 381,* ed.Thomas F. Torrance (Edinburgh: Handsel Press, 1981), xi.

48. I note again the important study by Wilfred Cantwell Smith, *What Is Scripture?*

49. I have chosen not to discuss the council held at Ephesus in 451 because its significance in doctrinal development is not as central as the other three and, to a degree, the council was outflanked by the reformulations of the Nicaean creed by the council at Constantinople, of which the participants at Ephesus were not fully aware, and also by statements made later at the council held at Chalcedon. See the brief, but authoritative, presentation of the ecumenical councils of the early church by Norman P. Tanner, *The Councils of the Church: A Short History* (New York: The Crossroad Publishing Co., 2001 [of the work first appearing in Italian in 1999, and in French in 2000]), especially pp. 13–45.

50. Alan Torrance, although slightly overstating his point, nevertheless cautions:

> What becomes unambiguously clear . . . is that the decisive doctrinal formulations in the christology of the early church show that, far from being "Hellenisers" of the gospel, Athanasius and the Nicene fathers set out to affirm its content precisely *over and against* Hellenistic disjunctions—between the divine and the contingent, between the eternal and the spatio-temporal, between mind and body, and between the intelligible and the sensible realms.

Alan Torrance, "Jesus in Christian Doctrine," *The Cambridge Companion to Jesus,* ed. Markus Bockmuehl (Cambridge: Cambridge University Press, 2001), 206.

51. So Norman P. Tanner in *Decrees of the Ecumenical Councils,* vol. 1: Nicaea I to Lateran V, ed. Norman P. Tanner, S.J. (Washington, DC: Georgetown University Press, 1990), 2. See also the very informative, insightful and sensitively written presentation on *credo* by Wilfred Cantwell Smith, *Faith and Belief,* 69–78. Note particularly Smith's point regarding the meaning of *credo* in light of its Sanskrit cognate, *śraddhā,* in the sense of "I set my heart on."

52. Tanner, in *Decrees of the Ecumenical Councils,* provides the text originally established by G. Alberigo, J. A. Dossentti, P.-P. Joannou, C. Leonardi, and P. Prodi, in consultation with H. Jedin. The pagination follows the presentation of the Greek and Latin texts with the English translations on facing pages numbered consecutively and preceded by "*." Hence our reference here is p.*5, with Greek and Latin inserted from p. 5.

53. Tanner, *The Councils,* 23–24. This creed of 381 has provided the basic structure for what, even today, is called the Nicene Creed.

54. Tanner, *Decrees of the Ecumenical Councils,* 1:86–*86.

55. On docetism, monarchianism, patripasianism, Sabellianism, modal monarchianism, Arianism, Apollinarianism, Nestorianism, Pelagianism, gnosticism, see the succinct and very helpful work by Henry Bettenson, ed., *Documents of the Christian Church.*

56. Leonard Prestige, in "ΠΕΡΙΧΩΡΕΩ and ΠΕΡΙΧΩΡΗΣΙΣ in the Fathers," *The Journal of Theological Studies* 29 (1928): 242–52, notes how John of Damascus, whose thinking has played an important role in the Eastern Orthodox Church, utilized the term *perichōrēsis* / περιχώρησις with some lack of subtlety regarding the role of Christ but with considerable theological insight into the relationality of the Trinity. Prestige says of John's usage that it was "really unsuited to Christology but admirably expressive of Trinitarian unity." Ibid., 244. It is *perichōrēsis* in relationality that one has a remarkable example of a brilliant formulation of the uninterrupted connectivity between a personal soteriological realization of the abiding efficaciousness of the Holy Spirit leading to an encounter with the Son and engaged acknowledgment of God as Father.

57. A comparativist has some difficulty with the conceptualization of "modernism" and "postmodernism," as with "modern world" and "postmodern world." It is hardly clear what "modern" means, nor is it less ambiguous to use the term to refer to one's own way of thinking, or that of one's colleagues, or those with whom one wishes to identify, as representing, in any way that could be cogent, the world, globally, as we know it to be.

58. Colin E. Gunton, *The One, the Three, and the Many: God, Creation, and the Culture of Modernity* (The Bampton Lectures, 1992) (Cambridge: Cambridge University Press, 2002 [the seventh printing of the work first published in 1993]), 7. Gunton, at ibid., note 53, p. 37, clarifies how he uses "relationality," paralleling to some extent my observation regarding thought and speech. Gunton writes, "By relationality I do not mean what is sometimes taught, that things can be known only in so far as they are related to us, but rather the realistic belief that particulars, of whatever kind, can be understood only in terms of their relatedness to each other and the whole."

59. Ibid., 135.

60. Ibid., 142–43.

61. Ibid., 163–64.

62. Thomas F. Torrance, *The Christian Doctrine of God, One Being Three Persons* (Edinburgh: T and T Clark, 2001 [first published in 1996]), 102. Jürgen Moltmann also discusses the *perichōrēsis* of the Trinity noting, of the Father, Son, and Holy Spirit, "In the perichoresis, the very thing that divides them becomes that which binds them together." Jürgen Moltmann, *The Trinity and the Kingdom: The Doctrine of God* (Minneapolis: Fortress Press, 1993), 175.

63. Gunton, op. cit., 165.

64. Ibid., 170.

## CHAPTER 13. FROM CONTROVERSY TO UNDERSTANDING

1. The revised Gregorian calendar was finally adopted in England in 1752, about the time a delegation from Sri Lanka was in Thailand or Siam making arrangements that would be efficacious for the reestablishment of the higher ordination, *upasampadā,* of the Saṅgha in Sri Lanka.

2. Some of us have decided on starting with the lives of the Christ, the Buddha, an event in the life of Muhammad, a dynasty, a period or periods of imperial rule, even, for a time, with the overthrow of a monarchy as in 1792, in France.

3. Until approximately three decades ago, published books would often note both systems of calculating: preferring *kristu varṣa,* year with regard to the Christ, for *anno dominum*, year of our Lord, and *buddha varṣa,* year with regard to the Buddha. On occasion, an author or publisher would note only the latter. Occasionally, one would meet CE, "Christian era," with BE, "Buddhist era." More recently, CE is occasionally used, primarily in the text of some works, to designate "common era." In general, in more recent years, Christian authors and works published in English would note the year according to the Gregorian calendar. Works published in Sinhala tend to vary: some providing only the number of the year according to the Gregorian calendar, without accompanying abbreviations, others according to a reckoning with the life of the Buddha providing the beginning point for the numerical series.

4. Noteworthy is the participation of Dutch representatives in the relationship between Sinhalas and Siamese or Thais. Of the return of this delegation to Sri Lanka, it has been said, "The Dutch governor of the time, Joan Gideon Loten (1752–57), whose relations with Kandy were not entirely cordial, observed in his *Memoir*: 'But in the year 1753 there was no lack of evidence of good understanding and friendship, the Court being extremely gratified at the long desired arrival of the priests of the Buddhist doctrine from Siam who arrived safely on the 5th of May in a Company's ship at Trincomalee, whence they set out for Kandy.'" Kitsiri Malalgoda, *Buddhism in Sinhalese Society, 1750–1900*: *A Study of Religious Revival and Change* (Berkeley: University of California Press, 1976), 62. And yet, while on this occasion the Dutch were supportive of Buddhists, Roman Catholics in Sri Lanka were experiencing the repressive weight of religious persecution under the Dutch.

5. The major "breakthrough"—through and beyond—regarding the limiting inadequacy of reified concepts, such as "religion," and "Buddhism," and "Christianity," to lead subtly into greater mutual religious understanding in human discourse was made by Wilfred Smith in *The Meaning and End of Religion,* to which we have referred above.

6. I have touched on these debates in a chapter entitled "The Coming of *Early Buddhism* to Sri Lanka," and again, briefly, in a chapter, "There Are Buddhists Living in Sri Lanka Today," in *On Understanding Buddhists,* 27–35, 115–31.

7. An event related by the Rt. Revd. Monsignor Dr. W. L. A. Don Peter in his article, "The Catholic Presence in Sri Lanka Through History, Belief, and Faith," *Religiousness in Sri Lanka,* ed. John Ross Carter (Colombo: Marga Institute, 1979), 243.

8. Donald G. Dawe, "Christian Faith in a Religiously Plural World," in *Christian Faith in a Religiously Plural World,* ed. Donald G. Dawe and John B. Carman (Maryknoll, NY: Orbis Books, 1978), 30.

9. Eugene B. Borowitz, "A Jewish Response: The Lure and Limits of Universalizing Our Faith," ibid., 62.

10. Mahinda Palihawadana, "*Dhamma* Today and Tomorrow," in *Religiousness in Sri Lanka,* ed. John Ross Carter (Colombo: Marga Institute, 1979), 139–40.

11. Wilfred Cantwell Smith, *Faith and Belief,* 7.

12. Ibid., 146–47.

13. See Wilfred Cantwell Smith, "Part Two: The Christian in a Religiously Plural World," in his *The Faith of Other Men* (New York: Harper Torchbooks, 1972),

113–40, which part Smith has retitled, "The Church in a Religiously Plural World," in the new and revised issue of this work, *Patterns of Faith Around the World* (Oxford: Oneworld, 1998), 121–45.

14. Raimundo Panikkar, *The Intrareligious Dialogue* (New York: Paulist Press, 1978), 26. Apparently this observation was made a decade earlier by Panikkar in his article, "The Rules of the Game in the Religious Encounter," *The Journal of Religious Studies* (Punjabi University) 3, no. 1 (Spring 1971).

15. Panikkar, *The Intrareligious Dialogue,* 40.

16. Ibid., 71–72.

17. One notes the regular meetings of the International Association for Shin Buddhist Studies held in August in such places as Honolulu, Berkeley, and at Otani University in Kyoto on two occasions. Our chapter 8, "'Relying Upon' or 'Taking Refuge' as a Genuinely Human Activity," was delivered at a meeting of the International Association for Shin Buddhist Studies at Otani University, August 3, 1993. Chapter 11 got its start at an IASBS meeting in August 1987, at Berkeley. And "Will There Be Faith on Earth?", our chapter 18, arose in an IASBS meeting at Otani University, Kyoto, on August 2, 2001.

Two moments are instructive in light of our focus on Sri Lanka. The first is our chapter 17, "Buddhist and Baptists: In Conversation into Our Common Future," which was originally presented as the O. H. de A. Wijesekera memorial oration held in Colombo on August 13, 1993. Numerous representatives of Christian denominations, particularly Baptists, were in attendance along with Buddhist scholars and academics who paid their respects to Professor Wijesekera, the "Dean of Sanskrit studies in Sri Lanka," filling the large auditorium.

The second moment was August 29, 2003, in the chapel of Chapel House located on the campus of Colgate University, a highly selective liberal arts institution of higher learning in upstate New York. An alms ceremony (*dāna*), on this occasion, a gift of food, was held for four Sri Lankan Theravāda Buddhist monks: Venerables K. Piyatissa, K. Kondañña, Seelavimala, and Seelānanda. The *dāna* was the third-month anniversary commemorating the passing of H. G. Marthina (1928–2003), who with her family was forced to leave Teldeniya, an upcountry village in Sri Lanka, because of a massive dam, reservoir, and irrigation project, to begin life anew in Sandamadulla. Mrs. H. G. Marthina, who had lived in villages all of her life in Sri Lanka, was the mother of four children before witnessing the death of her youngest child. Two of her daughters were recently Resident Supervisors at Chapel House, a center for prayer and meditation on Colgate's campus. They were joined by an older friend of many years, a Christian, my wife, a graduate of Baylor University, a Baptist university in Texas, and the three, dressed appropriately in white saris, sat before the monks. They were joined by others: professors and students—a Comparativist who is also an ordained Christian minister, a Muslim Scholar of Islam, scholars of the Hindu and Native American traditions, students of different religious backgrounds, or none, and others. In his homily, Ven. Piyatissa drew attention to the underlying purpose of our ritual act: celebrating the virtuous life of an impressive woman. No explanation was needed, no rationale or apology provided. He knew that all persons present were able to reach agreement on the value of virtuous living. The language of the chanting was Pali and of the homily, English. A thread was extended through all hands, reverently held in pressed palms, from a pot of water to all and back to the monks. We were observing and receiving *pirit*

(Pali, *paritta*), protection for those yet living and for those who have passed on. The theme of the service, the aspiration of the *dāna,* was to realize a profound sense of personal enhancement in a recognition that we had discerned an authentic act in becoming ever more fully human (*puñña*: often translated "merit") in order to extend the quality arising from this recognition to others. Persons present that day realized that they had received far more from the occasion than what was given to the monks by way of food or honoraria to a foundation. Uniformity in recognition of some of what is involved in being fully human was seen and celebrated that day in a religiously plural context—the real context of our world today.

CHAPTER 14. RELIGION AND THE IMPERATIVES FOR DEVELOPMENT

1. John Ross Carter, "Introduction," *Religiousness in Sri Lanka,* iv–v.
2. Ibid., vii.
3. Luo Zhufeng, ed., *Religion under Socialism in China,* trans. Donald E. MacInnis and Zheng Xi'an (New York: M. E. Sharpe, 1991).
4. H. Richard Niebuhr, *Faith on Earth,* 48.
5. Ibid., 1.
6. *The Dīgha Nikāya,* 2:72ff. The discussion dealing with the Vajjians and the elaboration of the qualities of humane living that are associated with growth treated here is also recorded in the *Vajjī-vagga* of *The Aṅguttara-nikāya*, pt. 4, ed. Prof. E. Hardy (London: Published for the Pali Text Society by Luzac, 1958 [of the work first published in 1899]), 16–27.

CHAPTER 15. GETTING FIRST THINGS FIRST

1. B. Ananda Maitreya Nayaka Thero, "Buddhism in Therāvada Countries," in *The Path of the Buddha: Buddhism Interpreted by Buddhists,* ed. Kenneth W. Morgan (New York: Ronald Press Co., 1956), 113–52. In this book, which appeared approximately fifty years ago, Morgan, my predecessor at Colgate University, introduced the leading Buddhist contributors, and of Ven. Balangoda Ananda Maitreya he wrote that he "was recommended by Buddhists in Thailand and Burma as well as his own country [Sri Lanka] as a man who can speak for all Theravāda countries. He has traveled widely and writes from a background of years of practice and observation of Theravāda Buddhism." Ibid., v.
2. This film produced by Peter Montagnon for the BBC, 1977, was one of thirteen films that appeared in a series entitled "The Long Search" and distributed by Time-Life Video. The film appeared in both 16 mm and ¾' VHS videocassette formats. About our distinguished monk, a reviewer of this film wrote, correctly, "Ananda Maitreya, the chief monastic informant, is memorable throughout." *Focus on Buddhism: A Guide to Audio-Visual Resources for Teaching Religion,* ed. Robert A. McDermott (Chambersburg, PA: Anima Books, 1981), 22.
3. For the Pali and English translation see *The Dhammapada,* 243–44. The English translation only of this scripture (the verse is 183) has appeared as *The Dhammapada: Translated with an Introduction and Notes,* by John Ross Carter and Mahinda Palihawadana, "Oxford World's Classics" (Oxford: Oxford University Press, 2000).

4. *The Dīgha Nikāya,* 49. The verse has been translated variously and well. One attempt reads,

> Work ye no evil; give yourselves to good;
> Cleanse ye your hearts,—so runs the Buddhas' word.

*Dialogues of the Buddha* [pt. 2], translated from the Pali by T. W. and C. A. F. Rhys Davids (London: Published for the Pali Text Society by Luzac, 1959 [of the work first published in 1910]), 38.

5. Sukumar Dutt, *The Buddha and Five After-Centuries* (London: Luzac, 1957), 76.

6. *The Dhammapada,* 244.

7. The gloss on our verse, verse 183 of *The Dhammapada,* provided in the *Dhammapadaṭṭhakathā,* is as follows:

> (Refraining) from all that is detrimental:
> *sabbapāpassa (akaraṇaṃ)*
> From every [kind of] unwholesome deed.
> The attainment (of what is wholesome):
> *(kusalassa) upasampadā*
> The generation of the wholesome and the development of what is [so] generated—from the setting forth [into religious life] to the path of Arahantship.
> The Purification of one's mind: *sacittapariyodapanaṃ*
> Causing one's mind to be cleansed of the five hindrances.
> This is the instruction of Awakened Ones: *etaṃ buddhāna sāsanaṃ*
> This is the teaching of all the Buddhas.

*The Dhammapada,* 244.

8. I use "belief" in its withered recent sense. Wilfred Smith has done much to help us understand the history of our handling (insouciant misuse?) of this word. At one place he writes,

> The English 'belief', which used to be the verbal sign designating allegiance, loyalty, integrity, love, commitment, trust and entrusting, and the capacity to perceive and to respond to transcendent qualities in oneself and one's environment—in short, faith; the Christian form of God's most momentous gift to each person—*has come to be* [emphasis mine] the term by which we designate rather a series of dubious, or at best problematic, propositions.

Wilfred Cantwell Smith, *Belief and History* (Charlottesville: University Press of Virginia, 1977), 69. See also his important companion volume, *Faith and Belief,* previously cited.

9. Henry S. Olcott, *The Buddhist Catechism* (Colombo: Publication Division of the Ministry of Cultural Affairs, n.d. [my copy indicates a "forty-second edition" with a preface dated 1908, and also a "certificate to the first edition" dated 1881]). Olcott placed this verse as a response to question number 145, of his 383 questions, "Has not the Buddha summed up his whole doctrine in one gātha, or verse?" The answer is "Yes." The passage follows in Pali with an English translation,

To cease from all evil actions,
To generate all that is good,
To cleanse one's mind:
This is the constant advice of the Buddhas.

Ibid., 30.

10. I have addressed the force of the term *Buddhist* as adjective and as noun in "There Are Buddhists Living Today in Sri Lanka." See my *On Understanding Buddhists,* 115–31.

11. See ibid., 65–69. This chapter, "The Notion of Refuge," appears there with some revision and originally appeared in *The Threefold Refuge in the Theravāda Buddhist Tradition,* ed. John Ross Carter with George Doherty Bond, Edmund F. Perry, and Shanta Ratnayaka (Chambersburg, PA: Anima Books, 1982).

12. S. F. de Silva, E. R. Eratna, and S. Vanigatunga, *Buddhadharmaya* (Colombo: Śrī Laṅka Prakāśaka Samagama, 1964), 1. This book was an approved text for upper-kindergarten children.

13. Rerukane Chandavimala, *Pohoya Dinaya* (Colombo: Anula Press, 1966), 34.

## CHAPTER 16. TRANSLATIONAL THEOLOGY

1. John Ross Carter, "Translational Theology: An Expression of Christian Faith in a Religiously Plural World," in *Christian Faith in a Religiously Plural World,* ed. Donald G. Dawe and John B. Carman (Maryknoll, NY: Orbis Books, 1978), 168–80.

2. Ibid., 152.

3. Wilfred Cantwell Smith, *Faith and Belief* (Princeton: Princeton University Press, 1979, 1998).

4. I queried in a note to my chapter in *Christian Faith in a Religiously Plural World,* "On a generic level, one could, conceivably, organize a symposium on faith, rather than 'Christian faith,' in a religiously plural world with a series of seminar discussions on the significance of Scripture for religious persons in the major religious traditions of humankind." Ibid., 180 n.1. In my undergraduate teaching, I taught a senior seminar entitled "Christian Faith in a Religiously Plural World," but have found over the years that the evidence has supported a more recent focus and title, "Faith in a Religiously Plural World."

5. "Like a koan, the problem of relating the particularity of Christian faith to its claim to universality is a paradox worthy of consideration. It is a moral, spiritual, and intellectual problem that is crucial for the continuing vitality of the Christian community. Like the koan this paradox admits of no simple or already evident solution. It calls for serious reflection to stretch, indeed to transcend existing lines of thought and even of belief, to encompass what has long remained unnoticed and unbridgeable. Finally, we would have to say that the koan for Christians may require sustained meditation to give us new light on how loyalty to Jesus Christ and his lordship is to be conceived in a religiously plural world." Minor Lee Rogers, "Introduction," in *Christian Faith in a Religiously Plural World,* 7.

6. Wilfred Cantwell Smith, "The Study of Religion and the Study of the Bible," *Journal of the American Academy of Religion* 39, no. 2 (June 1971): 131–40. In his magisterial work, *What is Scripture?*, Smith extends his insightful investigation to include

the place of scripture in the lives of persons participating in the great religious traditions of the world.

7. Donald G. Dawe, "Christian Faith in a Religiously Plural World," in *Christian Faith in a Religiously Plural World,* 30.

8. John B. Carman, "Religion as a Problem for Christian Theology," in *Christian Faith in a Religiously Plural World,* 96.

9. Dawe, "Christian Faith in a Religiously Plural World," 28.

10. Not only did this work facilitate the Christian attempts to share their vision of the saving activity of God in Christ but quite possibly it contributed to some degree to that vision, as, in the case of Paul's interpretation of "law" or *nomos* (νομος), which appeared in the Septuagint, behind which stood "teaching" or "law," Torah, in the Hebrew.

11. Futuristic considerations are tantalizing. What might be some ramifications within the Christian community, in AD 2195, if the most exact edition of the Greek New Testament were that compiled by Japanese Buddhists and if the most precise, erudite translation were that rendered by Japanese Buddhists in Japanese? Conceivably, Christian historians would obviously do well to learn Japanese, and they would also turn to the Hindus and Buddhists in this our current century to be informed by their interpretations of and responses to Western scholarship as it deals with their own religious traditions. More could be said, of course, but I leave this aside.

12. I refer to *Nava Givisuma, The Sinhala New Testament: A Common New Translation* (approved by the Bible Society and the Catholic Bishops' Conference in Sri Lanka), 1975. The first printing of this translation was in 1973, of five thousand copies. The second printing, 1975, was of three thousand copies. This translation is relational in an additional sense because of its ecumenical base within the Christian community in Sri Lanka. It is endorsed by both Protestants and Roman Catholics.

13. Reference is to my *Dhamma,* as noted previously and below in the bibliography.

14. Strictly speaking, the recent Sinhala translation does not convey the notion "enfleshed" held in the Greek at John 1:14 (*sarx egeneto* / σὰρξ ἐγένετο) but says "the *Dharma*-person became a human being" (*dharmayāṇō minisathava gena*) differing from Sinhala translations of 1921 and 1931, "the Word-person became flesh" (*vākyayāṇō māṃsavatva karuṇaven*).

15. *Nava Givisuma, The Sinhala New Testament: A Common New Translation,* reading "word of God" (*deviyanvahansēgē vacanaya*), as do the other standard translations, might conceivably read in the future, "Dharma of God" (*deviyanvahansēgē dharmaya*).

## CHAPTER 17. BUDDHISTS AND BAPTISTS

1. Why not, one might ask, rather speak more comprehensively of Buddhism (or something so conceptualized) and Christianity (also, as something so conceptualized) as is the current practice? I have done this indirectly, somewhat as asides, in various places over the years and have found that what I have taken, *generally,* to be central to Christianity tends to be *particular*, not only regarding one or another historical period, drawing upon this or that theological theme but also regarding one's own perspective. We have spoken of *Buddhism* and *Christianity* in very broad strokes, and the debates have yielded to dialogue, perhaps also to colloquia, and some of us have learned from others of us. This process involves a risk, however, of dealing with such abstract, even reified, generalities or with such narrow, specialized, topics that the majority of observers might

perceive the activity as aloof, remote from the life situation of their attempts to live a religious life. A circle of like-minded theologians and buddhologists involved in colloquia would do well to continue outreach to the great majorities of the two traditions who neither participate in the proceedings nor, evidence tends to indicate, agree with the conclusions. We participants in Buddhist-Christian dialogue or colloquia must strive to avoid being seen as a kind of conference-coterie perceived as a clique of sorts involved in a closed discussion. One way we might avoid this wrong perception would be to keep our focus on the particulars, on (the absence of?) discussions among Buddhists themselves on this matter of interreligious understanding, on (the absence of?) discussions among Presbyterian and Baptist denominational missionary boards on the future of Christian missions, on particular experiences of Buddhists and Christians and their encounters with the faith of each other (which have been manifold, assuredly).

2. *The Dhammapada,* trans. John Ross Carter and Mahinda Palihawadana (Oxford University Press, 1987, 1988, "World Classics," 2000).

3. This interpretation finds its metaphorical paradigm in the words of Jesus to James and John, the sons of Zebedee:

> "What do you want me to do for you?" And they said to him, "Grant us to sit, one at your right hand and one at your left, in your glory." But Jesus said to them, "You do not know what you are asking. Are you able to drink the cup that I drink, or to be baptized with the baptism with which I am baptized?" (Revised Standard Version [*RSV*] Mark 10:36–38)

4. Today the Roman Catholic and Eastern Orthodox Churches hold seven such rites ordained by Jesus to be sacraments: baptism, confirmation, the Eucharist, penance, holy orders, matrimony, and extreme unction. Protestants tend to hold only two: baptism and the Eucharist or the Lord's Supper, and they differ as to whether these rites are sacraments or rather, in a different sense, acts of profound affirmation and remembrance.

5. There are many subgroups constituting denominations of Baptists in the United States. The largest is the Southern Baptist Convention. Of note, also, is the denomination known as American Baptist Churches in the U.S.A. It has been my delightful opportunity to have been long affiliated with both, having attended Baylor University and the Southern Baptist Theological Seminary, having served in a pastorate in an American Baptist church in Deputy, Indiana (which church requested my ordination to the Gospel ministry by a Southern Baptist church in Texas), and having been a member of the First Baptist Church of Hamilton, New York. This Baptist church in Hamilton was in existence long before a split occurred, accompanying the American Civil War, which produced the Southern Baptists. The church in Hamilton is affiliated with the American Baptist Churches in the U.S.A.

6. Robert G. Torbet, *A History of the Baptists* (Philadelphia: Judson Press, 1959), 33.

7. We know of exceptions, of course, the ironic and somewhat lamentable occurrence of Buddhists and Baptists, in the name of institutional coherence, launching drives toward uniformity that cut at the base of this religious liberty. I am aware of the disconcerting turmoil in which the Southern Baptist Convention, the largest Protestant denomination in the United States, now finds itself. That turmoil is not so much between conservatives and liberals as between those who have forgotten their not easily wrought Baptist heritage and have displayed a peculiar kind of arrogant certainty,

and those attempting to maintain hard-won Baptist distinctives, such as the fundamental commitment to freedom of conscience in matters of faith and practice.

8. Sukumar Dutt, *The Buddha and Five After-Centuries,* 106–107.

9. *The Dīgha Nikāya,* 2:101. *Ye hi keci Ānanda etarahi vā mamaṃ vā accayena atta-dīpā viharissanti atta-saraṇā anañña-saraṇā, dhamma-dīpā dhamma-saraṇā anañña-saraṇā, tamatagge me te Ānanda bhikkhū bhavissanti ye keci sikkhā-kāmāti.*

10. Ibid., 154. *Siyā kho pan' Ānanda tumhākam evam assa: 'Atītasatthukaṃ pāvacanaṃ, n'atthi no Satthā' ti. Na kho pan' etaṃ Ānanda evaṃ daṭṭhabbaṃ. Yo vo Ānanda mayā Dhammo ca Vinayo ca desito paññatto, so vo mam' accayena Satthā.*

11. Ibid., 124–26. The translation is of a standard phrase, *sutte otāretabbāni Vinaye sandassetabbāni.* See also Dutt, op. cit., 98.

12. *The Aṅguttara-nikāya,* pt. 1, 190–91. A similar setting occurs at *The Aṅguttara-nikāya,* pt. 2, 190–94, where the Buddha enters a discussion with one Bhaddiya, a Licchavī, in much the same way about much the same issues. The dispositions toward, or appeals to, authority being challenged (at *A.* 2:191) are (1) by oral transmission from of old (*anussavena*), (2) tradition (*paramparāya*), (3) by reported account (*itikirāya*), (4) by correspondence with a collection of teachings (*piṭakasampadānena*), (5) by theoretical speculation (*takkahetu*) and (6) by mere inference as to cause (*nayahetu*), (7) by speculative analysis as to condition (*ākāraparivitakkena*), (8) by acquiescence with regard to customary opinions (*diṭṭhinijjhānakkhantiyā*) (9) by apparent likelihood (*bhavyarūpatāya*), and (10) by veneration of one's advisor (*samaṇo no garu*). See also *Niddesa II: Cullaniddesa,* ed. W. Stede (London: Published for the Pali Text Society by Humphrey Milford, Oxford University Press, 1918), 108, for a slight variation.

The overriding issues in these contexts are establishing for oneself a basis for shifting loyalties from one teacher to the Buddha, on such matters as the possible benefit of greed, of malice, and the like. The implication seems to be that one should try the methods to determine for oneself which leads most wholesomely to the eradication of greed, malice, and so forth.

13. See the discussions on the issue of authority in K. N. Jayatilleke, *Early Buddhist Theory of Knowledge* (London: George Allen and Unwin, 1963), especially 390.

14. *Dīgha Nikāya,* 2:154–55.3

15. *Sutta-Nipāta,* v. 884. See also *Buddha's Teachings,* ed. Lord Chalmers, v. 884, 210. Chalmers translates this, engagingly, "There's one sole 'Truth' (not two)." Ibid., 211. In *Woven Cadences of Early Buddhists,* trans. E. M. Hare, 130, the passage is translated, "Single indeed is truth nor is there twain." K. N. Jayatilleke, op. cit., 353, takes it as "truth is one without a second."

16. Many have chosen not to commit themselves to this idea of truth being one. We do well to reconsider the issue not in terms of proof or disproof of the affirmation but in terms of choice and commitment. The choice one makes can be consequential especially at a time like ours in which so many argue with such assurance that so little can be known with certainty. Consider a summary observation provided by Francis Fiorenza about significant changes

> that contemporary theories of knowledge bring to our understanding of "disciplinary knowledge." These changes include the criticism in epistemology of universalistic conceptions of rationality, the criticisms in pragmatism

> of foundationalism, the criticism in hermeneutical theory of subjective certainty, the critique within post-empiricist philosophies of science of objectivism, and the criticism within post-modern social theory of progressive meta-narratives of history. These changes increasingly question the nature of rationality, as universal, objective, and neutral.

Francis Schüssler Fiorenza, "Theology in the University," *Bulletin of the Council of Societies for the Study of Religion* 22, no. 2 (April 1993): 35.

17. *Sakaṃ hi dhammaṃ paripuṇṇaṃ āhu;*
*aññassa dhammaṃ pana hīnam āhu.*
*Evam pi viggayha vivādiyanti,*
*sakaṃ sakaṃ sammutim āhu saccaṃ.*

*Sutta-Nipāta,* v. 904.

18. Wilfred Cantwell Smith, "Conflicting Truth-Claims: A Rejoinder," in *Truth and Dialogue: The Relationship between World Religions,* ed. John Hick (London: Sheldon Press, second impression, 1975 [of the work first published in 1974]), 156.

19. Ibid., 158–59.

20. Ibid., 160.

21. Ibid., 162.

22. *Niddesa I: Mahāniddesa* (1917), 2:292 (on *Sutta-Nipāta*, v. 884).

23. *Ekaṃ saccaṃ nirodho maggo vā. Sutta-Nipāta Commentary: Being Paramatthajotikā II,* vol. 2, ed. Helmer Smith (London: Published for the Pali Text Society by Humphrey Milford, Oxford University Press, 1917), 555.

24. *Saddhamma-pajjotikā: The Commentary on the Mahā-Niddesa* I, 2:361 (commenting on the *Mahāniddesa* passage at 2:292).

25. *Visuddhimagga of Buddhaghosācariya, HOS,* chap. 16, par. 26: *Ekaṃ hi saccaṃ na dutīyan ti ādisu paramatthasacce nibbāne c'eva magge ca.*

26. *Paramatthamañjūsā of Bhadantācariya Dhammapāla Thera: Or The Commentary of the Visuddhimagga,* 526.

27. Among the most grievous offenses that a monk might commit (*pārājikā*) one finds the act of exaggerating one's supernatural powers of performing miracles (*uttarimanussadhammam. iddhipāṭihāriya*). *The Vinaya Piṭakaṃ,* 2:112. See also C. S. Upasak, *Dictionary of Early Buddhist Monastic Terms* (Varanasi: Bharati Prakashan), 158. Richard F. Gombrich, in *Theravāda Buddhism: A Social History from Ancient Benares to Modern Colombo* (London: Routledge and Kegan Paul, 1988), 104, draws attention to this *Vinaya* passage and observes, "The same thinking lies behind the general principle that monks are not to talk about or make a display of their religious progress, whether in frugality or in meditation."

28. Graham N. Stanton, *The Gospels and Jesus* (New York: Oxford University Press, 1989), 102–103.

29. John Ashton, *Understanding the Fourth Gospel* (Oxford: Clarendon Press, 1991), 214.

30. Stanton, op. cit., 103.

31. This growing community Raymond Brown calls "the Community of the Beloved Disciple" and provides a list of the "others" at the time, six groups in all. See Raymond E. Brown, S. S., *The Community of the Beloved Disciple* (New York: Paulist Pres, 1979), 62–84.

32. John Painter, *The Quest for the Messiah: The History, Literature, and Theology of the Johannine Community,* 2nd ed. (Nashville: Abingdon, 1993), 425.

33. Raymond Brown, op. cit., 56, elaborates,

> [I]n no stage of *pre-Gospel* history do I see evidence of sharp internal struggle within the Johannine community; its battles were with outsiders. This helps to explain the deep sense of "us" against "them" which we shall see . . . when we study the Johannine relations with other groups at the time the Gospel was written.

34. Charles H. Talbert, *Reading John: A Literary and Theological Commentary on the Fourth Gospel and the Johannine Epistles* (New York: Crossroad, 1992), 200–201.

35. Ibid., 202.

36. One will have noted the absence of the English definite article in my translation of this famous passage. The Greek article *hē* / ἡ is present, but, since there is no indefinite article in Greek, one does not detect so much the force of exclusivity or specificity in the use of the article, as, rather, a demonstrative force with emphasis. The force of *hē* / ἡ, therefore, would seem to be an emphasis of personal engagement: that way, that truth, and that life which has been made evident, which will lead on. In a sense the reply to Thomas's asking about how one is to know the way is something like, "For heaven's sake, Thomas, *I'm* that *way*," rather than primarily carrying the implication, "I am the way, the only way, and there is indeed no other." And further, perhaps the most striking contribution of Jesus (and hence the force of "through me") to the thinking of his day among men and women who were Jewish, who were living in response to God, was the discernment of God as Father. Here, too, there would be emphasis: through this one, the sent *Son*, is God known as *Father*.

This recognition of God as Father continues in the recognition of Christians of their own sonship. H. Richard Niebuhr puts it well in *The Responsible Self: An Essay in Christian Moral Philosophy* (New York: Harper and Row, 1963), 176, "When the Christian addresses the Determiner of Destiny actually, not merely verbally, as Father, he knows he does it in the name, because of the presence in him, of Jesus Christ. When he feels and knows himself to be a son of God, an heir in the universe, at home in the world, he knows this sonship, this at-homeness, as not only like Jesus Christ's but as actualized by him."

37. *Papañcasūdanī Majjhimanikāyaṭṭhakathā of Buddhaghosācariya,* pt. 1, 131.

38. Joachim Jeremias, *The Prayers of Jesus*. Although James Barr, in "Abba Isn't 'Daddy'," *Journal of Theological Studies* 39 (1988): 28–47, and "'Abba, Father' and the Familiarity of Jesus' Speech," *Theology* 91 no. 741 (1988): 173–79, argues, on the whole persuasively, against *'abbā* = "Daddy" popularized by Jeremias, both scholars agree on the emphasis given by Jesus to his relationship with God as Father.

39. Ashton, op. cit., 492, indicates two "characteristically Johannine terms for God, Father and Sender."

40. C. K. Barrett observes, "Undoubtedly he [the evangelist, the author of this Gospel] believes that the Son of God who was incarnate in Jesus of Nazareth inhabited eternity with the Father." He notes regarding "the meaning of sonship: both moral likeness and essential identity are included." C. K. Barrett, *The Gospel According to St. John: An Introduction with Commentary and Notes on the Greek Text*, 2nd ed.

(Philadelphia: Westminster Press, 1978 [1955]), 72. See, further, Charles Talbert's comments on the incarnate Jesus in this Gospel, op. cit., 205.

41. From μένω, which Arndt and Gingrich gloss, "fig., of someone who does not leave the realm or sphere in which he finds himself: *remain, continue, abide,*" and about which phrasing they say it "is a favorite of J[ohn] to denote an inward, enduring personal communion." William F. Arndt and F. Wilbur Gingrich, *A Greek-English Lexicon of the New Testament and Other Early Christian Literature* (Chicago: University of Chicago Press, 1957), 505a.

42. Stanton, op. cit., 103, turns to this passage as an example of this anti-Jewish posturing. He writes,

> One example will suffice. We quoted earlier the words of Jesus: "You will know the truth and the truth will make you free" (8:32). But in its context this is not, as it is often taken to be, an aphorism of universal validity for men of goodwill. These words occur in the middle of a lengthy and ferocious dispute between Jesus and "the Jews." At its climax there is some rather unpleasant name-calling.

J. Louis Martyn, *History and Theology in the Fourth Gospel (*Nashville: Abingdon, 1979 [revised and enlarged of the work first published in 1968]), 16, draws attention to this "disquieting, sharp, even unpleasant exchange between Jesus and a group of Jews." Martyn continues, "Jesus accuses his questioners of trying to murder him, contests their claim to be descended from Abraham, and furthermore suggests that these Jews have as their father neither Abraham nor God, but the devil."

43. Hermann Oldenberg and Richard Pischel, eds., *The Thera- and Therī-gathā: (Stanzas Ascribed to Elders of the Buddhist Order of Recluses)*, 2nd ed., with Appendices by K. R. Norman and L. Alsdorf (London: Published for the Pali Text Society by Luzac, 1966), v. 303,35. *Dhammo have rakkhati dhammacāriṃ, dhammo suciṇṇo sukham āvahāti: es' ānisaṃso dhamme suciṇṇe, na duggatiṃ gacchati dhammacārī.* See, further, my *Dhamma,* 144–46, for a brief discussion of this passage and its occurrence in several Pali and Sinhala sources.

44. *Saṃyutta-nikāya, 2:178. Anamataggāyaṃ bhikkhave saṃsāro pubbākoṭi na paññāyati avijjānīvaraṇānaṃ sattānaṃ taṇhāsaṃyojanānaṃ sandhāvataṃ saṃsarataṃ.* This general theme appears elsewhere. See *Aṅguttara-nikāya,* 5:113. *Purimā bhikkave koṭi na paññāyati avijjāya 'ito pubbe avijā nāhosi, atha pacchā sambhavī ' ti, evañ c'etaṃ bhikkhave vuccati.* "O monks, the point of origin of ignorance is not apparent so that one may say 'formerly there was no ignorance, then later it was produced'."

45. Mahinda Palihawadana, when reading a volume by James Leo Garrett Jr., one of my Baptist seminary professors, *Systematic Theology: Biblical, Historical, and Evangelical,* vol. 1 (Grand Rapids: Eerdmans, 1990), serendipitously hit upon this point of agreement between Buddhists and Baptists, and made a similar point in his presentation, as an O'Connor Visiting Professor of Literature, "Sin and *Dukkha*: the question of their comparability," at a Humanities Colloquium at Colgate University on Tuesday, May 4, 1993.

46. The great Greek term *euaggelion* / *εὐαγγέλιον*, meaning originally "a reward for good news," coming to mean "good news," of which the English "gospel," itself of interesting Anglo-Saxon derivation, is now the standard translation, has come into bad

times recently in such English usage as "evangelical" or "evangelist." These English words have tended to be used pejoratively, unfortunately, as have other great words such as "pious," "piety," and "dogma."

47. The point has been put this way:

> The Clear Comprehension of Reality (lit.: of Non-delusion) removes, through the clear light of an unclouded comprehension of actuality, the deepest and most obstinate delusion in man: his belief in a self, a soul, or an eternal substance of any description. This delusion, with its offspring of craving and hatred, is the true motive power of that revolving Wheel of Life and Suffering to which, like to an instrument of torture, beings are bound, and on which they are broken again and again.

Nyanaponika Thera, *The Heart of Buddhist Meditation* (York Beach, ME: Samuel Weiser, 1984), 51.

> Stressing the self-agency of the arising of insight again tends to miss the profound significance of the occasion. Bhikkhu Khantipalo has written, "It [insight-knowledge] leads, not to further entanglements, but to relinquishment. And it is fresh, new and quite different to what one had known before." He continues, "The Buddha also called this insight 'direct knowledge', direct, that is, without the intervention of the conceptualizing mind and direct because it gets to the heart of impermanence, dukkha and not self." Bhikkhu Khantipalo, *Calm and Insight: A Buddhist Manual for Meditators* (London: Curzon Press, 1981), 69.

48. Buddhaghosa puts it this way:

> Although it [change-of-lineage-knowledge] is not itself [this] turning [to the path], having been established in the position of this turning and, as if having given a sign to the path "Now, arise!", it ceases. And having not abandoned that sign given by it [i.e., by change-of-lineage-knowledge], following upon that knowledge in uninterrupted continuity, the path (*magga*) arises, breaking through and exploding the mass of greed, the mass of hatred, the mass of delusion, not penetrated before, not exploded before.

*Visuddhimagga of Buddhaghosācariya*, *HOS*, chap. 22, par. 10–11, 579. On this general topic, see also Mahinda Palihawadana, "Is There a Theravāda Buddhist Idea of Grace?", 186ff.

## CHAPTER 18. WILL THERE BE FAITH ON EARTH?

1. H. Richard Niebuhr, *Faith on Earth,* 1.
2. Ibid.
3. We sometimes see a reflection of this disintegration of grounded relationships when persons refer to the motivation for their acts. "It's nothing personal. It's just business," one might hear when an associate makes a cutting business deal. Or in being interviewed after a heroic act, one might hear another reply, "I was just doing my job" or "That's my job." Now, of course, such person being interviewed might have said this because he or she was self-effacing, wishing not to draw attention to himself or herself,

letting the matter pass quickly. But he or she also might well have given this interpretation because it was the socially safe or correct thing to say. He or she did what he or she was paid to do. He or she responded on the basis of a fiduciary contract rather than because he or she recognized swiftly and cogently that he or she had a human responsibility to rescue others, that persons have—or ought to have—this trust in others also to act likewise.

4. Niebuhr provides a succinct summary of his approach at *Faith on Earth,* 83; see also 39–40.

5. Niebuhr continues immediately, "In Him we live and move and have our being not only as existent but as worthy of existence and worthy in existence." Although preferring the personal pronoun throughout, Niebuhr makes it clear that in the final analysis, one moves beyond this mode of reference in speaking of the One. See, on these categories, his chapter "The Idea of Radical Monotheism," in *Radical Monotheism,* 32.

6. Niebuhr, *Faith on Earth,* 84. See also his *Radical Monotheism,* 33 n. 7.

7. See Wilfred Cantwell Smith, *Faith and Belief.*

8. I do not wish to enter a discussion about "selves" as interpreted by Christians and Buddhists. Let it be sufficient to say that I intend here the empirical ego; the person that I consider myself to be in my becoming ever more thoroughly known to myself. Whether there is a metaphysical, ontological component to this self or these selves is beyond my comprehension. That I am a person capable of loving and forgetting, being faithful and inadequate in my responsibilities, I can hardly contest.

9. Niebuhr draws our attention to this in his discussion of the collapse of "henotheism" into "polytheism":

> The great alternative to henotheism with its relative unification of life is pluralism in faith and polytheism among the gods. Historically and in the contemporary scene such pluralism seems most frequently to follow on the dissolution of social faith. When confidence in nation or other closed society is broken, *men who must live by faith* [emphasis added] take recourse to multiple centers of value and scatter their loyalties among many causes. When the half-gods go the minimal gods arrive. *Radical Monotheism,* 28.

In speaking of "radical monotheism," Niebuhr again notes faith as a given quality: "Radical monotheism . . . is a form of human faith, that is, of the confidence and fidelity *without which men do not live* [emphasis added]." Ibid., 38. In speaking generally about a quality of person, Niebuhr writes, "As that faith that life is worth living, as the reverence of life is a source of meaning and value, as the practice of adoration and worship, it [religion in this sense] *is common to all men* [emphasis added]" in his Supplementary Essay, "Faith in Gods and in God," ibid., 118.

10. Smith, *Faith and Belief,* 135. He continues, "This is so, however pure or distorted it or they may statistically prove to be empirically in any given situation." Smith shares the fruit of his labors: "Faith, then, so far as one can see as one looks out over the history of our race, is an essential human quality. One might argue that it is *the* essential human quality: that it is constitutive of man as human; that personality is constituted by our universal ability, or invitation, to live in terms of a transcendent dimension, and in response to it." Ibid., 129.

# A Bibliographic Note on the Context of Origin and Subsequent Versions of the Chapters in this Volume

It is a pleasure to have the opportunity to bring together into one volume, with appropriate revision throughout, a body of work for the most part variously offered before in lectures and talks, in almost all cases for, and at the invitation of, Buddhists, and subsequently published in three countries around the world. This context of origin is reflected in the title: *In the Company of Friends.* I acknowledge my appreciation for permission granted by editors and publishers of volumes and journals to revise and here present the chapters of this volume.

Chapter 1, "On Understanding Religious Men and Women," delivered at Otani University, Kyoto, Japan, in January, 1986, first appeared in *Kenkyūsho hō,* no. 14, January 31, 1986, published by Otani University, 20–26. Chapter 2, "Truth and History in Interreligious Understanding—A Preliminary Inquiry," was presented at a Buddhist-Christian colloquium held at Loyola Marymount University, Los Angeles, September 10–12, 2001, and was discussed at a meeting with colleagues of the Otani University Shin Buddhist Comprehensive Research Institute on October 12, 2001. A memorial volume for the late Godwin Samararatne provided the opportunity to publish our chapter 3, "Interreligious Understanding as a Religious Quest," previously entitled "On the Search for Interreligious Understanding," and appearing in *Approaching the Dhamma: Buddhist Texts and Practices in South and Southeast Asia,* edited by Anne M. Blackburn and Jeffrey Samuels (Seattle: BPS Publications, 2003), 69–87. "*Saṃvega* and the Incipient Phase of Faith," our chapter 4, was first placed in the hands of Buddhists and subsequently appeared in *Kalyāṇī: Journal of Humanities and Social Sciences of the University of Kelaniya* XIV–XXVI (1995–2007): 13–22. Our chapter 5, "*Shinjin*: More than 'Faith'?" was first given as a lecture at the Shin Buddhist Comprehensive Research Institute in the spring of 1986 and subsequently appeared in *Annual Memoirs of the Otani University Shin Buddhist Comprehensive Research Institute*, Volume 4 (1986), 1–40.

"Celebrating Our Faith," chapter 6, is a revision of an address entitled "On Celebrating Our Faith," given to students and faculty of Ryukoku University, Kyoto, Japan, in the spring of 1986, and first appeared in *The Shinshugaku: Journal of Studies in Shin*

*Buddhism* 78 (March 1988): 25–43. Chapter 7, "Colloquia In Faith," was first published as "On Conferences And Faith" in *Japanese Religions* 14, no. 4 (July 1987): 14–30. Chapter 8, "'Relying Upon' or 'Taking Refuge' as a Genuinely Human Activity," was delivered in Panel 1, "*Ōjo*: The Problem of Salvation in the Contemporary World," on August 3, 1993, as part of the Sixth Biennial Conference of the International Association of Shin Buddhist Studies held at Otani University, the text of which appeared in the *Proceedings,* published by Otani University in 1994, 27–52, while the entire text and notes appeared in *Annual Memoirs of The Otani University Shin Buddhist Comprehensive Research Institute*, Volume 11 (1993), 17–42. "Love and Compassion as Given," chapter 9, a first draft of which was presented on August 10, 1987, at a seminar entitled "Agape and compassion—their relation to insight or faith," as part of an international conference, "Buddhism and Christianity: Toward the Human Future," held at the Graduate Theological Union in Berkeley California, subsequently appeared in *The Eastern Buddhist* XXII, no. 1 (Spring 1989): 37–53. Chapter 10, "Toward an Understanding of What Is Inconceivable," appeared in *The Eastern Buddhist* XX, no. 2 (Autumn 1987): 32–52. "The Arising of Salvific Realization as Buddhists and Christians Have Affirmed," our chapter 11, drew upon some previous work published as "The Arising of *Magga* and *Shinjin,*" which was presented first at the Third Biennial Conference of the International Association for Shin Buddhist Studies, August 1987, at Berkeley, California, and appeared in *The Pure Land: Journal of Pure Land Buddhism,* (New Series) no. 3 (December 1987): 95–106. It was developed further in a consultation with Buddhist and Christian colleagues held at Chikushi Jogakuen, Dazaifu, Japan, on October 10, 2001. Chapter 12, "Relationality in Religious Awareness," evolved from a contribution dedicated to Masatoshi Nagatomi, one of my advisors during my years in graduate studies at Harvard University: "Identity in Relation: The Buddha and the Availability of Salvific Truth," *Pacific World: Journal of the Institute of Buddhist Studies* (Third Series) no. 5 (Fall 2003) [which first appeared Spring 2005] (a Special Section in Memory of Masatoshi Nagatomi): 35–53. During October 2006, the work underwent extensive revision to include testimonies of Pure Land Buddhists and Christians, and appeared as "Relationality in Religious Awareness," in *The Shinshugaku: Journal of Studies in Shin Buddhism* no. 118 (March 2008): 1–39.

"From Controversy to Understanding: More than a Century of Progress," chapter 13, appeared as the third chapter in *Don Peter Felicitation Volume*, presented to Right Reverend Monsignor Welgama Lekam Appuhamilage Don Peter, former rector of Aquinas College, Colombo, edited by E. C. T. Candappa and M. S. S. Fernandopulle (Colombo: Don Peter Felicitation Committee, 1983), 19–33. "Religion and the Imperatives for Development," which is our chapter 14, first appeared in *Marga Quarterly Journal* 12, no. 3, a volume dedicated to the memory of Gregory Kurukulasuriya (Colombo: Marga Institute, 1992), 15–22. Chapter 15, "Getting First Things First: Some Reflections on a Response by Venerable Ananda Maitreya," was originally published in *Ven. B. Ananda Maitreya Birth Centenary Felicitation Volume, 1896–1996/Baḷangoḍa Ānanda Maitreya Mahā Nāgimi* (Ratmalana, Sri Lanka: Sarvodaya Vishva Lekha, 1996), 128–30.

Chapter 16, "Translational Theology: An Expression of the Faith of Christians in a Religiously Plural World," formed a part of *Christian Faith in a Religiously Plural World,* edited by Donald G. Dawe and John B. Carman (Maryknoll, NY: Orbis Books, 1978), 168–80, and was developed from a paper, "The New Testament in Asian Languages," presented at the conference "Christian Faith in a Religiously Plural World," held at Washington and Lee University, Lexington, Virginia, April 22–24, 1976. Chapter 17,

"Buddhist and Baptists: In Conversation into Our Common Future," was revised from the O. H. de A. Wijesekera Memorial Oration given in Colombo, August 13, 1993, and printed by Sridevi Printers, Dehiwala, Sri Lanka, 1993. And our final piece, Chapter 18, "Will There Be Faith on Earth?," was presented as part of a plenary panel, "Jōdo Shinshū and the Human Crisis of the Modern World," at the International Association of Shin Buddhist Studies Conference at Otani University, Kyoto, August 2, 2001.

# Bibliography

In some cases, the more customary transliterations of titles of foreign language texts have been incorporated into the text of this volume. However, the form of presentations occurring in the Notes and Bibliography follows the format of title pages of the noted published works. There should be no difficulty in recognizing the sources mentioned in the text and the documentation of published works noted below in the Bibliography.

*A Buddhist Manual of Psychological Ethics.* Translated by Caroline A. F. Rhys Davids. London: Pali Text Society (distributed by Routledge and Kegan Paul), 1974 (of the work first published in 1900).

*The Aṅguttara-nikāya.* Part 1. Edited by the Rev. Richard Morris. 2nd ed. revised by A. K. Warder. London: Published for the Pali Text Society by Luzac, 1961.

*The Aṅguttara-nikāya.* Part 2. Edited by the Rev. Richard Morris. London: Published for the Pali Text Society by Luzac, 1955.

*The Aṅguttara Nikāya.* Parts 3–5. Edited by E. Hardy. London: Published for the Pali Text Society by Luzac, 1958.

*The Apostolic Fathers: With an English Translation.* Vol. 1. Kirsopp Lake. The Loeb Classical Library. Cambridge: Harvard University Press, 1952.

Arndt, William F., and F. Wilbur Gingrich. *A Greek-English Lexicon of the New Testament and Other Early Christian Literature.* Chicago: The University of Chicago Press, 1957.

Arulchelvam, Maheswari M. "The Gift Immutable." In *Of Human Bondage and Divine Grace: A Global Testimony,* ed. John Ross Carter, 47–55. La Salle, IL: Open Court, 1992.

Ashton, John. *Understanding the Fourth Gospel.* Oxford: Clarendon Press, 1991.

*Aṭṭhakathāsūci.* Part 3. Edited by Pandita Kosgoda Sirisumedha Thero. Revised by Pandita Dhammavaṃsa Thero. Colombo: M. D. Gunasena, 1969.

Augustine, Morris. "The Buddhist Notion of Faith," an unpublished dissertation submitted to the Faculty of the Graduate Theological Union in partial fulfillment of the requirements for the degree of Doctor of Philosophy, Berkeley, California, May 1978. Ann Arbor, Michigan: University Microfilms International, printed by microfilm/xerography in 1982.

Baillie, D. M. *God Was in Christ: An Essay on Incarnation and Atonement.* New York: Charles Scribner's Sons, 1948.

Baillie, John. *The Idea of Revelation in Recent Thought.* New York: Columbia University Press, 1956.

———. *Our Knowledge of God.* New York: Charles Scribner's Sons, 1939.

Barr, James. "'Abba, Father' and the Familiarity of Jesus' Speech." *Theology* 91, no. 741 (1988): 173–79.

———. "Abba Isn't 'Daddy'." *Journal of Theological Studies* 39 (1988): 28–47.

Barrett, C. K. *The Gospel According to St. John: An Introduction with Commentary and Notes on the Greek Text.* Philadelphia: The Westminster Press, 1978.

Bettenson, Henry. *Documents of the Christian Church.* London: Oxford University Press, 1959 (of the work first published in Oxford's The World's Classics series in 1943).

*Biblia Hebraica.* Edited by Rud. Kittel. Stuttgart: Württenbergische Bibelanstalt for the American Bible Society, 1937.

Borowitz, Eugene B. "A Jewish Response: The Lure and Limits of Universalizing Our Faith." In *Christian Faith in a Religiously Plural World,* ed. Donald G. Dawe and John B. Carman, 59–68. Maryknoll, NY: Orbis Books, 1978.

Brown, Raymond E., S.S. *The Community of the Beloved Disciple.* New York: Paulist Press, 1979.

Buddhadatta Mahāthera, A. P. *Concise Pāli-English Dictionary.* Colombo: The Colombo Apothecarie's Co., 1968.

Burbidge, John, ed. *Modern Culture from a Comparative Perspective,* by Wilfred Cantwell Smith. Albany: State University of New York Press, 1997.

Carman, John B. *Majesty and Meekness: A Comparative Study of Contrast and Harmony in the Concept of God.* Grand Rapids: Eerdmans, 1994.

———. "Religion as a Problem for Christian Theology." In *Christian Faith in a Religiously Plural World*, ed. Donald G. Dawe and John B. Carman, 83–103. Maryknoll, NY: Orbis Press, 1978.

———, and Frederick J. Streng, eds. *Spoken and Unspoken Thanks: Some Comparative Soundings.* Center for the Study of World Religions, Harvard University, and Center for World Thanksgiving, Dallas, Texas, 1989.

———. *The Theology of Rāmānuja: An Essay in Interreligious Understanding.* New Haven: Yale University Press, 1974.

Carter, John Ross. *Dhamma: Western Academic and Sinhalese Buddhist Interpretations—A Study of a Religious Concept.* Tokyo: Hokuseido Press, 1979. This work has appeared in a Sinhala translation: *Dhamma: aparadiga śāstrajña-saha sinhala bauddha artha kathana āgamika saṃkalpayak pilibaňda adhyayanayak,* trans. W. S. Karunatilake. Colombo: M. D. Gunasena, 1985; reprinted, with an abbreviated title, *Dhamma,* in 1999.

———, and Mahinda Palihawadana. *The Dhammapada: A New English Translation with the Pali Text and the First English Translation of the Commentary's Explanation of the Verses with Notes Translated from Sinhala Sources and Critical Textual Comments.* New York: Oxford University Press, 1987. First issued as an Oxford University Press paperback in 1998. The English translation with a new introduction and explanatory notes appeared in the Oxford World's Classics series in 2000.

———, ed. *Of Human Bondage and Divine Grace: A Global Testimony.* La Salle, IL: Open Court, 1992.

———, ed. *On Living Life Well: Echoes of the Words of the Buddha from the Theravāda Tradition.* Onalaska, WA: Pariyatti, 2010.

———. *On Understanding Buddhists: Essays on the Theravāda Tradition in Sri Lanka.* Albany: State University of New York Press, 1993.

———, ed. *The Religious Heritage of Japan: Foundations for Cross-cultural Understanding in a Religiously Plural World.* Portland, OR: Book East, 1999.

———, ed. *Religiousness in Sri Lanka.* Colombo: Marga Institute, 1979. This work has been translated into Sinhala as *Śrī Laṅkāvē āgamika bhāvaya* by the translation staff of Marga Institute. Colombo: Marga Institute, 1985.

———, ed. *The Threefold Refuge in The Theravāda Buddhist Tradition.* With George Doherty Bond, Edmund F. Perry, and Shanta Ratnayaka. Chambersburg, PA: Anima Books, 1982.

———. "Translational Theology: An Expression of Christian Faith in a Religiously Plural World." In *Christian Faith in a Religiously Plural World,* ed. Donald G. Dawe and John B. Carman, 168–80. Maryknoll, NY: Orbis Books, 1978.

Chalmers, Lord [Robert]. *Buddha's Teachings: Being the Sutta-Nipāta or Discourse-Collection edited in the original Pali text with an English version facing it.* Cambridge: Harvard University Press, 1932.

Chandavimala, Rerukane. *Pohoya Dinaya.* Colombo: Anula Press, 1966.

*The Collected Works of Shinran.* Vol. 1, *The Writings.* Translated with introduction, glossaries, and reading aids by Dennis Hirota (Head Translator), Hisao Inagaki, Michio Tokunaga, and Ryushin Uryuzu. Shin Buddhist Translation Series. Kyoto: Jōdo Shinshū Hongwanji-ha, 1997.

Coomaraswamy, Ananda K. "Saṃvega, 'Aesthetic Shock.'" *Harvard Journal of Asiatic Studies* 7, no. 3 (February 1943).

Corless, Roger Jonathan. "T'an-luan's Commentary on the Pure Land Discourse: An Annotated Translation and Soteriological Analysis of the Wang-Shêng-lun Chu," a PhD dissertation in Religion, University of Wisconsin, 1973. Ann Arbor, Michigan: University Microfilms, Inc., 1973.

Cullmann, Oscar. *Christ and Time: The Primitive Christian Conception of Time and History.* Translated from the German by Floyd V. Filson. Philadelphia: Westminster Press, 1950.

Dawe, Donald G. "Christian Faith in a Religiously Plural World." In *Christian Faith in a Religiously Plural World,* ed. Donald G. Dawe and John B. Carman, 13–33. Maryknoll, NY: Orbis Books, 1978.

———, and John B. Carman, eds. *Christian Faith in a Religiously Plural World.* Maryknoll, NY: Oribis Books, 1978.

de Silva, S. F., and E. R. Eratna, with S. Vanigatunga. *Buddhadharmaya.* Colombo: Śrī Laṅka Prakāśaka Samagama, 1964.

*The Dhammapada: A New English Translation with the Pali Text and the First English Translation of the Commentary's Explanation of the Verses with Notes Translated from Sinhala Sources and Critical Textual Comments* by John Ross Carter and Mahinda Palihawadana. New York: Oxford University Press, 1987. First issued as an Oxford University Press paperback in 1998. The English translation with a new introduction and explanatory notes appeared in the Oxford World's Classics series in 2000.

*Dhammapada Vivaraṇaya* by Morogallē Siri Ñāṇobhāsa Tissa. Colombo: M. D. Gunasena, 1962.

*Dhammapāla's Paramattha-Dīpanī,* Part 4, Being the Commentary on the *Vimāna-Vatthu.* Edited by E. Hardy. London: Published for the Pali Text Society by Henry Frowde, Oxford University Press, 1901.

*Dhampiyā-aṭuvā-gäṭapadaya.* Edited by Professor D. E. Hettiaratchi. Published by the Press Board of the Sri Lanka University at the University Press, 1974.

*Dialogues of the Buddha.* Part 2. Translated from the Pali by T. W. and C. A. F. Rhys Davids. London: Published for the Pali Text Society by Luzac, 1959 (of the work first published in 1910).

*The Dīgha Nikāya.* Vol. 1. Edited by T. W. Rhys Davids and J. Estlin Carpenter. London: Published for the Pali Text Society by Luzac, 1949.

*The Dīgha Nikāya.* Vol. 2. Edited by T. W. Rhys Davids and J. Estlin Carpenter. London: Geoffrey Cumberlege, Oxford University Press for the Pali Text Society, 1947 (of the work first published in 1903).

Don Peter, W. L. A. "The Catholic Presence in Sri Lanka through History, Belief, and Faith." In *Religiousness in Sri Lanka,* ed. John Ross Carter, 243–72. Colombo: Marga Institute, 1979.

Dutt, Sukumar. *The Buddha and Five After-Centuries.* London: Luzac, 1957.

Edgerton, Franklin. *Buddhist Hybrid Sanskrit Grammar and Dictionary.* Vol. 2, *Dictionary.* New Haven: Yale University Press, 1953.

*The Expositor.* Vol. 1. Translated by Pe Maung Tin. Edited and revised by Mrs. Rhys Davids. London: Published for the Pali Text Society by Luzac, 1958 (of the work first published in 1920).

Fiorenza, Francis Schüssler. "Theology in the University." *Bulletin of the Council of Societies for the Study of Religion* 22, no. 2 (April 1993).

Garrett, James Leo. *Systematic Theology: Biblical, Historical, and Evangelical.* Vol. 1. Grand Rapids: Eerdmans, 1990.

Geertz, Clifford. "Religion as a Cultural System." In *Anthropological Approaches to the Study of Religion,* ed. Michael Banton, 1–46. New York: Praeger, 1966.

Geiger, Wilhelm, and Magdalene Geiger. *Pāli Dhamma: vornehmlich in der kanonischen Literatur.* "Abhandlungen der Bayerischen Akademie der Wissenschaften; Philosophisch-philologische und historiche Klasse," Band 31, 1. Abhandlung (vorgelegt am 1 Mai 1920). München: Verlag der Bayerischen Akademie der Wissenschaften, 1920.

Gerrish, B. A. "Friedrich Schleiermacher." Vol. 13 of *The Encyclopedia of Religion,* Mircea Eliade, Editor in Chief. New York: Macmillan, 1987.

Gethin, Rupert. *The Foundations of Buddhism.* Oxford: Oxford University Press, 1998.

Gibb, H. A. R., and J. H. Kramers, eds. *The Shorter Encyclopaedia of Islam.* Edited on behalf of the Royal Netherlands Academy. Ithaca: Cornell University Press, n.d.

Gombrich, Richard F. *Theravāda Buddhism: A Social History from Ancient Benares to Modern Colombo.* London: Routledge and Kegan Paul, 1988.

Gómez, Luis O. *Land of Bliss: The Paradise of the Buddha of Measureless Light,* Sanskrit and Chinese Versions of the Sukhāvatīvyūha Sutras, Introductions and English Translation. Honolulu: University of Hawai'i Press, 1996.

Gunton, Colin E. *The One, the Three, and the Many: God, Creation, and the Culture of Modernity.* The Bampton Lectures, 1992. Cambridge: Cambridge University Press, 2002 (7th printing of the work first published in 1993).

Halverson, Marvin, and Arthur A. Cohen, eds. *A Handbook of Christian Theology: Definition Essays on Concepts and Movements of Thought in Contemporary Protestantism.* New York: Meridian, 1958.

Hare, E. M. *Woven Cadences of Early Buddhists.* Vol. 15, *The Sacred Books of the Buddhists.* London: Geoffrey Cumberlege, Oxford University Press, 1947.

Hartshorne, M. Holmes. *Kierkegaard Godly Deceiver: The Nature and Meaning of His Pseudonymous Writings.* New York: Columbia University Press, 1990.

———. "Of Human Bondage and Divine Grace." In *Of Human Bondage and Divine Grace: A Global Testimony,* ed. John Ross Carter, 274–90. La Salle, IL: Open Court, 1992.

Hazelton, Roger. "Salvation." In *A Handbook of Christian Theology: Definition Essays on Concepts and Movements of Thought in Contemporary Protestantism,* ed. Marvin Halverson and Arthur A. Cohen, 336–39. New York: Meridian, 1958.

Hirota, Dennis. "Breaking the Darkness: Images of Reality in the Shin Buddhist Path." *Japanese Religions* 16, no. 3 (January 1991). This work appears as chapter 1, "Images of Reality in the Shin Buddhist Path: A Hermeneutical Approach," in *Toward a Contemporary Understanding of Pure Land Buddhism: Creating a Shin Buddhist Theology in a Religiously Plural World*, ed. Dennis Hirota, 33–72, Albany: State University of New York Press, 2000.

———. (Head Translator) with Hisao Inagaki, Michio Tokunaga, and Ryushin Uryuzu. *The Collected Works of Shinran.* Vol. 1, *The Writings.* Translated with introductions, glossaries, and reading aids. Shin Buddhism Translation Series. Kyoto: Jōdo Shinshū Hongwanji-ha, 1997.

———. "Religious Transformation in Shinran and Shōkū." *The Pure Land* (New Series), no. 4 (December 1987): 57–69.

———. "Revelation as Sacrament in Shinran and Karl Barth." In *Across the Pacific with Love,* "Leroy Seat Commemorative Book," 137–54. Fukuoka, Japan: Touka Shobo, 2006.

———. "Shinran's View of Language: A Buddhist Hermeneutics of Faith." *The Eastern Buddhist* 26, no. 1 (Spring 1993): 50–93.

———. "Truth as Dialogic Event and Authentic Life in Shinran." *Shinshūgaku* (March 2006), 7–9.

*The Holy Qur'ān: Text, Translation, and Commentary,* by A. Yusuf Ali. Printed in the United States by McGregor and Werner, copyright 1946.

Hooper, J. S. M. *Greek New Testament Terms in Indian Languages.* Bangalore: The Bible Society of India and Ceylon, 1957.

*Hymns on the Pure Land: A translation of Shinran's Jōdowasan.* Yoshifumi Ueda, General Editor. Shin Buddhism Translation Series. Kyoto: Hongwanji International Center, 1991. *The Collected Writings of Shinran,* Vol. 1, 319–23.

*Hymns of the Pure Land Masters: A Translation of Shinran's Kōsō wasan.* Yoshifumi Ueda, General Editor. Shin Buddhism Translation Series. Kyoto: Hongwanji International Center, 1992. *The Collected Works of Shinran,* Vol. 1, 359–93.

Inagaki, Hisao. *T'an-luan's Commentary on Vasubandhu's Discourse on the Pure Land.* Kyoto: Nagata Bunshodo, 1998.

———, in collaboration with Harold Stewart. *The Three Pure Land Sutras: A Study and Translation from Chinese.* Kyoto: Nagata Bunshodo, 1994.

*Iti-vuttaka*. Edited by Ernst Windisch. London: Published for the Pali Text Society by Geoffrey Cumberlege, Oxford University Press, 1948.

*The Jātaka: Together with Its Commentary*. Vols. 1–7. Edited by V. Fausbøll. London: Published for the Pali Text Society by Luzac, 1962 (Vol. 1), 1963 (Vols. 2–5), 1964 (Vols. 6–7).

Jayatilleke, K. N. *Early Buddhist Theory of Knowledge*. London: George Allen and Unwin, 1963.

Jeremias, Joachim. *The Prayers of Jesus*. Philadelphia: Fortress Press, 1984 (Chapter 1 first published in 1967).

*The Jōdo Wasan: The Hymns on The Pure Land*. Translated and annotated by Ryukyo Fujimoto, Hisao Inagaki, and Leslie S. Kawamura. Ryukoku Translation Series. Kyoto: Ryukoku University, 1984 (2nd edition of the first, 1965).

Khantipalo, Bhikkhu. *Calm and Insight: A Buddhist Manual for Meditators*. London: Curzon Press, 1981.

Kitagawa, Joseph M., and Mark D. Cummings, eds. *Buddhism and Asian History: Religion, History, and Culture—Readings from the Encyclopedia of Religion*. Mircea Eliade, Editor in Chief. New York: MacMillan, 1989.

*The Koran Interpreted* by Arthur J. Arberry. New York: Macmillan, 1955.

*The Kōsō Wasan: The Hymns on the Patriarchs*. Ryukoku Translation Series. Kyoto: Ryukoku Translation Center, Ryukoku University, 1974.

*The Khuddaka-Paṭha: Together with Its Commentary Paramatthajotikā*. Vol. 1. Edited by Helmer Smith from a collation by Mabel Hunt. London: Published for the Pali Text Society by Luzac, 1959.

*Kyō Gyō Shin Shō (Ken Jōdo Shinjitsu Kyōgyōshō Monrui): The Teachings, Practice, Faith, and Enlightenment: A Collection of Passages Revealing the True Teaching, Practice, and Enlightenment of Pure Land Buddhism*. Vol. 5. Translated and annotated by Hisao Inagaki, Kosho Yukawa, Thomas R. Okano, under the direction of Mitsuyuki Ishida. Ryukoku Translation Series. Kyoto: Ryukoku Translation Center, Ryukoku University, 1983 (2nd edition of the first, 1966).

Lake, Kirsopp. *The Apostolic Fathers: With an English Translation*. Vol. 1. The Loeb Classical Library. Cambridge: Harvard University Press, 1952.

Lear, Jonathan. *Aristotle: The Desire to Understand*. Cambridge: Cambridge University Press, 1999 (of the work republished numerous times since 1988).

Lester, Robert C. "Rāmānuja and Śrī-vaiṣṇavism: The Concept of Prapatti or Śaraṇāgati." *History of Religions* 5 (Winter 1966): 266–82.

*Letters of Shinran: A Translation of Mattōshō*. Yoshifumi Ueda, Editor. Shin Buddhism Translation Series. Kyoto: Hongwanji International Center, 1978. *The Collected Works of Shinran*, Vol. 1, 557ff.

Luo Zhufeng, ed. *Religion Under Socialism in China*. Translated by Donald E. MacInnis and Zheng Xi'an. New York: M. E. Sharpe, 1991.

*The Mahāvaṃsa; or, The Great Chronicle of Ceylon*. Translated into English by Wilhelm Geiger, assisted by Mabel Haynes Bode. Colombo: Published by the Ceylon Government Information Department, 1960 (of the work first published in 1912).

Maitreya Nayaka Thero, B. Ananda. "Buddhism in Theravada Countries." In *The Path of the Buddha: Buddhism Interpreted by Buddhists*, ed. Kenneth W. Morgan, 113–52. New York: Ronald Press, 1956.

*Majjhima-nikāya*. Vol. 1. Edited by V. Trenckner. London: Published for the Pali Text Society by Luzac, 1964.

*Majjhima-nikāya*. Vol. 2. Edited by Robert Chalmers. London: Published for the Pali Text Society, 1960 (of the first edition, 1898).

Malalasekera, G. P. *Dictionary of Pāli Proper Names*. London: Luzac, 1960 (of the work first published in 1938).

Malalgoda, Kitsiri. *Buddhism in Sinhalese Society, 1750–1900: A Study of Religious Revival and Change*. Berkeley: University of California Press, 1976.

*Manorathapūraṇī: Buddhaghosa's Commentary on the Aṅguttara-nikāya*. Vol. 1. Edited by Max Walleser. London: Published for the Pali Text Society by the Oxford University Press, 1924.

*Manorathapūraṇī: Buddhaghosa's Commentary on the Aṅguttara-nikāya*. Vol. 2. Edited by Max Walleser and Hermann Kopp. London: Published for the Pali Text Society by the Oxford University Press, 1930.

*Manorathapūraṇī: Commentary on the Aṅguttara Nikāya*. Vol. 5, with Indexes to Vols. 1–5. Edited by Hermann Kopp. London: Published for the Pali Text Society by Luzac, 1956.

Martyn, J. Louis. *History and Theology in the Fourth Gospel*. Nashville: Abingdon, 1979.

*Matthews' Chinese-English Dictionary*. Revised American Edition. Cambridge: Harvard University Press, n.d. (1943?) (of the work first published in 1931).

McDermott, Robert A., ed. *Focus on Buddhism: A Guide to Audio-Visual Resources for Teaching Religion*. Chambersburg, PA: Anima Books, 1981.

*The Milindapañho: Being Dialogues between King Milinda and the Buddhist Sage Nāgasena*. Edited by V. Trenckner. London: Published for the Pali Text Society by Luzac, 1962.

Moltmann, Jürgen. *The Trinity and the Kingdom: The Doctrine of God*. Minneapolis: Fortress Press, 1993.

Morgan, Kenneth W., ed. *The Path of the Buddha: Buddhism Interpreted by Buddhists*. New York: Ronald Press, 1956.

Ñāṇobhāsa Tissa, Moragallē Siri. *Dhammapada Vivaraṇaya*. Colombo: M. D. Gunasena, 1962.

Narayanan, Vasudha. "*Karma, Bhaktiyoga*, and Grace in the Śrīvaiṣṇava Tradition: Rāmānuja and Kāraṭṭāḷvāṇ." In *Of Human Bondage and Divine Grace: A Global Testimony*, edited by John Ross Carter, 57–73. La Salle, Il: Open Court, 1992.

*Nava Givisuma: The Sinhala New Testament—A Common New Translation*. Colombo: The Bible Society, 1975. The first printing of this translation was in 1973, of 5,000 copies. The second printing, 1975, was of 3,000 copies.

Nelson, Nathaniel. *The Modern Reader's Japanese-English Character Dictionary*. 2nd revised edition. Rutland, VT: Charles E. Tuttle, 1985.

*The Netti-pakaraṇa*. Edited by E. Hardy. London: Luzac, 1961.

*Niddesa I: Mahāniddesa*. Vol. 2. Edited by L. de La Vallée Poussin and E. J. Thomas. London: Published for the Pali Text Society by Humphrey Milford, Oxford University Press, 1917.

*Niddesa II: Cullaniddesa*. Edited by W. Stede. London: Published for the Pali Text Society by Humphrey Milford, Oxford University Press, 1918.

Niebuhr, H. Richard. *Faith on Earth: An Inquiry into the Structure of Human Faith*. New Haven and London: Yale University Press, 1989.

———. *The Meaning of Revelation.* New York: Macmillan, 1946.

———. *Radical Monotheism and Western Culture: With Supplementary Essays.* New York: Harper and Row, 1960 (another edition by Westminster / John Knox, 1990).

———. *The Responsible Self: An Essay in Christian Moral Philosophy.* New York: Harper and Row, 1963 (reprinted, Louisville: Westminster / John Knox Press, Library of Theological Ethics, 1999).

Nomura, Nobuo. "Shinran's View of True Religion—From Amida Worship to the True and Real Religion." In *The Religious Heritage of Japan: Foundations for Cross-cultural Understanding in a Religiously Plural World,* ed. John Ross Carter, 117–31. Portland, OR: Book East, 1999.

*Notes on "Essentials of Faith Alone": A Translation of Shinran's Yuishinshō-mon'i.* Yoshifumi Ueda, General Editor. Shin Buddhism Translation Series. Kyoto: Hongwanji International Center, 1979. *The Collected Works of Shinran,* Vol. 1, 449–69.

*Notes on the Inscriptions on Sacred Scrolls: A Translation of Shinran's Songō shinzō meimon.* Yoshifumi Ueda, General Editor. Shin Buddhism Translation Series. Kyoto: Hongwanji International Center, 1981. *The Collected Works of Shinran,* Vol. 1, 491–520.

*Notes on Once-calling and Many-calling: A Translation of Shinran's Ichinen-tanen mon'i.* Yoshifumi Ueda, General Editor. Shin Buddhism Translation Series. Kyoto:Hongwanji International Center, 1980. *The Collected Writings of Shinran,* Vol. 1, 471–90.

*Novum Testamentum Graece,* cum apparatu critico curavit Eberhard Nestle. Stuttgart: Privileg. Württ. Bibelanstalt , for the American Bible Society, n.d.

Nyanaponika Thera. *The Heart of Buddhist Meditation.* London: Rider, 1962.

Nyanatiloka. *Buddhist Dictionary: Manual of Buddhist Terms and Doctrines.* 3rd revised and enlarged edition. Edited by Nyanaponika. Colombo: Frewin, 1972.

Nygren, Anders. *Agape and Eros.* Translated by Philip S. Watson. Philadelphia: The Westminster Press, n.d. (1953?) (of the work first published in an English translation by S.P.C.K. House: Part 1, 1932; Part 2, Vol. 1, 1938; Part 2, Vol. 2, 1939).

———. "Eros and Agape." In *A Handbook of Christian Theology: Definition Essays on Concepts and Movements of Thought in Contemporary Protestantism,* trans. Werner Rode, ed. Marvin Halverson and Arthur A. Cohen. New York: Meridian, 1958.

Olcott, Henry S. *The Buddhist Catechism.* Colombo: Publication Division of the Ministry of Cultural Affairs, n.d. (My copy indicates a "forty-second edition" with a preface dated 1908, and also a "certificate to the first edition" dated 1881.)

Oxtoby, Willard G., ed. *Religious Diversity: Essays by Wilfred Cantwell Smith.* New York: Harper and Row, 1976; and New York: Crossroad, 1982.

Painter, John. *The Quest for the Messiah: The History, Literature, and Theology of the Johannine Community.* Nashville: Abingdon, 1993.

*The Pali Text Society's Pali-English Dictionary.* Edited by T. W. Rhys Davids and William Stede. London: Luzac, 1966 (an edition of the work first published in fascicles, 1921–25).

Palihawadana, Mahinda. "*Dhamma* Today and Tomorrow." In *Religiousness in Sri Lanka,* ed. John Ross Carter, 129–47. Colombo: Marga Institute, 1979.

———. "Is There A Theravada Buddhist Idea of Grace?" In *Christian Faith in a Religiously Plural World,* ed. Donald G. Dawe and John B. Carman, 181–95. Maryknoll, NY: Orbis Books, 1978.

Panikkar, Raimundo. *The Intrareligious Dialogue*. New York: Paulist Press, 1978.

———. "The Rules of the Game in the Religious Encounter." *The Journal of Religious Studies* (Punjabi University) 3, no. 1 (Spring 1971).

*Papañcasūdanī Majjhimanikāyaṭṭhakathā of Buddhaghosācariya*. Parts 1–2. Edited by J. H. Woods and D. Kosambi. London: Published by the Pali Text Society, distributed by Routledge and Kegan Paul, 1977 (Part 1, of the work first published in 1922; Part 2, of the work first published in 1928).

*Papañcasūdanī Majjhimanikāyaṭṭhakathā of Buddhaghosācariya*. Parts 3–4. Edited by I. B. Horner. London: Published for the Pali Text Society by the Oxford University Press, 1933 (Part 3), 1937 (Part 4).

*Paramattha-Dīpanī: Iti-Vuttakaṭṭhakathā (Iti-Vuttaka Commentary) of Dhammapālācariya*. Vols. 1–2. Edited by M. M. Bose. London: Published for the Pali Text Society by Humphrey Milford, Oxford University Press, 1934 (Vol. 1), 1936 (Vol. 2).

*Paramattha-Dīpanī Theragāthā-Aṭṭhakathā: The Commentary of Dhammapālācariya*. Vols. 2–3. Edited by F. L. Woodward. London: Published for the Pali Text Society by Luzac, 1952 (Vol. 2), 1959 (Vol. 3).

*Paramattha-Dīpanī Udānaṭṭhakathā (Udāna Commentary) of Dhammapālācariya*. Edited by F. L. Woodward. London: Published for the Pali Text Society by the Oxford University Press, 1926.

*Paramatthajotikā, 1.* See *The Khuddaka-Pāṭha: Together with Its Commentary Paramatthajotikā, 1.* Edited by Helmer Smith from a collation by Mabel Hunt. London: Published for the Pali Text Society by Luzac, 1959.

*Paramatthamañjūsa of Bhadantācariya Dhammapāla Thera: Or The Commentary of the Visuddhimagga*. Vols. 1–3. Edited by Morontuḍuwē Dhammānanda Thera. Colombo: Mahabodhi Press, 1928 (Vol. 1), 1930 (Vol.2), 1949 (Vol. 3).

*Passages on the Pure Land Way: A translation of Shinran's Jōdo monrui jushō*. Yoshifumi Ueda, General Editor. Shin Buddhism Translation Series. Kyoto: Hongwanji International Center, 1982. *The Collected Works of Shinran,* Vol. 1, 293–317.

*The Path of Purification (Visuddhimagga) by Bhadantācariya Buddhaghosa*. Translated by Bhikkhu Ñyāṇamoli. Colombo: M. D. Gunasena, 1964.

Prestige, Leonard. "ΠΕΡΙΧΩΡΕΩ and ΠΕΡΙΧΩΡΗΣΙΣ in the Fathers." *The Journal of Theological Studies* 29 (1928): 242–52.

*Pūjāvaliya*. Edited by Kiriällē Ñāṇavimala Thera. Colombo: M. D. Gunasena, 1965.

Rhys Davids, Caroline A. F. *A Buddhist Manual of Psychological Ethics*. London: Published for the Pali Text Society and distributed by Routledge and Kegan Paul, 1974 (originally published by the Royal Asiatic Society, 1900).

Richardson, Alan. "Repent, Repentance, Convert, Conversion, Turn, Return." In *A Theological Word Book of the Bible,* edited by Alan Richardson, 191–92. New York: Macmillan, 1951.

Rogers, Minor Lee. "Introduction." In *Christian Faith in a Religiously Plural World,* ed. Donald G. Dawe and John B. Carman. Maryknoll, NY: Orbis Press, 1978.

———. "Shin Buddhist Piety as Gratitude," an unpublished paper delivered at a seminar on "Acts of Thanksgiving and the Virtue of Gratitude in Hinduism, Buddhism, and Islam," held in Dallas, Texas, December 17–19, 1983. This work has appeared in John B. Carman and Frederick J. Streng, eds., *Spoken and Unspoken Thanks: Some Comparative Soundings* (Dallas: Center for the Study of World Religions, Harvard University, and Center for World Thanksgiving,1989), 93–111.

———, and Ann Rogers. *Rennyo: The Second Founder of Shin Buddhism*. Berkeley: Asian Humanities Press, 1991.

*Saddharmālaṅkāraya*. Edited by Kiriällē Ñāṇavimala Thera. Colombo: M. D. Gunasena, 1954.

*Saddhamma-pajjotikā: The Commentary on the Mahā-Niddesa 1.* Vols. 1–2. Edited by A. P. Buddhadatta. London: Published for the Pali Text Society by Humphrey Milford, Oxford University Press, 1931 (Vol. 1), 1939 (Vol. 2).

*Saṃyutta-nikāya*. Parts 1–5. Edited by Léon Freer. London: Published for the Pali Text Society by Luzac, 1960.

*Sārattha-ppakāsinī: Buddhaghosa's Commentary on the Saṃyutta-nikāya*. Vols. 1–3. Edited by F. L. Woodward. London: Published for the Pali Text Society by Humphrey Milford, Oxford University Press, 1929 (Vol. 1), 1932 (Vol. 2), 1937 (Vol. 3).

*Septuaginta id vestus testamentum graece iuxta LXX interpretes*. Editio sexta. Vol. 2. Edited by Alfred Rahlfs. Stuttgart: Privile. Württ. Bibelanstalt for the American Bible Society, New York, n.d.

*Shinshū Shōgyō Zensho*. Vol. 2. Kyoto: Ōyagi Kōbundō, 1984.

*The Shōshin Ge: The Gāthā of True Faith in the Nembutsu*. Translated and annotated under the direction of Fugen Daien. Ryukoku Translation Series. Kyoto: Ryukoku Translation Center, Ryukoku University, 1984 (5th edition of the first, 1961).

*Shōzōmatsu Wasan: Shiniran's Hymns on the Last Age*. Vol. 7. Translated and annotated in the Ryukoku University Translation Center. Ryukoku Translation Series. Kyoto: Ryukoku University Press, 1980.

Smith, Jonathan Z. "The Influence of Symbols upon Social Change: A Place on Which to Stand." In *The Roots of Ritual,* ed. James D. Shaughnessy. Grand Rapids: Eerdmans, 1973.

Smith, Wilfred Cantwell. "A Human View of Truth." In *Modern Culture from a Comparative Perspective,* ed. John W. Burbidge, 99–119. Albany: State University of New York Press, 1997. This work appeared in *Studies in Religion / Sciences Religieuses* (1971) 1, 1:6–24; reprinted in *Truth and Dialogue: The Relationship between World Religions,* ed. John Hick. London: Sheldon Press, 1974; and *Truth and Dialogue in World Religions: Conflicting Truth Claims.* Philadelphia: Westminster Press, 1974.

———. *Belief and History*. Charlottesville: University Press of Virginia, 1977.

———. "Conflicting Truth-Claims: A Rejoinder." In *Truth and Dialogue: The Relationship between World Religions,* ed. John Hick. London: Sheldon Press, second impression, 1975 (of the work first published in 1974).

———. *Faith and Belief.* Princeton: Princeton University Press, 1979. This work has been reissued with a different subtitle, *Faith and Belief: The Difference Between Them* (Oxford: Oneworld, 1998).

———. *The Faith of Other Men*. New York: Harper Torchbooks, 1972. New and revised as *Patterns of Faith Around the World* (Oxford: Oneworld, 1993).

———. *The Meaning and End of Religion: A New Approach to the Religious Traditions of Mankind*. New York: Macmillan, 1962. This work was published in paperback as "A Mentor Book" (New York: New American Library, 1964), and in paperback through Harper and Row (San Francisco: Harper and Row, 1978); and more recently, again in paperback, and without the subtitle (Minneapolis: Fortress Press, 1991).

———. *Modern Culture from a Comparative Perspective*. Edited by John W. Burbidge. Albany: State University of New York Press, 1997.

———. *Modernization of A Traditional Society.* Bombay: Asia Publishing House, issued under the auspices of the Indian Council of World Affairs, 1965.

———. "Objectivity and the Humane Sciences: A New Proposal." In *Modern Culture from a Comparative Perspective,* ed. John W. Burbidge. Albany: State University of New York Press, 1997. (This chapter was originally published in *Transactions of the Royal Society of Canada,* Series 4, 12: 81–102; reprinted in *Symposium on the Frontiers and Limitations of Knowledge/Colloque sur les frontières et limites du savior,* ed. Claude Fortier et al. [Ottawa: Royal Society of Canada, 1974]; and as chapter 9 in *Religious Diversity: Essays by Wilfred Cantwell Smith,* ed. Willard G. Oxtoby [New York: Harper and Row, 1976; and New York: Crossroad, 1982].)

———. "The Study of Religion and the Study of the Bible." *Journal of the American Academy of Religion* 39, no. 2 (June 1971): 131–40.

———. *Towards A World Theology: Faith and the Comparative History of Religion.* Philadelphia: The Westminster Press, 1981.

———. *Questions of Religious Truth.* New York: Charles Scribner's Sons, 1967.

———. *What Is Scripture? A Comparative Approach.* Minneapolis: Fortress Press, 1993.

Soothill, William Edward, and Lewis Hodous. *A Dictionary of Chinese Buddhist Terms.* Taipei: Ch'eng Wen Publishing Company, 1970 (originally published by Kegan Paul, Trench, Trübner, 1934 [?]).

Sorata Nayaka Thera, Wälivițiyē. *Śrī Sumaṅgala Śabdakoṣa: A Sinhalese-Sinhalese Dictionary.* Colombo: Anula Press, 1963.

*Śrīmadbhagavadgītā Śrīśaṅkarabhagavatpādācāryaviracitena bhāṣyeṇa sahitā: The Bhagavad-Gītā with the Commentary of Śrī Śaṅkarācārya.* Critically edited by Dinkar Vishnu Gokhale. Poona Oriental Series, No. 1. Poona: Oriental Book Agency, 1950.

*Śrī Saddharmāvavāda Saṃgrahaya.* Edited by Vēragoḍa Amaramoli Thera. Colombo: Ratnākara Mudraṇālayaya, 1956.

*Śrī Sumaṅgala Śabdakoṣa: A Sinhalese-Sinhalese Dictionary.* By Sorata Nayaka Thera. Wälivitiyē. Colombo: Anula Press, 1963.

Sri Srutaprakaasika Acharya. *Sri Bhagavad-Ramanuja's Saranaagati Gadya with English Translation of the Text and Its Commentary.* Prepared under the guidance of Abhinava Desikka Sri Uttamur Viraraghavacharya Swami by K. Bashyam. 3rd edition. Madras: Published by Visishtadavaita Pracharini Sabha, 1970.

Stanton, Graham. *The Gospels and Jesus.* New York: Oxford University Press, 1989.

*Sumaṅgala-vilāsinī: Buddhaghosa's Commentary on the Dīght-Nikāya.* Part 1. Edited by T. W. Rhys Davids and J. Estlin Carpenter. London: Published for the Pali Text Society by Henry Frowde, Oxford University Press, 1886.

*Sumaṅgala-vilāsinī: Buddhaghosa's Commentary on the Dīgha-Nikāya.* Parts 2–3. Edited by W. Stede. London: Published for the Pali Text Society by Humphrey Milford, the Oxford University Press, 1931 (Part 2), 1932 (Part 3).

*Sutta-Nipāta.* New edition by Dines Andersen and Helmer Smith. London: Published for the Pali Text Society by Geoffrey Cumberlege, Oxford University Press, 1948.

*Sutta-Nipāta Commentary: Being Paramatthajotikā II.* Vols. 1–2. Edited by Helmer Smith. London: Published for the Pali Text Society by Humphrey Milford, Oxford University Press, 1916 (Vol. 1), 1917 (Vol. 2).

Talbert, Charles H. *Reading John: A Literary and Theological Commentary on the Fourth Gospel and the Johannine Epistles.* New York: Crossroad, 1992.

Tanner, Norman P. *The Councils of the Church: A Short History*. New York: Crossroad, 2001 (for the work first appearing in Italian in 1999, in French in 2000).

———, S.J., ed. *Decrees of the Ecumenical Councils*. Vol. 1, *Nicaea I to Lateran V*. Washington DC: Georgetown University Press, 1990.

*Tannishō: A Primer—A Record of the Words of Shinran Set Down in Lamentation over Departures from his Teaching*. Translated by Dennis Hirota. Introduction by Tokunaga Michio [Michio Tokunaga]. Kyoto: Ryukoku University, 1982. *The Collected Works of Shinran,* I, 659–82.

*The Tanni Shō: Notes Lamenting Differences*. Vol. 2. Ryukoku Translation Series. Kyoto: Ryukoku Translation Center, Ryukoku University, 4th edition (of the first, 1962).

*The Thera- and Therī-gathā: Stanzas Ascribed to Elders of the Buddhist Order of Recluses*. Edited by Hermann Oldenberg and Richard Pischel. 2nd edition, with Appendices by K. R. Norman and L. Alsdorf. London: Published for the Pali Text Society by Luzac, 1966.

Tillich, Paul. *Dynamics of Faith*. New York: Harper and Brothers, 1958.

*The Tiruvāçagam: The Tamil Text of the Fifty-one Poems*. Translated by Rev. G. U. Pope. Oxford: Clarendon Press, 1900.

Tokunaga, Michio. "The Dialectic of *Shinjin*." In *The Religious Heritage of Japan: Foundations for Cross-cultural Understanding in a Religiously Plural World,* ed. John Ross Carter, 133–43. Portland, OR: Book East, 1999.

———. "The 'Non-Self' Aspect in Shinran's Concept of 'Faith.'" An unpublished paper presented at the Second Biennial Conference of the International Association of Shin Buddhist Studies, Honolulu, Hawaii, August 3, 1985.

———. "Other Power and Social Ethics: The Bifurcation of Shinran's Teaching." In *The Religious Heritage of Japan: Foundations for Cross-cultural Understanding in a Religiously Plural World,* ed. John Ross Carter, 145–56. Portland, OR: Book East, 1999.

Torbet, Robert G. *A History of the Baptists*. Philadelphia: The Judson Press, 1959.

Torrance, Alan. "Jesus in Christian Doctrine." In *The Cambridge Companion to Jesus,* ed. Markus Bockmuehl, 200–19. Cambridge: Cambridge University Press, 2001.

Torrance, Thomas F. *The Christian Doctrine of God, One Being Three Persons*. Edinburgh: T and T Clark, 2001 (first published in 1996).

———. "Introduction." In *The Incarnation: Ecumenical Studies in the Nicene-Constantinopolitan Creed A. D. 381,* ed. Thomas F. Torrance. Edinburgh: Handsel Press, 1981.

*The True Teaching, Practice and Realization of the Pure Land Way: A Translation of Shinran's Kyōgyōshinshō*. Vol. 1. Yoshifumi Ueda, General Editor. Shin Buddhist Translation Series. Kyoto: Hongwanji International Center, 1983. *The Collected Works of Shinran,* Vol. 1, 1–292.

*Udāna*. Edited by Paul Steinthal. London: Published for the Pali Text Society by Geoffrey Cumberlege, Oxford University Press, 1948.

Ueda, Yoshifumi, and Dennis Hirota. *Shinran: An Introduction to His Thought—With Selections from the Shin Buddhism Translation Series*. Kyoto: Hongwanji International Center, 1989.

Upasak, C. S. *Dictionary of Early Buddhist Monastic Terms*. Varanasi: Bharati Prakashan, 1975.

*Vaṃsatthappakāsinī: Commentary on the Mahāvaṃsa*. Vols. 1–2. Edited by G. P. Malalasekera for the Government of Ceylon. London: Published for the Pali Text Society by Humphrey Milford, Oxford University Press, 1935.

*The Vinaya Piṭakam*. Vols. 1–5. Edited by Hermann Oldenberg. London: Published for the Pali Text Society by Luzac, 1964.

*Visuddhajanavilāsinī nāma Apadānaṭṭhakathā*. Edited by C. E. Godakumbura. London: Published for the Pali Text Society by Luzac, 1954.

*The Visuddhi-magga of Buddhaghosa*. Vol. 1. Edited by C. A. F. Rhys Davids. London: Published for the Pali Text Society by Humphrey Milford, Oxford University Press, 1920.

*Visuddhimagga of Buddhaghosācariya*. Edited by Henry Clarke Warren. Revised by Dharmananda Kosambi. Vol. 41. Harvard Oriental Series. Cambridge: Harvard University Press, 1950.

Watt, W. Montgomery. *Companion to the Qur'ān: Based on the Arberry Translation*. London: George Allen and Unwin, 1967.

Whitney, William Dwight. *The Roots, Verb-forms and Primary Derivatives of the Sanskrit Language*. Vol. 30. American Oriental Series. New Haven: American Oriental Society, 1945 [as a supplement to his *Sanskrit Grammar* (London: Trübner, 1885)].

Woodward, F. L. *The Book of the Kindred Sayings*. London: Luzac, 1954 (of the work first published in 1925).

# Index

Abba, as Daddy or Father, 64, 238nn1–2, 282n38, 292
academic tradition, 14, 98, 193
*Agapē*, 99–105, 107, 180, 252–3n6, 253nn9, 11–12, 254n16, 255n30, 288, 298
Ajātasattu, 39, 178
Allah, 65
Amaradeva, W. D., 105
*amen*, as having gone around the world, 246n25, 251n89
Amida, xxix, 20, 48–51, 53, 55, 57–58, 67–72, 82, 90–97, 106–108, 111–121, 123, 135, 146–147, 149–152, 157, 230, 245n21, 246n22, 236n28, 247n34, 248n50, 250n71, 251n90, 254n28, 256n3, 256n8, 257n8, 259n24, 263n33, 298
Ānanda, 42, 179, 205–206, 280n9, 280n10
Ānanda Maitreya, Balangoda. 181–185, 275nn1–2, 288
Anurādhapura, 105, 141, 153, 167
*aparihāniyā dhammā*, human qualities for development 178
Aquinas, Thomas (Saint), xiii, 15
Aristotle xiv, xvii, xix, 25, 29–33, 233n4, 296
Arulchelvam, Maheswari, 89, 244–5nn13–14, 291
*äsala perahära*, 164
assurance of birth, *yokushō*, 48, 82, 118, 120
attainment of birth, 95, 236n15
Augsburg Confession, 132
August, the month of, xix–xx, 163–6, 168, 173
Augustine, 102
Augustine, Morris, 235n1
authority, quest for among Buddhists, 206
*Avatāra* , 65

Bach, Johann Sebastian, 164
Bacon, Francis, 221
Baddēgama, 166, 226n10
Baillie, Donald M., 132–133, 263n29, 233n31
Baillie, John, 131–132, 263n25, 292
Baird, Robert D., 225n3
baptism, 68, 153, 201–204, 212, 279nn3–4
Baptist, xi, xiii–xiv, xvi–xvii, xxiv, xxx, 4, 8, 11, 19, 163, 196, 199–209, 211–3, 222n2, 274n17, 278–9n1, 279nn5–7, 283n45. 289
Baptist Education Society of the State of New York, 227n2
Barth, Karl, 151, 270nn43, 45
Baylor University, 8, 274n17, 279n5
becoming genuinely human 32, 69, 222
believe, drift in meaning of the word, 13, 144, 183, 221
*Bhagavadgītā*, xxix, 16, 193, 243n6, 303
*Bhagavan*, as Auspicious One, 104, 138–9, 142–3, 263n4, 265–6
Bible xxix, 64, 110, 152, 164, 187, 189–93, 196, 209, 242n2, 226n3, 252n2, 253n13, 277n6, 278n12, 292
Bible, particularity of for Christians, 189
Bodhidharma, 46